The Battle for Algeria

PENNSYLVANIA STUDIES IN HUMAN RIGHTS

Bert B. Lockwood, Jr., Series Editor

A complete list of books in the series is available from the publisher.

The Battle for Algeria

Sovereignty, Health Care, and Humanitarianism

Jennifer Johnson

PENN

UNIVERSITY OF PENNSYLVANIA PRESS

PHILADELPHIA

Published by
University of Pennsylvania Press
Philadelphia, Pennsylvania 19104-4112
www.upenn.edu/pennpress

Printed in the United States of America on acid-free paper
10 9 8 7 6 5 4 3 2 1

Library of Congress Cataloging-in-Publication Data
Johnson, Jennifer, author.
    The battle for Algeria : sovereignty, health care, and humanitarianism / Jennifer Johnson.
        pages cm. — (Pennsylvania studies in human rights)
    Includes bibliographical references and index.
    ISBN 978-0-8122-4771-8 (alk. paper)
    1. Algeria—History—Revolution, 1954–1962. 2. Algeria—Politics and government—1830–1962. 3. Decolonization—Algeria. 4. Medical care—Algeria—History—20th century. 5. Humanitarianism—Political aspects—Algeria. 6. Jabhat al-Tahrir al-Qawmi. 7. Red Cross and Red Crescent—Algeria—History. I. Title. II. Series: Pennsylvania studies in human rights.
    DT295.J625 2016
    965'.0461—dc23
                                                            2015016155

For my mom

Contents

ACICR	Archives du Comité International de la Croix-Rouge
AJAAS	Association de la Jeunesse Algérienne pour l'Action Sociale
ALN	Armée de Libération Nationale
AMG	Assistance Médicale Gratuite
AML	Amis du Manifeste et de la Libérté
ANA	Algerian National Archives
ANOM	Archives Nationales d'Outre-Mer
ASSRA	Adjointe Sanitaire et Sociale Rurale Auxiliaire
CCE	Comité de Coordination et d'Exécution
CH	centres d'hébergements
CMI	centres militaires d'internés
CNRA	Conseil National de la Révolution Algérienne
CRA	Croissant-Rouge Algérien
CRF	Croix-Rouge Française
CTT	centres de tri et de transit
ECPAD	Établissement de Communication et de Production Audiovisuelle de la Défense
EMSI	Équipe Medico-Sociale Itinérante
FIS	Front Islamique du Salut
FLN	Front de Libération Nationale
GPRA	Gouvernement Provisoire de la République Algérienne
ICRC	International Committee of the Red Cross
IGRP	Inspection Générale des Regroupements de la Population
IJMES	*International Journal of Middle East Studies*
MAE	Ministère des Affaires Étrangères
MNA	Mouvement Nationale Algérien
MTLD	Mouvement pour le Triomphe des Libertés Démocratiques
NARA	National Archives and Records Administration

NATO	North Atlantic Treaty Organization
OAS	Organisation Armée Secrète
PAM	prisonnier pris les armes à la main
PCA	Parti Communiste Algérienne
PPA	Parti du Peuple Algérien
RPF	Rassemblement du Peuple Français
SAS	Sections Administratives Spécialisées
SHAT	Service Historique de l'Armée de Terre
UDMA	Union Démocratique du Manifeste Algérien
UGEMA	Union Générale des Étudiants Musulmans Algériens
UGTA	Union Générale des Travailleurs Algériens
UN ARMS	United Nations Archives and Records Management Section
UNICEF	United Nations Children's Emergency Fund
UNOG	United Nations Office at Geneva Archives

Note on Sources, Names, and Spellings

This study uses a diverse set of sources in Arabic, French, and English drawn from Algeria, France, Switzerland, and the United States.

I am among the first group of scholars to work on the Provisional Government of the Algerian Republic (Gouvernement Provisoire de la République Algérienne, GPRA) documents and those of the Algerian Red Crescent in the Algerian National Archives. My sources, which include correspondence between the Algerian political leadership in Algeria and abroad, internal strategy memorandums, medical reports, and personal letters, contribute to a more comprehensive understanding of nationalist policy during the war from the Algerian participants themselves. The cataloging system for these collections changed between 2007 and 2012. When I conducted my research in 2007 and 2008, the GPRA collection was arranged by box and file number and was separate from the Algerian Red Crescent collection. When I returned in 2012, the two collections had been combined into one GPRA collection and the numbering system had changed. The book uses the two notation systems and provides as much detail as possible about the document in the hopes that scholars will be able to find them. I used a variety of French archives in Paris and Aix-en-Provence. The IH series is the most important fonds at the French military archives in Vincennes (Service Historique de l'Armée de Terre, SHAT) for the Algerian war. At the Archives Nationales d'Outre-Mer (ANOM; formerly Centre des Archives d'Outre-Mer, or CAOM) I used 81F (Ministère chargés d'affaires algérienne), the Sections Administratives Spécialisées (SAS), and the Gouvernement Générale (GGA) files. These sources include recently declassified French government materials, such as police reports, Special Administrative Sections program documents, and French military medical unit reports that contextualize and explain the colonial position. A considerable amount of archival material that deals with the Algerian war still requires a dérogation.

The International Committee of the Red Cross (ICRC) in Geneva, Switzerland, released records on the Algerian war in 2004. I relied on these records (subfonds A AG, 1951–1965) to help supplement gaps in the Algerian and French archives. They offer a unique perspective about the process of negotiation that international organizations engaged in during decolonization. Moreover, they show internal differences among personnel about how the Red Cross should respond to the many complexities the Algerian war presented.

I consulted the United Nations Office at Geneva (UNOG) archives in Switzerland. SO 215/1 ALG and SO 215/1 France reveal extensive complaints about human rights violations committed by both sides. The UN records indicate that its members confronted these allegations beginning in 1956 into the postindependence period. These complaints complicate French and Algerian health care and medical initiatives that presented a strictly humanitarian face. I consulted the United Nations Archives and Records Management Section (UN ARMS) in New York. Three series, S-0188-0005, S-0442-0189, and S-0884-0001, were especially important in explaining how Arab, African, and Asian allies campaigned on Algeria's behalf at the UN. Furthermore, I read published United Nations General Assembly and Security Council minutes. These records provide accounts of the vivid and passionate debates on the Algerian question that took place at the UN. They highlight multiple perspectives on the issue. I concentrate on those from previously colonized countries.

I examined the records of the U.S. Department of State (RG 59) at the National Archives and Records Administration (NARA) in College Park, Maryland, and the *Foreign Relations of the United States* series. These documents elucidate the American position on Algeria during decolonization.

In addition to the archival material, I rely on a small number of oral interviews with Algerian medical personnel and former war participants that I conducted over a three-year period. They provide critical insight into the history of medical services under French rule and during the war. When it was possible, I corroborated their recollections with other written sources.

My research uses newspapers, museum exhibits, published pamphlets, and photographs in French, Arabic, and English. Unless otherwise noted, all translations are my own.

In November 2012, the *International Journal of Middle East Studies* (*IJMES*) published a special issue on the Maghrib. In the foreword of the issue, the editors explained how the Maghrib, and especially Algeria, posed a transliteration problem. Even though France colonized Morocco, Algeria, and Tunisia, as well as parts of the Middle East, archival material varies across the region. French records on Algeria use the French spelling of names and places. For example, most French documents use "Mohammed," instead of the *IJMES* transliteration of the same name ("Muhammad"). Moreover, Algeria was under French rule for 130 years, frequently resulting in Algerians adopting French spellings of names and places. For instance, Hussein Lahouel, an FLN representative who toured Asia in the spring of 1956 and solicited financial and political support for the nationalist effort, signed his name "Hussein." "Husayn" is an alternate spelling that conforms to *IJMES* transliteration regulations. Throughout the book, I use the spelling of Algerian names published in Achour Cheurfi's *Dictionnaire de la révolution algérienne*. In Lahouel's case, I use "Hocine" to spell his first name. The same applies for Hocine Aït Ahmed, GPRA minister of state. I use the commonly accepted form of Egyptian president Gamal Abdel Nasser, as opposed to "Jamal 'abd al-Nasir" or "Nassar."

Introduction

On 24 September 1958, Ferhat Abbas (Figure 1), the newly appointed president of the Provisional Government of the Algerian Republic (GPRA) and longtime figure in Algerian nationalist politics, wrote a memorandum from Cairo to Léopold Boissier, the president of the International Committee of the Red Cross (ICRC). Abbas was responding to Boissier's letter from May of that year, in which Boissier proposed to the National Liberation Front (FLN) and the French government that they both commit to upholding the 1949 Geneva Conventions, a step that he believed would "humanize the Algerian conflict." In his lengthy reply, Abbas expressed his willingness to cooperate with the proposed terms if Boissier removed the expression that the "conflict did not have an international character." This condition, though politically charged and controversial, was only the first of many shrewd requests. Abbas laid out five issues to which the French government would have to agree before the Algerian nationalists would publicly pledge to follow the Geneva Conventions: the colonial administration would treat civilians and unarmed soldiers humanely, the wounded and sick would receive medical treatment, captured members of the armed forces would be granted prisoner of war status, the French government would inform the ICRC of any intended legal action against members of the Algerian armed forces, and, last, reprisals of any kind would not be permitted.[1]

Abbas's conditions indicate an astute understanding of the political landscape and moral stakes of the moment. He had the ear of the man running the most influential humanitarian organization of his day and he wanted to make sure he played the opportunity correctly. Abbas demonstrated intimate knowledge of the Geneva Conventions, which helped redefine human rights for individual civilians and noncombatants by extending basic physical and legal protections to previously excluded categories of people.[2] The revised Geneva Conventions were a significant victory for anticolonial national

Figure 1. Ferhat Abbas in his office in Tunis, 1961. (Getty)

liberation armies because they chipped away at colonial hegemony and opened the door for nonstate actors in an internal colonial conflict to make claims about their fundamental human rights.

Two years later in April 1960, after numerous exchanges with the ICRC, highly publicized prisoner release ceremonies, and international campaigns in support of Algerian independence, Abbas finally replied that the GPRA agreed to uphold the Geneva Conventions despite the fact that French president Charles de Gaulle did not promise to meet all of the aforementioned conditions. Abbas made a calculated decision. He showed that he knew the intricacies of the Geneva Conventions and he, along with various Algerian nationalist branches, spent years demonstrating their steadfast commitment to them in the international arena. By the time the GPRA officially signed the conventions on 11 June 1960, it was largely a symbolic gesture.[3] Countries and organizations around the world already perceived the Algerians fighting for liberation as humanitarians capable of running a modern nation-state.

This book offers a new interpretation of one of the most violent wars of decolonization: the Algerian war (1954–1962). I argue that the conflict was about who—France or the FLN—would exercise sovereignty of Algeria. The fight between the two sides was not simply a military affair; it also involved diverse and competing claims about who was positioned to better care for the Algerian people's health and welfare.

Even though the French outmaneuvered the Algerians on the battlefield, ultimately, the FLN was more successful at achieving its aims. To better understand the conflict and the unlikely triumph of the FLN over one of the most powerful Western countries in the world, I argue that one must examine the local context of the war as it evolved in Algeria as well as its international dimensions, which played out in every corner of the globe. I rely heavily on Algerian sources, which make clear the centrality of health and humanitarianism to their war effort. They reveal how the nationalist leadership constructed national health-care institutions that provided critical care for the population and functioned as a proto-state. Moreover, its representatives used postwar rhetoric about rights and national self-determination to legitimize their claims, which led to international recognition of Algerian sovereignty.

Scholars have examined the diplomatic dimensions of Algerian nationalists' efforts to internationalize the conflict, but they did not focus on Algerian agency nor did they significantly rely on Algerian archives.[4] Other scholars have analyzed the military and political dimensions of the war and many placed a heavy emphasis on colonial violence, torture, and terror committed by the French military and police during this period.[5] Frantz Fanon, the noted revolutionary theorist from Martinique who penned the scathing critique of colonialism *The Wretched of the Earth*, has also left us with enduring observations about the corroding nature of French colonial rule and violence during the war. His cautionary message in "Concerning Violence," that violence begets violence, proved all too true in Algeria.[6] Fanon's training in psychiatry and his years treating Algerian and French patients enabled him to share insights that few of his contemporaries could. Yet, he was not Algerian and his work frequently lapses into Manichean generalizations. As such, the book uses him sparingly. The extreme violence and atrocities committed by both sides, like Fanon, also remain in the background here.

Instead, this study analyzes the war through the eyes of the Algerian participants and privileges their voices and agency. It concentrates on French and Algerian efforts to engage one another off the physical battlefield and highlights the social dimensions of the FLN's winning strategy, which targeted the local and international arenas.

Both sides mobilized recently redefined notions of welfare and rights to appeal for support from a wide array of sources. The colonial administration used medicine and health care to try to win the hearts and minds of the population. The Sections Administratives Spécialisées (SAS), the most comprehensive wartime initiative, aimed to facilitate political rapprochement between the Algerian population and the colonial state. A significant portion of their efforts focused on medical care.[7] Teams of physicians, nurses, and assistants visited rural areas and provided free care, taught hygiene classes for women, and offered vaccinations. In some cases, their visits were the first time state services penetrated the interior, and the administration devoted serious attention toward remedying this neglect through peaceful pacifiers, instructed to conquer with medicine rather than bullets.[8]

Algerian nationalists also used the provision of medicine, health care, and personnel to win over the Algerian people by showing them "that they could care for the welfare of 'their' populations better than [could an] alien colonial government," as did other anticolonialists in the Third World.[9] Nationalists worked to construct an organized and vibrant health-services division that could rival that of the French state and convince locals that not only could they assume responsibility for the people's care, but that they were ready, effective immediately, to do so.[10] Anticolonial leaders across the globe, including India and Southeast Asia, engaged in similar endeavors that showed their willingness and readiness to care for the local population.

The health-services division was a key component of the internal FLN strategy to establish and project state power in Algeria to Algerians. Consequently, the division's duties targeted different groups within Algeria, including Algerian soldiers, Algerian civilians sympathetic to the FLN, and Algerian civilians who may have supported political rivals. Moreover, the health-services division sent a clear message to the people and the French administration that the nationalists were capable of building and running public welfare institutions.

In addition to FLN domestic medical efforts, the nationalists embarked upon international diplomatic and humanitarian initiatives. Starting in 1957, the nationalists concentrated on expanding their health-care initiatives beyond Algeria and sought international aid and support through a refined humanitarian message. The Algerian Red Crescent (Croissant-Rouge Algérien, CRA), the primary vehicle for disseminating this position and soliciting financial and material aid abroad, and its leadership appropriated the universal language of humanitarianism and rights to substantiate their claims for sovereignty. Nationalists built upon Arab alliances and viewed the internationalization of medical aid outside of Algeria as a critical tactic in gaining additional support. They believed an organization with international ties and widespread appeal would be most successful in projecting their cause to a global audience.

Algerian leaders continued their international outreach by lobbying the International Committee of the Red Cross and the United Nations to recognize Algerian independence. They fought to capitalize on the organizations' moral and political authority and manipulated the language within their founding documents to make strong arguments for why the nationalists were entitled to rule Algeria. They were extremely shrewd political weapons deployed against their colonial opponent.

FLN representatives set up an Algerian Red Crescent office in Geneva and they met frequently with ICRC delegates. These meetings put the international organization and its staff in a difficult position and highlighted the limitations of their humanitarian mandate.[11] On the one hand, the Red Cross was committed to providing aid regardless of race, religion, or gender. On the other hand, the organization did not have clear guidelines for how to handle internal conflicts, as many wars for decolonization were classified. Therefore, by meeting with and supplying assistance to Algerians, the Swiss representatives found themselves embroiled in a politically explosive diplomatic situation with the French colonial administration. The FLN understood the moral capital the ICRC could provide and they used it to their advantage.

Unlike the ICRC, Algerian nationalists were unable to represent themselves at the UN. The FLN therefore mobilized Algerian delegates to secure support in Asia, the Middle East, and Africa, regions with a shared religious tradition and colonial past that were committed to Third World solidarity, with the expectation that representatives from these allied countries would present the Algerian case at the UN on their behalf. The FLN further solidified its strategy for internationalizing the conflict and campaigning for inscription onto the General Assembly agenda by sending Algerian delegates to New York to set up an office from which to publicize the war in the United States and target the United Nations from closer range.

The FLN diplomatic corps acted as political and social attachés and represented another dimension of the nascent Algerian state. They refined the nationalist message for external audiences and presented an alternative version to the world to that of the French government's portrayal of Algerian "terrorists." Similar to the nationalists' domestic health-care campaigns and Red Crescent efforts, the FLN wanted to prove that not only did it understand the international diplomatic norms and rights of the day but it could also put them into practice. The nationalists' efforts evoked the actions of a state before it was officially recognized as such, and they paid particular attention to establishing internal and external recognition of their right to rule Algeria.

In the end, the nationalists were more successful in using notions of welfare and rights to their advantage. They exposed the hypocrisy of selectively applying universal discourse and provided a blueprint for claim making that nonstate actors could emulate. Consequently, anticolonial leaders throughout the Third World saw Algeria as a model for success in developing platforms for claiming sovereignty. Furthermore, the Algerians helped transform international organizations by forcing them to reconsider their purpose and mandate in a postcolonial world. Analyzing the war in this manner provides a different interpretation of the conflict and offers new directions for studying nationalist movements and concepts of sovereignty.

Sovereignty lies at the heart of this study. Dating back to Jean Bodin, a sixteenth-century French jurist and political philosopher, scholars have grappled with defining the idea in theory and in practice.[12] While most agree that sovereignty means fully controlling the state, there are myriad ways of establishing and maintaining sovereignty. This is especially true in an imperial context, where the concept was constantly in flux and redefined.[13] For our purposes, a sovereign derives its source of authority from being able to regulate the internal and external affairs of the state. From a domestic point of view, sovereigns need to control the physical space and the people within the territorial borders. The people also must recognize the sovereign's authority, and, in return, they frequently expect the state to take care of and provide for their welfare. From an external point of view, sovereigns are in charge of international relations and conduct in war. Therefore, sovereignty has two inextricably linked parts, domestic and international recognition.[14] A state cannot be sovereign without meeting both criteria. But the process of asserting and establishing that power is often fraught.

The FLN constructed a plan that, if successful, would satisfy the two required components of sovereignty. Its leadership developed a domestic strategy that (frequently through the use of force) eliminated its political rivals and provided social services, both of which contributed to the Algerian people recognizing the FLN's authority. The FLN's health-care outreach also helped cement its supremacy over other groups, such as the Algerian National Movement (MNA), and provided life-sustaining care for Algerian soldiers who were then able to continue fighting for national liberation. The numerous target audiences highlight the complicated Algerian landscape through which the FLN had to navigate during the war. Furthermore, the FLN's international strategy sought external recognition from a wide array of sources, such as sovereign countries, Arab, African, and Asian allies, and international organizations. The Algerians' approach challenged the French state's claims to Algeria and offered a clear alternative, especially when it came to questions of the people's health and welfare. Nationalist movements throughout the Third World were engaged in this contested process of claiming sovereignty, and many turned to Algeria for inspiration.

My work, therefore, is part of a growing comparative history of decolonization and international history that concentrates on how newly independent countries and nationalist movements throughout the Third World impacted the metropoles and made their way into the international order. John Darwin and Dane Kennedy wrote pioneering studies about the end of empire, arguing that a robust "history of decolonization requires the careful fusion of three 'sub-historiographies.'"[15] To be sure, developments in the metropole, national liberation movements in the colonies, and superpower politics each played an individual role in the formal transfer of power. But, according to Darwin and Kennedy, in order for scholars to fully understand the process of decolonization, one must examine and combine local, national, and international perspectives, as this study does.

Recent scholarship on North Africa and the Middle East continues to challenge an area-studies framework that previously analyzed social and political movements as local, unique, and disconnected from global politics.[16] In addition to deprovincializing North Africa and the Middle East, these studies have forced Cold War and foreign relations scholars to contend with the periphery between Washington and Moscow and take non-European actors in the postwar period seriously.

Scholarship on Algeria, a burgeoning field in the last twenty years, usually takes one of two forms: nationalist studies framed by nationalist agendas and international approaches devoid of Algerian actors. But it rarely integrates the local, national, and international dimensions that Darwin and Kennedy argued were necessary for understanding decolonization. French and Algerian national histories perpetuate the notion that the practices in Algeria between 1954 and 1962 were separate and distinct from one another, rather than related and interconnected to strategies that other nationalists used in Africa, Asia, and the Middle East to achieve independence from European powers.

After 1962, according to Benjamin Stora, the French national conscious-ness underwent "historical amnesia" for nearly thirty years.[17] For the next quarter century, the subsequent governments, former soldiers, and the one million repatriated European settlers tried to put Algeria behind them by concentrating on domestic issues.[18] With the hope of forgetting the violent separation between the two countries, President Charles de Gaulle pardoned prominent military generals who previously attempted to assassinate him, and the state absorbed a large European settler community that, in many cases, had never lived in France. In school, the history of the French empire, including the 132 years in Algeria, was glossed over until February 2005 when a controversial French law stipulated that school curricula emphasize the "positive role" of colonialism, especially in North Africa.

As archival material gradually became available in France in the late 1980s, histories about Algeria, in particular the war years (1954–1962), pro-liferated. A new generation of French scholars shattered the silence and con-fronted difficult questions about the nature of the colonial relationship in the North African territory, exploring military and judicial abuses that chal-lenged official French narratives.[19] This prompted national public outcry, which continued in 2001 when former general Paul Aussaresses wrote *Special Services, 1955–1957* and discussed torture openly. Aussaresses coolly stated that the French military commonly employed it and that he had no regrets because he was acting in service of his country.[20] Personal accounts of torture inflicted by the French military fueled the national conversation and opened the door for academics to engage in spirited debate.[21]

Recently, scholars have started analyzing the history of previously over-looked political parties in France and Algeria.[22] To be sure, they add an im-portant layer of texture to a complicated decolonization story. However, these studies concentrate on what the revelations mean for French history and/or Franco-Algerian history. Their conclusions rarely touch on the implications for histories of the Third World, comparative empire, and international history.

Algerian histories of the war are equally myopic. Unlike French history, Algerian history after independence frequently celebrated and commemo-rated the eight-year struggle. Former participants and their families fre-quently publish their memoirs.[23] The Algerian government awards maquisards and their descendants benefits and pensions and these individuals are re-vered throughout the country.[24] The plethora of personal accounts served to bolster an official state narrative that lionized the FLN and contended that the entire population rose up against their French colonial oppressors and contributed to their overthrow.

Algerian scholars slowly chipped away at this narrative. Mohammed Harbi, an Algerian historian who used personal materials to challenge the postcolonial nationalist version of history, argued that even though the FLN steered the country to independence, it was not the only political group invested in the process. He, along with historians Gilbert Meynier, Daho Djerbal, and Nedjib Sidi-Moussa, have shown the internal fractures within the FLN and exposed the violence they committed to the other major political force at the time, the Algerian National Movement (MNA).[25] Celebrating national heroes and lionizing the victorious political parties are common in postcolonial African countries and are subjects that invite comparative analysis. But Algerian scholarship rarely situates its independence movement within contemporary currents of decolonization.

Despite the Algerian conflict's centrality to the post–World War II international political climate, it was not until the first decade of the twenty-first century that scholars began to tackle this issue.[26] Most prominently, Matthew Connelly's *A Diplomatic Revolution* examines the international dimensions of the Algerian war and shows how Algerian nationalists gained independence through their international diplomatic efforts at the United Nations.[27] Connelly focuses on the Cold War context and demonstrates that Algerian leaders intentionally exploited the American-Soviet rivalry for political gain. *A Diplomatic Revolution* emphasized that Western countries and the Soviet Union did not have a monopoly on international relations. There were additional actors to consider in the political negotiations and outcomes of the 1950s and 1960s.

Connelly's work remains critical for scholars of Algeria, the Cold War, and diplomatic history. However, his work largely concentrates on American foreign policy during the Cold War as the two superpowers battled for influence in Africa during decolonization. The Cold War is the main axis of his analysis, not the war itself. He privileges the FLN's diplomatic efforts over the armed struggle and eclipses crucial local dimensions of the conflict. By placing Algeria at the epicenter of international change, with Washington, Moscow, and Beijing as the centers of power, Algerian voices are overshadowed and numerous questions remain about the Algerian leaders themselves and the war on the ground as they experienced it within Algeria and beyond its borders.

Since the publication of *A Diplomatic Revolution*, the Algerian National

Archives have released a considerable amount of material pertaining to the FLN and the Provisional Government of the Algerian Republic (GPRA), allowing scholars to pose new questions about the internal struggle and nationalist strategy. Jeffrey James Byrne's work stands out because he was among the first to obtain Algerian material on the post-1962 period, allowing him to draw conclusions about Algerian domestic and foreign policy as planned and described by the Algerians themselves.[28] This important body of scholarship engages with the postwar international political climate, but it does not adequately deal with international organizations and rights discourse that emerged alongside it.

In the years after 1945, international organizations and universal declarations about peace, security, and human rights proliferated. They articulated a renewed commitment to global cooperation and aimed to offer protection to men, women, and children around the world regardless of a person's race, gender, or religion. However, these noble intentions, as Mark Mazower has demonstrated, were not necessarily intended for everyone, namely colonial subjects. Emergent international organizations merely masked "the consolidation of a great power directorate."[29] In many cases, French and British officials expressed trepidation over the wording of these important documents. They worried that ideas and the vocabulary within them would serve as a guide and purveyor of rights for anyone able to read them.[30] Western leaders did not heed the lessons from the global impact of Woodrow Wilson's Fourteen Points on mobilizing the colonized.[31]

Prior to decolonization, Western powers benefited nearly exclusively from international organizations and rhetoric about individual freedom.[32] However, after 1945, a new global order provided a different vocabulary and vision of the future that anticolonial nationalist leaders appropriated and exploited for their own political gain.[33] Postwar international organizations offered additional forums in which nationalists could be heard, and rights discourse afforded them with new political possibilities.[34]

The war in Algeria demanded that the international community rethink the meaning of humanitarianism and human rights.[35] After World War II, especially 1945–1950, a period some scholars call "the human rights revolution," significant advances were made to protect individuals from physical, mental, and emotional abuse.[36] During these five years, the United Nations was created, the Universal Declaration of Human Rights and the Genocide Convention were finalized, the Fourth Convention was added to the Geneva Conventions, and the European Convention for the Protection of Human

Rights and Fundamental Freedoms of 1950 was signed. They provided the legal and moral framework for the dawn of a new world. However, they were hardly enforceable, and imperial powers, mainly France and Britain, strongly protested their universal applicability, fearing that anticolonial nationalists might use them against the colonial state. Their fears were warranted.

To be sure, human rights are difficult to define. They range from political and social rights to economic and legal rights. Their meaning has changed over time, frequently subject to interpretation depending on the context, culture, and location.[37] In the 1940s they pertained more to political rights. In the 1950s and 1960s, self-determination became a human rights focal point. By the 1970s, they expanded to include the right to health, food, shelter, women's rights, and economic prosperity.[38] Despite the challenges of an ever-expanding rights arsenal, a useful way to think about human rights is as an effort "to make claims across borders in the name of basic rights."[39] This broad definition provides a common thread throughout the history of human rights and highlights several reasons why the FLN strategy resonated across the globe in the 1950s and 1960s. The events and actions in Algeria inspired revolutionaries from Cuba and the United States to Moscow and China, and the Algerian nationalists' political success became emblematic of reconfigured post–World War II diplomatic possibilities.

The Battle for Algeria combines these histories and argues that Algerian decolonization should be considered part of human rights history. Too frequently, human rights literature "jumps" from the 1940s to the 1970s, bypassing decolonization.[40] Contrary to what Sam Moyn has argued, anticolonial nationalists used rights discourse as tools for their liberation.[41] Algerian nationalists were not on the periphery watching rights debates happen around them. They were at the center of them, shaping many of these political contests and defining their outcome. They seized words and ideas, albeit in a piecemeal approach, that could benefit their nationalist cause. In many cases, they thrust themselves onto the international stage armed only with universal terminology about health, humanitarianism, and self-determination.

With the help of universal rights, as broadly defined by Kenneth Cmiel, the FLN acted as a functional state before Algerian independence in 1962. Algerian leaders juggled the provision of medicine and health care, aid, and political representation at the International Committee of the Red Cross and the United Nations, and combined these efforts with a laser-sharp deployment of recently reconceived terms, ideas, and concepts. The massive changes to the international system enabled Third World actors to seize their place on the political battlefield, articulate claims, and seriously challenge their European oppressors in a way that was never possible on a military battlefield.[42]

The exchange between Ferhat Abbas, president of the Provisional Government of the Algerian Republic, and ICRC president Léopold Boissier illuminates how Algerian nationalists tested the principles and limits of the postwar order to claim sovereignty of Algeria. The FLN took advantage of all the available tools—ideological, political, and rhetorical—and developed a comprehensive domestic and international strategy to claim Algeria as its own. Nonstate actors around the world would emulate this strategy, transforming international understandings of sovereignty and rights.[43] This transformation begins in Algeria with the FLN forcing the world to consider the Third World.

Chapter 1

The Long Road to War

On Monday, 20 August 1956, a warm summer day two years into the Algerian war, six National Liberation Front (FLN) leaders, Mohamed Larbi Ben M'hidi, Ramdane Abane, Amar Ouamrane, Belkacem Krim, Lakhdar Bentobbal, and Youcef Zighoud, gathered in northern Algeria, in the Soummam Valley, to convene the Soummam Congress and discuss the future of their struggle for national liberation. The previous twenty-one months had been disappointing for FLN leaders. They struggled to recruit participants, obtain vital arms and financial support, eliminate and absorb their political rivals, and simultaneously combat aggressive French military action and repressive policies such as the April 1955 State of Emergency and March 1956 Special Powers Law, both of which suspended civil liberties and granted the military carte blanche. The FLN needed revitalization and a renewed focus and the Soummam Congress was just the event to do so.

Ben M'hidi and Abane, two central FLN figures who did not live to see independent Algeria, worked together to create an agenda for Soummam.[1] The men prioritized ten major areas to cover throughout the day, including financial and political matters, administrative and material needs inside and outside of Algeria, engaging with the United Nations and negotiating ceasefire terms.[2] The wide variety of agenda items targeted local, national, and international dimensions that facilitated controlling the land and people within Algeria's territorial borders and could yield external recognition of Algeria's right to sovereignty.

Belkacem Krim, one of the six men who planned the 1 November 1954 attacks that began the war and whose name by the summer of 1956 had taken on a "quasi mythical dimension," gave the first substantial regional report on Kabylia. He explained significant progress had been made in recruitment and finances. He claimed that the number of FLN soldiers had risen from 450 in November 1954 to 3,100 in August 1956. Krim shared similarly impressive financial increases for the same period, noting that at the start of the war Kabylia had one million francs, whereas at the time of the Soummam Congress, it held 445 million francs. He told the other five men that the people and combatants' spirits were "very good," but that "everyone is asking us for arms."[3] Amar Ouamrane, a former soldier in the French army who belonged to several political parties in the late 1940s and early 1950s before joining the FLN in 1954, delivered a report for the Algiers region that revealed miniscule soldier numbers in November 1954 (only fifty). But he presented the steady increase to one thousand in August 1956, and he boasted 200 million francs in the region's war chest. Ben M'hidi gave the status update for the Oran region and, although the number of soldiers had not surpassed 1,500 in May 1956, he proudly conveyed "excellent" relations between the FLN-ALN and the people. Ben M'hidi echoed Krim's words when he told the room that the people and combatants' spirits were "very good."[4] They concluded the morning session by outlining their principal political tasks that lie ahead, organizing and educating the people and propaganda. They also reiterated the importance of "psychological war," which the minutes explained as establishing "relations with the people, the European minority, and prisoners of war."[5] This revised political agenda would contribute to strengthening how the FLN operated, in general terms, in Algeria.

During the afternoon sessions, the nationalists discussed political structures and international efforts that would secure external recognition of their right to rule Algeria. They created the thirty-four-person National Council of the Algerian Revolution (Conseil National de la Révolution Algérienne, CNRA), which they wanted "to meet annually as long as the hostilities continue."[6] They also established the five-member Coordination and Execution Committee (Comité de Coordination et d'Exécution, CCE), made up of Ben M'hidi, Abane, Krim, Benyoucef Benkhedda, and Saad Dahlab, and granted it "the power to control the political, military, economic, and social organisms."[7] The congress participants specified "political primacy over that of the military" and the supremacy "of the interior over the exterior," taking direct aim at FLN comrades abroad.

It was the Soummam Congress's ninth agenda item, calendar of work, where Abane, Ben M'hidi, Ouramane, Krim, Zighoud, and Bentobbal revealed the depths of their political acumen and demonstrated an appreciation for the international political climate and mastery of acceptable codes of conduct. The men agreed that "only the National Council of the Algerian Revolution is authorized to order the cease-fire whose framework will be based on the United Nations platform. . . . The interior will have to provide all of the information we have to facilitate the task of our representatives at the United Nations." They issued strict orders to soldiers regarding their treatment of civilians and prisoners and said, "no officer, no matter his rank, henceforth has the right to pronounce a death sentence . . . slitting throats is formally forbidden in the future, those sentenced to death will be shot. The accused has the right to choose a defense. Mutilation is officially prohibited." They banned "the execution of prisoners of war" and advised that "a prisoner of war service be created in each *wilaya* [province]," for in their estimation, "it would be essential in popularizing the legality of our struggle." In closing, they briefly mentioned the need to build up a health-services division and that "each new recruit undergo a medical visit, when possible."[8] The leadership's attention to these particular matters suggests a fluency with the contemporary state of international laws of war, most notably the Geneva Conventions of 1949, and their desire to transform the FLN and ALN into modern entities their allies and opponents would have to recognize. They wanted to implement humane practices at every level and send a clear message that the FLN was committed to and capable of running a modern nation-state, even though it would not be internationally recognized as such for six more years.

This historic one-day event, initiated at the behest of Ramdane Abane, was one of the most important political developments for the Algerian nationalist side throughout the eight-year conflict. The Soummam Congress crystallized the direction of the party for years to come and influenced the shape and tenor of the liberation struggle until its conclusion in 1962. The summit's positive outcomes, however, could not mask harsh political realities and internal conflicts within the FLN. Nationalist representatives outside of Algeria, notably Ahmed Ben Bella, future first president of independent Algeria, Mohamed Khider, future Provisional Government of the Algerian Republic (GPRA) minister of information, and Hocine Aït Ahmed, future GPRA minister of state, were not present at Soummam. In fact, they had been deliberately excluded from the meeting's proceedings and received a summary account after the fact. In an early fall 1956 letter, Ben Bella wrote to the internal FLN delegation and expressed his disappointment at having been marginalized from such a significant event. He asked that they "postpone the publication of [the Soummam] decisions until all points of view of all of the brothers . . . are considered."[9] Ben Bella's wish was not fulfilled. On 22 October he was arrested when his plane, scheduled to fly from Rabat, Morocco, to Tunis, was intercepted over French airspace and he was imprisoned until the Evian negotiations six years later.

These initial glimpses into the FLN leadership present an alternative narrative about the nationalist movement. They raise questions about how the FLN ultimately became *the* nationalist party that diplomatically defeated the French, as Matthew Connelly has shown, and claimed sovereignty of Algeria. The FLN of 1962 was not the only party vying for power and its vision for how to achieve liberation was not the only course explored.

The long history of French colonial rule in Algeria is littered with instances of violence, legal and political inequality, a small but extremely influential European settler population, and repeated failure by innumerable colonial administrators to implement meaningful reform. Beginning in the 1920s, Algerian elites began formulating political groups, and for the next thirty years before the official start of the war for national liberation they pursued avenues ranging from assimilation to a Pan-Islamic 'umma (community). Important moments in Franco-Algerian relations during the 1930s and 1940s further strengthened nationalist sentiment, yet I argue World War II outcomes—the 1941 Atlantic Charter, the American presence in Algeria beginning in the fall of 1942, the May 1945 Sétif and Guelma massacres, the creation of the United Nations and its charter, the Universal Declaration of Human Rights, and the Geneva Conventions of 1949—were the most critical developments for Algerian nationalists. The texts provided a new discourse about rights from which anticolonial activists drew liberally, depending on the time and place.

By 1954 when the FLN announced itself as the leading nationalist group, its representatives, many of whom had been active in politics for several decades, used these changes to the international system to their political advantage and started cultivating their winning strategy of deploying universal rights rhetoric in order to appeal to an international audience. Despite their uneven use of rights discourse, Algerians most certainly relied upon the concepts of self-determination and international law to build their case for national sovereignty. The nationalists combined this international approach with an equally important local strategy in Algeria. Their quest for national liberation from France could not, and did not, hinge solely on the international arena, as some historians suggest.[10]

Origins of Nationalism, 1900–1940

The French began colonizing Algeria in June 1830. Close to forty thousand troops landed on the northern coast thirty miles from Algiers, under the pretext of avenging an alleged fly-whisk incident, which caused outrage in diplomatic circles. This inauspicious beginning led to one of the longest and most unique instances of colonialism.[11] Throughout the remainder of the nineteenth century the nature of French rule changed frequently. During the period of military rule (1830–1870), officials employed extreme violence to quell resistance and passed a series of laws, such as the 1846 Land Ordinance and the Senatus-Consulte of 14 July 1865, which were quite detrimental to the Algerian population.[12] Civilian rule (1870–1940) further segregated Algerians from settlers and Jews and solidified French political control of Algeria.[13] By the turn of the century, after seven decades of French colonial rule, the Algerian population had been marginalized in virtually every aspect of life and faced acute hardship. With educational opportunities curtailed and no political rights to speak of that would have enabled meaningful change in Algeria, their options for social and economic advancement were routinely hampered.

Beginning in 1910 several groups emerged that asked for varying degrees of reform from the French colonial state. The Young Algerians, who numbered no more than 1,200, were the first such group. These educated elites aspired to assimilate with France and its political institutions.[14] The 1912 Young Algerian Manifesto was among their most political acts.[15] In it, they requested that Algerian servicemen be treated the same as French soldiers. Furthermore, they asked for more Algerian representation in the Algerian assemblies and equitable taxes.[16] The Young Algerians only alluded to French citizenship and at no point did they demand independence. They wanted political recognition for risking their lives alongside French soldiers.

In World War I, 173,000 Algerian men fought for France. Of that total number, 25,000 were killed and roughly 60,000–70,000 men were wounded.[17] Those years were formative ones for many Algerians and other colonial conscripts throughout the European empires.[18] Their mass mobilization initiated a political awakening that extended beyond the educated elite. However, the Young Algerians remained the mouthpiece for reform after 1918. Even though governor-general Charles Jonnart was amenable to increasing political rights for a certain Algerian (male) demographic, he struggled to placate the vocal settler lobby that vehemently opposed additional rights for the

Algerian population. He passed the Jonnart Law of 1919, which expanded the Muslim electorate to 425,000 but still did not define a clear path to French citizenship and was a meek reflection of what the Young Algerians demanded.

President Woodrow Wilson's 8 January 1918 address to Congress, which later became known as the Fourteen Points, also had a profound impact on Algerian educated elites and anticolonial activists. Wilson's Point 5, "A free, open-minded, and absolutely impartial adjustment of all colonial claims, based upon a strict observance of the principle that in determining all such questions of sovereignty the interests of the populations concerned must have equal weight with the equitable claims of the government whose title is to be determined," was likely the most inspiring for Third World leaders.[19] It gave them hope that they would be able to choose their form of government.

Historian Erez Manela has described the "Wilsonian Moment" as the months from the fall of 1918 to the spring of 1919, when the American president made speeches and public pronouncements about the right to self-determination.[20] These ideas circulated globally and elites in India, Egypt, Korea, French Indochina, and China thought Wilson would support their demands for self-rule, when, in fact, Wilson had no intention of doing so. His rhetoric, at best, was intended for European allies, not colonized peoples in the Third World. Some Maghribi elites, including Tunisian professors Salah Cherif Ettounsi, Mohammed Elkhedir Ben el Houssine, and Emir Khaled, an Algerian who served in the French army in World War I but refused to be naturalized before the French implemented meaningful political reforms, wrote about Wilson's Fourteen Points. They criticized the French government for agreeing to them while still maintaining colonies.[21] As the Paris conference drew near, groups became disillusioned as they realized that Wilson would not take up their cause in the French capital. Their disappointment sowed the seeds of colonial discontent and sparked nationalist movements.

Despite their firm assimilationist and secular agenda, the settler lobby in Algeria demonized the Young Algerians for "nationalist" and "dogmatic" tendencies and, by the end of the decade these educated elites were no longer the only group endorsing reform and change in Algeria. By the 1920s, Algerian veterans, workers, and the educated elite were disillusioned by the nominal political changes in Algeria, and they began seeking alternative ways to unite and advance their goals, but still within a French-Algerian context. In the three decades before the FLN emerged as the nationalist leader, over ten

bona fide political parties and visions were tested and refined as they struggled to live within an increasingly contradictory and restrictive Algeria.[22]

Two men in particular, Ferhat Abbas and Messali Hadj, represent the two
most influential political courses explored during the 1920s and 1930s. Ferhat Abbas, born in the eastern village of Chahna in 1899 to a prominent local
family, received a degree from Algiers University and had early contact with
other Algerian *évolués* (educated elites). He spoke fluent French and was a
product of a French colonial education as put on display in his 1931 book,
The Young Algerian, in which he argued for assimilation with France.[23] His
ideas were an extension of the Young Algerians. He believed that political
lobbying would be more successful than mass action, and during the 1920s
and early 1930s he participated in local politics around Sétif and was elected
municipal councillor and Financial Delegation (Délégations Financières)
representative in Algiers.[24] He served in other political positions in which he
continued to work toward an assimilationist agenda. After the 1927 creation
of the Federation of Elected Muslims, Abbas and another elite, Mohamed
Salah Bendjelloul, co-led the organization and attempted to bridge the gap
between colonial officials' repressive policies and the federation's desire for
reform.

Abbas's foray into politics during this period proved eye-opening and
frustrating because his aspirations for large-scale integration were never realized. On an individual level, Abbas achieved political and personal success,
but he repeatedly confronted French officials' unwillingness to reform their
discriminatory policies toward the rest of the Algerian population. In an un-
finished book titled "My Political Testament," likely written in the 1930s,
Abbas wrote about the need to elevate the Algerian peasantry, for without
their emancipation Algeria would never become modern. He explained that
"it is the fate of this man, his happiness or his misfortune, which will determine Algeria's future. It is not the problem of the elite . . . if it were, it would
be so easy to resolve! Rather it is the problem of the masses, of the continually
uncultivated, miserable bankrupt masses, [and] when that mass understands
its condition [it will be] frightening in its explosions of hatred and anger."[25]
He understood his privilege did not extend to the masses and that Algeria's
future depended on uniform efforts to cultivate and educate the population.
By 1936, after nearly fifteen years in politics, Abbas's assimilation resolve
began to waver. In failing to offer meaningful reform, French administrators
started losing a dedicated advocate, whose longtime political philosophy was
"La France c'est moi."

Abbas never outright supported revolutionary violence, which a considerable portion of FLN members practiced between 1954 and 1962. But beginning in the late 1930s and especially after World War II, his political views
crept more and more toward Algerian independence. In January 1956, fourteen months into the war for national liberation, Abbas gave an interview to
the Tunisian newspaper *L'Action* in which he described his political evolution
and deference to the FLN. "My role today is to defer to the leaders of the
armed resistance. The methods I have defended for fifteen years—
cooperation, discussion, persuasion—proved ineffective."[26] Shortly thereafter, he spoke with the Swedish press and outlined four essential points to
achieving Algerian freedom. For him, obtaining the recognition of popular
sovereignty was the most important point among them.[27] Abbas's advocacy
for Algerian independence and support of the FLN was a marked departure
from his earlier beliefs. While he maintained that any political solution required negotiation, he was open to pursuing other avenues that he would not
have twenty years prior.

The Young Algerians and Ferhat Abbas represent efforts to implement
reform in Algeria during the first three decades of the twentieth century. But
the first group to articulate a nationalist agenda was the North African Star
(Étoile Nord-Africaine), cofounded by Messali Hadj in 1926 in Paris.[28] Messali Hadj, a twenty-eight-year-old former World War I conscript who was
born in Tlemcen in 1898, had long opposed French colonial rule and built a
coalition based on a trade union. In the wake of the Young Algerians' failure
to achieve concrete political advances, he pursued a mass mobilization approach, based on the tenets of the French left and the French Communist
Party. The North African Star quickly attracted members in Paris from the
growing emigrant population from Algeria. By the mid 1920s, nearly 100,000
Maghribi men fleeing poverty lived in Paris and were looking for work, and it
was this group of people, socially and culturally isolated from their home,
that formed the backbone of the party. His rise in politics and strand of nationalism "called for independence from France, withdrawal of the army of
occupation, building of a national army, abolition of the [Native Code], freedom of press and association, an Algerian parliament chosen via universal
suffrage, and municipal councils chosen via universal suffrage."[29] Historian
Emmanuel Sivan maintains that the North African Star was the first movement "dedicated to the idea of Algerian independence," an important distinction from Messali Hadj's contemporaries, and given the nature and total
reach of French colonial rule in Algeria and the absorption of the indigenous

elite class, it makes sense to him that the ideas would originate outside of Algeria.[30]

It took ten years for Messali Hadj's ideas to reach across the Mediterranean and spread through Algeria. But long before Messali Hadj had the opportunity to return to Algeria for this purpose, the French cabinet under André Tardieu banned the North African Star in 1929. He resurrected the party as the Glorious Star in France in 1933, but once again it was short-lived and lasted only one year. Undeterred, Messali Hadj recreated the party a third time in 1936, this time in Algeria, and called it the Algerian People's Party (Parti du Peuple Algérien, PPA). During the summer and fall months of that year, he toured the country and taught people about the need for Algeria's total independence from France. The PPA motto, "Neither assimilation nor separation, but emancipation," was by far the most radical and threatening to the French authorities, which accounts for his numerous arrests in 1939 and 1941. Messali Hadj's prominent rise represented a turning point in the emergence of nationalism. Starting with the Young Algerians, the majority of political leaders were educated elites who had studied and/or worked abroad. When Messali Hadj returned to Algeria in 1936 he helped encourage and inspire a new generation of local activists with more ties to the Algerian people who adhered to his independent Algeria aspirations.

However, eighteen years remained between Messali Hadj's 1936 arrival in Algeria and the 1954 FLN attacks that launched the war. Several key moments—the failure of Popular Front reforms, World War II, and severe French colonial repression in Sétif and Guelma in the spring of 1945—eroded the possibility of compromise and reform and hardened previously amenable leaders, such as a Ferhat Abbas, to the point where they embraced national independence.

Between 1935 and 1937, during a rare moment of political unity in France that would have significant implications on Algerian politics, French socialists, communists, and radicals came together and formed the Popular Front "to build," writes Martin Evans, "the broadest possible coalition against Fascism."[31] As part of a symbolic demonstration of this new alliance, men from the various groups gathered in the streets of Paris on 14 July 1935 and were joined by North African Star members, including Messali Hadj, who, according to Evans, "expected a future left-wing government to satisfy their [political] aspirations."[32] The coalition strategy worked. In May 1936, Léon Blum became the first Socialist prime minister of France. Algerian reformists, educated elites, and proto-nationalists eagerly awaited Blum's political rise, given their heartfelt frustration over former governor general Maurice Viollette's failure in 1930 and 1931 to increase Algerian political representation and grant citizenship to a limited and highly educated sector of the population who would not have been required to renounce their Muslim status.[33]

Immediately after his election, Blum appointed Viollette as minister of state of the Popular Front, and they embarked on another round of reform efforts that were not dissimilar in nature from Viollette's five years earlier. Both men firmly believed in the "necessity of integrating the Algerians" into France and their Blum-Viollette Bill, which proposed expanding the Algerian electorate by 25,000, reflected that.[34] But once again, the settler lobby, especially at the local and municipal levels in Algeria, vehemently rejected the bill. Several newspapers published inflammatory headlines claiming that if one voted for the "Viollette project, it's voting for civil war," and the "Viollette project, it's a new anti-France wing."[35]

In reality, the Blum-Viollette Bill was moderate and, had it succeeded, would have represented the possibility of a different political course, rather than an actual change in course. For that reason, explains John Ruedy, "it assumed enormous symbolic importance both for the Algerian opposition and the colon administration that was trying to hold the line." Overnight, the bill became "a litmus test," for both sides, "of the Popular Front's intentions regarding the Algeria question."[36] Its defeat and that of the Popular Front in 1937 permanently altered the climate of Algerian politics. The optimism and willingness of Ferhat Abbas, the 'ulamā, and the Young Algerians to explore assimilation, reform, negotiation, and Algerian-French coexistence began to unravel, and a new generation of nationalists, many of whom fought in World War II, eclipsed the earlier guard and set their sights on total independence. This progression mirrored what then governor-general Maurice Viollette cautioned against in 1926 when he wrote to the minister of the interior about the educated elite, or évolués, claiming that "six out of ten . . . are ready to adopt the French fatherland without second thoughts, but if the French fatherland rejects them, raises itself so high that they cannot reach it, they will make their own fatherland, and we will have willed it."[37]

World War II: Expanding the Political Discourse

World War II erupted on the heels of the recently dissolved Popular Front and its Algerian counterpart, the Muslim Congress, a 1936 coalition between the *élus*, the *'ulamā*, and the communists that worked with the Blum-Viollette government. It aroused a political hard-line and permanent disillusionment with French colonialism. By 1939, repressive French policies successfully weakened Algerian political parties by forcing them underground, arresting prominent figures such as Messali Hadj and banning the printing and circulation of newspapers advocating communist, leftist, or anticolonial views. Colonial suppression, however, did not halt nationalist pursuits. For example, Dr. Lamine Debaghine, clandestine Algerian People's Party (PPA) leader while Messali was in prison and future Provisional Government of the Algerian Republic (GPRA) minister of foreign affairs (1958–1959), and additional members Filali Abdallah, Ahmed Bouda, and Ahmed Mezerna continued pursing Messali's anticolonial objectives.[38]

Nazi Germany invaded Poland on 1 September 1939, setting off a firestorm of territorial expansion throughout Europe, including the Nazi invasion of France in the summer of 1940. The German occupation and resulting Vichy regime (1940–1944) under Marshal Philippe Pétain temporarily suspended colonial authorities' cracking down on Algerian political parties. Reflecting on "France's misfortunes of 1940," Algerian leaders Ferhat Abbas and Mohamed Bendjelloul, another advocate of Franco-Algerian integration, wrote that they thought "the settler [*colon*] . . . would reconsider the Algerian problem." But "no more than the 1918 victory," they lamented, "does the metropole's defeat" inspire self-reflection.[39] Even when faced with a humiliating foreign occupation, French administrators were unwilling to acknowledge their contradictory position on empire and claim to Algeria.

Beginning in November 1942, Algerian nationalists, spanning the full political spectrum, received an unexpected boost from the British and American presence in Algeria. The Allies' landing in North Africa, aimed as a staging ground to attack Germany, had a huge impact on the future revolutionary guard, such as M'hamed Yazid, PPA member and GPRA minister of information (1958–1962), Ramdane Abane, Soummam Congress architect, and Benyoucef Benkhedda, second GPRA president (1961–1962), for not only did they encounter political alternatives and Western generosity, but they formed important contacts with foreigners upon which they later relied.

Hocine Aït Ahmed, a founding FLN member who traveled to New York in the late 1950s in preparation for United Nations sessions and served as GPRA minister of state (1958–1962), recalled in his memoirs the impact of the Allied landing. "One can say that opinion, as a whole, moved on to the

Allied side . . . the population sympathized with the American army. There was a democratic side to the way in which the officers and soldiers behaved."[40] At the time, Ferhat Abbas thought the Americans would make Algeria "an American protectorate that Roosevelt would emancipate at the end of the war."[41] Their presence in North Africa inspired a spirit of optimism among Algerian leaders who hoped the Americans would at the very least support the idea of an Algeria federated with France. They would soon be disappointed to learn defeating Germany was the Allies' priority, not liberating the Maghrib from the throes of French colonialism.[42]

In the ensuing fifteen months, a broader coalition of Algerian activists produced three critical documents that increasingly articulated a position for separation and independence. In December 1942, Ferhat Abbas, a former proponent of assimilation, and twenty-four other Algerian leaders wrote a "Message from the Algerian Muslim Representatives to the Responsible Authorities" to protest the governor-general's conscription preparation, and they presented it to the Allies and French government officials. In it, Abbas recalled "the American President's commitment to the liberation of peoples, drawing attention to the unfree status of Algerians, and calling for a Muslim conference to draft a new economic, social, and political status for Algeria. In return for its implementation," the Algerian Muslim Representatives "committed Algerians to sacrifice themselves wholeheartedly for the liberation of metropolitan France."[43]

The language Abbas included in this "Message" referenced American president Franklin Roosevelt and British prime minister Winston Churchill's August 1941 Atlantic Charter. These towering wartime figures met to discuss postwar goals, which included limiting territorial expansion, economic cooperation, disarmament, and international peace and security. Yet, for anticolonial activists around the world, the charter's most relevant and useful principle was number three, that the United States and the United Kingdom respect "the right of all peoples to choose the form of government under which they live; and they wish to see sovereign rights and self-government restored to those who have been forcibly deprived of them."[44] The Atlantic Charter targeted Western Europe and the United States, but as would become a frequent problem with post–World War II international doctrines, the language was vague. Therefore, African nationalists appropriated the content in these doctrines and argued that they applied to them, as well as to Europeans and Americans.[45]

Even though Abbas did not specifically cite the Atlantic Charter in his 1942 message, he reminded Allies and French government representatives that the Algerian people remained under forced colonial domination. There-fore, according to the charter's third principle, they should be working to-ward Algerian self-government and sovereignty. Abbas's appeal, based on a set of widely circulated and supposedly universal ideas at the time, shows the antecedents of the FLN's strategy. By the mid-1950s, the FLN had additional universal discourses and international charters to choose from, as well as prominent international organizations at which to address their claims.

Abbas and his coauthors failed to receive the response they wanted and continued to lobby the colonial authorities for change. In February 1943, Abbas wrote the "Manifesto of the Algerian People," a nine-page reflection on the realities of colonialism and the Algerian condition. He reminded his readers that "in his declaration [the Atlantic Charter]," President Roosevelt gave assurances that in a postwar world "the rights of all peoples, big and small, would be respected."[46] Based on Roosevelt and Churchill's words, Abbas called for the "condemnation and abolition of colonization" and an Algerian constitution that guaranteed:

1. The absolute freedom and equality of all its inhabitants without dis-tinction as to race or religion.
2. The abolition of feudal property by a major agrarian reform and the right to well-being of the immense agricultural proletariat.
3. The recognition of the Arabic language as official on the same basis as French.
4. Freedom of press and association.
5. Free compulsory education for children of both sexes.
6. Freedom of religion for all inhabitants and the application to all reli-gions of the principle of separation of church and state.[47]

For Abbas, these were basic freedoms to which all people in Algeria, regard-less of their ethnic or racial origins, were entitled. Even though the manifesto did not state independence as the ultimate goal, its language indicated that Abbas was quite knowledgeable about rights and liberties enjoyed by French citizens and that his political vision demanded more and more equal mea-sures between French and Algerians, a concession Marcel Peyrouton, the governor-general of Algeria, was still unwilling to grant. Moreover, he tried to hold President Roosevelt and his allies accountable to the ideas within the Atlantic Charter by highlighting that Algerians did not choose nor did they want "the form of government under which they lived."[48]

Angered over its dismissal, Abbas gathered additional signatures and verbal support from Messali Hadj who was still in prison, and wrote what is commonly referred to as "An Addition to the Manifesto" (*Projet de réformes faisant suite au Manifeste*). This document, which demanded "the political autonomy of Algeria as a sovereign nation with *droit de regard* by France and Allied military assistance in case of conflict" after World War II, went farther than the two previous ones in articulating a desire for Algerian sovereignty, distinct and separate from France.[49] The addition to the manifesto also represented a rare moment when Abbas and Messali worked together, highlighting how once disparate Algerian political agendas were starting to converge.

Newly appointed governor-general Georges Catroux rejected the manifesto. General Charles de Gaulle, head of the Comité français de libération nationale, tried to appease the activists by passing a 7 March 1944 ordinance that granted citizenship to 65,000 Algerians. Furthermore, he abolished the Native Code that had been in place since 1881. Although de Gaulle's initiative still focused on preserving and strengthening the colonial relationship, it also marked the first significant political reforms in Algeria since 1919. Despite de Gaulle's marginal concessions, many Algerian political activists, including Ferhat Abbas, Messali Hadj and his followers, and the reformist 'ulamā rejected the ordinance as inadequate.

Exactly one week after the 7 March 1944 ordinance, Abbas founded the Amis du Manifeste et de la Liberté (AML), another attempt to build a broad coalition between the 'ulamā and the Algerian People's Party followers. He envisioned a more popular movement working toward "an Algerian nation," an "autonomous republic federated to a new, anticolonial, and anti-imperial French republic."[50] According to the AML statute, Abbas created the group to "familiarize and defend the 'Manifesto of the Algerian People' in front of French and Algerian public opinion and to reclaim the freedom of speech and expression for all Algerians." A second and related goal, Abbas wrote, was for the Amis du Manifeste et de la Liberté to "participate in the birth of a new world," which would respect human dignity.[51]

During the spring of 1944, Abbas moved closer toward Messali Hadj's political position of total separation from France. For example, on 22 May 1944, at a meeting in Constantine, Abbas announced that he was against "the politics of annexation and assimilation," and on 15 June, he discussed "forcing the French hand, to make them understand our will."[52] This rhetoric was not that of the same man who led the Federation of Elected Muslims in the late 1920s. By the end of 1944, the Amis du Manifeste et de la Liberté counted

500,000 members, thanks to Messali Hadj's open support. And yet, tensions between the two ideologues persisted; Abbas wanted to keep working with American president Franklin Roosevelt and French moderates to achieve a peaceful solution to the Algerian question, whereas Messali Hadj increasingly called for insurrection. The AML dissolved by 1 May 1945 and seven days later, after a series of tragic events, radical Algerian nationalists received an unexpected boost in men willing and eager to pursue independence at any cost.

One of the most violent and significant episodes in colonial Algerian history occurred while many people in Algeria and France celebrated the end of the war on 8 May 1945. In the eastern Algerian city of Sétif, 8,000–10,000 Algerian protesters carrying homemade banners and Algerian flags gathered in the streets. A scuffle erupted between them and the police, and by the end of the day twenty-nine Algerians were dead.[53] A similar scene played out in Guelma, a nearby town in the Constantinois close to the Tunisian border. However, a major distinguishing factor between the two cities is that settler militias carried out the reprisals in Guelma.[54] Threatened by what they considered to be a nationalist uprising and with the support of local subprefect André Achiary, the 4,000 settlers in Guelma organized themselves and killed 1,500 Algerians, mostly men between the ages of twenty-five and forty-five, by the end of the month.[55] The number of Algerians arrested soared in the weeks that followed. One estimate claims 5,560 individuals were rounded up for questioning.[56] Sétif and Guelma were turning points in solidifying nationalist sentiment. They hardened the political line for both French and Algerians and were a chilling indicator of the war to come. For advocates of *Algérie française,* Achiary's militias demonstrated the lengths they were willing to go to protect themselves and their interests. For anticolonialists, these events represented a definitive rupture in assimilationist policies. AML members recalled "the fallen innocent victims" who died as a result of "criminal acts" and vowed to push for stronger democratic reforms.[57] Be that as it may, I do not agree with historians such as Jean-Pierre Peyroulou who argue that May 1945 started the war for national liberation. To be sure, it was a defining moment in the evolution of Algerian nationalism. However, important domestic, regional, and international developments that contributed to the FLN's winning strategy for claiming sovereignty of Algeria had yet to take place.

Anticolonial Influences: North Africa and Indochina

In 1946, Ferhat Abbas and Messali Hadj continued to dominate the domestic political scene and a new generation of Algerian nationalists still had a choice between Abbas's recently formed Union Démocratique du Manifeste Algérien (UDMA) and Messali Hadj's latest political party, the Mouvement pour le Triomphe des Libértés Démocratiques (MTLD).[58] World War II radicalized Abbas, and even though both men wanted the same outcome for Algeria, independence, they did not agree on the approach and pace at which this was to happen. Abbas and his reformist supporters thought a gradual timeline achieved through diplomatic and democratic steps was the best way to attain independence from France, whereas Messali Hadj thought military action would yield the most successful results. Due to Messali Hadj's unwillingness to compromise, according to former FLN member Mohammed Harbi, by 1953, he was squeezed out of the MTLD by allies who were drawn to the UDMA's gradual approach.[59]

On the eve of 1 November 1954, three major political strands competed for power: the Messalists who advocated for independence through armed struggle; the centralists who attracted students and intellectuals with their message of political pluralism; and, last, the men who founded the FLN on 23 October 1954, who wanted to take up arms against the French colonial regime immediately.[60] One might notice that the Messalists and the FLN had extremely similar goals. They differed on one small point. Messali Hadj wanted to unite the various nationalist coalitions before initiating violence because he believed they stood a better chance of defeating the French. The FLN did not think that step was necessary and went ahead without the support of all Algerian nationalists. This rupture between the nationalists and lack of consensus reverberated into the early years of the struggle for national liberation as evidenced by the internal FLN divisions debated at Soummam in August 1956. It was also suggestive of the violent process by which Algerian nationalist "consensus" was established. Despite his being one of the most influential and experienced nationalist leaders dating back to the 1926 North African Star, Messali Hadj was marginalized by the FLN and postcolonial Algerian literature and relegated to the periphery of Algerian nationalist history. His charismatic personality and thirty years in Algerian politics threatened to undermine the FLN's message of unity under one party supported by the entire Algerian population. As a result, he was largely written out of the nationalist record until the late 1980s.[61]

In the decade after 1945, the Maghrib underwent considerable political changes that influenced Algerian nationalists and expanded their political options.[62] Immediately after World War II, Tunisian, Moroccan, and Algerian nationalists met to discuss pan-Maghribi action against French imperialism. Algeria's "wings," both French protectorates, were embroiled in similar nationalist mobilizations.[63] In Tunisia, Habib Bourguiba, the leader of the Neo-Destour Party and future first president, was convinced that "only a combination of Tunisian opposition and international pressure on France would create a political climate conducive to terminating French rule."[64] In March 1945, he traveled to Egypt to solicit help from the recently formed League of Arab States. The six nations in the League—Egypt, Iraq, Transjordan, Lebanon, Saudi Arabia, and Syria—were more focused on the Palestine question and thus unable to deliver the kind of support Bourguiba desired. However, the League's mere existence coupled with the Palestinian crisis inspired a "strong sense of Arab and Islamic identity" and propelled Pan-Arabism.[65] In 1947, Bourguiba joined forces with Moroccan and Algerian nationalists and created the Arab Maghrib Bureau in Cairo "with the purpose of coordinating propaganda and agitation against French rule," a tactic the FLN would soon adopt.[66] One year later, representatives from all three North African countries formed the Arab Maghrib Liberation Committee to carry out complementary initiatives. During the war for national liberation, the FLN relied on these regional connections for support ranging from material aid and arms to physical space to set up offices and organizations.

In the five years before the Algerian war, Algerian leaders witnessed armed struggle take off in the region. In 1949, the UN passed a resolution stating Libya would become independent, foreshadowing the important role the organization would play in decolonization. In 1950, Bourguiba attempted another round of political negotiations with the French administration when he presented it with the Neo-Destour's proposal to redefine the Franco-Tunisian relationship and his vision for Tunisian independence. In December 1952, tensions reached an all-time high in Tunisia when French terrorists killed Tunisian trade leader Ferhat Hached, setting off union strikes across the Maghrib. In the summer of that year, Nasser launched a revolution in Egypt and in August 1953, the French exiled then Moroccan sultan Mohammed V, which sparked violent protests. The Maghrib was rife with instability and the French were losing their grip on power.

The Algerians were not the only ones struggling to cast off a European oppressor. They now had tangible examples and models from which to draw.

The Vietminh's struggle to oust the French in Indochina between 1946 and 1954 arguably served as the FLN's direct inspiration when it launched its anticolonial movement in Algeria.[67] The Vietminh fashioned itself as a revolutionary group committed to creating a new political, economic, and social order. Its leadership, including Communist Party head Ho Chi Minh and senior military strategist Vo Nguyen Giap, developed a multipronged strategy that relied on mobilizing the indigenous population, solidifying regional alliances, and obtaining aid (especially from the People's Republic of China after 1949), which enabled them to strengthen their military efforts, construct a propaganda machine, and turn Cold War concerns into political gains. The FLN would emulate the Vietminh's blueprint for success and add a few more elements to its particular recipe for victory over the French. The consequences of a French defeat in Indochina reverberated for years to come and influenced how the French and the Algerians engaged each other on and off the battlefield.[68]

When World War II ended, recently liberated France set out to rebuild at home and reassert its power internationally. Reconstructing the Indochina federation was part of the latter task. But French political and military leaders faced numerous setbacks in 1945 and 1946, most notably tumultuous political transitions in the territories of Indochina, a vicious famine that caused up to two million deaths, and Charles de Gaulle's resignation as head of the French government, which splintered any hope of consensus on Indochina.

At the outset of the Franco-Vietminh war, which officially started on 19 December 1946, the French military unquestionably outnumbered and outperformed the Vietminh forces. However, by the conflict's end, culminating in a devastating and humiliating military defeat at Dien Bien Phu in the spring of 1954, the Vietminh had reversed these dynamics. It did so by spending years honing the above-mentioned strategy. Vietminh forces also benefited from mounting opposition to the war in France. Initially, domestic public opinion did not pay much attention to the conflict. The French press did not cover the events, and the majority of those fighting were either private soldiers or colonial troops. By 1953, the new French government, under Joseph Laniel, faced a concerned citizenry that questioned the purpose and cost of the war.[69] Dien Bien Phu was the last straw and eliminated any justification for France's continued presence there. Little did the subsequent French government, under René Coty, know, it would soon encounter a comparable enemy, much closer to home, that had studied the Vietminh and refined its techniques.

International Transformations: Standardizing
Health Care and Universalizing Rights

The domestic and regional contexts provided the FLN with the foundation to launch the war in 1954. But it was the international transformations and ensuing doctrines that emerged in the decade after World War II that furnished its leaders with critical tools for their winning strategy. International discourses on health care and welfare, so essential to the Algerian nationalists' campaign, evolved significantly from the 1850s to the 1950s.

International Sanitary Conferences, the first of which took place in France in 1851 and the last in 1938, were among the first attempts to create health codes governing the human body that would reduce the spread of disease throughout the world.[70] The League of Nations Health Organization, founded after World War I, represented a second attempt at formulating global health policy and introduced a common vocabulary about hygiene, which the FLN used during decolonization. Its efforts, along with those of the Epidemic Commission, the Rockefeller Foundation, and the Pasteur Institute, yielded important biological and epidemiological discoveries, but, with the exception of malaria research, their combined work had a minimal effect on the daily lives of those living in the global South.[71]

During the 1920s and 1930s, language about the right to health and welfare of all people around the world was slowly crystallizing. In some cases, colonial representatives and missionaries brought ideas of health and disease control to rural areas and contributed to what Nancy Hunt calls "a colonial lexicon" that altered the ways in which African women understood reproduction and maternity.[72] In other cases, a select number of local medical auxiliaries were trained to assist colonial physicians and to educate native populations about hygiene.[73] These intermediaries were critical in connecting biomedical ideas with those of the native populations and helped create a hybrid form of medicine and care.[74] But overall, imperial powers did not try to consistently educate the next generation of African physicians, nor did they focus on ways to improve the health of native populations over the long term as they discussed doing for their own populations at the League of Nations. Attempts to address disease-borne illnesses such as malaria and sleeping sickness were the most prominent health-care initiatives throughout colonial Africa. However, these targeted programs did not tackle social root causes and structural inequality that produced disease and ill health.[75] In the immediate aftermath of World War I, health care in colonial contexts dealt almost exclusively with disease prevention and was connected with the civilizing mission. It was not yet inextricably linked with humanitarian crises.

French and British administrators were forced to think about health, and specifically colonial health, differently when they encountered a crisis in production in the 1920s and 1930s and had to increase the colonial workforce. Officials admitted that they would need to improve health conditions for laborers if they were going to be subjected to longer hours, dangerous migration patterns, and unsanitary urban dwellings. In Algeria, for example, the Muslim population in urban centers increased dramatically between the 1920s and 1940s. In twenty years it more than doubled from 508,235 to 1,129,482. Population growth in rural areas and in the southern regions of Algeria expanded at a smaller rate (15–25 percent).[76] Despite the discrepancy, French administrators had to contend with the reality of sustained and close proximity of Algerians and settlers as well as the demand and pressure for improved health care. For the first time, officials had to address "the shortage and inefficiency of manpower due to debilitating diseases and unsanitary conditions" and quickly find ways to resolve the problem.[77]

In Algeria, this realization prompted administrators to prioritize the health of the natives, for not only would their well-being effect production but also it stood to boost the metropolitan economy. Certain progressive administrators such as Albert Sarraut believed that Algerian workers would work harder if they were granted some measures of protection, but his was not a widely held position in the 1930s. Not all men in power at the time envisioned benefits from what would have been a significantly different policy approach.

Reluctance to standardize health and labor conditions in the colonies changed after World War II. Empires presented both a challenge and a solution to the crisis of capitalism. On the one hand, the colonies contained an endless supply of laborers who could work toward more production and greater profit. On the other hand, those individuals needed to be healthy to work and required infrastructure to support their transportation and housing needs. Aiming to resolve this particular conundrum, colonial administrators and development experts throughout the French and British empires devised numerous five- and ten-year plans to expand schools and hospitals, build new roads, improve public facilities, and grow industry.[78] Although more attention was paid to native health and improving nutrition, colonial officials did not address the social roots of inequality.[79]

The accelerated pace of development between 1945 and 1955 did not last nor did it generate the sought-after capital to revitalize the French and British metropoles. But the decade-long push created a universal set of terms about health care, development, and modernity that Algerian nationalists were quietly absorbing.[80] They observed postwar health-care debates and armed themselves with a fresh understanding of international language. They soon deployed this language to articulate political claims and demonstrate their ability to care for the Algerian population, discussed in depth in Chapters 3 and 4.

Western European and American officials did not anticipate the use by Third World actors of medicine and health care terminology, and that was not the only area from which their language would be appropriated. The rise of international organizations that promoted human rights and a revised commitment to the principles of humanitarianism after World War II fundamentally altered international politics and rewrote the rules of political engagement. Human rights and humanitarianism provided universal ideas that were devoid of race, gender, or religious preferences and therefore were easily transferable to whoever had knowledge of them. These words were disseminated through radio broadcasts and newspaper headlines that the entire world could consume. This was not the first time in the twentieth century that anticolonial actors appropriated Western rhetoric. However, two important features distinguished the 1940s and 1950s: first, the volume of charters and agreements produced, as well as the number of signatories, far exceeded the interwar period, and, second, the level of anticolonial sentiment was at an all-time high.[81]

The severity and extreme violence of World War II left many Western nations vulnerable and their leaders eager to find solutions that would prevent that scale of war from ever repeating itself. For the second time in twenty-five years, international cooperation became their focus as exemplified by numerous rights-based declarations, including the Atlantic Charter, the UN Charter, the 1948 Universal Declaration of Human Rights, the Convention for the Protection of Human Rights and Fundamental Freedoms, and the Geneva Conventions of 1949.[82] However, these documents were intended to ensure Western security and European power, not enfranchise the entire world.

The United Nations, created in 1945, was the cornerstone of this internationalist spirit and served as the foundation for the ideals of global governance.[83] There had been three prior comprehensive attempts at international treaties: the Peace of Westphalia (1646), the Congress of Vienna (1815), and the Treaty of Versailles (1919), none of which were able to definitively resolve the tension between international cooperation and domestic jurisdiction.[84] These agreements also disproportionately favored Western European nations and the United States, a trend that bristled against the sweeping changes that decolonization introduced to international politics after World War II. The geographic span and the number of people affected by the war instilled a sense of urgency to work together, and notably every continent except Antarctica was represented in the original UN membership in 1945. But this unprecedented level of representation also meant that national delegates each had their own vision and priorities for the organization and they struggled to agree on the contents of the charter.

Algerian nationalist Ferhat Abbas closely followed the UN proceedings. On 29 April 1945, he publicly stated that "the United Nations conference assured the liberty of all people," which he thought would soon translate into Algerian independence.[85] But neither the charter nor the representatives who met in California that spring guaranteed independence, and the colonial question dominated internal debates for years to come. For example, in an effort to clarify the UN's position on anticolonial movements, several committees debated the rights of non-self-governing territories in the early 1950s, an issue the General Assembly revisited year after year.[86] Members struggled to include a colonial policy clause that, on the one hand, supported the right of all people to self-determination as articulated in Article 1(2) of the UN Charter and, on the other hand, permitted colonial governments to run their own affairs.[87] By the end of the decade, as "anti-colonialism gathered momentum," the UN had no choice but to adapt itself despite "objections from the Western powers involved."[88]

Western countries tackled the conundrum of trying to ensure peace without dissolving their right to rule within their borders by intentionally omitting enforcement mechanisms.[89] For instance, in a private meeting, Eleanor Roosevelt, a U.S. representative at the United Nations, who also played a critical role in writing the Universal Declaration of Human Rights in 1948, reportedly explained that the best way "to deal with Resolution A [on self-determination] was to amend it so that neither the timing nor the means of applying the principle would be automatic or rigid."[90] Even an eminent leader in the fight to protect all people acknowledged the interests of imperial nations behind closed doors. None of the agreements were legally binding nor could any member state or fellow signatory require that another party follow the prescriptions. Meaningful assistance and intervention of any kind were nearly impossible under these conditions often leading the Great Powers to use their commitments to human rights and humanitarianism as a weapon against each other rather than as a firm anchor to protect individuals.[91]

The United Nations and its charter became a prominent feature of post-war politics. Their architects had no control over who and how they were appropriated. The French did not intend to extend political rights to their empire, and colonial officials were unprepared when nationalists started articulating claims to French representatives and international organizations couched in the same terminology. But this is precisely what Algerian FLN members did. As discussed in Chapter 6, the FLN appealed to the United Nations, which provided a physical and theoretical stage for them to be heard by a broad audience and where colonial inequalities were mitigated.[92] The General Assembly floor in New York, and, by extension, international organizations, temporarily removed the preeminence of state sovereignty and leveled the political playing field. Algerian nationalists expressed their grievances and publicly exposed what sovereigns previously strained to keep private, transforming international organizations and the nature of political power and authority in the twentieth century.

The revised Geneva Conventions of 1949, what historian David Forsythe calls "a moral pillar for international relations after 1945," were a third international development upon which the Algerian nationalists later relied to claim their sovereignty.[93] Between 1946 and 1949, the International Committee of the Red Cross (ICRC) led a team of international jurists, Red Cross delegates, and state government representatives in updating the three existing Geneva Conventions and ensuring better protection for civilians during times of war.[94] The prestigious international organization, a beacon of moral authority in world affairs, recognized a need for broadening the scope of its humanitarian safeguards and embarked upon a contentious process during which officials struggled to balance national sovereignty and more rigorous international laws.[95]

State power and global security often interfere with one another, as national delegates discovered in San Francisco when they met to create the United Nations. However, ICRC neutrality was supposed to eliminate politics and national interests from the equation. But, as Mark Lewis has shown, that was not the case during the Geneva Convention revision debates.[96] "The revision project," he writes, "was dominated by a European/North American perspective, reflecting both post-war imperial politics and the ICRC's Eurocentric perspective."[97] In light of the ICRC's overall neglect of the Jewish population during the war and the harsh criticism it received for this, in 1946, acting president Max Huber was interested in revising the conventions in order "to gain enhanced powers to inspect prisons and camps, improve the rules for the treatment of POWs, establish baseline rules for the treatment of detained civilians, and strengthen the ICRC's legal and practical ability to deliver food and clothing to POWs."[98] The legal parameters set out in the final version of the Geneva Conventions did not pertain to civil or internal conflicts, technically what the French colonial administrations called the Algerian war. Yet, they provided a legal framework that was respected by its signatories and recognized worldwide as an ideal to strive for. Algerian nationalists would work both of these angles, especially after 1957. The FLN and the Algerian Liberation Army became well versed in the Geneva Conventions and tried to hold the French government, a signatory of the 1949 conventions, and its military accountable to them, while also claiming to recognize and follow the prescribed guidelines for proper codes of conduct in war. This post–World War II text laid out a how-to guide for nonstate actors to engage in diplomatic, military, and humanitarian negotiations with powerful army leaders and representatives from the renowned ICRC.

Conclusion

The evolution of nationalism in Algeria was a competitive forty-year process, the results of which could not have been predicted even in 1950. FLN members in 1954 lived through numerous iterations of political parties and failed reforms and most felt they had exhausted every viable option for achieving their aims. The FLN had a firm agenda for complete independence and was in a unique position in November 1954 to set off coordinated attacks throughout Algeria. However, as the opening vignette on the 1956 Soummam Congress showed, not all Algerian nationalists agreed that the FLN was the sole party capable of winning the war for the Algerian people, and, beyond that, there were massive divisions within the FLN reflecting decades of ideological sparring. The nationalist leadership continued to work through these differences that threatened to derail their ultimate objective.[99] In spite of these differences, the FLN managed to keep a firm grasp on dissenters and detractors and forge ahead in its mission of attracting international attention and support for its cause.

But for all of the nationalists' ingenuity and creativity, other tectonic shifts at the regional and international levels enabled them to attain their position and experience an unprecedented degree of success in shaping public opinion and forcing the French to recognize Algerian sovereignty. FLN representatives explored numerous diplomatic and military strategies. But, as the following chapters demonstrate, it was their appropriation of medicine and health-care, humanitarianism, and rights discourses, all products of World War II, that yielded the most successful results. The nationalists deliberately used them as political tools and selectively deployed them depending on the moment and target audience. The FLN mastered these rhetorics and built a comprehensive strategy that operated at the local, regional, and international levels and could not be ignored. We now turn to the first layer of the FLN's plan of attack, constructing a wartime health-services division and battling the French over winning the hearts, minds, and bodies of the population.

Chapter 2

Medical Pacification and the Sections Administratives Spécialisées

On 31 October 1954, nine "historic leaders," Mourad Didouche, Hocine Aït Ahmed, Mohamed Boudiaf, Mohamed Larbi Ben M'hidi, Ahmed Ben Bella, Mustapha Ben Boulaïd, Mohamed Khider, Rabah Bitat, Belkacem Krim, bound by their belief that independence was only possible through armed struggle and revolution, drafted the Proclamation of the National Liberation Front. This document, released in conjunction with the coordinated attacks of 1 November 1954 the next day, announced the beginning of the Algerian war for national liberation.

The proclamation, addressed to the Algerian people, emphasized that "after decades of struggle, the nationalist movement had reached its final phase. . . . Our action is solely directed against colonialism, a stubborn and blind enemy who has always refused to grant the slightest liberty by peaceful means. Those are," its authors believed, "sufficient reasons why our movement comes under the label of the National Liberation Front . . . offering the opportunity for all Algerian patriots from all social classes . . . to integrate themselves into the liberation struggle without any other consideration." The FLN's primary goal, as defined by the proclamation, was national independence by restoring "the sovereign, democratic, and social state of Algeria within the framework of Islamic principles" and by respecting "fundamental freedoms for all."[1]

The nationalist leaders carefully outlined internal and external objectives that guided their activities through 1962 and that they believed would secure Algerian sovereignty. Domestically, they aimed to restore the national revolutionary movement to its true place by "ridding it of all vestiges of corruption and reformism" and to "gather and organize all the sound energy of the Algerian people to liquidate the colonial system." The proclamation specified three external goals: internationalizing the Algerian problem, solidifying North African unity within an Arab Muslim context, and relying upon the United Nations Charter to demonstrate and attract solidarity for the principles articulated within it.[2] This sophisticated and multidimensional FLN platform was the result of decades of political activity and reflected an engagement with contemporary trends such as Pan-Arabism and human rights, broadly defined, in the post–World War II era. Moreover, the platform reflected the central tenets of what Algerian nationalists thought would prove their sovereignty to the Algerian people, French colonial officials, and world leaders.

Despite the FLN's announcement, the French government of Pierre Mendès-France neither recognized nor acknowledged a war was under way. Just a few weeks earlier, in October 1954, François Mitterand, minister of the interior, had traveled throughout Algeria and concluded in a report to French premier Mendès-France that "the climate is getting worse over there," and he "recognized the urgent need . . . to integrate more Algerians into the colonial administration."[3] These cautionary words could not have been more true.

The French administration was not prepared for the long-term political divisions and struggles that would follow between moderates and ultraconservatives who ardently believed in *Algérie française* and were prepared to take any necessary steps to ensure its survival. For Mendès-France, who advocated a reformist agenda, navigating these factions immediately became a problem after 1 November. At the 12 November National Assembly meeting, he declared his unequivocal support that "the Algerian departments are part of the French Republic. They have been French for a long time, and they are irrevocably French. . . . Between them and metropolitan France there can be no conceivable secession."[4] For the remaining three months that Mendès-France's government was in power, he grappled with accommodating various viewpoints and trying to find a peaceful solution similar to French policies in Morocco and Tunisia.[5]

One of Mendès-France's most significant appointments during this period, before his government crumbled and that of Edgar Faure replaced it, was naming Jacques Soustelle as governor-general of Algeria in January 1955.[6] Soustelle had long been active in French politics, dating back to World War II, when he joined Charles de Gaulle's Free French Resistance movement. The two men remained close, and Soustelle served as secretary-general from 1947 to 1951 in de Gaulle's Rassemblement du Peuple Français (RPF) party and he would later prove instrumental in orchestrating de Gaulle's return to power in May 1958. Mendès-France anticipated that in addition to Soustelle's World War II credentials his considerable political experience and acumen would serve to quiet opponents concerned that Algeria would be a third humiliating military loss in recent memory. French military defeats in 1940 when the Vichy government came to power in France and in 1954 at Dien Bien Phu in Indochina weighed heavily on the national consciousness, and military officials could not imagine suffering another defeat in Algeria.[7]

Soustelle had a reputation for being liberal and many hoped he would help reshape the contentious politics of the moment in Algeria.[8] He had publicly advocated for Algeria's integration with France and in the months leading up to his confirmation as governor-general, he wrote several articles that described "his ideas for a French Federation, in which Algeria would find its place."[9] Soustelle knew the settler lobby in Algeria distrusted him but that did not "detract him from accelerating reform that would win over the Muslim majority."[10] He traveled through Algeria on his first official visit in the winter of 1955 and witnessed the abject poverty and poor conditions in which many Algerians lived. His trip revealed the state's failure to penetrate the territory after 120 years of colonial rule, but he also learned that the recently formed FLN had not gained the people's support. With this picture in mind, he went on to develop the Special Administrative Sections (Sections Administratives Spécialisées, SAS), "precisely with the goal of elevating the quality of life of the [Algerian] population" and showing it an alternative for the future.[11]

The Special Administrative Sections were conceived broadly as a program that would facilitate political rapprochement between the Algerian population and the colonial state. They targeted a variety of areas that would improve the Algerian people's daily life and relieve dire economic conditions in which many lived. The SAS built roads and bridges and conducted censuses in order to better understand the welfare needs of different communities. They repaired schools and enrolled young boys and girls in primary classes. SAS teams also constructed houses for displaced families, oversaw local elections, and built work camps for unemployed men.[12] These programs went a long way toward pacifying the population and disincentivizing Algerians from joining the FLN.[13]

Medical outreach was a central component of the SAS program; it offered a dramatically different view of the French and their violent military campaigns. Teams of physicians, nurses, and assistants visited rural areas and provided free care, taught hygiene classes for women, and offered vaccinations. In some cases, their visits were the first time state services penetrated the interior, and the administration devoted serious attention toward remedying this neglect through peaceful pacifiers, instructed to conquer with medicine rather than bullets.[14] To be sure, SAS health-care programs and French military counterinsurgency operations shared a common end goal. However, the humane approach to Algerians' health and well-being transformed the way some Algerians perceived the colonial state.

These programs were not an original idea about how to manage North Africans. The initiative closely resembled the Bureaux Arabes in nineteenth-century Algeria and the Service des Affaires Indigènes in early colonial Morocco.[15] Furthermore, the colonial authorities in Algeria made efforts between 1904 and 1960 to train *auxiliaires médicaux* who were responsible for providing medical treatment and hygienic instruction exclusively to Muslims. This small group of Muslim men who totaled fewer than three hundred worked under *médecins de colonisation* and helped administer rural life in the first half of the twentieth century.[16] What makes the SAS noteworthy is the extreme lengths to which Jacques Soustelle and his colleagues went to extend social services in the 1950s. For nearly 130 years, the colonial state did not provide Algerians with adequate education and professional training opportunities equivalent to those offered to French citizens. French administrators did not build vital medical and social institutions that all Algerians could access, nor were Algerians permitted to actively participate in the political sphere. As such, the government found itself needing to "reconquer" and integrate Algerians into what Frantz Fanon has called a dying colonial regime in the 1950s and 1960s.[17]

The state of native health care spoke volumes about government allocation of resources and chronic underdevelopment. The war called attention to these deficiencies but it also presented the administration with an opportunity to offer care and establish itself in the hearts and minds of people in desperate need of medical attention and supplies. As such, the SAS often were met with little resistance and embraced by local communities, a fact that French military publications used for propaganda purposes.

The native population had largely been excluded from medical training when the war broke out. Despite facing extreme hardships, the nationalist leadership watched the French implement the SAS programs and capture the hearts and minds of the population through health-care campaigns. They witnessed the powerful effect the SAS had in rehabilitating the French colonial state and how the French military used medicine as a propaganda tool. The FLN emulated these programs and did so by creating its own health-services division, which did not take off in earnest until 1956 (discussed in more detail in Chapter 3).

This chapter examines the genesis of French colonial medical pacification campaigns, dating back to the nineteenth century, and shows how the French military resurrected these ideas and practices a century later during the war for national liberation. The Special Administrative Sections were one of the largest French wartime initiatives and yielded an unintentional result. The nationalists developed their own domestic medical services to care for the Algerian people, thus taking their first steps toward acting and performing like a state.

Medicine and Imperialism in Nineteenth-Century North Africa

Thousands of French soldiers and military physicians disembarked from ships in the 1830s, 1840s, and 1850s in Algeria, armed with what they considered a potent tool of conquest, *la mission civilisatrice*. These men firmly believed they were more enlightened and that they were "charged with a universal mission" to spread civilization to less developed peoples and places.[18] They viewed themselves as missionaries and apostles who were engaged in a global project of elevating civilization.[19]

The French conquered Algeria first during a period of military rule (1830–1870) and then administered the country for nearly a century under civilian rule. During the former, military personnel targeted the coastal cities of Algiers, Oran, and Constantine, and by 1848, they established thirty-three hospital facilities that primarily serviced the European population. Although the doors were open to the local Arab inhabitants, many hesitated to cross the threshold due to uncertainty and fear. Several French physicians developed medical initiatives that aimed to gain the confidence of chiefs and marabouts, inspire belief in French medicine, and attract Algerians to hospitals.[20] These military medical efforts were part of a larger pacification campaign to reduce Algerian resistance and demonstrate French superiority.[21] Even though the physicians strongly believed in the efficacy of their treatments, important discoveries in bacteriology and immunology had not yet been made.[22]

Upon their arrival in Algeria in the mid-nineteenth century, military doctors noted how rare it was to see hospital establishments.[23] They remarked how medicine and religious practices were often associated with one another and how "European medicine was often unconvincing" to Algerians.[24] The physicians hoped their tools of empire—medical care and other social services—would ease Algerian resistance and suspicion to the colonial project.[25] If their medicine was effective in treating disease, Algerians might be grateful and share their success stories with friends and family, and the French might be better prepared to penetrate into the heartlands of Algeria without encountering resistance. The early administrators recognized that conquering a foreign territory could be difficult. They encountered many barriers— unfamiliar geography, unknown territories, cultural and linguistic differences, shortage of supplies—and were unable to swiftly implement their social programs. Officials tried to overcome these challenges by establishing hospitals or clinics in more populated areas and treating Algerians in these facilities. French medical personnel hoped that after receiving medical care, Algerian patients would go home, eager to relay their positive experiences with others, consequently establishing French rule and authority in the process.[26]

Confronted with rampant disease and poor public health measures, the military regime prioritized "maintaining the health of the soldiers" and "bringing the benefits of our civilization to the Arabs."[27] The language used to describe medicine and health was often moralistic and judgmental. Those involved in the early settlement of Algeria witnessed local medical practices and concluded that they were backward, outdated, or nonexistent, and typically based on notions of fatalism.[28] Fatalism was one reason why many Algerians did not want to be vaccinated or interact with French physicians.[29] In other cases, fear and resistance to the colonial project explained why the French were able only to administer twelve vaccinations from 1845 to 1848.[30] These explanations exonerated the French of responsibility for the effects of their violent settlement campaign, including the seizure of land and massive local displacement.[31] If the Algerians would not take advantage of their offerings, it was not France's fault. Rather, it was the fault of the Algerians whose actions were informed by an inferior worldview.

Doctors played a central role "in creating Algeria" and enabling effective colonial governance.[32] Initially, they were sent to look after the troops settling the colony but the French medical corps' responsibilities soon extended beyond this primary objective as they began interacting with indigenous populations. They were often the first contact Algerians had with the French and would therefore serve as an extension of the emerging colonial state, an idea and practice that was resurrected during the war for national liberation. The physicians wanted to make a positive lasting impression, and they assumed bringing free medical care would be an easy way of psychologically disarming the Algerians. These early interactions and the written observations about the Algerians shaped colonial and metropolitan perceptions of the indigenous population and later served to categorize and marginalize them. Seldom were their observations and conclusions impartial; rather, they were wrought with racism and prejudice.[33] Much of the military corps' work in the first four decades of French rule laid the foundation for future colonial attitudes and policies in Algeria.[34]

Providing medical treatment to the Muslim population was an integral part of the colonizing process in Algeria. However, due to budgetary constraints, insufficient personnel, and growing Algerian and settler populations, colonial officials did not devote equal or consistent efforts to medical training and care throughout the first half of the twentieth century. This does not mean that French administrators ignored the strategic value of providing medicine and health care, as evidenced by governor-general Charles Jonnart's 1903 speech in Tunis. In his remarks, he noted "the doctor is the true conqueror, the peaceful conqueror. . . . If [the French] wish to penetrate their hearts, to win the confidence of the Muslims, it is in multiplying the services of medical assistance that [the French] will arrive at it most surely."[35] This is the same explanation the government used in Algeria during the period of military rule and identical to the justification it would employ a century later when it sent teams of physicians and nurses to rural areas during the Algerian war. The image of the doctor as conqueror resurfaced quickly in the 1950s. The nineteenth-century French pacification efforts provided the historical and intellectual tradition that later made the Special Administrative Sections possible and informed Algerian nationalist health-care efforts.

Medicine, Training, and Facilities, 1900–1954

After the initial conquest of Algeria and the transition from military rule to civilian rule, the French continued to erect medical infrastructure and provide some free health-care services such as medical consultations.[36] However, the primary objective of these projects was no longer to pacify the Algerians but rather to protect and serve the growing European settler population and effectively govern the population.[37] Hospitals and clinics were built in major cities, thereby largely neglecting rural areas. These facilities were so far removed from the majority of the Algerian population who lived outside of the major urban centers that they were unable to travel to receive medical assistance. While some colonial administrators and doctors attributed their absence in the clinics to superstition or indifference, some understood that the physical distance between the Algerian communities and the clinics in urban locations prevented them from coming in for checkups and medicine. Dr. E. L. Bertherand of the Algiers Bureau Arabe recognized that Algerians were less likely to leave their families and travel great distances to French-run hospitals. He suggested traveling to meet the natives in the same way that the military physicians had decades before them.[38] Moreover, some French doctors noticed contesting medical epistemologies that required negotiations between themselves and their patients.[39]

The authorities also hoped to recruit local medical auxiliaries to ease the load of French physicians and establish permanent contact with Algerians.[40] The Native Auxiliary Medical Corps was created in 1901 to provide doctors with local assistants.[41] In the decade following its creation, Algerians between the ages of nineteen and twenty-four were recruited to attend a two-year training program at the School of Medicine and Pharmacy of Algiers and complete an internship at Mustapha Hospital, after which they would assist doctors in distributing and administering certain medications, vaccinating patients, and preparing them for medical procedures.[42] By 1912, when its population was roughly 5.5 million (4.75 million Algerians and 750,000 Europeans), Algeria had fifteen civil hospitals, five military hospitals, and three hospices in Algiers, Constantine, and Oran. Seventy-eight physicians, surgeons, and pharmacists worked in these establishments. It is unclear how many, if any, of the seventy-eight were Algerian.[43] These statistics indicate that the facilities were understaffed and the medical personnel were overworked, which led to insufficient or otherwise poor care.

Despite the limited and inadequate care the French were able to administer, they remained optimistic in light of recent scientific discoveries and medical advances made at the Pasteur Institute. The government proceeded to build hospitals and training facilities in the interwar period, the most notable of which included the Hygiene and Colonial Medicine Institute (1923) and several auxiliary hospitals. The number of civil hospitals and hospices grew from twenty-one in 1920 to forty-five in 1932.[44] World War II delayed most projects of this nature, including education initiatives.[45] Immediately following the war, the planned expansion of medical facilities was temporarily suspended. The government conducted studies and surveys and discovered serious hospital deficiencies. These results spawned initiatives to reorganize and expand medical services in Algeria. With a renewed interest in reform, the French government invested in structural improvements. Following World War II, it increased the number of hospital beds from 16,000 in 1944 to 26,166 by March 1955.[46] But the number of hospital beds in Algeria paled in comparison to the number of beds in the metropole. The former had one or two beds per one thousand inhabitants, while the latter averaged twelve beds per one thousand residents.[47] Yet, the administration continued its expansion projects. Between 1947 and 1955, construction began on seventy health centers, of which fifty-six had been completed at the end of the period. Of seventy-one consultation rooms planned, fifty-five were completed. The administration also turned its attention to fighting tuberculosis and distributing vaccinations. The number of beds for tuberculosis patients grew from 800 in 1944 to 5,000 in March 1955, and by January 1954, 1.3 million people had been vaccinated.[48]

Looking at these improvements would suggest that the colonial regime was dedicated to extending medical services to Algerians. However, when the growth of the population is factored into these statistics, the expansion of medical care is less impressive. Following World War II, the Algerian population had reached 8.5 million and yet the country was only equipped with twenty-eight civil hospitals and nineteen auxiliary hospitals.[49] It would have been physically and financially impossible to properly service the medical and health-care needs of the population in these limited facilities. The southern regions of Algeria had been mostly neglected before World War II and remained so during the government's planned expansion. Although the number of physicians in the area nearly doubled between 1943 and 1955, from twenty-five to forty-five, this increase kept pace neither with the growth of the region's population nor with the expansion in medical care elsewhere in Algeria.[50] Even with a renewed commitment to providing more doctors, these statistics highlight how much of Algeria and its population lay beyond the reach of the colonial state.

After 1945 French health administrators took a proactive step toward expanding the medical corps by issuing a series of ordinances and decrees updating rules and regulations regarding who was permitted to practice medicine in France and Algeria.[51] They generally stipulated that physicians, dentists, and nurses were required to have a diploma issued by the French state, have French citizenship, or have recognized diplomas from Morocco or

Tunisia. Vaccines and preventative care were regulated through the Public Health Code, which discussed methods for staying healthy for those living in France and Algeria. The Public Health Code also included details about hospital operations, the ways in which the regional, departmental, and national medical profession should be organized, and the nature and role of hospitals and public clinics.[52] As of 1953, the French did not differentiate between how medical institutions and their staff members were expected to operate in France and in Algeria. Even though the medical infrastructure varied greatly in the two places, the government conceptualized them as similar and subject to the same rules.

One way to help further alleviate these stresses would have been to train more Algerian doctors in the new medical schools and institutes the French were erecting around the country. But as one prominent doctor who participated in the national liberation struggle remembered, in his medical school class of more than thirty students only one or two of them were Algerian in the early 1950s.[53] Algerian women were even less likely to enter medical school, as one of the few trained female doctors of the time recalled.[54] High illiteracy rates and poor early education excluded most Algerians from becoming competitive medical school applicants and often relegated them to inferior positions such as medical assistants. On the eve of the war for national liberation, Algerians had been marginalized in the medical sphere for decades. But they witnessed the power, both literally and ideologically, that medicine could have over the population.

The French had created a significant gap in knowledge and access to information, leaving them ill-equipped and unprepared to deal with the medical crisis that would erupt during the war. The medical sector in colonial Algeria was seriously underdeveloped and in need of significant financial resources, as well as training opportunities and staff. These conditions set the stage for French medical campaigns to take advantage of the health-care vacuum, the result of decades of colonial failure, when the war for national liberation began and attempts were made to use them for political gain. The FLN watched closely and gained inspiration from them, implementing nearly identical medical programs in Algeria after 1956.

The Sections Administratives Spécialisées

As the war forged ahead and tensions escalated between the two sides following the August 1955 Philippeville massacres, a turning point in the war, Soustelle began implementing social and economic programs he hoped would
mitigate Algerian resentment and combat nationalist propaganda.[55] Even
though the administration's initial response to the FLN attacks was simply to
reinforce police efforts, by 1955, and especially after Philippeville, it became
clear that a larger, less conventional conflict was under way. Soustelle knew
winning the battle for Algerian hearts and minds would be critical to winning
the war, a fact to which many military officers recently returned from Indochina attested.[56] He realized that the French army, once again, faced an unconventional opponent in Algeria and would need to use different methods to
vanquish the enemy. As such, he drew from French military strategies that assumed the nature of war had become increasingly "subversive, fought not with
regular armies but with bands of guerrillas or people's armies . . . finding refuge
and support among the population."[57] Militias around the world utilized revolutionary warfare as their dominant strategy, and Algeria was no exception.[58]
From its first set of coordinated attacks, the FLN employed guerrilla tactics that
were meant to destabilize French rule throughout the country. In response, the
French military adopted counterrevolutionary measures that were applied in
conjunction with a series of programs intended to destroy Algerian political
networks, collect intelligence, and win over the local population.[59]

The Sections Administratives Spécialisées were the cornerstone integra-
tion program, and by 1961 more than seven hundred existed in Algeria.[60]
Despite French claims throughout colonial rule that Algerians could become
French citizens, few actually obtained citizenship because in order to do so
Algerians were required to abandon their Muslim personal status. During
the 1950s and 1960s, in an effort to quell the war, French politicians adopted
a more flexible approach to officially incorporating Algerians into France.[61]
Alongside meager political openings, the government pursued integration
policies that officials hoped would "overcome [the Muslim community's]
overwhelming poverty and that independence would be prevented by integrating Muslims fully into modern French society."[62] But there was a certain
irony to the urgency of the SAS. Had the French previously educated Algerians, granted them political rights, or consistently provided social services,
the Pierre Mendès-France and Edgar Faure governments may not have
needed Soustelle to devise an integration campaign.[63]

Nearly six months after his initial trip through the Algerian countryside, a 26 September 1955 decree permitted Soustelle to establish the Special Administrative Sections. In a December 1955 pamphlet he explained that in light of the current situation, he decided to create the SAS "to ensure the retaking of the population in regions where terrorists are active or those at risk of being contaminated." The heart of the mission was "to reestablish contact with the Algerians, renew their confidence in the French, and report information back to civil authorities."[64] To help SAS personnel accomplish these goals, Soustelle authorized them to "exercise certain administrative functions that will permit them to service the population" and help it "recover a taste for and respect of the French presence."[65] He divided up the country into zones, and the SAS would operate within those areas that Soustelle believed harbored rebels. Soustelle specified that an Algerian Affaires officer would head each SAS unit and a member of the Algerian Affaires Attaché Corps, medical personnel, a protection force, a vehicle and radio, and construction supplies, would be at his disposal.[66] This team's objective, writes Jacques Frémeaux, was to "prevent losing Algeria" and "to construct an Algeria linked with France," not service the people simply for their own good.[67]

The December 1955 pamphlet obscures the degree to which SAS social programs were firmly subordinated to the military and its larger purpose of fighting the FLN. Its medical sector received instructions from the military and reported its progress and monthly activities back to military superiors. The various programs' materials and equipment were supplied by the military, and personnel were frequently hired through military channels. Any structural changes or reassignments came from military officials. In actuality, the SAS were simply an extension of the French military and carried out what one scholar calls "police missions."[68]

However, this new face of the military did not principally guard checkpoints or carry rifles. The SAS personnel arrived with more gentle weapons, medicine and health-care products, and, similar to military physicians who helped settle Algeria during the mid-nineteenth century, they became potent symbols of colonial development to which the French could point as showcasing their commitment to Algeria. How could the government be accused of neglecting the Algerians' welfare if it was offering free medical care and building new schools? Jacques Soustelle knew the colonial administration needed to concentrate on public relations and focus on strengthening relations with the Algerian population. For French general Raoul Salan, the SAS officers played a central role in this endeavor and were "the driving force behind pacification."[69]

From the inception of the SAS there was a distinction between the military objectives and the way the SAS portrayed its activities to the Algerian people. The military's dual mission was to subdue the local population by supplying social services and to collect intelligence for future military endeavors, just as doctors had done during the Algerian conquest beginning in the 1830s. Part of the comprehensive strategy in waging war against the FLN was to engage the population, take hold of it, rally it, and progressively utilize it.[70] The SAS were dispatched to areas of strategic value and they were supposed to operate with military precision when establishing contact with villages and attempt to neutralize their suspicion and hostility toward the French. SAS visits would demonstrate to the local population that not only could the colonial state provide for them but that it was also committed to improving their quality of life in ways that the FLN could not. At the same time, monthly medical reports about the number of men, women, and children would be sent back to military officials who would then convert the raw data into reliable intelligence about particular regions.[71] With this kind of information, soon the SAS could attempt "to balance in a short time, and with considerable effort, the administrative and social irresponsibility with which Paris had ruled Algeria for more than a century."[72] This was how the SAS were ideally supposed to function. As we will see, the reality of how the SAS operated was quite different.[73]

Recruiting Personnel

The administration turned its attention to finding qualified staff to carry out pacification, many of whom were likely unaware of the depth and breadth of the medical field's underdevelopment. This immediately posed a problem. Those that were hired came from a variety of backgrounds, including but not limited to Indochina veterans, Arabic linguists and specialists of the region, and regiment officers.[74] The diverse experience of participants made ideological coherence nearly impossible, and they were constantly caught between contradictory military and civilian priorities. Their "intermediary positions" were a source of tension from the outset and hindered what they would achieve.[75]

When the SAS started, there were fewer than four hundred military physicians working in Algeria and the state of medical facilities remained inadequate to offer comprehensive care to the roughly ten million Muslim and

European people living in Algeria at the time.[76] Public and private hospitals received twelve million francs between 1949 and 1954, and a May 1955 *Monthly Bulletin of General Statistics* applauded the expansion of hospital beds in that time from 21,218 to 28,018, but this number would hardly temper the devastation ahead and the deplorable conditions SAS teams encountered.[77] Given the nature of SAS units, officials preferred to place military doctors in designated medical positions; however, too few existed and the leadership began coordinating their efforts with civil physicians in Algeria.

The SAS recruited active officers in the French army and reserve officers at home. They were expected to serve anywhere from six months to three years and were enticed with salaries ranging from 5,000 to 18,000 francs, but even with these incentives, the number of volunteers remained feeble.[78] Armand Frémont attributes the difficulty of recruiting voluntary military and Foreign Legion enlistees to feelings of doubt and ambivalence about Algeria, some even protesting that "this war [is] not ours."[79] SAS medical officers, frequently drawn from the same pool of volunteers, had to temper these sentiments and find ways to continue their medical outreach to the Algerian people.

The SAS program, looking to develop its staff beyond military recruits, may have found a way of supplementing medical personnel with Algerian staff, but a series of applications from 1955 show that colonial officials privileged political allegiance over technical skill. Late that fall, several hundred men and women, the majority of whom were Algerian, submitted dossiers for consideration to work at hospital facilities such as the Psychiatric Hospital of Blida, the Algerian Cancer Center, the Oran Civil Hospital, and the Sétif Civil Hospital. Upon review, which consisted of checking the person's education, city and address of origin, police record, and personal conduct, a significant portion of the male applicants were rejected because of their political affiliation. The police wanted to know whether the applicant supported the French government and if he or she had any questionable political ties.[80]

Abderrahmane ben Abdelkrim Benzine, a twenty-two-year-old male with no prior police record, applied to work in one of the Algiers locations, but an Algiers prefect questioned his political allegiance. Benzine had been arrested in 1949 for distributing Parti du Peuple Algérien (PPA) tracts, and, even though he had not been formally charged with a crime, the prefect thought this provided sufficient evidence that he could not be trusted.[81] Benzine's current position at the Office of Public Transport and ability to speak Arabic and Kabyle were insufficient to influence a favorable recommendation. Instead, the prefect labeled him "a propagandist of separatist ideology," with a "hostile" attitude "toward the French cause."[82] The official overlooked Benzine's useful language skills and social connections in the area based on an event six years prior that may not have had any bearing on his ability to perform a job well.

Abdelkader Zerrouki, originally from Orléansville who moved to Tlemcen after the 1954 earthquake, was another young male whose application was rejected based on his alleged political leanings. In Zerrouki's file, Orléansville subprefect Platt wrote that he received "good information about the candidate's conduct and morality."[83] However, Platt noted that the applicant's father, M'hamed Zerrouki, "is a very active UDMA [Union Démocratique du Manifeste Algérien] militant," and he believed that Abdelkader "was a member of the UDMA in Orléansville," whose "politics aligned with those of his father."[84] Platt's general observations about the Zerrouki family led him to conclude that Abdelkader was not a suitable candidate for hire.

Half of the applicants were women, and they were typically recommended for employment. As with their male counterparts, the reviewer vetted their political histories, but unlike many of the men's applications, the women's background checks did not reveal a past of organized political activity. In fact, many of the female hopefuls were approved because they "did not express any political opinion," nor did they generate any concern "regarding their behavior and morality."[85] They were considered politically neutral and deemed less likely to bring their politics to work.

In the spring and summer of 1956, hospitals across the country received another batch of applications from doctors in Algeria and in France who requested personnel positions. In several instances, letters accompanied the file, asking that the application undergo further review. The available material did not provide conclusive information about each case, but some of the applicants were refused employment based on technical credentials. For example, Dr. Xavier Maurin applied for a surgical position at the Oran Civil Hospital in May 1956, but Robert Lacoste denied him the job in July 1956 because Maurin had only passed two of the three required exams.[86] This small series of applications revealed that people were applying for medical jobs in Algeria in 1955 and 1956, but a group of officials were not compelled to hire them. Moreover, it is troubling that candidates with viable skills sought out professional positions two years into the war and were passed over.

The SAS also recruited Algerian women to contribute to pacification and sought individuals who could assist them in practical matters such as translating Berber and Arabic and distributing medicine and emergency goods to their communities. If Algerians saw their own working alongside the French, they might be more inclined to receive medical treatment and send their children to school. The SAS drew upon a tested imperial strategy and relied on auxiliaries to promote medical programs and services.[87] In the past, they served as crucial linchpins between the indigenous population and colonial doctors, and the SAS recycled the idea in the 1950s.

One major SAS objective was to concentrate on women and the female domain in rural areas, and the Équipe Médico-Sociale Itinérante (EMSI) and Adjointe Sanitaire et Sociale Rurale Auxiliaire (ASSRA) were created in the spring and fall of 1957, respectively, with this aim. In confidential instructional manuals and correspondence, army officials acknowledged that finding trained personnel and providing medical care were "indispensable" first steps "in establishing contact with the Algerians," but that ultimately "medicine was secondary."[88] The "real objective" of these programs, notes Marnia Lazreg, "was to use sociomedical assistance as a medium through which to make contact with women, that is to say, to know, inform, educate, organize and guide them in preparation for their acceptance of the most French solution to the Algerian problem."[89] The EMSI and ASSRA staff were not benign agents of social change as the French tried to present them. They were responsible for diffusing French propaganda, educating women about emancipation, and carrying out psychological warfare.[90] As we will see in the next chapter, the FLN and its health-services division used Algerian women for similar ends.

French government and military officials made frequent mention of SAS recruiting and mobilization challenges that they struggled to address throughout the war. For instance, in 1959, French general Jacques Allard admitted to a serious physician deficit.[91] He estimated that one doctor was needed for every ten thousand inhabitants, and, at the time, there were only 220 French civil physicians in the entire country for a total population well over nine million. According to Allard's calculations, the medical sector needed nearly six hundred more doctors to meet the demand.[92] The military knew that even with six hundred more doctors participating in the Assistance Médicale Gratuite (AMG), a companion program created in 1956, and the SAS throughout Algeria, it would still require more staff to fill hospital positions in urban areas. The army counted on seven hundred reserve doctors to help alleviate the physician shortage. These statistics provide some perspective into the many recruitment challenges the SAS encountered and the dire need for more trained personnel willing to participate in the medical campaigns. Without them, Soustelle's intentions of winning over the countryside could not be realized. If the SAS and AMG units did not have sufficient staff, their visits would become irregular; the lines for consultations would be longer. Those waiting for hours to see the doctor might not make it to the front of the line, and, as one general in Oran noted, this could "diminish [the unit's] effectiveness" in the area.[93] Without continuity and sufficient medicine to distribute, personnel risked losing any inroads they had made with Algerians during previous visits and hampered their chances at fostering support for *Algérie française*.

Government officials devised new recruitment strategies that ranged from asking friends to temporary contracts. If current medical professionals told a friend or family about their work, perhaps they would be able to convince them that their service was needed. Colonial administrators considered altering the terms and conditions of medical contracts for they thought that shorter contracts might encourage people to work for state-sponsored programs. They debated the merits of a recruitment day and suggested making a tour in Algeria mandatory for sixth-year medical students in France, framing it in terms of national service and duty. They even alluded to financially rewarding doctors for performing more consultations.[94] All of these ideas could not mask the fact that the medical pacification programs were in trouble and in immediate need of reinforcements.

In response to this acute problem, the colonial administration amended medical decrees governing who was allowed to practice the profession and expanded the parameters to include foreign doctors, a group previously submitted to intense scrutiny when seeking employment in Algeria.[95] The French minister for Algerian affairs issued several legal amendments, beginning with the 23 October 1958 ordinance and followed by the decrees of 28 March 1960 and 9 April 1960, which stipulated that French nationals in the medical and pharmaceutical professions who had practiced in Tunisia, Morocco, or Indochina were now eligible to practice in France and Algeria.[96] Another decree issued on 19 April 1961 made additional concessions by authorizing foreign doctors with foreign diplomas to practice medicine in Algeria.[97] French officials received applications from doctors in Spain and Morocco, and in many instances they were recommended to come to Algeria; the 19 April 1961 decree was often cited as justification for their approval.[98] The scarcity of medical personnel was never eliminated during the war. However, French officials, realizing the potential advantages of medical pacification, increasingly broadened the health-care field by accepting individuals to serve their cause.

Another way the medical campaigns tried to compensate for insufficient staff and equipment was to improve coordination between military and civilian physicians who were already practicing in the country and did not require additional training. But the two groups, though linked conceptually, clashed over their approach to administering care. The SAS were instructed to visit remote locations and interact with Algerian locals. However, the military gave explicit instructions about guarding SAS safety and treating the population with caution. Due to the "subversive" nature of the conflict, the military inherently distrusted the Algerian people it was charged with helping and grew suspicious of their motives for coming to a mobile clinic; was it for medicine or an ambush? Therefore, the military advised medical personnel to be vigilant at all times. Army officials acknowledged that distributing medical care was an important French propaganda tool, but they insisted that medical personnel still approach Algerian patients as potential combatants. As such, sick Algerians were not to be brought to French hospitals, nor were they to be transported in French military vehicles.[99] In the event of an epidemic, the SAS were told to notify the closest civilian physician and await his response before responding. Above and beyond their moral responsibilities, the SAS were told to intervene only "in perfect security conditions."[100]

The French military grew increasingly suspicious of medicine and equipment requests submitted by medical teams, and letters and reports from top army officials reveal that they questioned whether doctors prioritized the military's goals over the patients' health. In June 1958, French general Raoul Salan wrote a letter stressing that "it is indispensable to recall [medication] requests must correspond to real needs," and they should never "be simultaneously addressed to multiple establishments."[101] His central concern was that medication and supplies could end up in the wrong hands and benefit the FLN, a situation that did occur. Salan therefore reminded doctors that they should only request products that were not "already in their possession" and cautioned against submitting requests more than once per month.

French Military Propaganda

Decentralized reports and propaganda efforts helped mask the complicated landscape and competing medical and military missions, permitting some program heads and French leaders to think the medical campaigns were more successful than they were. Alongside a voluminous collection of letters criticizing the underfunded and understaffed programs were success stories from medical personnel heralding the number of consultations they performed, progress female assistants were having with local Algerian women, and warm receptions they received from local populations around the country. It is precisely this kind of evidence to which colonial administrators could point to claim that these programs were working and provided a level of care far superior to that offered by the FLN and its health-services division.

An Assistance Médicale Gratuite team that was part of a Tizi-Ouzou SAS unit kept detailed consultation notebooks over a two-and-a-half-year period, which shed light on contemporary illnesses and the nature of relationships between the mobile medical staff and the local population. Every single page of two large notebooks beginning on 9 July 1958 and ending on 12 October 1960 was filled with patients' full names, their sex, age, date of visit, the town in which they resided, and their physical ailment. The first notebook, which chronicled a twenty-month period from July 1958 through March 1960, kept meticulous records that suggest during that time the AMG unit saw patients every single one of those days, well over five thousand patients in all. The second notebook, entitled *Assistance médicale des musulmans: Registre des consultations journalières*, begins on 21 March 1960 and ends on 12 October 1960, and, although the bookkeeping is not as consistent as in the first notebook, the records indicate that the medical professionals oversaw a total of 6,000–6,500 consultations, with consultations taking place nearly every day.[102] The most common sicknesses were pulmonary problems, bronchitis, meningitis, eye diseases, diarrhea, and general body wounds. These illnesses were largely unrelated to wartime military assaults but rather derived from poor medical care and impoverished living conditions over an extended period of time. The AMG team in Tizi-Ouzou was not treating battle wounds. Instead their job called for basic provision of care to groups of people previously neglected during the colonial period.

The SAS and AMG doctors improvised when it came to their offices. They set up tables outside and worked in abandoned buildings or from their vans. Their workstations were far removed from the government offices in Paris and Algiers, granting them a degree of flexibility. These doctors saw more men than women and a significant number of children under the age of twelve. The notebooks did not indicate which member of the medical team assisted which patient, but they did show a consistent and dedicated medical team that was able to consult with Algerians every day for fifteen months. They did not report supply shortages that would have prevented them from meeting with patients, nor did they report any Algerian animosity toward them or their medical initiatives. In fact, they demonstrated the opposite. The medical personnel were able to establish a permanent presence in the Tizi-Ouzou community and saw Algerian patients of all ages and genders regularly. What the notebooks do not confirm was whether the same physicians and assistants remained in Tizi-Ouzou for the duration of the time described in the consultation log. Judging by the pervasive shortage of doctors throughout the country, it is doubtful that those seeing patients in July 1958 were the same ones doing so in October 1960. In any event, their steady presence represented a marked departure from the period prior to 1955.

These notebooks, along with numerous others, obscured a reality that French military officials and colonial leaders did not frequently acknowledge.[103] The SAS targeted poor, hungry, and malnourished Algerians who might never have been to a doctor or interacted with a colonial official before in their lives. Therefore, this interaction may not have been wrought with as much suspicion as the theorist Frantz Fanon described. For him, "the French medical service in Algeria could not be separated from French colonialism in Algeria."[104] Even though Fanon did not write directly about the SAS, his observations about how connected medicine and colonialism were remained applicable to the wartime project.[105] Jacques Soustelle's reform initiatives were predicated on inherent power differentials, and the SAS were another opportunity to prove the administration's moral and physical strength. Medicine was a way for French politicians advocating *Algérie française* to hold themselves up as the savior and solution to Algerians' health problems, and they cast doctors and nurses in the role of benefactor to the millions of Algerians who were struggling to survive the war. But Fanon overstated the amount of resistance the French doctors encountered. He described how Algerians "rejected" and "mistrusted" doctors and how "the colonized person who goes to see the doctor is always diffident."[106] He imagined that every interaction between a French doctor and an Algerian patient was a colonial confrontation and could only be understood in dialectical terms. This was certainly not the case when SAS units drove into town and were surrounded by entire families who eagerly awaited their help.

The military captured these moments and published many of the images for the world to see (Figures 2 and 3). These were the kinds of interactions

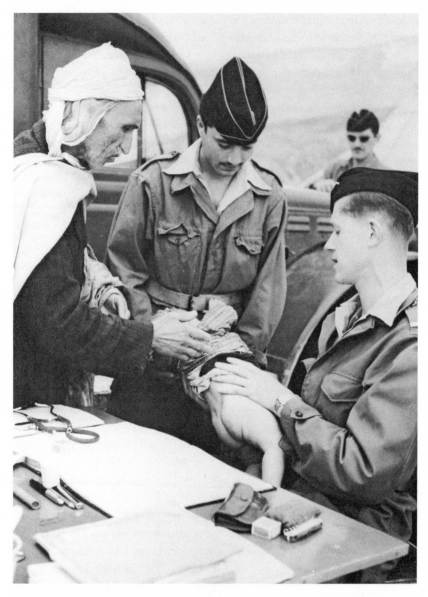

Figure 2. French medical personnel in Zemoura, Algeria. Dr. Resillot (*seated, right*) examines an Algerian infant, 1956. (Établissement de Communication et de Production Audiovisuelle de la Défense)

and benevolent behavior the army wanted to highlight—not the war tactics
behind them. In *Le Service de santé des armées en Algérie, 1830–1958*, the
military described its glorious history in Algeria from the time of the conquest up to the war and connected the achievements of the military doctors
in the nineteenth century to the current physicians working in SAS and AMG
teams.[107] The publication asked where the "native population" would be without the military's services and credited the military for bringing preventative
health care to Algeria.[108] What was more striking than the many chapters that
documented the army's accomplishments was how grateful and happy the

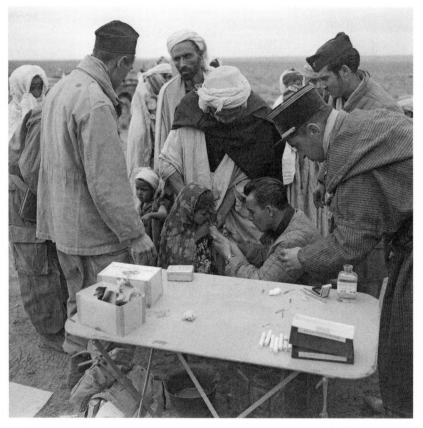

Figure 3. French medical personnel in Mecheria, Algeria. Chief of medicine
Dr. Clément and Sergeant Heurtaux treating Algerian patients, 1957.
(Établissement de Communication et de Production Audiovisuelle de la
Défense)

Algerians seemed to be when interacting with medical ambassadors of the colonial state. Long lines and crowds of people did not appear to discourage Algerians from waiting their turn to see a doctor. Men, women, and children of all ages gathered around the mobile health unit, their smiles revealing a level of excitement. Doctors cradled infants and caressed little patients who were timid and afraid. Nurses held women's hands as they waited their turn. Military personnel were seen laughing and at ease with Algerians. These were not the pictures of war, death, and devastation newspapers commonly printed. But that did not make them any less a tool of war. And as Chapter 3 shows, the FLN adopted this strategy and circulated images of their physicians treating Algerian soldiers and civilians.

Conclusion

The Special Administrative Sections were active through the end of the war, but some contend that the program was destined for failure once President de Gaulle came to power in 1958 and changed the political objectives of the war.[109] His advocacy of self-determination beginning in September 1959, and ultimately his willingness to negotiate the Evian Accords, were in direct competition with the policy of integration and thus undermined SAS objectives. In Jacques Soustelle's memoirs, he recalled how hopeful he felt about the possibility of integration in 1955 and 1956. At the time, he considered "the colonial phase" to be over and was committed to finding different solutions for France and its colonies.[110] He firmly believed integration initiatives, such as the SAS, would fuse the Algerian economy with that of the metropole and ensure the "survival and the development of Algeria." Additionally, "on the moral plan," he suggested that integration "would put an end to inferiority complexes that fed nationalism."[111]

When Soustelle created the SAS in 1955, he was drawing not only on his extensive political experience but also on an ideological tradition dating back over a century when French military physicians were sent to settle Algeria through medical pacification. The colonial administration launched the SAS and its complementary programs, Assistance Médicale Gratuite, Adjointe Sanitaire et Sociale Rurale Auxiliaire, and Équipe Médico-Sociale Itinérante, to reassert authority over the population through less violent measures and offer a viable alternative to the FLN. Medical personnel did not wear camouflage uniforms, and they were instructed to present themselves as "peaceful pacifiers." But at their core, these medical programs were first and foremost a military project whose social services were a necessary means to a desired military end, crushing the Algerian nationalists' war efforts and keeping Algeria under French control.[112]

But this tool of conquest did not lead to its intended goals. Even though the SAS grew to seven hundred units and the number of annual medical consultations exceeded several hundred thousand per year, persistent shortages of equipment, staff, and medicine curtailed the program's effectiveness and exposed the harsh realities of the French administration's long-term failure to develop and manage Algeria during the colonial period. The administration's focus on rapprochement through health was not misguided. However, its intense focus on its own programs led officials to severely underestimate and overlook the FLN's parallel medical initiatives that emerged simultaneously. The French did not have a monopoly on winning hearts and minds in Algeria. In fact, the FLN took advantage of this strategy and incorporated it into its domestic social outreach and went one step further by exporting it internationally.

Chapter 3

"See Our Arms, See Our Physicians":
The Algerian Health-Services Division

In March 1955, five months into the war, thirty-year-old doctor Michel Martini left Paris for Orléansville, a town 125 miles west of Algiers, to replace head surgeon Dr. Kamoun at the local hospital. This was not his first trip to Algeria. In 1946, he had accompanied his father, who went on business to oversee bank operations in Algiers, and it was during this initial visit that Martini "discovered" Algeria's unique place within the French empire. He returned eight years later in May 1954 and spent one month working as a surgeon in Miliana Hospital. After exploring different employment opportunities, in December 1954 he took a surgical certification exam in Algiers that permitted him to take the position in Orléansville three months later.[1]

When Martini arrived at the hospital, he observed that the available equipment was sufficient for general surgery. However, the operating tables were old and outdated and the collection of operating instruments seemed to have been assembled piecemeal. If his hospital's working conditions were any indication of the quality of public health in Algeria at the time, he wrote in his memoirs, then it bordered on rudimentary.[2] For the first six months, he planned to get to know the residents of Orléansville (approximately 50,000 inhabitants, 8,000 of whom were European), who were still reeling from the massive earthquake the previous September. By and large, Martini was able to do this because, according to him, the region between Algiers and Oran was calm and outside the areas of military activity.[3]

Even though Martini claimed to be beyond the spheres of physical fighting through the summer of 1956, he confronted political and moral dilemmas that many medical professionals encountered during the war much sooner. On 22 December 1955, one of Martini's Algerian colleagues, Masseboeuf, asked him if Mohamed Boudiaf, an FLN member, could stay with him. He was not seriously injured but he needed a place to hide for several days. Martini thought it prudent to check him into the hospital, where he could keep him over the Christmas holiday and run a number of tests. Reflecting on this incident many years later, Martini wrote that he was never convinced of the necessity of Boudiaf's "hospitalization." More likely, he thought, his comrades wanted to test his militant disposition before entrusting him with more important missions in the future.[4]

Michel Martini's experiences, while unique, raise a number of important issues about the state of health services in Algeria in the early war years and the vacuum the FLN health services would try to fill. First, when he arrived in Orléansville, Martini was struck by the poor medical facilities and equipment at his disposal. For him, not only was this a clear indication that Algeria was underdeveloped but also that, "medically speaking, Algeria was not France."[5] As a result, the local population did not have adequate treatment centers or medical personnel to meet their needs. And second, the FLN did not yet have its own health-care division, and some of its members relied on medical staff to treat them and, in some cases, provide cover while they hid from French authorities. In the first twenty-one months of the war, the Algerian nationalists needed to call upon a diverse network of trained professionals in order to sustain their efforts.

But after the summer of 1956, the FLN was much more proactive about constructing its own health-services division in Algeria. Doing so was one of the ways in which the nationalists combated the French at home and carried out their domestic wartime strategy. Even though the French Special Administrative Sections medical sectors and companion programs aimed at winning the local population's hearts and minds reported progress in this endeavor, they did not pose an insurmountable threat for the FLN. In fact, the Algerian leadership recognized that medicine and health care were vital necessities to claiming sovereignty of Algeria, and incorporated their provision into the national strategy.

This chapter argues that Algerian nationalists used the provision of medicine, health care, and personnel to win over the Algerian people and show them that the FLN was prepared to assume responsibility for their care. Nationalists built an organized and vibrant health-services division that they believed presented a viable alternative to that of the French administration and they anticipated that the Algerian people would choose its social services over those offered by the colonial state.[6]

The health-services division served two critical functions. First, it was a key component of the internal FLN strategy to establish and project state power in Algeria to Algerians. Consequently, the division's duties targeted diverse groups within Algeria, including individuals who were sympathetic to the FLN as well as some who may have supported political rivals. Second, the health-services division sent a clear message to the people and the French administration that the nationalists were capable of building and running public welfare institutions, thus lending additional weight to their claims for sovereignty.

However, before the nationalists were able to offer medical services to the people, they first had to work through internal FLN party divisions between 1954 and 1956. The FLN-ALN domestic Services de Santé (hereafter referred to as the health-services division) developed slowly during this time but expanded significantly following the May 1956 strike and the August 1956 Soummam Congress. These events contributed to transforming the FLN-ALN health-services division by increasing the number and visibility of doctors, nurses, and medical assistants committed to fighting for liberation. Furthermore, it helped the FLN gain legitimacy over competing political groups in Algeria.

The domestic medical sector repeatedly encountered obstacles, including French officials' seizure of medical supplies, Algerian doctors' arrests, and limited skilled health-care professionals. These challenges are not surprising in an imperial context. However, the nationalists continually cast themselves as modern statesmen dedicated to managing public health. They did this by issuing detailed instructions and directives regarding medical protocol, surgical procedures, treatment plans, and hygienic practices, all of which presented a stark contrast and direct rebuttal of colonial representations of the FLN. Though not as extensive as the French health sector in Algeria, nationalists integrated the health-services division with its army and combined forces with international doctors to reach a large number of people across the country and documented their outreach in pamphlets and newspaper articles in a calculated attempt to bolster sovereignty claims. The FLN developed a medical sector before it had a fully functioning government, highlighting a vital component of the nationalists' state-building project at home. Moreover, it demonstrates the leadership's attention to the high stakes of being able to take care of the people's welfare.

FLN-ALN Medicine and Health Care, 1954–1956

The FLN became the dominant mouthpiece of the anticolonial struggle but it did not start off that way nor did it enjoy uniform support. The lack of political consensus, especially during the first two years of the war, had far-reaching consequences on medical services in Algeria and hampered the kind of care the FLN was able to administer to soldiers and civilians.

Between 1954 and 1956, FLN representatives had to devote considerable time and effort ensuring their supremacy "by all means," observed former FLN member Mohammed Harbi, "including violence."[7] For example, during the first thirty months of the war, the FLN killed 6,352 Algerians as compared to 1,035 French.[8] By summer 1956, the FLN had nearly eliminated the Algerian National Movement (Mouvement Nationale Algérien, MNA), Ferhat Abbas's Union Démocratique du Manifeste Algérien (UDMA), and the Algerian Communist Party (Parti Communiste Algérienne, PCA). The newly formed General Union of Algerian Workers (Union Générale des Travailleurs Algériens, UGTA) also came firmly under its control. The FLN continued to use violence and purge its opponents throughout the war.[9]

FLN leaders cultivated the notion that 1954 was "year zero" and dismissed previous attempts at political reform, thereby casting themselves and the FLN as the sole "proprietors of the anticolonial revolution."[10] The FLN "myth of unity" masked a complicated reality of internal discord and violent power struggles, which made effective leadership difficult and had important implications for postcolonial politics in Algeria.[11] Comprehensive FLN unity may never have existed and at no other time was this fact more apparent than during 1954 to 1956 when four factions within the FLN struggled to control the nationalist organization and eliminate their rivals. The external delegation seated in Cairo (Aït Ahmed, Ben Bella, Khider, and Boudiaf), the internal delegation in Algeria, primarily located in Algiers and Kabylia (Bitat, Ouamrane, and later Ramdane Abane), the FLN commanders in the field, and the Fédération de France all competed for ultimate stewardship of the FLN.

The split between the internal and external delegations risked derailing the FLN early on in the war.[12] It also helps explain some of the difficulties the nationalists faced during the initial phase of the war. The most notable military offensive the FLN launched during this period was an attack in eastern Algeria in August 1955 during which the FLN killed 123 people (71 French, 21 Algerian civilians, and 31 members of the security forces). The French military retaliated and killed between ten and one hundred times as many Algerians.[13] Despite numerous attempts, the initial military achievements of the FLN were not impressive.[14] The FLN's lackluster military success record carried over into its medical sector, highlighting the detrimental consequences of political infighting. Moreover, it prevented the FLN from constructing, projecting, and controlling a national health-care message.

To be sure, the colonial state's chronic neglect and underdevelopment of education and social services throughout Algeria for over a century left a considerable chasm between Algerian and French technical and medical expertise. In December 1954, fewer than 1,900 doctors in Algeria (of whom only 75 were Algerian) served a population of roughly nine million Algerians and one million French settlers; put another way, almost 5,300 patients per doctor.[15] Of the total number of doctors, 75 percent (approximately 1,400) lived in the three major cities of Algiers, Oran, and Constantine, where the highest concentration of settlers resided.

Enrollment numbers at every educational level were dismal for Algerians. During the 1949–1950 academic year, 23,392 students attended secondary school. Of those students, 2,743 were Algerian and the rest were French. That same year, 110,000 French students and 177,000 Algerian students attended 2,086 primary schools.[16] The Algerian population outnumbered the French population nine to one at this time. The nearly comparable primary schooling statistics between the two groups expose the depths of inequality in colonial Algeria just four years before the war began.

In the fall of 1954, 5,308 Algerian students were registered in secondary schools and 686 in universities. These numbers indicate that only a mere fraction of local pupils were receiving specialized medical training.[17] At the beginning of the war, 86 percent of Algerian men and 95 percent of Algerian women were still illiterate, revealing what historian John Ruedy calls "a monumental indictment of a system that for more than a century had claimed to be civilizing the uncivilized."[18] Poor education rates and internal FLN party divisions presented nationalists with yet another set of obstacles to overcome in their quest for national liberation. Moreover, they hampered their ability to create a health-services division with uniform medical standards and protocols that would be able to treat Algerian soldiers and civilians effectively.

Nationalists and former medical personal rarely acknowledge this reality, and, in several memoirs and published accounts, they adamantly argue that the FLN-ALN health-services division was an integral part of their war effort beginning in fall 1954. For example, Algerian doctor and historian Mostéfa

Khiati writes that "from the moment the war for national liberation began on 1 November, FLN-ALN health services were in place."[19] According to Khiati, the revolution "was the culmination of a long process," and on its first day activists had already discussed "military, logistical, liaison, information matters . . . and health had not been forgotten."[20] He and Algerian doctors Mohammed Benaïssa Amir, Ahmed Benkhaled, and Mohammed Guentari claim that medical care existed throughout the war and featured prominently on the organization's agenda, yet they have difficulty providing substantiating evidence to this end for 1954–1956.[21]

Their insistence on early FLN care is best understood within the context and significance of nationalist unity and its ability to demonstrate continuous outreach to their reported constituents. They have a vested interest in shaping a narrative that portrays their actions as part of a meticulously planned organization that considered various social and political aspects before November 1954. Such a depiction infuses the FLN with additional legitimacy and credibility and supports Marnia Lazreg's claim that it "was eager to project an image of justice and concern for the welfare of the people."[22] While the nine "historic chiefs," Messali Hadj, Ferhat Abbas, and many other activists who had participated in politics for decades debated how best to pursue an independent Algeria and which issues were most critical to achieving success, they had not reached a consensus nor had they established operational and self-sustaining social and medical programs.

Several factors challenge the leadership's version of cohesion and suggest that the health-services division was weak and uncoordinated before 1956. First, the political history previously discussed reveals a divided and geographically dispersed FLN party. The level of disagreement over which individual or group of individuals represented the movement and the number of different commanders in the field raise questions about the logistical feasibility of running such a division. Second, the small number of trained Algerian doctors in the country at the time means that even if all of them joined the war effort and spread out across the expansive territory, they would have been unable to meet the demand for the most basic of care. Finally, former maquisards and fervent nationalists equally committed to supporting a laudatory version of the path to independence have written accounts that detail the daily difficulty they had finding care for themselves and providing it for their wounded peers, presenting a different and labored medical reality.

The most common observations emphasized by participants were the ad hoc nature of care and inadequate medical supplies during the war's initial years. Rabah Zérari, who published under his nom de guerre Commandant Azzedine, was an ALN commander in the Algiers region and severely wounded on numerous occasions. In one of his three memoirs, *On nous appelait fellaghas*, he reflected on the limited expertise of his peers and the necessity of making creative use of basic materials. Azzedine ran an infirmary in Zbarbar in Bouïra Province and remarked that, even though he happily accepted this responsibility, "we did not have doctors, nurses, or medication and we treated the wounded . . . with alcohol, mercurochrome, aspirin, and sulfonamides. . . . In serious cases, we improvised."[23] One day, Biskri, a former acquaintance of Azzedine, arrived in his barracks with extensive injuries that he claimed he received at Mustapha Hospital in Algiers. After patching Biskri up, Azzedine assigned him to guard three prisoners he classified as "traitors." When two escaped and one took a bullet that left "his brain swinging in the open air," the best treatment they could use to try to cauterize the bleeding was oil and honey, what he describes as "the poor man's remedy" and one that Azzedine later used on himself when an explosion smashed his right arm into pieces.[24]

Azzedine was not the only person who considered medical care extremely challenging during this phase of the war. Other accounts assert that organization between commanders was poor, pharmaceutical products were difficult to obtain, and each region "made do" with local resources.[25] Communication throughout the country was limited, and the ALN did not have standard procedures or trained personnel upon whom to rely, highlighted by the fact that men frequently drew from Boy Scout memories to perform basic first aid.[26] Youcef Khatib, who was known by his nom de guerre Colonel Hassan, also active in and around Algiers, shared his experience with wounded soldiers combining coffee and eggs to create a cast for a broken bone because those were the best options available to them.[27] Azzedine remembered nurses filling syringes with water in order to conserve medicine for the most severe ailments, and, though he applauds these efforts, he still calls the medical situation "catastrophic."[28] Mohammed Harbi offers a similar conclusion and labels health-care provisions "relatively inefficient" before 1956.[29]

Most of the available published sources on the Algerian medical sector during the war de-emphasize the 1954–1956 period and absorb it into the achievements of later years. For example, Ahmed Benkhaled's *Chroniques médicales algériennes* sets out to explore "the role of the medical corps and its activities in the maquis in the struggle for national liberation," yet its true emphasis lies on the health-services division after 1956.[30] Mostéfa Khiati's *Les blouses blanches de le révolution* includes a short section (3 pages of 516) entitled "1954–1956: Phase de mise en place" that admits "military matters" prevailed over those of health during this period and that ALN medical services "were embryonic."[31] Mohamed Teguia, a former FLN Fédération de France activist who returned to Algeria in 1958 to lead an FLN unit, wrote *L'Armée de libération national en wilaya IV* in which he conceded that only after 1956/1957 "was the organization of [health] services" consolidated and able "to treat wounded soldiers and the rural population."[32] None of these accounts minimizes improvised care nor do they take away from heroic measures individuals carried out to save lives. However, they challenge the nationalist narrative that claims it provided a viable alternative to colonial health-care services dating back to 1 November 1954. Furthermore, they suggest that the French Special Administrative Sections program, implemented in late 1955, likely influenced the FLN to develop its own health-services division.

The Student Strike and Soummam Congress, 1956

The FLN leadership took vital steps to change its political and social course, both of which benefited the health-services division, but not until 1956. Two particular events, the Student Strike of May 1956 and the Soummam Congress held in August of that year, had immediate and tangible effects on recruitment efforts and increased coordination and collaboration between its political representatives in Algeria and abroad.

Beginning in February 1955, the General Union of Muslim Algerian Students (Union Générale des Étudiants Musulmans Algériens, UGEMA) had chapters with a diverse membership in Algeria and France, the most active of which were in Paris and Algiers. In the weeks leading up to the strike, representatives debated the merits of school and continued education, especially for Algerian students in European institutions. Lamine Khène, a leading UGEMA figure and first secretary of state of the Provisional Government of the Algerian Republic (GPRA), remembered "the serious threats" Muslim students received in universities, culminating in the death of one Ben Aknoun "comrade."[33] On 18 May, the Algiers chapter convened to "evaluate the situation." In this meeting, "there were only a few students and we did not reach a consensus. We decided to meet again tomorrow, after spreading the word to as many people as possible." The next day, the hall was full, and though numerous UGEMA members had declared their allegiance to the FLN, "at no point" that day did anyone "pronounce the word FLN."[34] Khène's emphasis on the separation between groups reflects a desire to show that the UGEMA acted voluntarily, not under direct orders from the FLN, and better supports the nationalist claim that every sector of the Algerian population contributed to the war.[35]

On 19 May the UGEMA organized what turned out to be an extremely powerful tool for the wartime medical division and inaugurated a new phase of the conflict that infused the FLN with necessary manpower and young people who had various education levels and skills. In its first public address, the union called on Algerian students to walk away from their classrooms and devote themselves to national service. It questioned the nature of their coursework and the value of their diplomas in such a time of crisis, when their "mothers, spouses, [and] sisters are raped, when [their] elderly die by machine-gun fire, bombs, and napalm."[36] What are "we, the cadavers of tomorrow, training for . . . ? Our passivity in the face of war taking place right in front of our eyes makes us complicit. . . . Our false tranquillity . . . will no longer satisfy our conscience."[37] The UGEMA urged students in all disciplines to suspend their studies immediately and indefinitely, "desert university benches," and commit themselves to "more urgent and glorious tasks. You must join the National Liberation Army and its political organism the FLN en masse. Algerian students and intellectuals, for the world that is watching, for the nation that is calling you, for the heroic destiny of our country, will we be renegades?"[38]

Education statistics show that Algerian students in Algeria and France responded to the strike. During the 1955–1956 academic year, 684 students were enrolled at the university level in Algeria. Of that total number only 128 of them were studying medicine, compared to 267 the following year. The strike also impacted general education enrollment, which dropped from 5,198 to 4,700. A similar trend is visible with Algerian students in France, whose numbers shrank from 2,080 to 1,811 in the same period.[39] Mostéfa Khiati, an Algerian historian of medicine, argues that medicine and pharmacy enrollment numbers in Algiers "are even more striking" in showing the strike's success. In 1956–1957, 128 Algerian students were taking those classes, whereas, in the 1957–1958 academic year, student enrollment dwindled to a mere 17.[40]

The FLN and the student union encouraged a large percentage of new recruits to join the health-services division, marking a moment that Ahmed

Benkhaled calls "unquestionably, a crucial turning point in the history of the Algerian health services during the national liberation struggle."[41] Though many of them had not finished their schooling nor had they obtained diplomas, medical students' limited knowledge and skills were in high demand and considered a valuable asset for the FLN and ALN. The nationalists saw them as presenting an opportunity to teach rudimentary first aid, and they organized retreats for soldiers in the maquis.[42] *El Moudjahid*, the FLN wartime journal, reported that the ALN took time to train an elite cadre of medical personnel. Out of a group of roughly three hundred soldiers preparing for combat, forty of them were trained by the commanding physician, who was likely a former medical student. Their intensive instruction was intended to prepare them to perform triage and basic surgical procedures. After one month, they would be rotated back out to the larger group and forty more recruits would start their medical training.[43] The extent of medical preparation that the FLN and ALN were able to provide before their men and women met combat remains in question but *El Moudjahid*'s article suggests nationalists' continuous effort to use medical expertise to their advantage.

Many Algerian students interested in pursuing medical degrees had gone to France prior to the war, and they played an equally vital role in shaping the health-services division after the student strike. In 1955–1956 Montpellier University had the highest concentration of Algerian medical and pharmacy students outside of Algiers and Paris (106), followed by Lyon, Toulouse, Aix-en-Provence, and Marseille, and they watched the political and military developments at home closely.[44] After the French newspaper *Le Monde* reprinted the UGEMA's call on 19 May 1956, thirty-three Algerian medical students studying in France, including influential figures Bensalem Djamel-Eddine, Messaoud Djennas, Mustapha Laliam, and Mohamed Toumi, jumped at the chance to contribute to the national struggle.[45] Messaoud Djennas, a second-year ophthalmology student at the time, remembers having "only one idea in his head" the eve of the student strike, and that was to finish his medical degree.[46] But as soon as the UGEMA announced its initiative, Djennas and "a crushing majority" of his Montpellier colleagues "joined in the massive patriotic strike." He threw himself into the struggle, believing that through what he describes as "a sublime surge of uniform mobilization, Algeria was going to encounter its destiny."[47] In his memoirs Djamel-Eddine, a second-year medical student in the spring of 1956, explains with slightly less fervor how he left France on 31 December 1956 and took a boat to Tunisia, where he planned to meet up with his family. He practiced medicine in Sousse,

Tunisia, for several months and worked closely with Dr. Mohamed Nekk-ache, a member of the Algerian health commission in the east, before entering into Algeria in May 1957 and working in Wilaya 1.[48] Going to neighboring Maghribi countries first due to increased security measures and a growing French military presence was a common path for students coming from France, and, though their aim was to return to Algeria, they still contributed to the war effort in Morocco and Tunisia by treating wounded soldiers along the borders and, later, droves of Algerian refugees.

Trained Algerian women were in even shorter supply because fewer of them went to school. But this fact did not stop some from wanting to join the FLN-ALN ranks. Statistics are hard to come by, and it is difficult to determine the number of female students who responded to the union strike. One doctor places the figure under five.[49] However, we do know from personal accounts, such as Djamila Amrane's, that "some young women . . . were directly approached by the FLN to help them to take care of the wounded on the battlefield. Others were urged to take courses in first aid and join the guerrillas in the mountains, where their skills were needed."[50] In 1955 the FLN contacted Myriam Ben Mohamed, or "Mimi," as Commandant Azze-dine affectionately refers to her, about joining the war effort. Before November 1954, Mohamed worked as a nurse in Algiers and assisted Dr. Reda Zmirli administering shots to patients and bandaging up their wounds. Hamedet, the head of an Algiers FLN cell, enlisted her because she was "constantly in touch with physicians," and he deduced that her training and contacts would be an asset.[51] Mimi's service trajectory is emblematic of the 443 females nurses, fund-raisers, and procurers of medical and arms supplies Amrane estimates were active in the mid-1950s.[52]

FLN materials support Amrane's insistence on female involvement. In one pamphlet entitled *Aspects of the Algerian Revolution*, pictures showed Algerian women attending medical classes, serving as nurses, applying bandages, cleaning wounds, and sewing stitches, trying to highlight the strength of its health-services division and the depth, male and female, of its reserves (Figures 4 and 5). The images are reminiscent of the Special Administrative Sections pictures the French military circulated during the war. The images depicted Algerian women working for the nationalist cause, treating male soldiers, and learning nursing skills. The pictures invoked a community of dedicated and educated individuals willing to sacrifice for the greater food of their country.

The second major development in health-care recruitment and organiza-

Figure 4. Algerian female medical personnel assisting the population.
(Archives Nationales d'Outre-Mer)

tion in 1956 was the Soummam Congress, which took place on 20 August in the Soummam Valley. The main impetus behind the congress was political. The FLN needed to unite its different leadership factions, generate a coherent strategy, and refine its goals. This summit, attended by sixteen delegates from around the country, established political rule over the organization's military wing and prioritized the internal leadership over the external one operating in Cairo.[53] The attendees issued a platform outlining cease-fire and negotiation conditions. They discussed a variety of issues, including the role of women and youth, the FLN's relationship with peasants, trade unions, the Jewish community, communists, and settlers. They also divided Algeria into six *wilāyāt* (provinces) for organizational purposes and established new executive hierarchies throughout the country.[54]

After the fall of 1956, the FLN's wartime health-care system operated within the new territorial infrastructure of the *wilāyāt*, each of which was further divided into zones, regions, sectors, and finally subsectors. Each health-services unit within this hierarchy was expected to maintain detailed reports on the patients it treated and submit them to the unit above it. In theory, each level had an infirmary, supervised by a head medical assistant and staffed by traveling nurses, a structure evocative of the Special Administrative Sections

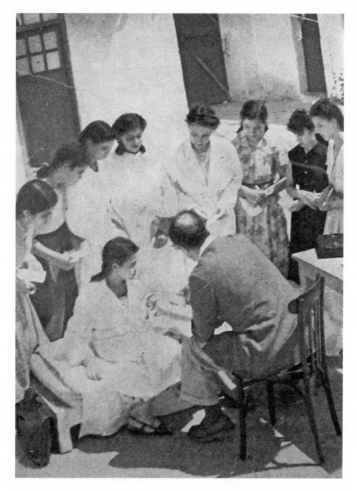

Figure 5. Young Algerian women receive nursing instruction. (Archives Nationales d'Outre-Mer)

mobile units.[55] The staff was expected to produce three copies of their monthly reports, and every three months medical personnel were supposed to meet to discuss all the monthly reports from the groups in their respective areas and send them to FLN and ALN representatives in order for them to track the number of wounded, the types of injuries soldiers sustained, average recovery times, and necessary supplies to restock and distribute.[56] For example, a zonal infirmary director of Wilaya 4, responsible for all personnel under him and civilian and military care in his area, wrote about his duties of "monitoring medication and ensuring an equal distribution throughout the zone, recording all admissions and discharges, and writing monthly reports that detailed the infirmary's patient, financial, and moral activities."[57]

This system, depicted by Ahmed Benkhaled and Mohammed Benaïssa Amir, suggests that nationalist leaders and health-care providers attempted to communicate better and coordinate the different territorial regions of Algeria and provide more efficient care for the injured and wounded. While nationalists' attention did lie in ameliorating conditions, Benkhaled and Amir's accounts present an idealized version of how the medical sector actually functioned, considering how often maquisards had to change locations to avoid detection, making record keeping of this nature unlikely. Little evidence exists that suggests that the FLN-ALN health-service division was able to operate this efficiently.[58] This small glimpse into the health-services division indicates that it developed more concretely after the summer of 1956 and improved upon previously disparate or nonexistent medical services, but neither the available sources nor personnel accounts confirm a fully operational system.

FLN Directives and Medical Propaganda

The nationalist leadership sought to improve the medical sector and began issuing strict instructions about health-service aims and propaganda that would increase its visibility among the population and offer a viable alternative to colonial medical facilities. Similar to strategies employed in other colonial contexts in Africa and the Middle East, the FLN tried to equate its own medical services with those of a future sovereign state and employed a social welfare framework that showed that it "[spoke] in the name of the demographic masses and their well-being, in contradistinction to the colonial state."[59]

The FLN used medicine to gain the people's trust and claim moral and social authority over their welfare. In one FLN-ALN service note, Lakhdar, a captain in Wilaya 4, reminded his personnel to "periodically visit and treat the population," a critical step in demonstrating the FLN's rapport with it.[60] In reports about morale and social conditions, medical officers often commented on their successes winning over Algerian civilians. "Mahmoud," an ALN member in Wilaya 4, wrote that "the population always receives [doctors and nurses] with great satisfaction. They never pass through a village without providing care to a large number of children and the elderly. The people know the difficulties we face in procuring medication and appreciate our efforts even more."[61] Monthly reports issued by the FLN and ALN observed "how happy civilians were to see Arab physicians" caring for and encouraging them and noted that medical care was "an excellent psychological weapon to use against the French" in projecting nationalist power.[62] Algerian doctor Djamel-Eddine remembers telling crowds of patients in rural villages that the FLN would "take care of them," that its leaders were "interested in their lives" and would "not let them die" in poor conditions.[63] He shouted "see our arms . . . see our physicians" as a way to project FLN power and reassure the people of its ability to provide state services, intending, to borrow an expression from Sandra Sufian, "heal the land and the nation."[64]

The French military noticed nationalists' health initiatives, and in June 1957 General Raoul Salan discovered that the FLN-ALN health-services division was not only treating soldiers but also Algerian civilians (Figure 6). Mobile medical teams passed through villages and the countryside—as did

Figure 6. Algerian doctors treating civilians. (Archives Nationales d'Outre-Mer)

the French Sections Administratives Spécialisées—offering treatment that was previously unavailable. In a letter to the interarmy Superior Command of the Tenth Military Region, Salan noted what a "psychological effect" the "rebel commanders" could have on the rural population. He thought offering medical treatment was one of the "best FLN propaganda tools" he had seen to date, and he commented on the important moral dimension of this kind of work.[65] Salan's remarks were a rare admission that French health professionals were not the only players on this field competing for the same prize.

Propaganda, directed at civilians and French officials, remained a nationalist priority, but the leadership also had to contend with continued supply shortages, security concerns, and limited medical expertise on the front lines and made decisions it believed would maximize the health-services division's success. A December 1956 FLN-ALN circular regarding rules and regulations for the Constantine area outlined conditions for service, stating that "only soldiers can be admitted to this post," and they must bring "a note from their military superior. No civilians should be admitted . . . those that are sick or wounded" can seek "medical treatment from the nearest infirmary."[66] The circular called for up to "six armed soldiers" to guard the facility who would be asked to assist in medical evacuations in the event of an emergency, and it emphasized the importance of discipline among patients who were instructed to "scrupulously adhere to doctors' orders." In cases of "serious disobedience and repeated infractions, medical sanctions can be taken," because ultimately "the infirmary is an ALN establishment and discipline should be carried out as it would in any other army unit."[67] The prescriptions reveal that in some instances, the ALN instructed medical units not to treat the local population and to concentrate their efforts on Algerian soldiers, a problem for winning over the people. It also indicates that at its core, the wartime health-services division was an Algerian military initiative, and soldiers' care remained vital to sustaining army operations.

Algerian military officials established a detailed protocol for the proper way to seek treatment and how soldiers should conduct themselves while patients in medical facilities. According to an ALN health-services announcement for Oran that the French military recovered from the body of an Algerian it shot down on 28 August 1957, thirteen kilometers west of Tiaret, "wounded Algerian combatants should only receive treatment from their fellow brother combatants. If the injury is minor," he should always maintain "his individual weapon" in his bed for protection.[68] The announcement's second chapter urged that each patient "be rapidly treated in order to rejoin his unit," and it reminded readers that the wounded "should never forget that he is a soldier and militant, and as a result, he is expected to continue educating the people and constantly serve as an example. In every interaction, the wounded should present himself as a disciplined soldier conscious of his mission," but guard military tactical plans.[69] It remains unclear how many patient combatants and medical personnel knew of these directives, yet they are significant in showing nationalists' attention in developing strict codes of conduct for soldiers and regular procedures.

Nationalists also went to great lengths to demonstrate the legitimacy of their army and to prove that the ALN advocated for the same medical standards as other military armies around the world. Dr. Mohammed Benaïssa Amir recollects rigorous hygiene protocols in Wilaya 5 health-services barracks, including patient beds being placed at least fifty centimeters from one another, proper ventilation, "the absence of parasites and the presence of sun," and regular kitchen and bathroom cleanings.[70] To protect and conserve soldiers' health, they were told to routinely clean their "bodies, hands, teeth," and it was forbidden "to share any personal hygiene products (towels, toothbrushes) or to change clothes with someone else." Regardless of whether they were in barracks or out in the field, combatants were expected only to consume proper drinking water, and if none was on hand, "water should be disinfected."[71]

A 1983 Algerian Health Ministry publication, *Seminar on the Development of a National Health System*, reinforces the notion that the health-services division during the war placed a strong emphasis on hygiene and prevention. It claimed that soldiers "strictly observed the following measures: daily beard shaves, very short hair, cut nails, clean uniforms . . . washing hands before each meal, this action became a ritual in the ALN, careful teeth brushing after each meal, [and] drinking water infused with 1 or 2 drops of chloride."[72] The FLN and ALN issued such rigorous health directives, one Wilaya 2 doctor explained, because the leadership wanted its members to be clean if they died in battle.[73] This attention to detail suggests that Algerian soldiers had a complex understanding of hygiene and the benefits of preventive care. It also sounds as though clean water was readily available, but, given the treacherous terrain they were often in and how frequently they moved, it is unlikely they washed and bathed regularly. Mohamed Teguia, an ALN lieutenant in Wilaya 4 wrote about how he and the men under his command constantly searched for water in places that were "difficult for the French to access." His troops sought small "natural water sources" that may not have appeared on French maps for sterilizing wounds and medical equipment. His descriptions of how difficult finding water could be indicate that the hygiene directives may have overstated its availability.[74] Despite this discrepancy, the directives show nationalists' awareness and commitment to constructing a preventive care model analogous to those of other international armies.

These rules also had a practical dimension. The FLN-ALN needed its men back out in the field, able-bodied and ready for combat, and could not afford long medical leaves of absence. Michel Martini, a French-born doctor who participated in the Algerian nationalist effort, has noted that the majority of those injured during military operations did not return to the maquis.[75] Nonetheless, the FLN and ALN health-services division's attempts to improve patient records provided them an opportunity to amass critical data and concentrate efforts on obtaining specific medications and supplies for particular injuries.[76] In 1957 an Algerian medical assistant in Wilaya 4 reported that the most common ailments were "diarrhea, general fatigue, colds, meningitis, dysentery, and abscess," justification for "antibiotics, eyedrops, vitamins, and respiratory medication" requests.[77] Later health-services division reports compiled lists of patients that used their services, if they were treated and how many remained. For example, in Wilaya 3 in July 1959, "Rachid" wrote that sixty-six individuals were hospitalized for unspecified conditions, nineteen were cured, and forty-five remained, whereas in the following month the infirmary recorded seventy-one patients, thirty-nine of whom were hospitalized, and thirty-two who were healed.[78]

FLN-ALN health-services directives began emphasizing qualified personnel with medical training and issued service notes about needing better-trained staff. The Union Générale des Étudiants Musulmans Algériens strike had supplied the medical division with students who inaugurated a new phase of the division. However, their numbers would not sustain the lengthy war effort and Algerian officials constantly confronted the need for additional recruits. This predicament might have convinced them to accept any and all health-care volunteers, but this was not always the case, especially for Algerian women. In a November 1957 French military report, an unnamed official in Constantine observed that in addition to "their role as nurses inside and outside of hospitals, rebel commanders intend to use [them] for social and political" purposes. "Female combatants," he said, "are called upon to be, even more than nurses, veritable political FLN agents."[79] His interpretations of broader FLN strategy for women is correct, as Marnia Lazreg, Diane Sambron, and Natalya Vince's work shows, yet his assumption that Algerian women automatically were admitted as nurses is not.[80] An FLN-ALN service note written after August 1956 devoted a section to "recruiting nurses" and explained that although "[they] are directed to the maquis, some of them are sent home. For the simple reason that they are not nurses. In the future, ask health-services division members for their diplomas."[81] The note specified a preference "that the [women] obtain parental consent; this will avoid the problem of having to send them back," and, last, that they "be questioned before they arrive in the maquis. In-depth inquiries will be made if any doubts surface. Do not underestimate the enemy," who would "try to place agents in our various services."[82] Nationalists wanted to verify their loyalty and ensure they were not French spies, a reasonable precaution to take, yet personnel shortages were so dire perhaps FLN service notes from the months following the Soummam Congress represent a desired outcome rather than the way in which recruitment and screening were actually carried out.

French Decrees, Medical Personnel, and State Repression

For seven of the eight years of conflict, on top of limited medical expertise, recruitment difficulties, and political infighting, the Algerian health-services division faced French government decrees aimed at restricting medical products' availability and circulation to rebels. On 21 November 1955, Robert Lacoste, resident minister of Algeria, issued a decree that forbade selling, transporting, and trading hygienic items, including bandages, hydrophilic cotton, and cellulose, in Algeria.[83] Working to supplement this decree, French officials dispensed a series of additional orders in 1955 and 1956 regulating the sale of chemicals and pharmaceutical products. In a 1955 "Official Notice on Nitrate and Chloride Products," the anonymous author explained that the recent decrees aimed to curtail "terrorists'" access to these important materials, which were essential for fabricating explosives.[84] However, in the same notice, officials also acknowledged that the Algerian people were "brutally deprived" of "essential products," thus conceding that this was a delicate issue as it pertained to the population's ability to protect itself during the war.[85]

Consequently, the notice insisted these measures were not meant to "block" or "ban" the products entirely, rather the restrictions "merely constitute a precautionary measure" that would neither disrupt "the pharmacy profession nor the normal provisions for the population."[86] It indicated an awareness of how negatively doctors and Algerian civilians could perceive these medical decrees, and the notice attempted to address this concern by reassuring the population that it would not suffer by their implementation. But in truth, the decrees represented a marked departure from previous ones, such as the law of 11 July 1938 and later updated in decree 51-497 on 2 May 1951, that outlined civilian protections during times of war.[87]

It did not take long before the government received complaints about the 1955 and 1956 regulations and their deleterious effects on patient care. On January 1957, the Sétif prefect closed the town's central pharmacy, and in May of that year, it remained shuttered. His intermediary, M. Moissenet, re-layed the prefect's insistence that his office take "stricter surveillance mea-sures to avoid attempts to steal medication."[88] The population could not receive care or basic supplies from this venue out of fear of their misappro-priation. He did not mention chlorides and nitrates, the intended targets of the decrees. Instead, the prefect liberally interpreted the decrees to justify stopping all medication provisions.

In March 1957, Pierre Hosteing, director of the civil cabinet, wrote a let-ter about his concerns over the additional hardships Algerian civilians en-dured as a result of the decrees. In it, he noted, "the ensuing inconveniences for [them] in having to present a medical prescription to buy ordinary phar-maceutical products. The price of the visit to obtain the necessary prescrip-tion is often more expensive than the medication and imposes a supplementary cost to the sick." Hosteing suggested "replacing the prescrip-tion requirement with a registry" patients would sign and pharmacists would keep, a method he thought "sufficient to control the frequency and delivery of certain products that rebels could eventually use."[89]

The director general of social action, M. Lafont de Sentenac, rebuked Hosteing's proposed changes. On 23 April 1957, "after having reviewed cop-ies of antibiotic request forms," he wrote to Hosteing, "it appears to me desir-able to preserve without modification, the 22 December 1956 special order. Prescriptions," show "the name of the prescriber" and instill accountability in him or her. Lafont de Sentenac did not completely ignore Hosteing's primary concern, the Algerian people. He ended his letter by saying, "I underline the fact that the special regulations will not disrupt the delivery of medication by medical directors in health centers or by [Special Administrative Sections] to needy populations, nor will the sick have any trouble receiving treatment in hospital establishments."[90] The exchange illustrates that despite officials' at-tempts to safeguard Algerian patient care and encourage them to continue frequenting colonial health-care facilities, the numerous medical decrees further reduced treatment options for the population and created an opportunity for the nationalist health-services division to argue it was more dedicated to and concerned with civilians' welfare.

Nationalists continued to acquire medical products despite the restrictive policies. French leaders saw evidence of this when military units recovered their own medical provisions on the battlefield. For example, in 1957, the colonial army retrieved a kit containing syringes, scissors, needles, pins, thermometers, gauze, and small vials of medication along the Tunisian border (Figure 7).[91] In the spring of 1960, according to French military intelligence sources, the FLN and ALN acquired bandages, antibiotics, vitamins, and

Figure 7. Medicine kit discovered on Tunisian border, 1957. (Établissement de Communication et de Production Audiovisuelle de la Défense)

anticoagulants. Though Colonel A. Brunet, French commander of the Oran Central Zone, could not confirm their origin, he believed that some of these items came from urban pharmacies, indicating that despite colonial officials' concerted efforts, nationalists found ways to circumnavigate them.[92]

Algerian political figures interpreted the medical decrees as yet another example of poor colonial management at their expense. In September 1957, Algerian Red Crescent president Omar Boukli-Hacène, chided the colonial administration for "depriv[ing] Algerians of physicians" and claimed the decrees eliminated "any hope of acquiring medication."[93] The restrictions on medicine and pharmaceutical products also afforded the FLN a chance to present a compelling case that French officials would target anyone, for any reason, and, as such, the Algerian population should completely avoid the French heath-services division and use the Algerian equivalent. Commandant Azzedine recalled the leadership forbidding the population "from going to French hospitals, infirmaries, or clinics." For him, "a sick person was very fragile, susceptible, ready to provide information to fix whatever ailed him. A harmless visit could end in an interrogation," and Algerian political and military officials could not risk patients divulging maquisards' locations and hiding spots in exchange for a shot or bandage.[94]

Nationalists publicized French officials' repressive actions toward (primarily Algerian) doctors, who were suspected of treating rebels, as further evidence of the colonial state's disregard for the people's welfare. Doctors Mustapha Laliam and Reda Zmirli, two well-known physicians dedicated to helping their compatriots and often mentioned by participants and fellow physicians for their important contributions in the late 1950s and early 1960s, were both arrested and imprisoned for what the French government considered major crimes.[95] Laliam went to Montpellier for his medical training and, like many in his previously mentioned cohort, felt compelled to return to Algeria after the Union Générale des Étudiants Musulmans Algériens strike. He followed a similar path to that of Djamel-Eddine and first practiced medicine in Tunisia in July 1957 before receiving an FLN summons to come to Algeria and put his skills to use. He successfully traveled to Kabylia that fall, answered to Colonel Amirouche, and four months later was promoted to the position of chief physician of Zone 3 for Wilaya 3. In a December 1958 letter to Léopold Boissier, president of the International Committee of the Red Cross, French Red Cross president André François-Poncet remarked that French authorities captured Laliam "when he, and a group of rebels, were trying to cross over into Tunisia. When they caught him, he had a revolver on him." Such an infraction, according to François-Poncet, "violated an essential rule that every member of the medical corps had the obligation to observe," but he still believed that Laliam's sentence of twenty years' hard labor was excessive and that he "had been charged and condemned not for his medical activity, but for his political activity."[96]

Reda Zmirli endured a similar fate when French officials arrested him the same year for treating Algerians in a secluded farmhouse, which they claimed Zmirli had "transformed into a clandestine hospital and refuge center for rebels." When French forces approached, he reportedly "defended himself with weapons."[97] On 15 March 1958 the FLN proposed in *El Moudjahid* that Zmirli's eight-year hard labor sentence for "associating with criminals" was the result of "a military tribunal" that argued that he treated wounded ALN soldiers. The article did not mention the alleged guns; rather it emphasized the political nature of the supposed crime. In *El Moudjahid*, nationalists accused the colonial authorities of deliberately targeting physicians, a violation of an international resolution unanimously agreed upon at the Nineteenth International Conference of the Red Cross in New Delhi, India, which stated, "in the event of internal troubles, the wounded will be treated without distinction to political affiliation and medication will not be disrupted in any manner." The medical domain, as the FLN understood the rules of war, "should be respected."[98] Algerian leaders' denunciations attracted several international supporters, including representatives from the Egyptian and Syrian Red Crescent societies and the Chilean, Colombian, Canadian, German, Swedish, Norwegian, and Bulgarian Red Cross societies, who challenged the legitimacy of the doctors' arrests and demonstrated a broader appeal to their cases.[99] Their fate did not only concern the FLN and the doctors' friends and family; their sentences had implications for what was possible and permissible in war.

French officials repeatedly denied allegations that they were targeting doctors and nurses. In December 1958, Henri Langlais of the French foreign ministry wrote to André François-Poncet that he "initiated an investigation, per your request, with regards to allegations that we are retaining a significant number of doctors and pharmacists that the Algerian population needs in our living centers [*centres d'hébergement*]."[100] He determined "the accusation made by enemies of France are absolutely without merit," and that currently "only eight doctors and three pharmacists are being detained."[101] Langlais boasted that authorities had released six doctors since January 1958, suggesting that nationalists had exaggerated the situation.[102] To be sure, reality resided somewhere between these polarized versions.

The number of Algerian doctors detained or imprisoned specifically for providing treatment to "rebels" remains difficult to ascertain, but the French medical decrees and fear of persecution drove many Algerian health-services division members to make strategic and painful decisions. Dr. Djamel-Eddine, who worked under Colonel Amirouche in Wilaya 3, recalled how medical personnel were trained to concentrate their efforts on the least injured patients who had a better chance of healing and recuperating and that he prioritized those requiring the least amount of care.[103] In his memoirs, Commandant Azzedine described how difficult it was to obtain medicine after 1955. Purchasing medicine in pharmacies, as many had previously done, became more complicated, and he increasingly relied on civilians and medical personnel to exchange products in secret, the most coveted of which were "antibiotics, mercurochrome, bandages, aspirin."[104] An Algerian without known political affiliations might have been able to acquire a few medical supplies and pass through checkpoints unnoticed, and these basic medications ensured weeks of care in the maquis.

The impact of French regulations on the acquisition of medical supplies continued to hinder the Algerian health-services division, as ALN reports after 1957 describe the "dearth of medication," one of Algerian medical assistants' "gravest concerns."[105] The Algerian leadership appealed to the population to find any kind of medication to help their "brothers who are falling everyday at the hands of murderous subversive organizations." A nationalist political tract published toward the end of the war reminded the people of the stakes at hand and asked them to contribute to "safeguarding human life" by locating medicine "immediately," because "tomorrow would be too late."[106]

French and International Physicians

Algerian civilians and doctors were not the only ones who participated in domestic wartime health-care initiatives. Medical personnel from all backgrounds contributed in a myriad of ways. Pierre Chaulet and Jeanine Belkhodja provide two notable examples of physicians who treated Algerians despite facing dangerous consequences and highlight that medical care transcended national and gender lines.

Pierre Chaulet was born in Algiers in 1930 to French parents who raised him in a Catholic household. He recalled that at a young age, he noticed disparity and inequality around him. Around the age of twenty Chaulet decided to pursue medicine because he thought it would enable him to relieve human suffering.[107] He was also concerned about changing society, and he wanted to raise social awareness with respect to French colonial practices. In the early 1950s, he became politicized, and it was during this time that he established meaningful ties with future FLN members, who in 1955 recruited him to start a health-services unit in Algiers. In a 2007 interview, he joked that calling it a functional medical service may have been "generous," but it did not detract from his dedication to assembling a group of people who could treat the wounded.[108] Chaulet successfully enlisted European doctors to help him circumvent French pharmaceutical bans that he said "targeted Algerians" and made his work more complicated. He insisted he was not deterred by these restrictive measures and began treating patients privately with supplies friends acquired from hospitals.[109] Prominent Algerian FLN members expressed their gratitude for his important contributions and applauded his efforts to teach them simple yet crucial skills, such as how to administer shots and how to apply stitches.[110] At the end of February 1956, the French authorities arrested Chaulet and forced him to leave Algeria. Even though Chaulet did not return to Algeria until 1962 after the cease-fire, he continued providing medical care by rehabilitating patients and treating lung and tubercular cases with his wife Claudine in Tunisia until the war's conclusion. When I asked him if he considered retiring after his expulsion, he quietly replied that the idea "had never occurred to [him]."[111]

Jeanine Belkhodja, one of the few trained female physicians in 1950s Algeria, is another prime example of a person driven to fight for the country's liberation by offering her medical expertise.[112] The child of a mixed marriage (her mother was French, her father was Kabyle), Belkhodja floated between Christian and Muslim groups, which introduced her to a variety of cultural and political perspectives from an early age.[113] As a young woman she was actively involved with the Communist Party, the *mutuelle d'étudiants* (a political organization that represented Catholics, Jews, Muslims, Communists, and Protestants), and finally with the FLN. In 1955, shortly after she completed her medical degree, FLN representatives contacted her. They asked if she would "transport medication, antibiotics, and bandages" through Tamzali, the clandestine organization that primarily shuttled medicine and other supplies between Kabylia and Algiers.[114] She recalled that this was a period "when it was not so easy [for the wounded in Algeria]. They were treated by Algerian and European civilian physicians. There were a decent number of European doctors who treated the wounded and sick without asking their exact origins."[115] She emphasized that in the police and military climate of that time, doctors were taking big risks seeing Algerian FLN and ALN patients.

She carried out secret operations in and around Algiers until her arrest in March 1957. When she went to trial three months later, she was accused of making explosives, not clandestinely treating enemies of the French state.[116] The French court condemned her to exile in France, a verdict that would theoretically remove her talent and skill from the war and sever ties with her affiliates. But this did not work. By November 1957, she was back in contact with FLN members, and shortly thereafter she was in Tunisia treating patients. She joined the health-services division there, consulted with French soldiers, and aided Algerian refugees. She and other physicians conducted missions along the border and treated patients for injuries they sustained while crossing the Morice Line.[117] She waited until the 19 March 1962 cease-fire to return to Algeria, but upon her arrival home, she discovered that "Algiers was truly divided in two. There were streets, that on one side were controlled by the FLN and on the other by the OAS [Organisation Armée Secrète]." Algiers remained at the mercy of the warring factions until "the second cease-fire," the OAS accords, a truce between the FLN and the Organisation Armée Secrète announced on 17 June 1962.[118] After the referendum, she returned to work in the hospitals in Algiers.

Although it is impossible to know fully the personal motivations of this latter group of physicians, which also included Jean-Paul Grangaud, a third prominent doctor of French descent who wanted to be a medical missionary and treated Algerian activists during the war, Martin Evans's work provides a useful framework with which to think about rare individuals and their commitment to medicine and Algerian independence.[119] For Evans, French history, family history, contemporary politics, and direct experience were the most common explanations for a person's political actions. Even though his study concentrates on people who resisted the war in France, the four categories he identifies apply to Chaulet and Belkhodja, who not only spent many years in Algeria but also were deeply affected by personal experiences and political developments they witnessed dating back to childhood.

Religion also played a role in doctors' willingness to provide care during the war. Mostéfa Khiati attributes Chaulet's engagement in the war to a more specific cause, his Catholic roots, which, he writes, predisposed him "to struggle against misery and violence."[120] Historian Darcie Fontaine, whose research focuses on Catholicism and decolonization in Algeria, argues that a small minority of "liberal" Christians who had lived there for decades worked to end *Algérie française* due to their previous involvement in social organizations and personal relationships with Algerians. In 1952, Pierre Chaulet, Pierre Roche, and Mahfoud Kaddache formed the Algerian Youth Association for Social Action (Association de la Jeunesse Algérienne pour l'Action Sociale, AJAAS), a notable example of this type of organization that aimed to foster Christian-Muslim dialogue and improve relations between the two groups through literacy programs, hygiene classes, and social aid. Fontaine maintains, "it was the burgeoning awareness of the economic, social, and political conditions of the Algerians, both through discussion, and through direct experience in the shantytowns and other social projects of the organization that led many Christian members of the AJAAS," such as Chaulet, "to a political awakening that eventually led them to understand the desire and justification for Algerian independence."[121]

Several non-Catholic French military medical personnel questioned the dubious professional medical practices the war encouraged, adding support to nationalists' claims that the colonial administration did not prioritize Algerians' health. Gérard Zwang, a military physician, Pierre Godeau, a doctor who practiced in Kabylia, and Marie-Claude Leloup-Colonna, who provided medical care in the second half of the war, spoke of challenges they encountered regularly and the empathy they felt for the wounded on both sides, a sentiment often lost in the competing rhetorics.[122] Joël Gaucher, who had Red Cross first-aid training and was called for military service in the spring of 1958, was one of the few French medical personnel who commented on difficult moral and ethical situations. When he arrived in Algeria, Gaucher thought the French army "committed several casting errors. [He] had a hard time imagining some [recruits] with a white assistant's coat. Undoubtedly they would have been more comfortable tending to cows and sheep."[123] He noticed their limited medical training, insufficient for most battle wounds, but especially for having to treat Algerian prisoner torture victims. Sometimes his superiors asked him to perform basic tasks such as administering penicillin and monitoring prisoners. When Algerian patients reached him requiring medical attention, Gaucher believed they "were unlikely to get out of the situation alive."[124]

Authorities and military personnel debated the merits of treating Algerians at all. They feared that transporting them to medical facilities created a security threat. Prefects and police commissioners voiced concern that hospitals were not a maximum-security facility, and they would therefore need to send reinforcements. They worried that without proper supervision patients could organize among themselves in the hospital or coordinate with others on the outside and execute an attack.[125] Gaucher was not concerned with these issues; he was dedicated to treating whoever came his way. For him, it would be disingenuous for the French military medical personnel to claim that they were unaware of French abuses because they routinely monitored the aftermath, a fact to which Henri Alleg attested in *La Question* (see Chapter 4). Unlike some of his fellow staff members, Gaucher treated Algerians who bravely came to the garrison for medical assistance and who were "likely openly engaged in the rebellion" against the French.[126] He realized that in the heat of the moment, when a dying body was placed in front of him, it did not matter who he thought was on the right or wrong side of politics. This is an important reality that is often overlooked in favor of discourse and politics. Faced with the option of prolonging life or hastening death by standing idle, many physicians may have defied government directives and put their potentially life-saving skills to use.

During the second half of the war, the FLN worked closely with Arab and Eastern Bloc governments to supplement the Algerian health-services division and the select number of French doctors' efforts. In December 1958, Egyptian president Gamal Abdel Nasser invited a group of Algerian nurses to participate in an internship at the Egyptian Red Crescent. He told *El Moudjahid* "he was convinced that if a young Algerian girl is determined to fight for her country, her faith will be rewarded and God will bestow victory and dignity upon Algeria."[127] European doctors devoted their skills too. Mohammed Benaïssa Amir, an Algerian doctor in Oran, noted that after 1961 coordination of supplies and personnel fell into place along the western border because of increased assistance from Casablanca, Paris, and Lebanon, and he credited Spanish doctors with providing assistance to refugees and injured ALN soldiers in the Moroccan Rif area.[128]

Nationalists also reached out to the Soviet Union, Yugoslavia, and Czechoslovakia for help. These governments developed a system that allowed the ALN to regularly send its wounded to treatment facilities abroad as described in several *El Moudjahid* articles.[129] On 31 August 1959, one reported that one hundred soldiers "left last week . . . for the Soviet Union and twenty-four others left [yesterday] for Czechoslovakia aboard a special plane that the Czech government chartered."[130] Jeanine Belkhodja cited Eastern countries' important role in providing treatment and physical therapy for the injured, a practice that continued after 1962, according to Ian Young's account of his time in Kabylia working for a Bulgarian gynecologist.[131]

Revolutionary sympathizers, such as Cuba's Fidel Castro, called on doctors to volunteer for service in Algeria in the early 1960s. After his first visit
to Algiers in 1962, he brought seventy-six wounded ALN soldiers and twenty
orphans to Havana, a political display of solidarity that, according to historian Piero Gleijeses, foreshadowed Castro's intention of projecting power in
Africa.[132] The FLN considered these "concrete gesture[s]" signifying a larger
commitment to independent Algeria, and they are illustrative of Cold War
Third World alliances that Matthew Connelly and Odd Arne Westad have
analyzed.[133]

The Algerian-Cuban relationship grew stronger after independence.
Ahmed Ben Bella, first president of independent Algeria, visited Cuba in October 1962 (Figure 8), and in return for his demonstration of friendship with
Cuba, in May 1963, Castro sent the first Cuban medical mission to Algeria.
The Cuban minister of public health, José Ramón Machado Ventura, accompanied "twenty-nine doctors, three dentists, fifteen nurses, and eight medical
technicians," forty-five men and ten women.[134] Many of the logistics had not
yet been worked out, including their length of stay and which government
would pay their salaries. Gleijeses calls the medical mission in 1963 "an un-
usual gesture" because "an underdeveloped country tender[ed] free aid to
another in even more dire straits. . . . It was an act of solidarity that brought
no tangible benefit and came at real material cost." Machado Ventura agreed.
He noted, "It was like a beggar offering his help, but we knew that the Algerian people needed it even more than we did and that they deserved it."[135]
Despite the hardship the medical mission may have caused the Cubans, it illustrates the FLN's widespread appeal and the lengths to which other developing countries were willing to go to contribute to the national cause, a
subject explored more thoroughly in the Chapter 4.

As these many examples indicate, the medical landscape in Algeria was
quite nuanced and layered. It was composed of Algerians, French, Arab,
Western, and communist health-care professionals working together to preserve human life and fighting for political liberation. Frantz Fanon was
among them; however, he drew very different conclusions about the medical
possibilities between the colonized and the colonizer.[136] But the doctors discussed above attest to the fact that there were many instances of cooperation
and mutual respect across ideological and political lines that show the significance of Algerian decolonization. These doctors repeatedly faced imprison-
ment and risked their lives to pursue what they thought was right during the
war and in the process formed a critical dimension of medical services that

Figure 8. Ahmed Ben Bella (*center*) visits Fidel Castro (*left*) in Cuba, 23 October 1962. (Getty)

nationalists could point to as evidence of their state-building aspirations and measures they would take to ensure Algerians' well-being.

Conclusion

Frequently, political and diplomatic histories of the war neglect important social dimensions of the FLN-ALN agenda. This chapter examined national-ists' efforts to develop and sustain a health-services division in Algeria and argues that it was an extremely important dimension of the FLN's overall strategy to legitimize itself to the local population and strengthen domestic support. A version of its services operated throughout the majority of the conflict, especially after the 1956 student strike and Soummam Congress. Even though the extent of its accomplishments is disputed by maquisards, its mere existence is notable given the extremely asymmetric nature of the war. Nationalists' political divisions hindered its initial formation, but following seminal student recruitment and increased organization and coordination within the *wilāyāt*, they were able to hone a clear message about their ability to protect and serve the Algerian population. They employed strategies similar to those of the French Special Administrative Sections, reinforcing their claims that the FLN and ALN represented a modern disciplined organization and army that valued the people's physical care.

Colonial officials went to great lengths to cripple the health-services division and Algerian doctors. Their restrictive medical policies and arrests of personnel interrupted supply circulation and, without question, impeded treatment for Algerian soldiers and civilians. But they did not eliminate it. In fact, these oppressive colonial measures motivated some health-care professionals to work harder in clandestine locations and along the Moroccan and Tunisian borders. International governments and doctors aided in buoying nationalists' health-care pursuits and demonstrated broad interest and commitment to Algerians' anticolonial struggle. Their contributions, impressive in their own right, represent only a fraction of the global support nationalists garnered through international outreach.

The next chapters explore how the FLN sought external support for the war effort. While some scholars have examined the diplomatic dimensions of Algerian nationalists' efforts to internationalize the conflict, they did not concentrate on the social dimensions of health care and humanitarianism, nor did they focus on Algerian agency.[137] The following chapters analyze the Algerian Red Crescent and how the Algerians brought their plight to the International Committee of the Red Cross and the United Nations. Moreover, they show how the Algerian nationalists transformed these international institutions at the apogee of decolonization.

Internationalizing Humanitarianism:
The Algerian Red Crescent

From the beginning of the anticolonial movement, the FLN attended to both local and international dimensions of its war effort, and this attention also applied to the medical division. The student strike, the Soummam Congress, and doctors of various backgrounds contributed to establishing a more sophisticated domestic health-services division, even while the brutal conditions of war made it difficult to adequately meet all of the population's needs. Starting in 1957, the nationalists concentrated on expanding their health-care initiatives beyond Algeria and sought international aid and support through a refined humanitarian message. The Algerian Red Crescent (Croissant-Rouge Algérien, CRA) was the primary vehicle for disseminating this position and soliciting financial and material aid abroad. Its leadership appropriated the universal language of humanitarianism and rights to substantiate their claims for sovereignty.

Nationalists built upon Arab alliances and viewed the internationalization of medical aid outside of Algeria as a critical tactic in gaining additional support. They believed an organization with international ties and widespread appeal would be most successful in projecting their cause to a global audience. The French Red Cross (Croix-Rouge Française, CRF) in Algeria could have potentially filled this role. Per International Committee of the Red Cross (ICRC) regulations, each sovereign country is permitted one national society to carry out humanitarian activities according to local needs. Though associated with the founding branch in Geneva and expected to uphold the principles of neutrality and impartiality, national societies approved by the central organization were not under its direct authority and maintained their own staff. In theory, the French Red Cross in Algeria could have been a place for French and Algerian doctors to join forces openly. Its facilities could have provided a haven for patients of all ethnicities and religions to feel safe from both French military and FLN attacks. Moreover, it could have served as a staging ground from which to launch international appeals for assistance. Instead, the French Red Cross found itself torn between a colonial mission and a humanitarian one and systematically assumed a position of sympathy for the metropole.

The nationalists called the French Red Cross a "vessel of French colonialism" and founded the Algerian Red Crescent as a counterpoint. They were neither deterred nor discouraged by the likely fact that the International Committee of the Red Cross would only grant their national society de facto status, if any status at all.[1] For them, the technical standing of the organization was inconsequential. What mattered to the Algerian Red Crescent leaders was that they had the opportunity to construct a different image of themselves. Their self-presentation was in direct contrast to that presented by French colonial officials and showed Algerian nationalists committed to and capable of adhering to international codes of conduct and humane practices. The Algerian Red Crescent and its representatives did this by focusing on four issues: controversy over French military use of torture, staging prisoner-release ceremonies, soliciting the vast International Committee of the Red Cross network, and campaigning on behalf of Algerian refugees. These tactics contributed to reshaping international perceptions of Algerians and their war for national liberation and recast the nationalists as humanitarians to the world.

The French Red Cross in Algeria

National Red Cross societies have always been an important component of the International Committee of the Red Cross, dating back to the 1860s. They were conceived as an extension of the Geneva-based organization and were predicated on the same principles of impartiality and neutrality. Furthermore, they were expected to provide aid and assistance to all people and avoid personal, religious, or national bias. National societies embraced these noble goals and were eager to join in an internationally recognized effort to prioritize care, especially during times of war. But in the 1870s, 1880s, and 1890s, European, American, and Russian leaders demonstrated a tendency to link society activities with their respective militaries and politicians, a phenomenon John Hutchinson says "was almost universal" by World War I. In peace times, royal families and high-ranking officials appointed delegates to national societies they anticipated would protect their interests. For example, in tsarist Russia, the empress personally "selected the president of the Red Cross society from a list of retiring generals."[2] National societies were never fully independent entities, argues David Forsythe, because individual states approved the first ones and established a precedent for a "historically deferential" relationship with states and their governments.[3]

As the humanitarian network expanded globally, ICRC delegates struggled to oversee national societies and ensure that they adhered to the Red Cross's original mission.[4] Gustave Moynier, an original founder of the Red Cross, noted in his 1896 book, *Notions essentielles de la Croix-Rouge*, that the International Committee of the Red Cross was expected to recognize new societies but was "never given the power to monitor their subsequent performance nor to bring them to heel for shortcomings or irregularities."[5] At the turn of the twentieth century, he witnessed national societies turning away from universalism toward nationalism and militarism, and he had little recourse to change their orientation.[6] National societies in the interwar period, most notably the German Red Cross, continually betrayed the ethos and spirit of universal care while laying claim to ICRC principles. In November 1933, new decrees were passed in Germany that inextricably linked the German Red Cross with the recently formed Third Reich, and, overnight, the national society "became directly responsible to the German government."[7] These statutes transformed the German Red Cross into "just another part of the German state machinery" with disastrous consequences for Jews, prisoners, and any other category of people deemed undesirable by the Nazi regime through 1945.[8]

This historical context sheds light on the French Red Cross and its activities and allegiance to the French military in Algeria throughout the war for national liberation. It was by no means the first national society to navigate the complexities of nationalism, war, and humanitarianism. However, colonial Algeria differs from previous cases because it was one of the few places where two national societies operated on the same terrain and competed against one another for national and international support.

The French Red Cross was founded in 1864. Its headquarters were in Paris, and the colonial outposts that operated throughout the Maghrib reported to that office. The French Red Cross in Algiers was an extension of the metropolitan one and designed to relieve (all) human suffering. Ideally, its personnel were committed to contributing "to all efforts related to social welfare, prevention, education and health care" and did not distinguish between the nature of its work and responsibilities in the metropole and the colony.[9] During the decades preceding the war for independence, the French Red Cross in Algeria organized national health days, contributed aid to tubercular North African patients in France, assisted veterans of World War II and Indochina, and matched Algerian host families with young French missionaries for Christmas and the New Year holiday.[10] Annual reports suggest that the national society performed services for the European and Algerian populations in Algeria, and it did not receive major criticism from either.

During this period the French Red Cross had difficulty recruiting local staff and overcoming religious differences. Just six months before the war started, the ICRC sent Mr. Lossier to conduct a brief study of Red Cross activities in Africa. He observed a near absence of Algerian male personnel in the French Red Cross in Algiers. Algerian women were more integrated into the national Red Cross society. They worked in small numbers as nurses and nursing assistants. But Lossier was weary of their abilities because "their evolution was still embryonic." Even though some were able to overcome "these obstacles," he thought the majority of Muslim women remained loyal to religious concepts that discouraged "rapid emancipation."[11]

The French Red Cross had limited Algerian staff but that did not prevent the national society from claiming to equally service French and Algerian communities. On his trip Lossier visited hospitals and dispensaries and reported that "Berbers, Arabs, and Europeans" were all treated in the same way. Based on the facilities that he saw, Lossier posited that 80–90 percent of French Red Cross beneficiaries were "Muslim," not European.[12] This is an unlikely statistic but it attests to the fact that the national society attempted to impartially administer care.

The French Red Cross did not maintain such a balanced position after 1954. As soon as the war broke out in November of that year, FLN leaders labeled the French Red Cross "a puppet of the French authorities."[13] To be sure, nationalist claims that the French Red Cross was overly sympathetic toward the colonial administration and its army served propaganda purposes. But the national society's own 1950s annual reports and newsletters reveal a disproportionate allocation of resources and services to the French army, and the political language they used to describe the conflict was analogous to that of the French state.

The French Red Cross's official organ, *Vie et Bonté* magazine, did not mention the war for several months. Instead it continued publishing human interest stories about physicians who fought in Indochina and debated, in general terms, the decay of medical infrastructure in times of war.[14] When *Vie et Bonté* did publish articles about Algeria, such as the September–October 1956 article summarizing French Red Cross president André François-Poncet's visit there, it detailed his numerous stops throughout the country to local chapters. But it failed to report specifics about the conflict. The piece emphasized "that everywhere [François-Poncet] went he saw Red Cross achievements, personnel that honor the national society, committee presidents who often face difficult tasks supporting one another, some assisting the military and others the Muslim [population]."[15] This kind of reporting, which showcases positive attributes of French Red Cross activities is not necessarily surprising. Yet its complete omission for the reasons behind François-Poncet's visit is. His trip was not routine. He was checking on regional capacity and distribution in light of military and political developments in the country.

French Red Cross annual reports for 1955 and 1956 maintain similar elisions about the war. Both devote considerable attention to the September 1954 Orléansville earthquake and ensuing efforts to provide relief to communities in the area. Assisting the French army was the second focus of these reports, with one-tenth of the twenty-million-franc operating budget spent in this domain.[16] Brief mention in official correspondence alluded to the current "situation." For example, Jacques Pernet, who worked in the Algiers prefect's office, wrote a short memo explaining the French Red Cross intended to collect funds for "those hit by the events" (French code for "war") but did not elaborate further.[17] The 1955 report referenced "the insurrectional state" and "distressing events that paralyzed some regional activity" in its opening lines and, like Pernet's letter, fell short of clarifying what those terms meant.[18] In a June 1956 letter to ICRC president Léopold Boissier, the general director of the French Red Cross in Algiers, Léonce Imbert, boasted of the French Red Cross's "humanitarian and social action toward those who suffer . . . during the difficult times at hand."[19] Imbert did not specify what or why Algeria was experiencing "difficult times." Despite chaos and repression erupting throughout Algeria, the French Red Cross was unwilling to officially acknowledge that a transformative war was taking place.

In a 1957 report, the French Red Cross finally directly acknowledged the conflict. It specified that the national society had "intensified its efforts . . .

despite difficulties from the insurrectional state" and pacification campaigns.[20] The report focused on the society's "social and humanitarian spirit"
that dispensed "charitable aid, without racial or religious distinction, to people in need, victims of natural disasters, and calamitous events, specifically
floods." But it only described victims in general terms. It did not profile aid
distributed to destitute Algerian civilians or ALN soldiers affected by the
war.[21] Financial and material consideration for the French army received sustained attention and French Red Cross personnel opened 170 files on behalf
of French military families, a number that grew steadily for the duration of
the war.[22] The national society's strong relationship with the army was also
reflected in numerous articles in the French newspapers *Le Monde* and *L'Echo
d'Alger* that described French Red Cross staff visiting French soldiers in hospitals and distributing cigarettes, candy, and games to raise morale.[23]

The imbalanced provision of care and allocation of resources in the first
years of the war made some former FLN participants and Algerian medical
personnel skeptical about French Red Cross neutrality. Colonel Hassan,
when asked to describe its role in the 1950s, laughed as if the notion of the
French Red Cross helping Algerians was inconceivable and implied that
many Algerian combatants did not trust the national society.[24] Soon-to-be
Algerian Red Crescent officials noted a French Red Cross presence in Algeria
but said "it was nothing other than a docile instrument" beholden to the
French authorities that only "serviced the French army."[25]

Other Red Crescent societies in the Arab world had the same negative
impression of the French Red Cross in Algeria. In July and August 1957, Dr.
M. Chaouky, the Syrian Red Crescent's vice president, and Dr. Moustafa
Khalifeh, president of the Jordanian Red Crescent, wrote separate letters to
the ICRC, strongly protesting the French Red Cross's "ill-treatment" of Algerian nationalists fighting to liberate their country.[26] Both men claimed that
the French Red Cross was not treating Algerian combatants and that staff
restricted care based on instructions from the French authorities.[27] If this
were true, the French Red Cross violated the major principles of the humanitarian organization and showed an allegiance toward the colonial state.

French Red Cross president André François-Poncet vehemently denied
these charges. François-Poncet assured ICRC president Léopold Boissier that
the Algerians "were treated like everyone else in the hospitals" and that the
French Red Cross devoted its resources to all victims of "the events," "whoever they may be."[28] But François-Poncet's use of "the events" betrayed his
political orientation, and other ICRC representatives questioned his ability to

carry out impartial care to Algerians.[29] That said, the reality of French Red Cross activity in Algeria probably falls between François-Poncet's description and that of Chaouky and Khalifeh. However, the perception that the French Red Cross discriminated against Algerians mattered and served as a catalyst to start a separate national society.

A Second National Society: The Algerian Red Crescent

The FLN leadership was consistently critical of the French Red Cross and in January 1957 decided to develop its own society, the Algerian Red Crescent (Croissant-Rouge Algérien, CRA). The Geneva-based International Committee of the Red Cross was unlikely to recognize the newly conceived CRA but that did not discourage nationalists. In his history of the Algerian Red Crescent, its former secretary-general Mustapha Makaci explained that "revolutionary Algeria was not in the position to fulfill ICRC conditions. . . . The Algerian government did not exist in this period. . . . Yet meeting the population's needs was urgent. We had to consider an intermediary solution."[30]

Members of the FLN chief executive body, the Comité de Coordination et d'Exécution (CCE), the precursor to the Provisional Government of the Algerian Republic (Gouvernment Provisoire de la République Algérienne, GPRA), believed it was necessary for "wounded Algeria to create and have at its disposal a mouthpiece close to the international committees of Red Crosses and Red Crescents, to solicit and receive aid."[31] They envisioned that the Algerian Red Crescent would work closely with the International Committee of the Red Cross. The Algerian Red Crescent's first president, Omar Boukli-Hacène, a lawyer from Tlemcén, expressed hope that "de jure recognition [of the CRA] would be linked to Algerian independence."[32] Boukli-Hacène's remarks underscore a central component of Algerian nationalist strategy. In lieu of being able to assert themselves through a military victory, the Algerian leaders aspired to seize their sovereignty through less conventional measures, such as the International Committee for the Red Cross officially recognizing one of their proto-national organizations. The Algerian Red Crescent would be the kind of organization that other countries around the world would respect. From its inception, Red Crescent delegates agreed that the national society would monitor and report French violations of human rights and the Geneva Conventions in Algeria.[33] The nationalists' early articulation of Algerian Red Crescent responsibilities shows a shrewd political awareness of the boundaries the new organization could contest and the issues it could exploit in the future.

Beginning in September 1956 Algerians met to discuss the possibility of forming a Red Crescent.[34] In December 1956, the Comité de Coordination et d'Exécution approved the creation of the Algerian Red Crescent, with the understanding that it would follow FLN directives and would be "perfectly integrated" into the existing executive FLN-ALN war branches. It would function as a much-needed social wing of the revolutionary movement, supplementing its primary political and military initiatives.[35] The Algerian Red Crescent would pursue a complementary agenda to that of the FLN and ALN, but it would have different responsibilities from those branches. It would use humanitarian ideals, principles, and rhetoric to expand support for the nationalist cause by merging Algerian "political questions with humanitarian ones," quite a dangerous combination according to ICRC representative Pierre Gaillard.[36]

Appropriating humanitarian language was a key component of Algerian Red Crescent strategy. Adopting this particular discourse showed that Algerian leaders were aware of and committed to international norms. Moreover, it demonstrated that the nationalists were capable of translating a vocabulary developed by international institutions that previously benefited Western powers into one that served their own ends and through which they could make sovereignty claims.[37] Algerian Red Crescent representatives drew freely from International Committee of the Red Cross literature in formulating the central elements of its mission, which included treating the injured, assisting war victims, serving as an intermediary between prisoners of war and their families, and facilitating ICRC missions to Algeria.[38] Additional Algerian Red Crescent concerns were to assist the growing Algerian refugee population in Morocco and Tunisia, supply medicine and medical personnel to the ALN-FLN health-services division, and integrate Algeria into a global international aid movement.[39]

The Algerians' international ambition to align themselves with the Geneva-based organization and its humanitarian principles was clearly defined from the Algerian Red Crescent's inception.[40] The CCE's detailed Algerian Red Crescent plan references conditions laid out in the Geneva Conventions of 1949, namely, paying special attention to victims of war. Given that French authorities routinely denied that the military action in Algeria constituted a war, the official status and applicability of international law was difficult to ascertain. However, in correspondence with the ICRC throughout the war,

Algerian nationalists claimed they followed the Geneva Conventions even though they were not signatories.[41]

The Algerian Red Crescent established its first offices in Tangiers and Tunis in early 1957. Later that year it created branches in Geneva and Cairo. The nationalists chose Geneva because it was where the Red Cross and other important international organizations were concentrated and Cairo because it could serve as a center "to receive donations and ensure their distribution."[42] A general overview of Algerian Red Crescent activities, likely written by one of its early officials highlighted Cairo's strategic importance for connecting with our "Middle Eastern brothers."[43] In the same report, the author recounted the day-to-day tasks that the Tangiers office performed, which included "continuous contact and discussion with ICRC representatives to make them recognize the CRA" and "sending propaganda documents," and encouraged those working in other cities to emulate them.[44] FLN delegates and early Algerian Red Crescent leaders considered contacting sympathetic organizations for aid and lobbying the International Committee of the Red Cross crucial components of their work. The Algerian Red Crescent set out to establish relationships with influential representatives of humanitarian organizations and communicate regularly with national Red Cross societies around the world, hoping to show the extent of its dedication to conducting the war in a humane fashion.

Just four weeks after radios announced the creation of the Algerian Red Crescent on 8 January 1957, at the height of the battle of Algiers and shortly before the FLN eight-day strike initiative, the new organization's representatives were sending letters to national societies abroad and enlisting their support.[45] For example, on 7 February Algerian Red Crescent president Boukli-Hacène wrote to the president of the English Red Cross in London telling him that the Algerian Red Crescent had been established in Tangiers and that it "pursued the exact same goals" as other national societies around the world. Boukli-Hacène stressed "the long-lasting feelings of solidarity that motivate your organization and your great nation" to act on behalf "of the suffering" and asked that the English Red Cross "respond with aid for Algerian soldiers, the sick and wounded, and orphans and refugees."[46]

By March 1957, Algerian Red Crescent leaders were writing to and meeting with International Committee of the Red Cross representatives. On 8 and 9 March, the Algerian Red Crescent's president, general secretary, and treasurer arrived in Geneva from Tangiers and met with FLN delegates and ICRC delegate Claude Pilloud.[47] Boukli-Hacène had prepared a lengthy memo explaining why the International Committee of the Red Cross should recognize the Algerian Red Crescent. However, none of the reasons given were tenable according to the ICRC conditions for an official national society. The two parties discussed prisoners, International Committee of the Red Cross visits to Algeria, and the possibility of sending trained medical personnel to aid the Algerians. The Algerian delegates also used the meeting to raise "a long list of French atrocities and inhumane treatment," including "executions, torture, hostages, attacks, pillages, and rapes" committed by French authorities.[48] Even though Pilloud did not make any definitive recommendations about how the international organization might proceed with the Algerians, securing a face-to-face meeting with the International Committee of the Red Cross was an achievement for the national society because it unofficially legitimized Algerian Red Crescent action.

The motivations for the creation of the Algerian Red Crescent were not lost on Pilloud. He quickly voiced concerns about the aims of the organization and "the delicate position" in which it placed the International Committee of the Red Cross. Pilloud remarked that "the goal of creating this organism is to have an institution, distinct from the FLN, that will be able to negotiate with the ICRC, and humanize the war. There is a tendency from my FLN interlocutors to send all problems that might interest the ICRC to the Algerian Red Crescent. . . . Upon their return to Tangiers, they were going to assemble the CRA committee and [re]examine the problem in light of [what I said]." He worried that by meeting with Algerian Red Crescent representatives he had recognized their activities and, by extension, their organization. He promised "to do my best to avoid difficulties for the ICRC," though "this will not be easy."[49] Pilloud's concerns were not unfounded. Association with the reputable humanitarian institution provided the Algerian nationalists an opportunity to present their agenda as analogous to that of the International Committee of the Red Cross and to create a broader international platform from which to make appeals.

The national society wasted no time doing so. By fall 1957, it set up a temporary office in Libya and was writing the Arab League, explaining its interactions with the International Committee of the Red Cross. In September of that year, French officials in Paris noticed that the Algerian Red Crescent established a branch in Zavia, Libya, devoted to receiving donations for Algerian civilians and soldiers. The national society appealed to Libyans to "donate part of their zakat to the organization, and any other food, money, or clothing they could spare for their Algerian brothers."[50] An October 1957 "information notice" described how on numerous occasions, Algerian Red Crescent representatives requested that the International Committee of the Red Cross send medical aid to help relieve "the large number of wounded and scarcity of medical products. The ICRC agreed to send it and [we] must follow-up. It has also taken an interest in the question of wounded war victims accommodations," but the notice added, "numerous obstacles, the most important of which is the lack of materials" have prevented progress. "It would be judicious, then, to work toward that end."[51] These two examples are a fraction of the initial Algerian Red Crescent outreach but highlight its representatives' efforts in forging relationships based on a sense of shared solidarity, moral obligation, and just practice, solicitation techniques they ameliorated throughout the war.

Since January 1957, Algerian Red Crescent leaders contacted other national societies through personal correspondence and met privately with Geneva Red Cross delegates. The Nineteenth International Conference of the Red Cross in New Delhi, India, October–November 1957, was the Algerian Red Crescent's first opportunity to simultaneously engage the International Red Cross network and petition its support for the Algerians' anticolonial movement. Due to Algerian Red Crescent de facto status, however, its representatives were unable to attend in an official capacity. Its leadership therefore enlisted Tunisian and Syrian delegations to appeal on their behalf and put out a call to help Algerian refugees. According to Mustapha Makaci, aid temporarily swelled after December, and the CRA collected the following types of donations: 50,000 Swedish crowns from the Swedish Red Cross, 10,000 Norwegian crowns from the Norwegian Red Cross, and medication from the Italian Red Cross.[52] Arab allies gave the nationalists' war effort vital exposure on an international humanitarian stage and introduced the Algerian Red Crescent to many who may not have known it existed.

A resolution mandating the protection of civilians, wounded, pharmacists, and physicians was a second major Algerian Red Crescent victory that emerged from the conference.[53] Attendees amended Article 3 of the Geneva Conventions, specifying that, "the wounded should be treated indiscriminately; physicians should not fear in any way the treatment they are called to give in these circumstances," and that "there should be no restriction on the free circulation of medication except for those [restrictions] defined by international legislation."[54] These provisions, though not specific to Algeria, had serious implications for the conflict that nationalists invoked immediately. On 15 December 1957, *El Moudjahid* published an article under the headline

"The International Red Cross Condemns the French Government Attitude" and reviewed the resolution for commensurate provision of medical care. The piece proclaimed "an important paragraph [in the resolution], particularly applicable to France, condemns all governments that create legislation limiting or impeding free circulation of medication in a conflict, even in a conflict where one of the two parties refuses to call it a war."[55] This pointed verbal attack was clearly intended to reproach French government policies discussed in Chapter 3. It also demonstrated involvement and engagement with ICRC policies. Nationalists, especially Algerian Red Crescent representatives, relied upon this method of incorporating ICRC language and absorbing it as part of their own agenda to showcase the extent of their commitment to international humanitarian practices, and they shamed their opponent for failure to do so. Domestic and global outrage over French military use of torture in 1958 provided the nationalists with an opportunity to do just that.

Capitalizing on French Military Use of Torture

The year 1958 was a turning point in the war. In May 1958 Charles de Gaulle returned to power, agreeing to take office on the condition that the French Constitution be rewritten to give the president sole executive powers.[56] In the four years since the outbreak of the war, France had appointed four different governor-generals of Algeria. French military offensives—including the Battle of Algiers—increased, as did the number of casualties on both sides, and a vocal settler constituency became more obstinate.[57] De Gaulle was perceived as a moderate figure to whom various political factions, from the French military to the European settler community, could all relate. The more conservative groups believed he would advocate for *Algérie française*, while those in favor of a return to civil authority expected that de Gaulle would make a concerted effort to rein in the military and try to end the war. As Alistair Horne points out, "the trouble was that each separate faction let itself wallow in the hopes that de Gaulle would be all things to all men."[58] In one of his first public addresses to a crowd of thousands of Algerians, de Gaulle infamously announced, "Je vous ai compris." For Algerians, including members of moderate political parties in the disputed territory and back in France, this speech signaled the slightest of compromises away from a hard-line, right-wing approach.

De Gaulle implemented major changes within months of assuming

power, the first of which was a referendum in September 1958. This vote—
the first one in which French and Algerians participated together in a single
electoral college—served to solidify the new constitution for the Fifth Republic.[59] De Gaulle would later suggest negotiating a *paix des braves* and most
notably, in September 1959, he made the "self-determination" speech, which
ultimately provided the kind of public concession the FLN and ALN needed
for their demands for national sovereignty to gain more political traction.

The Algerian leadership also underwent major political changes in the
fall of 1958. Many of the original FLN leaders, including Hocine Aït Ahmed,
Rabah Bitat, Mohamed Khider, and Mohamed Boudiaf, established the Provisional Government of the Algerian Republic (GPRA) in Cairo, which
served as their representative body for the remainder of the war.[60] As de
Gaulle spoke in Algeria in the summer of 1958, FLN leaders recognized an
important opportunity for their cause. They timed the GPRA announcement
for the week before de Gaulle's referendum anticipating their press conference in Cairo would disrupt and distract those in Algeria and abroad from
the positive momentum de Gaulle had generated in the preceding months.
Within days of the press conference, fifteen countries, from Morocco and
Tunisia to China and Vietnam, recognized the GPRA.[61] This demonstration
of international solidarity indicates not only that the GPRA had immediate
international allies but also that the Algerian liberation effort resonated beyond North African and Arab shores. Internationalizing the conflict through
diplomacy was always a central component of nationalist strategy, and after
1958 the GPRA was increasingly successful in achieving this aim.

Beginning in the fall of 1958, GPRA leaders, and its president Ferhat
Abbas in particular, expanded their diplomatic strategy. They worked closely
with the Algerian Red Crescent to create an image of themselves and the Algerian people as humanitarians and used the national society as a launch pad
to construct a version of the Algerian struggle it wanted the world to see.
They exploited confirmation of French torture—a dominant military strategy
until 1960—and recast the colonial administration as an abuser and violator
of its own republican ideals. Moreover, with the help of the Algerian Red
Crescent, the FLN shifted the focus of the debate, casting its members as liberal, generous humanitarians willing to voluntarily follow the Geneva
Conventions.

The French government passed exceptional legislative measures in Algeria in 1955 and 1956, which paved the way for the French army's system-
atized use of torture.[62] Rumors about torture circulated in Algeria and France

during this time, but they remained unsubstantiated. By spring 1957, French prime minister Guy Mollet came under criticism at home for failing to address the rumors. He responded by forming the Commission to Safeguard Individual Rights and Liberties (Commission de sauvegarde des droits et libertés individuels) to investigate and "clarify all of the accusations brought against the [French] army or government officials" and "calm public opinion" about FLN claims of torture.[63] The commission was based in France and made up of twelve men from different professions, ranging from lawyers to the president of the French Red Cross.[64] Mollet hoped the diverse membership would ensure its political independence from the military and reassure his constituents that he took this matter seriously.

Army officials in Algiers were abuzz when Mollet announced the commission's formation on 5 April 1957. Governor-general Robert Lacoste's cabinet set out to reassure the military that it would stand behind it, whatever the outcome. If the commission alleged that army officials abused their power, Lacoste's officials told them they would "defend the army in the face of slander."[65] The administration's tacit compliance was only one of the many challenges the commission faced during its short existence. It barely had its own budget and did not hold any real jurisdiction over access to information. As a result, the few trips commission members made to Algeria to investigate cases such as Maurice Audin's disappearance and Aïn Isser where prisoners died were short and largely limited to Algiers.[66]

Ultimately, the commission's twelve representatives had difficulty making uniform recommendations because they defined abuse and torture differently and the government restricted their access to numerous facilities. One report emphasized "the real and serious nature of the abuses" in Algeria, but said it did not find "a general system" of torture. Rather, the commission found that "sporadic acts" committed by individuals who acted without the consent of their superiors were more common.[67] Its conclusions were not consistent with later scholarly works that made use of declassified French army documents that confirmed systematic torture. Yet this discrepancy is not altogether surprising considering the army often oversaw the commission's visits.

Commission members repeatedly requested that French officials publish their results. They were denied. One of its members, Robert Delavignette, former governor-general of French West Africa, resigned over the matter and vowed to make the findings public. In December 1957, leading French newspaper *Le Monde* printed the findings, prompting a rapid response from

Robert Lacoste. His statement, which drew upon remarks Guy Mollet made at the National Assembly on 27 March of that year, reminded French citizens that "every time [abuse] cases were raised . . . sanctions were made." "The government," he added, "does not fear" pursuing the truth.[68] His strong words of conviction sounded powerful but did not initiate change. Several individuals named in previous reports for abusing their power still held those same positions at the end of December 1957.[69]

Henri Alleg's *La Question* was the first account French administrators and military officials took seriously. The reputable editor gave critics concrete evidence of torture and set off a firestorm of negative press about the war in France.[70] Alleg had been the editor of the communist newspaper *Alger Républicain* from 1950 to 1955 and had regularly published articles supporting Algerian independence. The French government banned the paper in 1955, forcing Alleg into hiding. On 12 June 1957 French paratroopers found him and arrested him for "endangering the safety of the state."[71] During his detainment, he endured mental and physical torture, as his interrogators tried to extract the names of individuals who had sheltered him while he was eluding the authorities. Ultimately, soldiers transferred Alleg to Lodi camp, where he recovered at a military hospital, fearing his disappearance or death would generate more controversy.

While he recuperated, Alleg penned *La Question* and smuggled it out. Portions of the manuscript appeared in French newspapers, but the government censored them. When the book came out in its entirety in 1958, officials tried to limit public debate and discussion about it and pulled newspaper editorials that addressed its contents. Two months after *La Question*'s initial publication, the government seized the remaining copies and banned its distribution in France. However, it continued circulating through clandestine channels.[72] French administrators denied Alleg's allegations, but religious groups and intellectuals campaigned and pushed for further inquiry into the torture question.[73]

As tension escalated surrounding allegations of torture, colonial administrators tried to deflect criticism onto the FLN and ALN who they claimed were "terrorists."[74] French colonial discourse had long portrayed Algerians as "savage" and "intensely violent by nature," a myth that predates 1830 but which the French military manipulated throughout the conquest in the nineteenth century. Similar claims were made during major uprisings against the colonial regime in the wake of World War II, notably after the Sétif and Guelma protests in May 1945.[75] The war for independence provided the

French government with a new occasion to demonize its enemy and accuse nationalists of "neglect[ing] all the laws and customs of war," even killing their own people.[76] On 28 and 29 May 1957, the ALN killings at Mélouza, which left three hundred Messali Hadj and Algerian National Movement (Mouvement Nationale Algérien, MNA) supporters dead, provided colonial officials with a perfect opportunity to depict the Algerians as savage.[77]

In the months after the Mélouza massacres, the administration used its own propaganda to exploit these deaths and show the world that the Algerian nationalists were in fact "brutal and irresponsible monsters."[78] In the summer of 1957, Robert Lacoste quickly compiled a brochure titled *L'Opinion mondiale juge les sanglants "libérateurs" de Mélouza et de Wagram*. In the fall, he issued a second booklet entitled *Aspects véritables de la rébellion algérienne* (also known as the "Green Book"), which was intended to show the kind of uncivilized opponent the French were fighting.[79] In the latter, Lacoste "unmask[ed] our adversary's propaganda" and analyzed his terror tactics.[80] The Green Book assembled horrifying pictures of French and Algerians—men, women, and children of all ages—who had been killed by the FLN for not supporting its war effort or for having violated FLN directives.[81] According to James Le Sueur, the Green Book was "the most explicit propaganda effort launched during the war," despite claims by the resident minister's office that it was an effort to "show in concrete and conclusive fashion, by irrefutable documents which can easily be verified, the methods employed by the rebels."[82] Mélouza and the damaging depictions of "Muslim fanaticism" and the gruesome images of the dead victims enabled the administration to try to "convince readers that reports of French military torture [paled] in comparison to what Algerians were capable of."[83] These promotional materials were not simply intended for a French audience. The technical consul to Lacoste's cabinet reported that the French ambassador to the United States approached him and suggested that the booklets could be "of great interest" for the United States and Great Britain and that they may be able to "turn public opinion against the Algerians."[84]

French officials persisted in their efforts to discredit disparaging remarks nationalists made. In a July 1960 report entitled "Torture: An FLN Propaganda Tool," the unnamed author asserted that Algerian reports of torture were fabricated and suggested the FLN had instructed Algerian rebels to hurt themselves and show their scars as evidence of abuse inflicted by the French army. "In order to give additional importance to his claims," the report stated, the FLN advised "the arrested Algerian patriot not to hesitate to burn himself when he is alone and to throw himself against the wall or a table, a way for him to show the evidence to the judge."[85] Colonial bureaucrats depicted nationalists as deceptive and vilified their opponents by accusing them of conniving behavior, unbefitting of state leaders. But French officials soon realized they faced a formidable adversary when it came to propaganda wars. The FLN, in conjunction with the Provisional Government of the Algerian Republic and the Algerian Red Crescent, took advantage of torture allegations and recast the imperial government and its military as barbaric and uncivilized. Prisoner-release ceremonies were particularly effective in this vein.

"Exploit This News": Prisoner Releases

The Algerian Red Crescent and International Committee of the Red Cross corresponded continually during the first eighteen months of the Red Crescent's existence, often about the issue of prisoners. Central elements of the International Committee of the Red Cross's mission included relief for prisoners of war on both sides, tracing missing persons, and reporting on the wounded.[86] To be sure, the nationalists studied the Red Cross agenda and modeled the edicts around it.

The Geneva Conventions of 1949 were the first to squarely address "armed conflict not of an international character occurring in the territory of one of the High Contracting Parties." Article 3 provided anticolonial leaders with the most leverage to try to force the French military into complying with the Geneva Conventions, which France had ratified. Furthermore, Article 3 gave the Algerians a very clear guide of how to conduct themselves in a manner that was "indispensible" to "civilized people." This included prohibiting "cruel treatment and torture" and "degrading treatment." Article 3 also stated that "the wounded and sick shall be collected and cared for."[87]

FLN and ALN records regarding POWs are difficult to come by. First, the maquis traveled by foot and frequently moved locations. Meticulous record keeping was not a top priority. Second, in 1957 French military action increased forcing portions of the Algerian leadership out of the country. And third, prisoners of any kind, French soldiers, Algerian civilians, and women and children, are a sensitive topic the Algerian National Archives have not yet made available. Despite these challenges, Raphaëlle Branche collected copious material from ICRC and French archives and conducted many interviews with former POWs and their families and recently provided one of the first comprehensives studies on prisoners during the war. She argues that for the Algerians prisoners were a central bargaining chip with the ICRC and the French military. Due to the asymmetric nature of the war, the FLN and ALN used their capture and treatment of French prisoners to show that the Algerian army was a regular army that followed the rules of war. Moreover, they aimed to negotiate with the French and exchange French prisoners for Algerian ones.[88] Prisoner exchanges rarely occurred because this would have meant the French recognized a legitimate military adversary. Therefore, the Algerian nationalists pursued other methods, such as prisoner-release ceremonies, a subject to which we will soon turn, to demonstrate their mastery of and commitment to the Geneva Conventions.

International Committee of the Red Cross delegates hoped that the Algerian Red Crescent would provide the international organization with information about French POWs, even though it was not officially recognized. (It asked the same of the French military regarding Algerian POWs.) Djilali Bentami, an Algerian doctor from Oran, set up an office in Geneva and served as the primary contact between the Red Crescent and the ICRC from 1957 to 1962. He led the effort to obtain reliable information about French prisoners from the FLN and ALN. Between 1957 and 1960, he had regular meetings with ICRC representatives, and he became a trusted intermediary for the international organization.[89] Bentami reached out to the nationalist leadership on numerous occasions but he was unable to deliver actionable information about French prisoners' whereabouts and well-being to the Red Cross.[90] He persisted in his quest and repeatedly assured ICRC representatives that he would obtain a list of all the prisoners the ALN had in its possession.[91] But this promise, as well as many others Bentami made over the years, went unfulfilled.

ICRC representatives became frustrated working with both sides because neither produced prisoner lists. The Red Cross could not force them to do so and was essentially beholden to their will. After a summer 1958 meeting in Geneva, Red Cross delegate I. Zreikat wrote that Dr. Bentami thought "it is very necessary for the FLN to make a gesture and observe the Red Cross humanitarian principles if it wants reciprocity."[92] Up until this point, he added, the FLN had not done so.

This changed later in the year with the creation of the Provisional Government of the Algerian Republic (GPRA). Abbas had been in contact with the International Committee of the Red Cross for nearly two years by the time he was named head of the Provisional Government of the Algerian

Republic and was thus familiar with Red Cross concerns about French prisoners. In one of his first officials acts, on 3 October 1958, Abbas, along with Belkacem Krim, GPRA vice president and minister of the armed forces, and Lakhdar Bentobbal, minister of the interior, issued a prisoner-release decree that extended "a general amnesty to certain categories of detainees."[93] It specified that "all detainees who were in local FLN and ALN units with the exception of those pursued or condemned for high treason or collaboration with the enemy" were entitled to amnesty and liberation. The official notice concluded that "certain French soldiers" held by the ALN would also "be liberated without conditions and returned to their families by delegates of the International Red Cross of Geneva."[94]

The amnesty decree would soon have an undeniable impact on improving relations with the International Committee of the Red Cross and on reshaping the image of Algerian nationalists. Members of the GPRA and Algerian Red Crescent had interacted with the International Committee of the Red Cross long enough to know that prisoner safety was one of the international organization's priorities. Abbas wanted to prove that he and Algerian Red Crescent representatives were worthy partners on whom the International Committee of the Red Cross could depend. The GPRA and Algerian Red Crescent also had a chance to combat the negative press, propaganda, and derogatory portrayals the French government was circulating globally.

The nascent Algerian government wanted to project a positive image of Algerian men and women fighting for national liberation, one that suggested they believed in human rights, treated French prisoners with respect, and embraced the Geneva Conventions.[95] Eleven days after the 3 October decree, "Nadir" who worked for the minister of external affairs discussed the potential impact prisoner releases could have on the organization and recommended that they should be brought to the attention of local press, political personalities, and organizations such as the Red Cross. He stressed that it was "very desirable that the accent be put on our liberalism and our concern for humanity."[96] In the event that prisoner releases "need to be explained in political terms to your interlocutors," he recommended, it should first be made clear that "it is an act of good will on our part [and] implies to our adversary that we respect the Geneva Conventions." Second, "it is from a position of strength that we are able to be liberal and generous. [Our actions] are not a sign of weakness." And third, "we await a French government response to our eminently humane initiative" that shows "the same good will." When possible, he concluded, "it is in this way that newspaper editorials should be oriented."[97] The nationalists' willingness to tackle the delicate matter of POWs was a deliberate strategy to demonstrate to the International Committee of the Red Cross and the world that they intended to comply with humane practices.

The Algerian leadership rapidly prepared its first prisoner-release cere-mony in Tunisia. Two and a half weeks after Abbas announced the decree, the ALN released four French prisoners it had captured near Sakiet Sidi Youssef on 11 January of that year and had held for ten months.[98] The Alge-rian Red Crescent worked with the Tunisian Red Crescent and organized a ceremony for their release on 20 October 1958. El Moudjahid reported that Aziz Djellouli, president of the Tunisian Red Crescent, and International Committee of the Red Cross delegates Jean de Preux and Pierre Gaillard pre-sided over the occasion, which lasted just under one hour. Roughly sixty members of the international press and radio were on hand to witness the French soldiers returning to their families.[99] Three groups, Actualités tunisi-ennes, Actualités françaises, and Fox Movietone, filmed the prisoners' re-lease.[100] In a press statement, an unidentified GPRA representative told the crowd that this occasion was a result of the 3 October decree and was not contingent upon the release of Algerian POWs by the French military.[101] This effort demonstrated the commitment of the Provisional Government of the Algerian Republic, the Algerian Red Crescent, and the Tunisian Red Cres-cent to work together and to distance themselves from the colonial adminis-tration's accusations that the FLN was a terrorist group. The Provisional Government of the Algerian Republic, in its infant stages, facilitated this event and successfully coordinated various Algerian organizations, signaling a renewed interest in incorporating Algerian Red Crescent work into the broader nationalist political strategy.

Additional prisoner releases throughout North Africa followed the initial one in Tunisia. On 3 November 1958, Colonel Amirouche, the influential leader of Wilaya 3, supervised the ALN release of six French soldiers in Kabylia. M'hamed Yazid, minister of information for the Provisional Gov-ernment of the Algerian Republic, wrote a memo from Cairo one week later, saying, "these six French prisoners publicly recognized, in declarations that were reproduced by the French press on 5 and 6 November, that they were well treated by the ALN." Yazid remarked that "global opinion will not fail to realize that this new release of French prisoners is taking place at a moment when the French government is violating international laws of war more than ever," publicly shaming his opponent and redirecting attention toward French transgressions.[102]

During the second week of December 1958, an International Committee of the Red Cross delegation assisted ALN officials and the Algerian Red Crescent in a prisoner-release ceremony in Morocco (Figure 9). According to "Nadir," a GPRA external affairs representative, the nationalists counted on "the maximum amount of publicity" of this event. If possible, the coverage should underscore that the Algerians' actions reflected their government's respect for the laws of war, which, Nadir claimed, the French army violated daily.[103]

In February 1959, two months after the first Morocco prisoner ceremony, the Algerian Red Crescent arranged a second one in Oujda and released six additional French military personnel. International Committee of the Red

Figure 9. Liberation of eight French prisoners by the ALN. ICRC delegates hand over the prisoners to the French Embassy, Rabat, Morocco, 3 December 1958. (International Committee of the Red Cross)

Cross delegates C. Vautier and Gaillard reported that the Algerian Red Crescent presented Lucien Louvet, Jean Coulos, Maurice Borel, Gilbet Fillieux,
Yvon Jacquey, and François Fournier to them. Following the ceremony, they
transported them to France and reunited the men with their families.[104]

These orchestrated events marked the new humanitarian face that would
define future GPRA, FLN-ALN, and Algerian Red Crescent politics.[105] In the
four months since Abbas announced the GPRA amnesty initiative, the Algerian Red Crescent worked with the Tunisian Red Crescent, Moroccan officials, and International Committee of the Red Cross intermediaries in three
Maghribi countries. These ceremonies provided a stark contrast to the images and stories about Algerian barbarism published in the French press.
They were meant also to serve as "positive gestures" that "clearly expressed"
the desire to "unilaterally humanize the conflict" and strengthen the Algerian
Red Crescent–International Red Cross relationship.[106]

El Moudjahid regularly included articles depicting Algerian leaders' actions aligning with international humanitarian principles. On 22 June 1959,
the FLN wartime journal printed an interview with new Algerian Red Crescent president Mostefa Benbahmed. The doctor, who was originally from
Constantine, underscored the reasons the national society worked to facilitate prisoner releases. For Benbahmed, the "successive liberations of a certain
number of French prisoners" illustrated the GPRA and CRA's "attachment to
the Geneva Conventions." The nationalists organized these events "not for
propaganda purposes, as our adversaries maintain."[107] His words embody the
spirit and essence nationalists wanted to convey to a broader international
audience about the numerous humanitarian virtues carried out by the Red
Crescent.

Upon their release, French prisoners sometimes issued statements about
their time in captivity, further emphasizing Algerian nationalists' commitment to international law. On 19 October 1958 "Georges" wrote such a letter.
In it, he explained he had been taken by the ALN in Algeria. But he wanted
people to know that the ALN "was not a savage army but rather a regular
army." He said Algerian soldiers had "treated him very well up until this point
and had fed [the prisoners] well." The ALN was planning to release Georges
on 1 November, the revolution's anniversary, and he asked the French government to allow the International Red Cross to enter into Algeria to assist in
the soldiers' release.[108] Three days later, Colonel Amirouche wrote a follow-
up letter to French military officers about "[their] son, [Georges]," who, he
said, was "treated humanely" according to laws of war.[109] It is unclear under

what conditions Georges penned his letter and, though little else is known about him, the language he and Amirouche used to speak about his capture indicate an attention to conveying a similar message about the nationalists. They were the ones going the extra measure, ensuring the safety of their prisoners (not the French military) even when technically they were under no obligation to do so.

The Algerian nationalist groups continued working together to broadcast French prisoner releases in newspapers and journals and on the radio throughout the remainder of the war. Beginning in 1959, they expanded their reporting to include their resolve to free other foreign nationals. In June 1959, *El Moudjahid* published a story about four Spanish soldiers who had been recently released by Algerian forces and returned to their families. Shortly thereafter, an FLN representative in Madrid wrote to the Provisional Government of the Algerian Republic minister of armed forces, asking him to please "exploit this news." He suggested collecting data about the four men and including that in the statement. The FLN representative received a response from Cairo within five days requesting the Spaniards' names and "all useful information" that would enable the FLN Madrid staff to issue "interesting propaganda about this subject."[110]

Prisoners of war, argues historian Dalila Aït-El-Djoudi, were part of a calculated propaganda effort aimed at winning over international public opinion. ALN members, she explains, were instructed to make sure that French prisoners were given accommodations and food. They should be permitted to write freely to their family and friends, and, above all, they should never be mistreated.[111] ALN commanders issued directives about indoctrinating the prisoners with the "spirit of the revolution," a practice that encouraged positive press such as Georges's letter and that produced immeasurable returns for their war effort.[112]

The nationalists, understandably, were concerned by reports that questioned their humanitarian image, such as *Le Monde*'s 12 May 1958 story alleging the ALN had killed three French soldiers in return for Algerian soldiers' deaths.[113] The Provisional Government of the Algerian Republic, the Algerian Red Crescent, and the FLN-ALN tried to minimize French government and International Committee of the Red Cross inquiries about missing French soldiers they could not account for and worked to preserve the impression that they continually searched for their whereabouts. During the summer of 1958 the International Committee of the Red Cross submitted a request for information on numerous French soldiers who disappeared in different regions of Algeria. On 28 July an ALN military chief wrote to an unspecified International Committee of the Red Cross delegate on behalf of Algerian Red Crescent president Boukli-Hacène that "despite meticulous research conducted by our general staff . . . the names of the servicemen you gave me do not appear on the list of prisoners held by the ALN. The soldiers, in our opinion were probably killed in combat."[114] He suggested the inquiry was a blatant propaganda attempt "orchestrated by the French government . . . to hide the death of their sons by making them believe that they are being held by the ALN." He proposed that the French soldiers in question could have died in a routine French military operation, been lost, or fallen into enemy hands. He concluded his letter with impassioned words: "we are very sensitive to these sad families' agony, but we cannot feed their fantasies."[115] The ALN chief and Boukli-Hacène knew prisoners were an International Committee of the Red Cross pressure point; they wanted to say whatever they could to maintain strong relations with the ICRC delegates, divert their attention away from possible Algerian army abuses, and cast doubts on the French army.

Instrumentalizing Refugees and International Aid

The Provisional Government of the Algerian Republic, the Algerian Red Crescent, and the FLN-ALN expanded their strategy for international recognition by publicizing the plight of Algerian refugees. Prisoner-release ceremonies had helped the nationalists define themselves as committed to the laws of war. Focusing on Algerian refugees would help them garner international sympathy for the consequences of such a brutal war and bring in significant financial and material aid from every continent. The refugee crisis, unlike prisoners of war, United Nations delegates would argue in the General Assembly in 1959, threatened international security due to the high numbers of displaced individuals who crossed Maghribi borders needing food and shelter. Displaced Algerians taxed the government budgets of recently independent Morocco and Tunisia.[116] Algeria's neighbors could not meet their needs on their own. Algerian Red Crescent officials adopted this outlook to appeal to national Red Cross and Red Crescent societies around the globe with staggering success and strengthened their campaign to prove the colonial government could not be trusted with the Algerian population's health and welfare.

The refugee problem steadily grew over the course of the war and can be largely attributed to regroupment centers, a small and disjointed military experiment that began in the Aurès in 1955. But by 1957, they had become a dominant army tactic to deny rebels of local support.[117] French military officials uprooted the Algerian population from their land and livestock, depriving them of their traditional agricultural economy, and relocated them to designated areas under their control. They believed, according to Michel Cornaton, these centers would cut off Algerian combatants from supplies and land used to launch attacks against the colonial regime.[118] In 1957, the military created two categories of centers, temporary and permanent ones. Temporary centers were destroyed after they fulfilled their initial relocation function. Permanent centers were geared toward more long-term goals. Military officers scouted areas with natural resources and a sustainable environment, places that could "display economic and sociological viability."[119]

The number of regroupment centers increased dramatically from this point on. In 1957, approximately 240,000 Algerians lived in 382 temporary and permanent centers. By early 1960, 1.5 million Algerians lived in over 1,700 regroupment centers.[120] Later that year, according to sociologists Pierre Bourdieu and Abdelmalek Sayad, the centers were so pervasive that nearly one-fourth of the Algerian population had been forcibly resettled into them.[121]

Two French military strategies, the Challe Plan and the *zones interdites*, or free-fire zones, help explain regroupment centers' exponential growth. In December 1958, President Charles de Gaulle appointed General Maurice Challe as commander in chief of the army to bring about "swift military successes before the spring" of 1959.[122] Previously, the military launched attacks across the Algerian countryside but often without a clear regional focus. General Challe implemented a system targeting mountainous areas and, one at a time, crushed ALN units within each sector. Once soldiers accomplished this task in one region, the general assigned them to move on to the next one. By July 1959, Challe's men had successfully attacked Oranais, Algerois, east Kabylia, and the Aurès. Free-fire zones, a military initiative that began in 1957, forced local populations off their land and mandated that they relocate without any prior notice or preparation. Once the area was checked and often burned to deprive the FLN of shelter or resources, anyone in it or passing through it, would likely be shot.[123] Keith Sutton argues that those areas "calculated as having a low pacification potential . . . were increasingly separated off" as free-fire zones.[124] Many regroupment inhabitants were victims of these two unforgiving policies.

The French army's efforts to relocate the population within Algeria wreaked havoc on civilians' daily lives. By 1959, over 200,000 Algerians had fled their homeland in search of basic essentials like food, clothing, and medicine. French officials downplayed the high figures of Algerian refugees and accused the ALN of inflating the numbers. A 1959 French Division of Information notice insisted that 90,000 refugees did not all flee during the war. Rather, that figure included three separate categories of people, approximately 50,000 Algerians who lived in Morocco at the beginning of the rebellion, between 30,000 and 40,000 refugees, who before the rebellion's extension into Oran, sought shelter, and roughly 4,800 ALN soldiers stationed in Morocco.[125] Nationalist "propaganda," the notice claimed, influenced the public into thinking that all 80,000–90,000 refugees in Morocco fled from colonial oppression, whereas French officials maintained half of them left before military action began. In a similar report on the status of Algerian refugees in Tunisia during the same year, the French Intelligence Division, which had conducted a study on the strategic significance of the Bizerte base, criticized the Tunisian government for doctoring refugee figures. It alleged that Tunisia was receiving "considerable international aid from which Algerian rebels could benefit. . . . In fact, the Tunisians came up with 125,000 refugees, while French military authorities estimate 100,000 Algerians went to Tunisia before the rebellion, and 15,000–20,000 refugees had arrived since 1957."[126] The Intelligence Division expressed disbelief at the escalating figures and demonstrated apprehension over Moroccan and Tunisian support but did not make any gestures, symbolic or otherwise, to alleviate refugee conditions. For French personnel, Algerian rebels profiting from refugee aid and supplies was a more pressing concern.

The Algerian Red Crescent took on the refugee issue and made it a centerpiece of the national society's agenda, refuting the colonial administration's position that the nationalists exaggerated the problem. It began producing pamphlets and memos detailing the plight of the displaced. One bilingual publication, titled *Les Réfugiés Algériens—The Algerian Refugees* (Figure 10), included graphic images of refugees and the deplorable conditions in which they lived due to the destructive nature of French military action.[127] The pamphlet stated that "every visitor to the Algerian-Tunisian and Algerian-Moroccan frontier areas" would be "appalled and horrified by the sight of perhaps the most pitiful human tragedy of our times." It called on readers to recognize common human characteristics and get involved in the Algerian Red Crescent relief effort.[128]

Figure 10. Cover image of *Les Réfugiés Algériens*. (Archives Nationales d'Outre-Mer)

The Algerian national society representatives took full advantage of the International Red Cross network and circulated its materials to as many national Red Cross and Red Crescent societies as it could contact. This dimension of Algerian propaganda aimed to publicize the war, familiarize the world with Algerian refugees, demonstrate severe financial, medical, and material need, and ask for aid. The Algerian Red Crescent refined this method of solicitation and received millions of dollars during the second half of the war.

Shortly after the Algerian Red Crescent distributed this pamphlet, French Lieutenant Colonel Bourdoncle observed that the bilingual publication was "edited by the FLN under the Algerian Red Crescent insignia." He conceded, "it was well presented and well translated and could be used as a White Paper in the United Nations and as a general propaganda document [for] Anglo-Saxon and Latin American countries. Even though the photographs of atrocities and torture are edited montages, they are sufficient to deceive unsuspecting readers."[129] Bourdoncle noted how the Algerian Red Crescent used several languages to communicate with more people and expand its circle of allies. He understandably dismissed the pamphlet's gruesome pictures of torture victims that were printed without context. However, he could not deny their powerful political and emotional effect.

The Algerian Red Crescent used this kind of material to send a "call on behalf of refugees" to Arab allies in Damascus, Beirut, Baghdad, Khartoum, Amman, Benghazi, and Jeddah, imploring them to apply pressure on their governments and on social organizations in their countries. In one 10 November 1958 letter, Benyoucef Benkhedda, GPRA minister of social affairs, described refugee conditions in Morocco and Tunisia and asserted that "more than 300,000 Algerians, 50 percent of whom are children, 35 percent women, and 15 percent elderly individuals," lived across the borders.[130] The Moroccan and Tunisian governments had made significant relief contributions, but they could not provide sufficient aid to meet the full demand. Therefore, Benkhedda was "reiterating the call . . . and asking again to kindly ensure that our representatives in the Arab world spare no effort in making this plea a crowning success."[131]

The Algerian Red Crescent campaign resonated with Algerian allies and raised funds from across the Arab world through 1962. Donations came in all materials and amounts and were sent to CRA offices in Tunis and Tangiers. The Moroccan and Tunisian Red Crescent societies also accepted donations on the Algerian Red Crescent's behalf because the national society did not operate in Algeria during the war. In January 1958 Jordan sent approximately 80,000 Swiss francs to the Algerian Red Crescent office in Tangiers.[132] In the fall of that year, Libyan Red Crescent representative Zahidallall Reish informed the Algerian Red Crescent that its council sent "by air mail, the sum of $2,500.00 to be used for child welfare work among refugees from the combat zones."[133] Internal Algerian Red Crescent reports for 1959 show Syria sent 60,000 French francs' worth of flour and cornmeal; Egypt sent over 450,000,000 French francs worth of flour, sugar, cloths, and blankets; Morocco shipped unspecified medications, and Kuwait packaged clothes worth more than 10,000 francs, to name just a few of the Arab nations that participated in the relief effort.[134] These were the most typical kinds of refugee assistance donations they sent and continued to send as indicated by Algerian Red Crescent reports for 1960 and 1961. In them, Tunisia and Lebanon feature most prominently for their medication and pharmaceutical contributions.[135]

The Algerian Red Crescent did not rely solely on correspondence to solicit aid from the Arab world. It also dispatched delegates to make a case in person. The year 1959 was especially productive. Before the 1959 World Health Organization (WHO) conference in Geneva, Algerian leaders worked with a host of countries—Saudi Arabia, Ghana, Guinea, India, Indonesia, Iraq, Lebanon, Libya, Morocco, Pakistan, United Arab Republic, Jordan, Sudan, Tunisia, Yemen, Afghanistan, and Ethiopia—and developed a platform they could present to the internationally assembled audience on behalf of Algerian refugees and those living in regroupment camps. The delegations' motion expressed how "deeply moved" they were "by the tragic nature of the situation that has caused thousands of people, the majority of whom are women, children, and the elderly, to suffer in camps." They urged the International Committee of the Red Cross to pressure the French government to "scrupulously observe the Geneva Conventions" and "protect civilians," and find ways to shut down the camps "and return the displaced to their previously inhabited land."[136] Their plea bears a strong resemblance to Algerian Red Crescent phrasing in pamphlets and correspondence, suggesting their representatives had a hand in drafting this motion and shaped it for consistency and continuity.

A second important illustration of the widespread diplomatic efforts in which the Algerian Red Crescent engaged was its proxy representation at an international Red Cross meeting in Athens, Greece in September 1959. During the months leading up to the meeting, Red Crescent representatives traveled to Jordan to request that its delegation represent their interests in Athens. Their efforts paid off. On 19 September 1959, FLN leaders received a telegram that Jordanian officials had sent through Syrian intermediaries, confirming that the Jordanian government "consented to include a CRA member in our delegation" at the upcoming event, securing an additional opportunity for the nationalists to broadcast the lengths they would go to protect the vulnerable Algerian population and condemn the colonial administration.[137]

But even more telling of the Algerian Red Crescent's solicitation success was the extent to which countries and organizations outside the Arab world responded to its calls for help. Countries such as Italy and Portugal began sending clothes, blankets, milk, and cloth as early as 1958, as did Japan, Canada, Chile, and Norway.[138] The East German Red Cross contributed 250,000 marks' worth of medication for refugees in February 1958.[139] North Vietnam sent medicine and rice to the Casablanca office and the Netherlands sent medicine, blankets, and clothing for refugees via the Moroccan Red Crescent.[140] After a visit from Algerian Red Crescent vice president Mostefa Lakhal, the Turkish Red Crescent donated thirty tons of sugar and medicine.[141] French military intelligence even noted the volume of medication, money, and bedcover donations the Algerian Red Crescent received from nations such as China and Sweden.[142] In November and December 1960 alone, the Algerian Red Crescent received seventy-five kilograms of "personal effects" from Italy and 410 kilograms of medication and general supplies from Switzerland.[143] International organizations also increased their aid after 1959. For example, UNICEF became particularly interested in Algerian refugees in Morocco and Tunisia and in July 1960 allocated $80,000 and $170,000, respectively, for each country.[144] In 1961, aid continued to stream into Algerian Red Crescent offices from diverse organizations. The Indian Congress Committee sent 550 cotton blankets, 427 pounds of tea, and 1,000 vials of penicillin to Tunis, and the Vatican pledged $100,000 for refugee relief work.[145]

The global response in the second half of the war is a powerful indicator of Algerian Red Crescent success in constructing a compelling humanitarian message that went beyond Arab alliances and anticolonial movements, yet one issue remains unclear. Algerian Red Crescent records inventoried remarkable donations, but they do not indicate how they were distributed to refugee communities or if they were used for other purposes. Alleviating the dire conditions of Algerian refugees across the Maghrib required extreme coordination and excellent communication to ensure that all of the aid reached those in need. One FLN member at Oued Rmel in western Tunisia told American activists Richard and Joan Brace that he "saw many lists of materials donated to the Red Crescent, but very rarely the materials themselves." He attributed the lack of supplies to "either ALN priority or Tunisian poverty, or both. Either source could have reduced his provisions."[146] This man raised an important practical issue that the Algerian Red Crescent literature does not resolve. Refugees were not the only ones waiting for food and medicine. ALN soldiers and Moroccan and Tunisian communities along the borders also lived in poverty and faced difficult conditions. Although the aid was earmarked for Algerian refugees, it is possible neighboring governments or ALN commanders diverted portions or entire shipments to provide for their people, a common practice in humanitarian crises necessitating further study.

Furthermore, the Algerian records celebrate the massive influx of international donations, but they do not adequately reflect the level of confusion and moral quandary some Red Cross employees experienced upon receiving materials from the Algerian Red Crescent. In 1959, Swedish and Netherlands Red Cross representatives wrote to the International Committee of the Red Cross in Geneva, explaining that the Algerian Red Crescent sent them information about the Algerian refugee crisis and requested in-person meetings.[147] Haakon Mathiesen, the president of the Norwegian Red Cross, wanted the ICRC to advise him on how he should receive the Algerian Red Crescent, given that it was not an officially recognized organization. Mathiesen noted, "It seems to us to be a somewhat difficult situation with a touch of political questions."[148] Mathiesen's delicate phrasing honed in directly on the contentious political questions Algerian Red Crescent activities raised.

Ten days later, Roger Gallopin, ICRC executive director, wrote to Mathiesen and said the ICRC "quite understand[s] that the request put forward in this [Algerian Red Crescent] letter is embarrassing for the Norwegian Red Cross," but he does not explicate why that was the case. He explained that even though the Red Crescent did not meet the criteria for recognition, "in view of the special circumstances prevailing in this case," the ICRC decided "to maintain de facto relations with this organization in order to carry out activities of a strictly humanitarian nature."[149] Once again, Gallopin did not detail the "special circumstances," but one can surmise that he meant the unique juridical challenges involved in the Algerian war. Gallopin told Mathiesen that it was up to the Norwegian Red Cross how it wanted to handle a Red Crescent meeting. Mathiesen sympathized with the refugee crisis and pointed out that for two years, the Norwegian Red Cross had donated on their behalf. However, he was not prepared to meet with Red Crescent delegates in an official capacity, only as foreigners, discussing common interests.[150]

Even though the Algerian Red Crescent encountered skepticism from a handful of Red Cross societies, overall its propaganda and solicitation efforts yielded significant results.[151] Frequently when Red Cross representatives did not officially recognize the Red Crescent, they would still donate money and/or supplies for Algerian refugees, as in the Norwegian case.[152] The Algerian Red Crescent's activities were commendable in scope and international support that, at a minimum, proved to colonial authorities that many individuals and organizations empathized with their humanitarian message.

Conclusion

When the FLN supported the Algerian Red Crescent's 1957 creation, its leaders envisioned the national society offering a viable alternative to that of the French Red Cross for Algerian refugees and ALN soldiers. They attacked the French Red Cross for prioritizing French military and government assistance over that of the local population, which for them breached the International Committee of the Red Cross's ethos of neutrality. Algerian Red Crescent activities operated primarily outside of Algerian borders between 1957 and 1962, and its representatives took on critical issues that, from the start, placed Algerian needs over those of anyone else. Algerian Red Crescent initiatives and records exhibited overt national self-interest, a phenomenon that has occurred throughout history, as many Red Cross scholars have shown, and one that logically develops in a decolonization setting.

What distinguished Algerian Red Crescent nationalism is how its representatives successfully translated humanitarianism vocabulary and concerns into political and material gain. It became an extension of the FLN, ALN, and Provisional Government of the Algerian Republic, and its delegates used it as a platform to counter French officials' claims that nationalists were barbaric and uncivilized. Instead they formulated a compelling image of the anticolonial struggle and those fighting for liberation. The national society took on French military torture and exposed French republican hypocrisy. It staged foreign prisoner-release ceremonies across North Africa demonstrating mastery of International Red Cross issues and constructed a case for nationalists' generosity and adherence to humane practices. And finally, it thrust regroupment camps and Algerian refugees' plight onto an international stage, and through relentless and sophisticated propaganda and solicitation, received significant donations for their relief.

The Algerian Red Crescent adopted an innovative approach for the time, one that nonstate actors frequently use today when interacting with humanitarian organizations.[153] Its founders and personnel wagered that their appropriation of universal language and practices would grant them honorary membership in an international community of like-minded people and organizations committed to justice and freedom. They were right and handsomely rewarded. Moreover, Algerian nationalists and the unique circumstances of a colonial war for national liberation had a direct impact on transforming the ICRC and the United Nations. They forced these organizations to amend their policies and consider the Third World, a process to which we now turn.

Chapter 5

The International Committee of
the Red Cross in Algeria

> It is undeniable that the 1949 Conventions were conceived according to
> and based on the experience of "classic" armed conflicts (conventional
> international wars).
> — René-Jean Wilhelm, ICRC delegate, 1965

In January 1960, at the height of African decolonization, the French newspaper *Le Monde* printed excerpts of the confidential report that the International Committee of the Red Cross (ICRC) submitted to the French government after its seventh mission to Algeria. The details within the report corroborated many of the Algerian Red Crescent's allegations about French wartime policies in Algeria. It exposed controversial information about prison conditions, routine torture by the French army, detention centers, and regroupment camps, each one a politically explosive issue that the French government went to great lengths to contain over the course of the Algerian war. In fact, the colonial administration claimed the "events" happening in Algeria were not a war and thus a sovereign French concern. Why, then, was the ICRC permitted in the contested territory in the first place and what circumstances led the self-defined neutral and apolitical organization to become embroiled in a public and political battle for the future of Algeria?

This chapter examines how after the atrocities of World War II the International Committee of the Red Cross revised the Geneva Conventions in 1949 in order to better meet the needs of civilians. Yet, despite its efforts to improve international relations and protect human life, neither the Geneva

Conventions nor the institution's leadership adequately anticipated the next political and international challenge: decolonization. The updated Geneva Conventions did not specify what response, if any, was required in an internal conflict. Practically speaking, this meant action in a colonial context was subject to interpretation, placing the International Committee of the Red Cross in a vulnerable position, easily manipulated by opposing sides.[1]

The International Committee of the Red Cross's long and largely distinguished history, dating back to the 1860s, enticed governments, nationalist movements, and individuals around the world.[2] They sought out the organization for material assistance but also for the moral authority it could lend to their particular cause. Despite its proven commitment to helping parties regardless of their race, religion, or gender, the International Committee of the Red Cross's actions, especially during decolonization, revealed a growing disconnect between its intended impartiality and political realities.

Internal conflicts presented the International Committee of the Red Cross with a new kind of quandary. They tested the limits of what its representatives could accomplish and increasingly paralyzed the organization. On the one hand, its mandate provided critical assistance and motivated civilians and governments to adhere to humanitarian principles. On the other hand, Red Cross representatives could neither enforce rules nor require changes. They were further constrained by an agreement that they were only permitted into a country on condition that their reports remain confidential. The threat of publicizing extremely sensitive state information obtained on government-sanctioned missions was the extent of the International Committee of the Red Cross's power.

Its universal mission had widespread appeal. In Algeria, as in other colonial contexts, both the French and Algerian leaderships wanted to work with the Red Cross. They gravitated toward ICRC principles and yearned to demonstrate that they were dedicated to enacting humanitarian codes of conduct. The ideas themselves were so powerful that French and Algerian officials self-regulated their behavior hoping to establish a favorable relationship with the organization's representatives. The French government worked with the ICRC to subdue international criticism, and Algerian nationalists pursued the Red Cross because they perceived it to be uniquely positioned to lend credibility to their war effort and substantiate their claims for sovereignty.

ICRC representatives did not agree on the course of action they should pursue in Algeria or if they should work with both sides. ICRC delegates used what power they had to influence numerous French governments and Algerian nationalists to uphold the Geneva Conventions and protect as many lives as possible. However, the humanitarian principles upon which the International Committee of the Red Cross was founded constantly bristled against the politics of the state and national sovereignty, exposing the fraught relationship between humanitarianism and politics that persists to this day.

Algeria remains one of the few cases in which the contents of a Red Cross report were made public during the conflict, and this breach of trust signals a significant moment in the organization's history. The incident suggested that the International Committee of the Red Cross had reached the limits of its moral authority. Through an analysis of the 1949 Geneva Conventions, ICRC positions on internal conflicts in the early 1950s, and its ten missions to Algeria between 1955 and 1962, this chapter shows the moral and practical obstacles the International Committee of the Red Cross faced during decolonization. Ultimately, the challenges its leadership encountered when trying to work with French colonial administrators and Algerian nationalists during the war prompted it to further amend Red Cross policies, transforming the organization in the process.

Revisions for a New World: The Geneva Conventions of 1949

The International Committee of the Red Cross decided to reevaluate its policies on prisoners and civilians during armed conflict after World War II in light of the tragic loss of human life. The existing three Geneva Conventions had proved inadequate during the war and needed revision to suit modern conditions of war.[3] Many of its members believed that the absence of a convention for the protection of civilians during the war "led to grievous consequences" in the 1940s.[4] Lengthy debates culminated in a fourth convention called the Convention for the Protection of Civilian Persons in Time of War.

ICRC leaders in Geneva met with national Red Cross societies and their representatives who were active during World War II and gathered recommendations on the kinds of improvements the ICRC could make. ICRC delegates continued meeting with and soliciting advice from governments for three years and worked on several drafts of the document that aimed to ensure that certain wartime protections were put in place for both military personnel and civilians.[5] On 12 August 1949, seventeen delegations signed the four conventions. Over the next six months, forty-four additional states signed them, bringing the total numbers of signatory states to sixty-one.[6]

The updated Geneva Conventions were intended for international wars and conflicts, noted ICRC delegate René-Jean Wilhelm, not civil and internal ones, which soon dominated warfare in the 1950s.[7] ICRC drafters knew at the time that the conventions were limited in scope, and as a result they tried to incorporate some safeguards for persons not taking part in the armed conflict. Article 3 of the 1949 Geneva Conventions was written specifically for conflicts not of an international character and states:

(1) Persons taking no active part in the hostilities, including members of armed forces who have laid down their arms and those placed *hors de combat* by sickness, wounds, detention, or any other cause, shall in all circumstances be treated humanely, without any adverse distinction founded on race, colour, religion or faith, sex, birth or wealth, or any other similar criteria.

To this end, the following acts are and shall remain prohibited at any time and in any place whatsoever with respect to the above-mentioned persons:

(a) violence to life and person, in particular murder of all kinds, mutilation, cruel treatment and torture;
(b) taking of hostages;
(c) outrages upon personal dignity, in particular, humiliating and degrading treatment;
(d) the passing of sentences and the carrying out of executions without previous judgment pronounced by a regularly constituted court, affording all the judicial guarantees which are recognized as indispensable by civilized peoples.

(2) The wounded and sick shall be collected and cared for.

Initially, a 1949 draft called for protection in civil wars and decolonization, but these suggestions never made it into the final version. Instead, writes Heather Wilson, Article 3 was "an attempt to apply the fundamental principles of the Conventions to non-international armed conflicts while not making the Conventions applicable in their entirety."[8]

The French delegation repeatedly delayed the revision process between

1946 and 1949. According to Fabian Klose, French representatives "submitted a proposal to apply not all Article 3 norms to internal conflicts but only the minimum ones." The French were not motivated "by a heartfelt commitment to the humanitarian protection of the colonial population during international unrest."[9] They already had an eye toward the potential applicability of the conventions in their colonies, and they expended tremendous energy trying to avoid such an outcome.

Even though Article 3 was a major development in international law, it only formally protected those not taking part in the conflict. It went a long way in instituting protective boundaries around civilians in internal conflicts yet the specific measures remained extremely vague because it did not delineate clearly to whom it applied.[10] Depending on one's interpretation, civilians, former military personnel, medical staff, or sick and wounded members of the armed forces were all entitled to receive care. During the Algerian war, French colonial officials and Algerian nationalists argued that they were applying Article 3 to their opponents, but the ICRC had no way of verifying the article's systematic implementation, nor could its representatives force them to adhere to Article 3. This central problem persisted throughout the conflict and exposed ICRC vulnerabilities for failing to anticipate a prominent new form of armed conflict on the horizon.

Internal Conflicts in a Colonial Setting

Indochina and Kenya were among the first anticolonial movements the ICRC confronted in the late 1940s and early 1950s, and they served as reference points for Algeria. The Presidential Council at the time did not know how to react or what role the ICRC should take on in what it called "internal troubles,"[11] although members recognized that they posed "a serious humanitarian problem."[12] A general report on ICRC intervention in internal conflicts stated that "it could not provide a precise definition of these situations, but that did not matter . . . what is important is to know when the ICRC can and should intervene."[13] It listed the following conditions for intervention:

1. The conflict must have a certain seriousness and consist of violent acts.
2. The events must be a certain length of time.
3. There must be a struggle between two or more groups that each possess an organization.

4. There must be victims.

5. Even if all four conditions are met, the ICRC is not obligated to intervene if the national Red Cross can act effectively and is willing to do so.[14]

Only in situations where conditions one through four occurred simultaneously would the ICRC consider taking action, and representatives would first collect information on the particular case before offering the organization's services.

The wars of decolonization easily met these criteria. However, the ICRC did not have any legal jurisdiction in Indochina and Kenya, and if it sent assistance or suggested conducting missions, it had to make requests through the European governments, not the nationalist organizations, for the countries were not yet sovereign. The Swiss delegations would neither question nor interfere in the politics on the ground and were only prepared to intervene on "moral grounds."[15] The ICRC's aim of abstaining from politics proved impossible in this new form of internal conflict.

In January 1955, ICRC delegates clashed over what the organization's official position should be on internal conflicts. They were perplexed by the unique challenges Britain and France posed for the ICRC. Both imperial powers had signed the United Nations Charter and the Universal Declaration of Human Rights less than a decade prior but were now engaged in practices in their colonies that blatantly violated them. Henri Coursier, ICRC representative and member of the ICRC legal department, noted in his observations about unrest in Kenya that "Great Britain did not solicit ICRC intervention" for help in respecting "the principles of civilization. We can imagine that such an intervention, in contrast, desired by the insurgents, could in diverse situations . . . render the conflict less savage."[16] He remarked that Britain signed the European Convention on Human Rights "undoubtedly with the best intentions to apply them in the countries [it] administered." Yet Coursier noticed colonial officials went to great lengths to cut off rebels from internationalizing the conflict and suppressing their ability to receive international protection. Coursier falls shy of openly criticizing British action in Kenya, a common refrain throughout the wars of decolonization, but his word choice and tone indicate he believes its colonial administration had forgotten the principles of civilization and needed a reminder. This is a strong indictment of British behavior and an implicit way of suggesting its officials openly violated acceptable codes of conduct.

In June 1955, six months after Coursier's internal report and three years into the violence in Kenya, ICRC representative Pierre Gaillard received a letter explaining how the British Red Cross might handle the consequences of conflict in Kenya. It explained that

> In the case of Kenya and the British Red Cross, I think it quite feasible that for reasons of expediency and prudence it has been decided to do nothing, as to avoid any possible objection and criticism. Chairman and Vice-Chairman of the British Red Cross are not of that social strata which has practical experience and knowledge of the position of the Colonies' indigenous people. They may even feel obliged—and justified from their own point of view—to decline any activity in order to avoid being reproached for intervening in colonial political affairs.[17]

His reply encapsulates all of the potential problems with a national Red Cross society in a colonial situation and the ICRC's inability to mandate changes. In this case, British Red Cross senior staff did not know enough about the local population to make meaningful contributions, and they were compelled to abstain from providing any assistance, fearing a negative reaction for intervening in politics. What, then, was the British Red Cross there for if not to alleviate the suffering of all people?

In 1957 Lady Limerick, vice-chairman of the British Red Cross, told ICRC president Léopold Boissier that ICRC intervention was unwelcome and that the "barbarian tribal unrest," not a civil war, was now under control. Numerous other individuals and organizations had already provided humanitarian assistance, and therefore she politely declined Boissier's overture.[18] Even if other groups had sent assistance, the national society interacted little with the local Kenyan population, and it likely did not receive this aid. But that disturbing fact did not unsettle Lady Limerick, and their lack of interest for equitable treatment would be a persistent source of frustration for the ICRC when trying to work with colonial governments.

In the weeks leading up to the first ICRC mission in Kenya, after five years of trying to schedule one, Pierre Gaillard vented his stress over being repeatedly denied entrance into the East African country during a Presidential Council meeting. He said, if the British deny the ICRC access once again, "a perfectly plausible hypothetical" situation, "we can at least have a piece [of paper] attesting that we tried to do something."[19] The British government and

British Red Cross positions during the Kenyan conflict set the stage for what ICRC representatives would encounter in Algeria and foreshadowed the limits of the organization's power when facing a European power that either refused to work with the ICRC or did so reluctantly and only for political purposes. The savvy Algerian Red Crescent leadership further distinguished the Algerian case.

The ICRC Goes to Algeria

When fighting broke out in Algeria in November 1954, ICRC representatives had not resolved the tension between alleviating suffering of *all* people and respecting colonial juridical boundaries. That did not stop them from discussing the merits of offering assistance in Algeria and working with the French Red Cross there in the early months of the conflict. Typically during international conflicts, the ICRC worked with existing national societies to coordinate aid distribution and gather credible information about prison conditions, necessary supplies, and medical shortages.[20] Although the French Red Cross (Croix-Rouge Française, CRF) was operational before and during the war, ICRC delegate Pierre Gaillard (Figure 11) characterized national Red Cross societies as "generally pro-government" and reluctant to get "their feet wet" in political affairs. Gaillard was correct (see Chapter 4). The French Red Cross did exhibit pro–French government leanings.[21] Drawing on his extensive experience in the Middle East and North Africa, Gaillard worried that the French Red Cross was poorly placed to intervene in the delicate political question that hinged on national sovereignty.[22] He urged the ICRC to "seriously question" the merits of involving the French Red Cross. If it did, Gaillard suggested limiting the national society's responsibilities to caring for the French and "loyal Arab" populations.[23]

Gaillard's concerns were already realized in Kenya, and there was a growing awareness of this problem among his colleagues. In a December 1955 letter, ICRC delegate William Michel alerted Jean Pictet, ICRC director of general affairs, to a statement made by the Vatican regarding its missions to Africa. Michel explained that Red Cross leaders "recognize that anticolonial nationalism is sweeping Asia and Africa and is tending to identify the Red Cross with . . . colonialists. It is the Red Cross's hope that shifting local Red Cross leadership to natives may help the Red Cross survive."[24] Michel noted that this observation did not reflect reality but that perception mattered. The

Figure 11. Pierre Gaillard, ICRC delegate. (International Committee of the Red Cross)

ICRC must remain vigilant in protecting its initiatives and "not be upstaged by the events," a prophetic warning the Algerian war rendered useless.

The ICRC followed the escalating "troubles" in the winter of 1954, and ICRC delegate Pierre Gaillard remembered "pushing [the Red Cross] to act in Algeria." He had worked in Palestine, Morocco, and Tunisia and, based on his experiences there, "it was clear" to him "that the [independence] movement was not going to bypass Algeria."[25] Gaillard knew the Geneva Conventions fell short of delineating rules for internal conflicts. However, he credited ICRC president Paul Ruegger (1948–1955) as being "fairly clairvoyant" for thinking "that the ICRC, given the evolution of the world, should be engaged in situations of internal troubles and assist political prisoners."[26] According to Gaillard, Ruegger commissioned a panel of international legal experts to help determine conditions for intervention, and based on their recommendations Michel drafted a letter to French leader Pierre Mendès-France, asking permission for the ICRC to visit Algeria.[27] On 2 February 1955 Mendès-France replied favorably on the condition that the findings remain private. He specified that "for obvious reasons of public order" the government would not give the ICRC the names of people who had been arrested up to that point. He claimed that this list served "no practical purpose" for the ICRC and assured Michel that "the majority of people in question were quickly released" from custody. Mendès-France authorized restricted access to detention centers and told Michel that Red Cross representatives could interview the detained without witnesses, but he remained adamant that ICRC action must not lead to any publicity.[28] The ICRC agreed to proceed "discreetly."[29]

The ICRC request placed the Mendès-France government in a difficult position. On the one hand, France did not want any third-party assistance in its internal matters. On the other hand, ICRC letters signaled a potential public relations disaster. As an early signatory of the 1949 Geneva Conventions and a proponent of republicanism, France needed to project the image that it followed these principles.[30] Denying the ICRC entrance into Algeria would have made France look like it had something to hide. Mendès-France also needed allies during this time of political unrest. When the ICRC contacted him, he was facing tremendous opposition in the National Assembly and his government would eventually fall days after the ICRC wrote him. In January 1955, he tried to merge French and Algerian police forces with the hope that if the two cooperated with one another they could bring the rebellion in Algeria under control. Mendès-France coupled that decision with appointing Jacques Soustelle the new governor-general to help restore order. Bringing in the respected humanitarian organization to assess the situation would demonstrate that his government was committed to humanitarian practices. Mendès-France did not realize that by authorizing the first visit, what Pierre Gaillard calls "a little miracle,"[31] he set a precedent that the ICRC would invoke in the future when seeking permission for subsequent missions.[32]

The first mission was organized very quickly. Gaillard, Michel, and

Jean-Pierre Maunoir arrived in Algeria on 28 February 1955 and spent the next seven weeks visiting prisons and detention centers in Algeria and Morocco.[33] At the time, according to the French General Security Division, Algeria had 113 penitentiary facilities.[34] During the initial tour, the ICRC team was escorted to forty-three of them. Delegates received little information about where they would visit, and they were not given a schedule for the following days. They were at the mercy of the French government and remembered feeling as if the authorities were "taking them for a ride."[35] Even though they had the government's consent, they encountered resistance from legal officials in Algeria, who considered the ICRC to be intruding in their domestic affairs. Many of the Algerian detainees had been charged with crimes (including beheadings and bombing public places), and the French administration intended to prosecute them according to their own legal code. In general, local officials did not think the ICRC threatened their jurisdiction and procedures, but, in some instances, French magistrates withheld their authorization and successfully delayed visits to detention facilities and limited access to prisoners.[36]

A distinct feature of ICRC missions was supposed to be unsupervised conversations with detainees. These private conversations were intended to facilitate an honest dialogue about the prisoners' conditions and how their captors were treating them. Unfortunately, the ICRC team was only allowed to speak to Algerian detainees without French supervision less than half of the time. The delegates' experience in Algeria was considerably different from their time in Morocco, where on the same mission Gaillard and his team were granted free access to prisoners and spoke to them without an interlocutor. The ICRC was told that due to the serious nature of the "events" taking place in Algeria, its members could not move about the prisons freely. French officials justified obstructing the ICRC team as a matter of national security and intentionally restricted access to Algerians and potentially useful information.

Despite the obstacles Gaillard, Michel, and Maunoir encountered on the ground in Algeria, they still managed to uncover police brutality in prisons. When talking to the ICRC, Algerian prisoners reported minor beatings and physical mistreatment, suggesting early evidence of police abuse. Michel, Gaillard, and Maunoir noticed that a significant delay persisted between the date of arrest and entry into a detention facility, raising questions about prisoners' treatment in the interim period.[37] But due to the organization's apolitical nature, beyond the threat of publicity, all the ICRC could do was record the complaints and file them in a report that was sent to the French prime minister in Paris after the completion of each mission.[38] The concluding remarks of the first mission's report, dated 16 May 1955, noted that "police action" toward those pursued in the "events" was the subject of "complaints that cannot be neglected." But beyond that, there were few explicit suggestions of what the French government should change.[39] Instead the report ended on a positive note, stressing that prisoners in and around Algiers remained in "good health" during their short stays and that correspondence with family members "appeared to function normally."[40]

After what the ICRC delegates had seen and the frustration they had experienced in Algeria during their two-month stay, why would the representatives submit this kind of laudatory report to the French government? The report did not criticize the French for their poorly equipped infirmary in Oran or for the insufficient medical supplies that Algerian detainees complained about.[41] It did not stress particular sites around Algeria that needed better sanitation, nor did it condemn French police brutality. The ICRC made tepid recommendations for improvements but, overall, remained a passive observer to these pressing issues.

Some scholars have argued that the ICRC's neutral position can be an obstacle to accomplishing the organization's goals. It is precisely because of the Red Cross's impartial and independent stance that it has been able to penetrate war-ridden areas and develop sufficient political and social clout to try to ameliorate conditions. The ICRC was not supposed to side with any party or group. Its sole purpose was to offer assistance, "regardless of the race, creed or nationality of the recipients and without adverse distinction of any kind."[42] Yet it was precisely because the ICRC did not have a political stake in any war or conflict that it was beholden to maintaining good relationships with its contacts and that it had to refrain from judging them and their actions. That was not the organization's job.

David Forsythe, in his history of the ICRC, problematizes the fact that the vast majority of ICRC literature is neither self-critical nor self-reflective. It does not address its claims of impartiality despite actions and policies that suggest national and factional motives.[43] Nicholas Berry, another historian of the organization, on the other hand, argues that the ICRC has a second mission, to sabotage and end war. Berry suggests that this is an inherently political goal, thus violating ICRC founding principles. He asks how the ICRC and national Red Cross societies can remain neutral if they are actively trying to relieve suffering and stalemate the conflict. They are often placed in a contradictory position because the international and national Red Cross organizations' success and access are in large part due to their impartial political, religious, and ethnic stance.[44]

In order to live out the ICRC mission of "affording impartially, without discrimination, protection and assistance to those who need it, in the event of armed conflicts," the reports had to be devoid of political language and analysis.[45] They served more as a reference point that demonstrated French commitment to humanitarian principles. ICRC reports, similar to the UN Charter and 1948 Declaration of Human Rights, were not enforceable or legally binding. They were mere suggestions, and yet they carried significant power in international forums. ICRC approval or condemnation, much like adherence to other international doctrines, was an outward symbol that governments could point to that demonstrated their willingness to follow international norms.

From William Michel's initial contact with Mendès-France, the ICRC was at the mercy of the French government. ICRC representatives would not have been allowed to enter Algeria without the French government's permission. They would not have been allowed to visit detention centers without the government's permission. They would not have been granted access to Algerian or French soldiers without the government's permission. Every aspect of the ICRC visit was controlled by the colonial administration. But Mendès-France likely felt equally constrained by the Red Cross investigating French affairs and as a result was compelled to carefully orchestrate a visit that would give the international delegates some information about the conflict without revealing anything too damaging.

During the first five months of the conflict, the ICRC corresponded primarily with the French authorities, but after the first mission Red Cross representatives realized that the politics behind this new conflict yielded restricted access to Algerian prisoners. In an effort to assist more people and collect additional information about conditions in Algeria, Pierre Gaillard suggested contacting the Algerian nationalists. In May 1955, Gaillard remarked in a note to the ICRC that the "internal troubles" were "less severe" at the beginning of the year. "Now," six months later, the situation had escalated, and the ICRC "cannot be disinterested in what is taking place or what will take place in Algeria."[46] He recommended committee members assemble a team for a second mission that could "take up and build upon the work of the first mission."

As the ICRC waited to hear back from Guy Mollet, Mendès-France's successor, about returning to Algeria, Gaillard thought it would be an appropriate time to contact "'the other party' (the rebels), probably outside of Algeria" in order to avoid a conflict with French authorities and risk a repeat of Indochina. Gaillard was reluctant to ascribe meaning to this olive branch to Algerian nationalists, but he was clear on the merits of encouraging "the respect of certain fundamental humanitarian principles, in this case, for example, Article 3, shared by all four 1949 conventions."[47] Gaillard's note articulates the already-evident tension between politics and humanitarianism. By virtue of acknowledging that the ICRC should concentrate its efforts on Algerian nationalists beyond Algeria's borders, Gaillard showed that he understood the potential consequences of angering colonial officials and how they might perceive ICRC contact with the Algerian leadership as hostile. However, he wanted to remain true to ICRC principles and offer aid to whoever needed it. If the French government would not be entirely forthcoming, he hoped FLN representatives would provide additional details about the events taking place on the ground and agree to respect humanitarian tenets of war.

In February 1956, eight months after Gaillard initially raised the idea, the ICRC contacted the FLN in Cairo. Mohamed Khider and Ahmed Ben Bella spoke on behalf of the nationalist group and demonstrated an immediate willingness to cooperate with the ICRC, but they made their actions conditional on those of the French. In their letter to ICRC representative David de Traz, they wrote, "the government of the French republic, which does not recognize that Algeria is in a state of war, is nonetheless . . . bound to the 1949 Geneva Conventions pertaining to the treatment of prisoners of war." Khider and Ben Bella asserted that "we are prepared to apply all of the dispositions of this convention to all French prisoners of war taken by the ALN as long as the French government reciprocated" with Algerian POWs.[48] The Algerian delegation in Cairo was well versed in the Geneva Conventions and tried to use them as leverage for achieving international support and recognition. They also tried to force their opponents' hand, for if the French government and military agreed to apply the Geneva Conventions to the Algerian case, they would have implicitly acknowledged that the events were actually a war between two separate parties.

In its capacity as a humanitarian organization, the ICRC was expected to refrain from becoming politically involved or publicly supporting one side of a conflict. But contacting the Algerians to inform them of the Geneva Conventions and asking them to respect French prisoners can be interpreted as both consistent with the ICRC policy and also as soliciting rebels in an internal state affair. The eight-month gap between Gaillard's first mention of contacting the Algerian leadership and David de Traz's letter to Cairo indicates a degree of hesitation by the organization's leaders. ICRC delegates who conducted the first mission in Algeria knew there was more to the story than what they saw, and they anticipated that the nationalists could act as a crucial partner in learning more about the conflict and supporting the Geneva Conventions.

In the spring of 1956, the ICRC received letters from concerned French citizens and intellectuals imploring the organization to do something about the conditions in Algeria, providing Red Cross members additional motivation for action. Albert Camus, along with professors, teachers, and religious figures, wrote to ICRC president Léopold Boissier, explaining that they were "completely torn apart by the events covering Algeria in blood," and implored that the ICRC "urgently intervene to ensure that the Geneva Convention of 12 August 1949 concerning the protection of civilians be respected" in Algeria. Camus and his compatriots reminded Boissier that the "French in France and in Algeria" have "very diverse opinions" and they considered themselves "interpreters of a large fraction of public opinion" in both places.[49]

The French government and military positions were not the only ones for the ICRC to consider. It now had to consider reputable French figures raising Geneva Conventions violations and demanding acknowledgment. Boissier's response to the group insisted "the events . . . in North Africa have not failed to retain our attention." Since the first mission in the spring of 1955, "the Committee has reached out on numerous occasions to M. Edgar Faure and M. Guy Mollet" for permission "to send a new mission to Algeria."[50] Boissier found himself in a conflicting position. He had numerous French and Algerian contacts, primarily outside of Algeria, asking that the Geneva Conventions be applied in Algeria, illustrating their social and moral currency. However, he still faced a reluctant French government that controlled Algeria, skirted ICRC requests for a second mission, and continually denied a war was taking place. This last point technically exonerated French military personnel from adhering to the Geneva Conventions. If the ICRC followed its own self-produced rubric, its representatives would have to wait for French government consent while managing external pressure to guarantee civilian and POW protection to those affected on both sides of the conflict. This conundrum only grew more pronounced as the conflict progressed.

The Limits of ICRC Power

In April 1956, after careful consideration, French prime minister Guy Mollet finally replied to ICRC president Léopold Boissier that a team of two or three Swiss nationals would be authorized to come back to Algeria for a second mission. Mollet outlined four objectives: visiting the internment camps; *initiating* visits to detention centers and on occasion having a conversation without a witness; *if necessary*, planning distribution of relief supplies; and making suggestions about additional humanitarian action that the French government could take in Algeria. He stipulated, however, that government authorization was conditional on the following: the mission could not be conducted as an investigation; rather, it must remain "strictly humanitarian" and "exclude any inquiry into the legal situation of concerned parties"; "aid must be distributed by French organizations registered with the government"; and "the findings and conclusions . . . must only be communicated to French authorities."[51] Mollet was clear and firm: under no circumstance should ICRC reports be made public. He, similar to his predecessor Mendès-France, struggled to define the parameters of the mission and walk the line between accommodating the ICRC and opening up a Pandora's box of legal questions and practices. Mollet was wary of any ICRC involvement, and his letter to Léopold Boissier indicates his apprehension about a second visit. Yet he had delayed an official response as long as was diplomatically permissible. The first mission had occurred without major incident, and Mollet's carefully constructed parameters aimed for the same with the next one.

Boissier agreed to Mollet's conditions and assembled Pierre Gaillard, Claude Pilloud, René Bovey, and doctors Hans Willener and Louis-Alexis Gailland for the second mission. From 12 May to 28 June these men visited sixty-one detention facilities and housing centers (*centres d'hébergement*, CH) and stopped by close to fifty prisons. In their report the representatives commented on "normal" prison conditions but noted that prisoners lived in overcrowded conditions and medical service was "insufficient." Several detained Algerians, some of whom they were able to speak with alone, complained that they were not allowed to see their families. In cases where prisoners expressed fear and anger over guards' physical abuse, ICRC delegates suggested "the responsible authorities begin an investigation" into what happened. They also recommended officials "strive to diminish as much as possible the delay . . . between an individual arrest and his presentation to a judge or his admission to a housing center."[52]

Mollet's administration was not obliged to implement the ICRC recommendations and could simply demonstrate diplomatic and humanitarian goodwill by permitting additional visits. However, French officials raised concerns about the implications of ICRC missions. In July 1956, one month after the second mission, Étienne Dennery, the French ambassador in Switzerland, wrote a letter to the minister of foreign affairs in Paris regarding the recent ICRC visits. He said, "Red Cross intervention in Algeria poses a juridical problem." It is not a conflict deserving of international law, but rather "a rebellion comparable to that of General Markos in Greece. The International Committee representatives must take into account the particular legal situation within French sovereignty."[53] For semantic purposes, if the war remained a rebellion, French leaders would have an easier time keeping the ICRC at bay and justifying an internal (French) state solution. However, as Dennery intimated, the ICRC's continued presence in Algeria might give its representatives and, more significantly, anyone sympathetic with the nationalist cause the impression that the conflict deserved an international designation and had exceeded French Red Cross capabilities.

Boissier pressed on and received permission for a third, fourth, and fifth mission to Algeria, all led by Pierre Gaillard and Dr. Louis-Alexis Gailland.[54] During this period, French prime ministers changed rapidly, and, in addition to Guy Mollet, the ICRC worked with Maurice Bourgès-Maunory and Félix Gaillard, both of whom were only in office for six months. Constant government turnover presented challenges for Pierre Gaillard and Dr. Gailland because they were dealing with new and tentative administrators on each occasion. However, as reflected in their reports, it also offered opportunities to pursue different sites and make alternate suggestions to a new group of people eager to explore more options for dealing with the escalating political and practical consequences of the war.

In these three missions, Gaillard and Gailland visited close to 175 sites at housing centers, prisons, hospitals, and "sorting" centers (*centres de tri et de transit*, CTT), a type of facility where the French held persons arrested for political activities or captured for their activities in the maquis.[55] Each stop afforded the ICRC representatives an opportunity to speak with a few more Algerians and, in fewer instances, French prisoners (Figure 12). Gaillard and Gailland heard complaints about instances of extreme confinement and learned of French military internment centers (*centres militaires d'internés*, CMI) and reeducation camps.[56] They repeatedly noted inadequate building conditions and inconsistent medical care.

Figure 12. Bir el Ater detention center. ICRC visit, Gaillard-Gailland mission, December 1957. (International Committee of the Red Cross)

But physical abuse was by far the most prominent issue in each ICRC report. The November 1956 report remarked that in "each camp visited," Dr. Gailland examined a number of individuals and witnessed the "aftermath of physical abuse in the form of cigarette burns," wounds on their wrists and ankles from chains, and surface burns resulting from "the application of electrodes with electric current."[57] The July 1957 report revealed that detainees singled out "interrogations, notably those conducted by the police," as a place where officers frequently "applied electric current" to the body, and, "in some cases, the International Committee delegates even observed obvious wounds on detainees leaving an interrogation."[58]

The fourth ICRC report reminded French general Raoul Salan and the Bourgès-Maunoury government that the two previous reports mentioned this critical issue. Once again, Gaillard and Gailland thought it imperative to bring to "the French government's attention" that these practices contradicted "the spirit of the 1949 Geneva Conventions, and its Article 3."[59] The March 1958 report used nearly identical language about government disregard for humane treatment, and it would be difficult for French leaders to claim they did not know the ICRC's position on this matter. Its delegates had seen, on numerous occasions and over the course of several years, a blatant disregard for Article 3, and in particular sections 1(a) and 1(c), for conflicts not of an international character, which states "the following acts are and shall remain prohibited at any time and in any place whatsoever with respect to the above-mentioned persons: (a) violence to life and person, in particular murder of all kinds, mutilation, cruel treatment and torture; . . . (c) outrages upon personal dignity, in particular, humiliating and degrading treatment."[60]

As requested, these ICRC reports were only sent to the French authorities, but Gaillard grew increasingly frustrated with the colonial leadership's lack of initiative to make systematic changes.[61] The confidentiality agreement insulated the French government from exposure and public critique and the only recourse Gaillard had was to use strong language denouncing excessive uses of force, which became more pronounced during missions three, four, and five.[62] By late 1957, it was evident to him that not only was Algeria a different kind of conflict but respecting ICRC neutrality and acting as a moral compass hoping to influence official French policy would only yield limited results. This "internal" problem required creative solutions that went outside the proverbial ICRC box without flagrantly trampling on the organization's founding principles.

The ICRC Pursues Both Sides

In 1957 the ICRC started working with the newly formed Algerian Red Crescent and it began requesting prisoner lists from the acting national society and the French military.[63] In reality, the ICRC was leaving no stone unturned by asking the French and Algerians for prisoner lists. The Algerian Red Crescent complied when it was politically advantageous for it to do so, a fact that did not escape ICRC delegates. In practice, Pierre Gaillard recalled, the FLN could not maintain prisoner camps given the guerrilla nature of the war.[64] Algerian soldiers had to move frequently to avoid detection, making regulated prisoners facilities near impossible. But the Algerian leadership corresponded frequently with the ICRC about prisoners and sponsored "cinematic liberations" in Tunisia and Morocco.[65]

Several French administrators expressed concern about ICRC interactions with Algerian nationalists and were bothered that it regularly corresponded with them. Colonial administrators rarely cooperated on the matter of prisoners and expressed "serious reservations" about providing lists because "this could potentially lead to legitimizing the FLN."[66] Another administrator said it was "out of the question" to supply the ICRC with prisoner lists because he considered all "arrested and detained FLN members" to be French citizens, whose "illegal activities were vigorously pursued by [French] law," therefore eliminating the need for external assistance of any kind. He questioned if a prisoner list would encourage Algerians to think of themselves as prisoners of war and would support their initiatives to negotiate with the French government as a separate party. He did think, however, that the ICRC should continue to pursue the names of citizens held by "the rebellion," because only then would the French be poised to intervene and liberate "those who were still alive" in rebel hands. He emphasized that in Algeria there could not be "two parties with equal rights." According to him, the French and Algerians were on the same side and to act differently would be a "flagrant contradiction of the founding principles" of Algérie française.[67]

The ICRC found itself in uncharted territory. It was volunteering its services to both sides of the conflict, but neither would agree unconditionally to its terms for assisting prisoners. On 28 May 1958, ICRC president Léopold Boissier tried another approach. In response to the escalation of fighting and violence in Algeria that spring, he sent French and Algerian leaders the same letter imploring them to consider observing Article 3 of the Geneva Conventions. He demonstrated an understanding of the political stakes and was careful to call attention to the fact that agreement by the Algerians would not mean ICRC recognition of the belligerent status of the ALN.[68] Boissier's memorandum specified additional provisions to which he hoped the French and Algerians would consent. First, "in the event of capture, members of the armed forces would not be legally pursued for solely having participated in the struggle." He asked that they would benefit from humane treatment and from all the essential guarantees granted to prisoners of war, that they could communicate with their families and be permitted visits from the ICRC. Second, he asked that if captured members of armed forces were subjected to legal proceedings, the organization be informed and given authorization to follow the case and assist in their defense. Last, he requested that all retaliatory acts, "whatever their motive," cease.[69]

Boissier's letter suggests that the ICRC had reached an insurmountable obstacle. Without prisoner lists or Algerian or French consent to visit and communicate with prisoners, the only information that the ICRC had about Algeria was what its delegates collected on their missions supervised by the French government, police chiefs, and lawyers, and the letters and meetings it conducted with Algerian Red Crescent delegates. The ICRC was unable to gather unfiltered information and continuously encountered international law constraints and the limitations of the Geneva Conventions for noninternational conflicts. ICRC prestige and opinion mattered to the French government only to the extent that the organization could potentially embarrass it on an international stage. This threat motivated colonial officials to regulate their behavior to a degree but not enough for ICRC delegates to have unrestricted access to any site or any prisoner during missions in Algeria and not enough for French officials to systematically implement their reports' suggestions.

French officials expressed "regret and surprise" that the organization wrote to them about adhering to Article 3. As an early signatory of the 1949 Geneva Conventions, one official claimed that he acted in accordance with the conventions and applied them "scrupulously." If a situation arose in which Article 3 was not followed, the responsible individual was "immediately" and "severely sanctioned."[70] In the same letter, the colonial administrator alleged French officials had cooperated with the ICRC since the early days of the conflict. They provided care to wounded Algerian soldiers and civilians and had given arrested Algerians the opportunity to appear before regular tribunals. If anyone should be reprimanded, it should be the "terrorists," he said, for they were the ones "killing civilians, slitting the throats of women and children, and mutilating the wounded."[71] The French were insulted that the ICRC had "placed them on equal footing" with a group of "rebels," who had repeatedly deprived parents of "any news about their children" and "committed crimes that would revolt the human conscience."[72] As the ICRC reports revealed, French officers, policemen, and soldiers were not as law-abiding as official discourse made them out to be. But despite feigned outrage at the ICRC for suggesting it was violating Article 3, the French leadership did not renew its pledge to the Geneva Conventions in writing.

The ICRC did not fare much better with the Algerian leadership. Nationalists expressed interest in applying Article 3 for its potential in bolstering their political agenda, but Boissier was unable to get a written commitment from them. He wrote to Ferhat Abbas, then president of the Provisional Government of the Algerian Republic, in October 1958 and again in December 1959. Boissier explained that the ICRC had been tirelessly pursuing the French government to accept Article 3, but to no avail. He reminded Abbas that the "elementary humanitarian rules" covered in Article 3 would save lives.[73] It took two years before Abbas finally replied favorably to Boissier's request.

The ICRC persisted in applying quiet pressure on French leaders and may have influenced their decision to take one step closer to recognizing Algerian "rebels" as proper combatants in 1958. During the war's first three years,

French military and judicial officers did not differentiate between Algerians accused of setting off an explosive or a bomb in a public place and those who openly carried weapons and wore a uniform. They were often put together in sorting centers and housing centers and handled in a similar manner. Individuals wearing uniforms were not recognized as official combatants, and they were guaranteed neither humane treatment nor medical care as prisoners of war. However, their ambiguous status started to change in the winter of 1958. In November 1957, General Salan signed a notice that remained confidential for several months that would distinguish "rebel prisoners captured with weapons," or *prisonniers pris les armes à la main* (PAMs), from other Algerian prisoners caught without weapons. In the notice, Salan specified that these individuals in question "should be treated as closely as possible to prisoners of war" without actually attaining prisoner of war status.[74] He wanted to "avoid any gesture or statement that could be interpreted as an infringement on the prisoners' personal dignity."[75]

Scholars have argued that Salan's new internment camps were a way to remove Algerian combatants from systematic legal proceedings.[76] ICRC president Léopold Boissier and his staff may have been aware of this possibility, given French treatment of prisoners they witnessed on numerous missions. However, they "congratulated" the French government for implementing PAM status and bringing Algerians one step closer to being protected by the Geneva Conventions. Red Cross representatives were using whatever methods of persuasion and flattery they could to recognize and encourage concrete action toward upholding humanitarian conduct.[77]

The ICRC's hands were tied, but this did not dissuade delegates from conducting a sixth and seventh mission to Algeria. In December 1958, Pierre Gaillard and Roger Vust spent almost three weeks touring sixteen CMI, CTT, CH, and prison sites. This was the first time the ICRC had returned to Algeria in its official capacity since Salan opened special holding facilities for Algerian prisoners, and days before the mission, Roger Gallopin, ICRC executive director, gave Gaillard specific instructions to assess them.[78] During private interviews they heard multiple complaints about "overcrowded" conditions in two new prisons, questionable "interrogation" methods, and water shortages. In their January 1959 report, Gaillard and Vust noted that "PAMs appear to be treated correctly," but not all of the prisoners felt comfortable speaking to them because they feared French authority reprisals. Treading lightly, Gaillard and Vust wrote that "they wanted to come back to the delicate question of interrogations."[79] They observed that "prisoners from a variety of categories" were "subjected to an arbitrary regime," a system, in their opinion, that should be better controlled.[80] They "hoped the French authorities would take into consideration the preceding reflections to modify and improve . . . the detention regime in Algeria." This mild reproach was as close as ICRC reports ever came to openly criticizing French operations in Algeria, and when they did include suggestions of this nature, they were qualified with accolades for minimal improvements. For example, immediately following Gaillard and Vust's tempered recommendation, they wrote, "It must be noted that improvements have already been made or are in the process of being made in certain centers [we] visited." They could not end the report, they said, "without reiterating our strong gratitude" for permission to come to Algeria.[81]

The ICRC reports, including the one filed after the seventh mission (Figure 13), all contain this amicable tone, which was crucial to maintaining good relations with French authorities.[82] The changing French leadership could point to ICRC visits as an indication of its commitment to liberalism and humanitarianism without the obligation of meaningful change, and the

Figure 13. ICRC delegate Pierre Gaillard meets with detainees at an Algerian detention center during the ICRC's seventh mission to Algeria, October 1959. (International Committee of the Red Cross)

ICRC could claim its delegates pursued ways to humanize the conflict. The reports, however, show a fragile and tenuous relationship between the colonial government and the international organization. Moreover, they reinforce that both parties had wildly different motives for working with one another, all of which came to light in an extremely public 1960 controversy.

Controversy and Scandal: *Le Monde* Prints ICRC Report

After previous missions, ICRC delegates compiled their detailed notes and wrote a report on each facility they had visited in Algeria and presented general remarks for consideration. These confidential reports were then sent from Geneva to the French Ministry in Paris, at which point authorities could make copies, if so desired, to distribute to French officials. Per the ICRC's 1955 agreement with Mendès-France, its delegates only transmitted them to the French government, and up until the seventh mission the information contained within them had remained private.

But on 5 January 1960, Hubert Beuve-Méry, editor of the leading French newspaper *Le Monde*, printed large excerpts of the ICRC report Pierre Gaillard, Roger Vust, and Dr. Jean-Louis de Chastonay submitted in mid-December 1959.[83] Scholars have speculated broadly about the source of the leak. Did it come from within the ICRC or was it someone in a position of power in the French cabinet? If the former, what does this tell us about the division between an institution's motto and the individual opinions of those who work to carry out that motto? If the latter, how does this broaden our understanding of internal fissures at the highest levels of colonial government as the war entered its sixth year?

Though difficult to confirm, multiple sources, including ICRC records, suggest that Edmond Michelet, French minister of justice from 1959 to 1961, was the source of the leak.[84] French president Charles de Gaulle appointed Michelet, who resisted against Vichy during World War II and previously served in prominent political positions, most notably as minister of the army in 1945–1946, as minister of justice to temper the warring "ultra" and "liberal" factions within his own administration. At the time, according to Joseph Rovan, one of Michelet's colleagues, the French Justice Department faced numerous sensitive legal issues, including the use of torture, disappearances, the Audin affair, hunger strikes, and the relationship between police and military powers.[85] Michelet, similar to many of his "liberal" contemporaries, "ardently

wished that Algeria would remain united to France" and enjoy "legal equality."[86] As the war raged on, this outcome became increasingly unlikely, and
Michelet began to forcefully oppose the dramatic suspension of Algerians'
legal rights. ICRC delegate Roger Gallopin suspected that the source of the
leak was from "someone high up" in the French government who wanted to
alter the course of the war.[87]

Michelet's politics and position make him the likely source. His strongest
adversary was Paris police chief Maurice Papon, who openly worked to erode
the rule of law pertaining to the rights of "terrorists" and ordered the October
1961 massacre.[88] During his tenure, Papon was "constantly dissatisfied with
the legal system," which according to Jim House and Neil MacMaster, "he
viewed as a fetter on the ability of his officers to crush terrorist organizations."[89] Moreover, he remained frustrated by Michelet and his aides who advocated for negotiations with the FLN. Papon perceived Michelet to place
debilitating limitations on his proposals, and in August 1961 he convinced de
Gaulle to fire him. But Papon was unable to muzzle Michelet before he had
the opportunity to play a role in publicizing the ICRC report.

In a 2004 interview ICRC delegate Pierre Gaillard identified Michelet as
the person "who diffused the report."[90] Pierre Vidal-Naquet claimed that Michelet's close associate and fellow Papon protester Gaston Gosselin used his
connections at Le Monde to disseminate the report, and Raphaëlle Branche
also pinpoints Gosselin as the source "in the Minister of Justice's cabinet."[91]
Regardless of whether Michelet himself contacted Le Monde editor Beuve-
Méry or it was his colleague Gosselin, the leak highlights the internal tension
within the French government and within de Gaulle's inner circle. This fact is
well known and contributed to the downfall of consecutive governments
during the Algerian war. What distinguishes this particular instance is that a
French cabinet member felt strongly enough to prioritize his personal con-
victions over his professional ones and risk embarrassing the French nation,
its president, and the military in Algeria on an unprecedented scale. And he
succeeded.

Le Monde printed extensive excerpts of the lengthy ICRC report, much of
which echoed the amicable tone delegates used in earlier reports. But for the
first time, the general public could read about the meetings Red Cross delegates had with Paul Delouvrier and General Challe and the sites they visited
while in Algeria. Any person could now obtain crucial evidence about prison
conditions and physical abuse in detention facilities and draw their own conclusions about the extreme measures the Fifth Republic was taking to

maintain *Algérie française*. Anticipating the controversy this information would cause, French prime minister Michel Debré issued a statement alongside the report. He said that although "this document reveals that errors and abuses continue to occur at times," it also showcased how detention centers had been improved over the course of ICRC visits.[92] In an attempt to defuse public reaction, Debré used the opportunity to chastise the Algerians for denying the Red Cross access to their detention facilities.

A vigorous debate ensued and lasted for several days in the French press. On 6 January 1960, *Le Monde* included a section on the aftermath of the International Red Cross report it had published the day before. Several other newspapers picked up the story and faced consequences for their critical remarks. For example, Maurice Papon ordered that the early edition of *Libération* be seized because of its analysis of the report.[93] An editorial in *L'Humanité* remarked that torture had not ceased in Algeria and that it probably happened on a daily basis. The 10–11 January *Le Monde* edition reprinted editorials from the *Journal de Genève, Paris-Normandie,* and the *Daily Herald*, which all expressed concern about the report's contents. International papers, including the *Egyptian Gazette*, the *Japan Times*, and *Hindu*, a paper in Madras, India, also picked up the story.[94] The French public and the world now had evidence from a reputable organization confirming Algerian nationalists' allegations about French crimes, which the colonial authorities could no longer deny.[95]

The leak blindsided the ICRC staff. Representatives questioned whether it came from someone in-house, a French official, or a French journalist, and they were adamant about identifying the person who put their efforts in jeopardy.[96] ICRC president Léopold Boissier issued an informational notice explaining the Red Cross's role in internal conflicts.[97] The organization, he said, was limited to a few activities to help humanize the conflict. It could offer assistance to both sides and visit at the government's discretion. The Red Cross had been doing that since 1955. Moreover, ICRC reports were only submitted to the government that granted permission for the mission. The ICRC, Boissier wrote, did not publish its reports. But he made clear that "governments . . . are free to do so."[98]

Publishing the report in *Le Monde* not only challenged the word of the French military and called into question the legality of the measures the French employed in Algeria, but it also dismantled ICRC legitimacy and put lives at risk. The Red Cross had spent the past five years working with numerous French governments to improve conditions for Algerian detainees in military centers, and their relationship with the ever-changing authorities was always contingent upon a confidentiality agreement that Pierre Mendès-France and Guy Mollet made very clear from the beginning. Whatever the ICRC saw in Algeria, wherever the delegates were taken, and whatever suggestions the reports made were acceptable as long as the public did not hear about it. *Le Monde* ruptured the balance between the French government and the ICRC in order to expose French military and judicial misconduct that up until that point had been difficult to prove. *Le Monde* thrust the ICRC into the middle of French politics, a position the organization had actively tried to avoid, and to this day Red Cross delegates insist that they did not provide the newspaper with the report.[99]

Until the report was made public, key ICRC personnel had been frustrated by the narrowly circumscribed limits of their power given the organization's self-defined apolitical position. Adhering to this neutral approach mandated discretion from Red Cross delegates and its president. This position, historian Caroline Moorehead points out, "demonstrated one of the fundamental contradictions in International Committee work: that the price paid for being allowed to be a witness is to remain silent about what is seen."[100] This paradox was always a feature of ICRC work dating back to its creation in the 1860s. However, during decolonization dying colonial French governments took advantage of the ICRC's self-produced rubric and wagered that it would remain silent regardless of what delegates saw in Algeria. French officials, similar to the Algerian Red Crescent leadership, used the ICRC for political self-aggrandizement.

The leak removed the reins of power from the conservative faction of de Gaulle's regime and forced French officials to respond publicly about military and police action in Algeria. They no longer controlled the unidirectional flow of ICRC information and were compelled to explain and justify their behavior to a wider audience, a significant departure from their early insistence that Algeria was not an international concern. The French also found themselves in this position at the United Nations, the subject of Chapter 6, where they were forced to comment on and respond to the remarkable efforts of the Algerian nationalists who sought to publicize and internationalize the conflict. On the opening pages of the leading French newspaper, prime minister Debré reassured *Le Monde*'s readers that the government "naturally holds in the highest esteem ICRC conclusions and can only celebrate the assistance that this organism brings in the pursuit of rendering each day more humane."[101] Rarely had Debré, or any top French official, engaged with the

ICRC and its recommendations in such a public manner. Equally seldom did a French administrator stress in the press a synergetic relationship with the ICRC in their commitment to carrying out humane behavior in Algeria.

The alternative, complete disavowal of the ICRC report or denying future ICRC missions, may have further compromised French government standing in the eyes of the French public and jeopardized continued ICRC support. France had become increasingly isolated on the international diplomatic stage, as we will soon see, and de Gaulle could hardly afford another scandal further eroding his credibility. His administration needed to show a firm and sincere dedication to humanitarian practices, and restoring its relationship with the ICRC was a vital step in this direction. This process was not easy. The ICRC was not permitted to return to Algeria until January 1961. But after being publicly humiliated, more than ever, the colonial administration sought Red Cross approval to show the world that it had learned from the errors of its ways and that it was committed to making improvements.

Three Final Red Cross Missions

The ICRC conducted two missions before the cease-fire (19 March 1962) in January and February and November and December 1961. Pierre Gaillard and Roger Vust led both of them and visited a combined 112 sites. The eighth report did not directly mention *Le Monde*, but it made subtle references to the time elapsed since the ICRC's last visit. Overall, Gaillard and Vust concluded, "the ICRC recognizes, that since 1959, a large effort has been made to improve a number of detention facilities in Algeria." They hoped, though, that "the French authorities would take into consideration the findings and suggestions," in particular, measures to improve "the interrogation centers."[102] Questions of physical abuse and lengthy detention periods without formal charges remained a persistent problem through 1961.

One change that appeared in the ninth report was that Gaillard and Vust placed a greater emphasis on the treatment of European activists in Algerian prisons and Algerians that had been expelled from France, foreshadowing major issues that the outgoing French government and incoming independent Algerian government would have to tackle in 1962.[103] By December 1961 de Gaulle and the Provisional Government of the Algerian Republic were engaged in serious diplomatic negotiations, and perhaps this was the ICRC's way of introducing these issues for consideration.

When the ICRC conducted its final mission in Algeria from 25 May to 29 June 1962, the physical and political landscape was dramatically altered from that of 1955. Instead of repeated complaints from Algerian prisoners about interrogation methods, the tenth ICRC report emphasized European detainees' anxieties about their fate after French rule ended.[104] Algerian nationalists were liberated from facilities around the country; hundreds of thousands of European settlers embarked for France; and the Provisional Government of the Algerian Republic (GPRA) leadership headed back to Algeria. All eyes, with the exception of the Secret Army Organization (Organisation Armée Secrète, OAS), were looking forward toward the improbable realization of Algerian independence.[105]

The ICRC offered its services to Algerian leaders during the political transition and remained steadfast in finding missing persons and protecting *harkis*.[106] In October 1962 Pierre Gaillard and Roger Vust went to Algeria to meet with the Algerian regime and discuss these two matters. Upon their return they wrote, "Despite assurances that we received [from Colonel Houari Boumediene, the minister of the interior, the director of national security, and the director of the penal system], there is little hope of finding the majority of missing Europeans alive."[107] Their remarks about the *harkis* were equally dismal. According to the Evian Accords, *harkis* would not be pursued or condemned after the cease-fire. But after meeting with Boumediene, who affirmed his position that *harkis* were "war criminals" that should face justice, Gaillard and Vust noted that they would "energetically continue their efforts on [the *harkis'*] behalf." For them, "if the Algerian authorities actually engaged in legal proceedings against [them], it would be a flagrant violation of the Evian Accords. But, for its part, the ICRC is not responsible and it falls on the French authorities to act."[108] The Algerian leadership quickly adopted a rationale vis-à-vis the ICRC and sensitive political questions that emulated the outgoing colonial administration's stance. So much had changed in Algeria. Yet, once again ICRC delegates were working with a government that did not want them poking around in its internal affairs, and the ICRC had little recourse to require change.

For the three years of his presidency (1962–1965), Ahmed Ben Bella permitted the ICRC to continue its efforts in locating missing persons and working toward implementing safety precautions for the *harkis*. Shortly after coming to power, Ben Bella signed an agreement with the ICRC pledging his cooperation "in facilitating the action of delegates in every possible manner" and according "them complete freedom to move throughout Algeria."[109] The

ICRC had heard this kind of language before. Colonel Boumediene's remarks about *harkis* make it difficult to believe the official Algerian government position had shifted that dramatically. The divergence in discourse may best be understood if one looks to the political conundrum previous French leaders attempted to navigate. Ben Bella likely signed the ICRC agreement for the same reason Pierre Mendès-France permitted the first mission in 1955. The newly independent Maghribi country had much to prove domestically and internationally, and engaging with the ICRC demonstrated a renewed commitment to the humanitarian principles that the Algerian Provisional Government, Algerian Red Crescent, and FLN had espoused during the war. Moreover, Ben Bella's willingness to welcome the ICRC showed the ICRC's appeal in a postcolonial world and is a testament to its lasting symbolic importance.

Conclusion

The Algerian case represents a pivotal moment in ICRC history and shows the potential political power of the organization and its humanitarian agenda. Algeria was one of the first major anticolonial conflicts the ICRC debated, and its actions there served as a precedent for future interventions in internal conflicts.[110] ICRC delegates faced extenuating circumstances and years of unrequited requests from the French and Algerian leaderships, and yet the ICRC continued to conduct missions and make recommendations for tempering the devastating effects of war. Based on the apolitical principle of neutrality, the ICRC was compelled to help both sides of the conflict regardless of their unfulfilled promises.

The ICRC attempted to abstain from politics, but from the moment representatives requested to visit Algeria in 1955 it became embroiled in contentious questions about statehood and sovereignty. Delegates endured numerous frustrations; based on the organization's self-produced rubric and the inadequacy of the Geneva Conventions for internal conflicts, they were only able to exert a quiet moral pressure, not enforce meaningful change throughout the Algerian war. Some may consider this a failure, but it may be more productive to consider the nature of the organization's role as a silent watchdog. Its continued presence in Algeria, if nothing else, put French officials, and later Algerian officials, on notice that someone somewhere was a witness to this conflict and its aftermath. A group of individuals who came back mission after mission were keeping a detailed record and trying to hold governments accountable for their policies at a time when no one else could.

The ICRC's moral authority also succeeded in helping regulate state behavior and establish parameters of acceptable conduct in Algeria, but this authority had limits as evidenced by the seventh mission report leak. This episode, though disruptive and embarrassing for all parties involved, exposed a serious institutional deficiency and contributed to the ICRC changing intervention protocol in internal conflicts. The ICRC had reached a threshold beyond which lay additional suffering and casualties of war, and the lessons delegates learned in Algeria served as a catalyst for change.

Subsequent conflicts, such as the Nigerian civil war between 1967 and 1970, the Yemeni conflict in 1970, and failed ICRC attempts in Vietnam during the 1960s and 1970s after the United States replaced the French there highlighted the organization's shortcomings. This realization, coupled with increasingly vocal independent states in the Third World speaking out against the 1949 Geneva Conventions because they did not participate in their creation, prompted the ICRC to add two additional protocols to the conventions in 1977. The first one dealt with international armed conflict, and the second one supplemented the general provisions of common Article 3 from the 1949 Geneva Conventions and became the first treaty to deal specifically with internal conflicts.[111] The ICRC could no longer ignore this issue. If it did, it would remain constrained in the future and risked being eclipsed and discredited by the evolving landscape of twentieth-century warfare.

Chapter 6

Global Diplomacy and the Fight for Self-Determination

Nothing contained in the present Charter shall authorize the United Nations to intervene in matters which are essentially within the domestic jurisdiction of any state or shall require the Members to submit such matters to settlement under the present Charter; but this principle shall not prejudice the application of enforcement measures under Chapter VII.

—Article 2(7), Charter of the United Nations

The Security Council may investigate any dispute, or any situation which might lead to international friction or give rise to a dispute, in order to determine whether the continuance of the dispute or situation is likely to endanger the maintenance of international peace and security.

—Article 34, Charter of the United Nations

Any Member of the United Nations may bring any dispute, or any situation of the nature referred to in Article 34, to the attention of the Security Council or of the General Assembly.

—Article 35(1), Charter of the United Nations

The International Committee of the Red Cross was not the only international organization struggling to adapt to the particular challenges of decolonization. In the 1950s, the United Nations (UN) also encountered a changing world, and UN members, especially those from Western countries, confronted a set of international problems for which they were unprepared. The

Algerian nationalists saw numerous opportunities in taking their cause to the United Nations, where they could exploit international relations. Staying true to their political platform of internationalizing the conflict and swaying public opinion in favor of their sovereignty claims, they deliberately targeted the United Nations in the same way they did the International Committee of the Red Cross, hoping it would legitimate their cause.

While scholars have examined ways in which the United Nations served as a defining diplomatic battleground for the Algerian question, too frequently these histories have been written from a Western perspective, not that of the Algerian actors themselves.[1] This chapter reevaluates how the National Liberation Front (FLN) devised and managed its campaign for external recognition. It shows the leadership's fluency with the contents of the UN Charter and how they used the document's ambiguities to their political advantage. Moreover, it shifts the focus to the extensive networks Algerian anticolonial leaders constructed in the Third World, which proved essential in their quest for sovereignty.

Nationalists knew as long as the French government claimed sovereignty over Algeria they would not be able to represent themselves at the United Nations. Therefore, the FLN mobilized Algerian delegates to secure support in Asia, the Middle East, and Africa, regions with a shared religious tradition and colonial past that were committed to Third World solidarity. The Algerian leadership expected that representatives from these allied countries would present the Algerian case at the United Nations on their behalf, thereby taking up the mandate that Robert Malley calls "Third Worldism."[2] The FLN further solidified its strategy for external recognition and campaigning for inscription onto the General Assembly agenda by sending Algerian delegates to New York to set up an office from which to publicize the war in the United States and target the United Nations from closer range.

By sending representatives around the world and soliciting diplomatic support, the FLN leadership executed yet another layer of its political vision; it acted and performed like a state. FLN representatives assembled a diplomatic corps and refined their message for particular audiences. In doing so, they presented an alternative version to the Algerian people and the world to that of the French government's portrayal of Algerian "terrorists." Similar to the nationalists' domestic health-care campaigns and Red Crescent efforts, the FLN wanted to prove that not only did it understand the international diplomatic norms of the day but it could also enact them.

This chapter shows an important component of the FLN's strategy and explains how and why African, Asian, and Middle Eastern countries acted as Algerian nationalists' proxies at the United Nations. The advent of decolonization changed the UN's demographic and these new members were an increasingly powerful voice in the General Assembly.[3] In the Algerian case, countries in the Third World, especially representatives from Arab nations, used the UN Charter language to make self-determination claims that contributed to Algerian sovereignty. Their instrumentalization of human rights rhetoric was important in shifting global opinion about Algerians' rights, but their meaning and content were highly dynamic.[4] They supported the Algerian anticolonial struggle by sending letters to the Security Council and making lengthy remarks about the war during their addresses in plenary meetings, repeatedly citing Articles 34 and 35 of the charter as grounds for why UN members must discuss the situation. Despite their well-reasoned arguments and passionate pleas, the French government position on Algeria remained unchanged throughout the 1950s. Algeria was part of France, and per Article 2(7) of the UN Charter, members were not permitted to "intervene in matters which are essentially within the domestic jurisdiction of any state."

The different and contradictory interpretations of the institution's founding document reveal an unsettling and complicated reality behind the United Nations. Theoretically, member states, big and small, would enjoy the same benefits of protection and responsibility to uphold peace. But in practice, Western countries, and particularly the five permanent members of the Security Council, worked together to ensure their national and colonial interests.[5] Even though they belonged to a global cooperative, they remained adamant that other members stay out of what they considered their internal affairs. Nowhere was this tension between domestic jurisdiction and a commitment to international security more apparent than during the Algerian war. UN members had been discussing the organization's position on colonial policy prior to the outbreak of the war.[6] However, the Algerian case exposed a new level of institutional hypocrisy, highlighting the shallow rhetoric of post–World War II pledges.

French UN representatives relied upon Western political alliances and select portions of the UN Charter to protect their reputation and the territory colonial officials considered an extension of France. But they proved insufficient against the comprehensive FLN strategy. The growing tide of anticolonial sentiment exemplified in the Bandung Conference and the confluence of Moroccan and Tunisian independence, the Suez crisis, the Hungarian Revolution, and Cold War tensions also significantly impacted how UN members handled the Algerian question. The stakes for all sides—sovereignty, empire, and self-determination—were extremely high and set the stage for many heated debates at the United Nations. What distinguishes this critical juncture in the 1950s and 1960s was that it finally presented nonstate actors and newly independent countries with an opportunity to form a coalition against European colonialism and successfully articulate claims based on universal rhetoric on a globally respected stage.

The FLN Lobbies International Allies

From the FLN's inception and first day of coordinated attacks in November 1954, the revolutionary group stated that its two main objectives were independence and international recognition. The FLN proclamation identified internal and external goals, and in the latter category, it referenced the United Nations' utility in the nationalists' quest for independence. It vowed to use "the charter's framework" to "strengthen sympathy from all nations who support our liberation movement."[7] FLN leaders enlisted allies that were UN members to assist them in this endeavor.

One month after the FLN launched its quest for national liberation, Mohamed Khider, Algerian representative to the Arab League in Cairo and one of the two most crucial external FLN delegates tasked with exporting the nationalist cause, wrote to the Saudi Arabian king inquiring if he would be willing to send a letter to the UN Security Council alerting it to warlike conditions in Algeria.[8] On 14 December 1954 Abed Bou Hafa sent a telegram to Khider confirming King Saud's consent for him to work with the Saudi ambassador to defend Algeria at the United Nations. Bou Hafa requested that Khider "Please Send By Cable Regularly Detailed Information About Military Operation and Casuelties [sic] STOP Send All Information Available By Air and Request Friends In Press Do Likewise STOP Case Be Presented When Preparation Concluded."[9] Khider began assembling as much data as possible with which to provide the Saudi ambassador. He wanted current and pointed information, and he focused on UN priorities that the Security Council would have difficulty ignoring.

In the days and weeks immediately following the FLN attacks, as Khider was reaching out to potential supporters, French leaders did not think they had reason for concern. They noticed disturbances throughout Algerian cities, but they did not consider them the opening offensive of a large-scale and long-term conflict that would become a focal point of numerous General Assembly sessions. Under the headline "Terrorism in North Africa," a 2 November article in the leading French newspaper *Le Monde* reported four deaths from "deliberate action" officials believed "were part of an organized plot by the nationalists."[10] But the following day, the front-page headline of the same newspaper declared "Calm Restored in Algiers and Oran."[11] Colonial officials learned otherwise as they were soon confronted by sympathetic interlocutors at the United Nations who began an aggressive campaign for Algerian independence.

On 5 January 1955, Saudi Arabian UN representative Asad Al-Fiqih warned the Security Council president of the "the grave situation in Algeria," which "is likely to endanger the maintenance of international peace and security" under Article 35.[12] He stated that the nationalist uprising was "one of the gravest insurrections that France has faced in thirty years" and called the French administration "repressive and unjust." He asked that the president circulate the note among the members of the Security Council.[13] He claimed the existing colonial military and police forces proved insufficient to quell the FLN and that French premier Pierre Mendès-France had dispatched additional troops to Algeria.[14] Al-Fiqih was deeply concerned by the discrepancy in force as reported by French newspaper *Le Monde* and the *New York Times*. According to Al-Fiqih's sources, in December 1954 over 40,000 French troops were sent to liquidate "some 4,000 nationalists" that French government officials stated "were in uniforms and armed with guns, and operating from headquarters in the region of the Aurès."[15] What is striking about Al-Fiqih's letter is the speed with which he assembled information about the situation in Algeria. Khider likely heeded Bou Hafa's call for "all information" on Algeria enabling Al-Fiqih to draft a compelling plea that initiated a subsequent deluge of appeals.

Before the FLN assembled a team of "guerrilla diplomats" bound for Asia, the Middle East, and Africa to solicit the kind of support Al-Fiqih demonstrated, the leadership benefited greatly from the Bandung Conference.[16] For one week in April 1955, twenty-nine African and Asian states, most of which were newly independent, met in Indonesia to discuss economic and cultural cooperation, collective opposition to colonialism, and the Non-Aligned Movement.[17] This gathering was a diplomatic and symbolic event marking the politics of the moment—decolonization, the Cold War, and a new world order—and pointed toward "possible futures of the postcolonial world."[18]

Indonesian president Ahmed Sukarno opened the conference on 18 April

1955 with these words: "For many generations our peoples have been the voiceless ones in the world. We have been the unregarded, the peoples for whom decisions were made by others whose interests were paramount, the peoples who lived in poverty and humiliation. Then our nations demanded, nay fought for independence, and achieved independence, and with that independence came responsibility. We have heavy responsibilities to ourselves, and to the world, and to the yet-unborn generations."[19] His rousing speech signaled an irrefutable critique of colonialism and announced a turning of the tide to former Great Power nations. Not only did the conference take place outside of a colonial metropolitan center, it also assembled an assorted group of delegations from the Third World, each with unique colonial histories and diverse religious and cultural backgrounds. For seven days they put aside any differences they had and came together, united in their commitment to forging a new international system.[20]

The FLN sent Mohammed-Seddik Benyahia, a founder of the General Union of Algerian Muslim Students (UGEMA) and representative at both rounds of Evian Accords negotiations in 1961 and 1962, to Bandung, where he was able to generate interest in the Algerian cause and contextualize it within a framework of global anticolonial struggle. Even though Benyahia did not present a motion identifying FLN positions, he discussed Algeria in tandem with Morocco and Tunisia, both in the midst of their own liberation struggles, and pushed for their respective "rights" and "independence."[21] The Pakistani delegation in turn declared its support for "the right of the people of Algeria to self-determination," a sentiment Iraqi and Egyptian representatives also shared.[22] An unnamed FLN member later remembered Bandung as "the realisation by the newly independent countries that they must work together, on the one hand, to consolidate their freshly acquired independence and, on the other, not to fall into either of the two blocs' lap, whose mutual philosophy might be based on [U.S. secretary of state John] Foster Dulles' strange and dangerous notion: those who are not with us, are against us."[23]

Securing a place at Bandung was an early diplomatic victory for the FLN and enabled the leadership to establish strong ties with the Afro-Asia bloc, which would be absolutely vital to bringing Algeria to the United Nations. In the immediate aftermath of the conference, international support for Algerian sovereignty increased, and several Bandung participants and sovereign UN members worked together to request including the Algerian question on the agenda at the General Assembly's tenth session. On 29 July 1955, representatives of Afghanistan, Burma, Egypt, India, Indonesia, Iran, Iraq,

Lebanon, Liberia, Pakistan, Saudi Arabia, Syria, Thailand, and Yemen wrote a letter to the secretary-general emphasizing the right to self-determination and the protection of rights in general terms and discussed the "deteriorating situation in Algeria" that not only threatened peace but also "may lead to international friction." They urged the United Nations "to bring about a situation conducive to negotiations between France and the true representatives of the Algerian people."[24] Similar to Saudi representative Al-Fiqih's January 1955 letter, these representatives knew the important pressure points to stress when addressing the United Nations—international peace and stability. They needed to convince other members, especially European and American delegates, that French military action in Algeria violated Article 34 of the UN Charter and risked disrupting international relations in the area. They also wanted to show the strength and unity behind the principles of Bandung and the Non-Aligned Movement to which FLN foreign policy was very dedicated.

They nearly succeeded in this endeavor. During six meetings in the General Assembly, delegates debated Algeria, and based on the General Committee's recommendation not to include it as an agenda item on 30 September 1955 it was narrowly defeated by 28 votes to 27 with 5 abstentions. According to voting records, countries voted in bloc groups; 94.25 percent of Asian and African delegates voted against the General Committee's position, whereas 83.34 percent of Western countries voted for it.[25] These alliances remained relatively intact throughout the duration of the war, but as the number of newly independent Asian and African nations grew so too did their voting power in the United Nations. In calling on the General Assembly to discuss Algeria, the Afro-Asia bloc was asking the UN and its members to reconsider the definition of sovereignty and statehood.

The mere idea of inscribing Algeria onto the General Assembly agenda angered the French to such a degree that their delegates walked out on 1 October 1955 and did not return until the end of November. Before exiting, French minister of foreign affairs and UN delegate Antoine Pinay told the General Assembly that "France cannot tolerate insults and slander directed against its work for the benefit of civilization." Trying to dissuade members from putting Algeria on the agenda, he said, "in my country's opinion, the decision taken by the Assembly will be more serious for the United Nations than France. The very future of our Organization will be at stake," for "what would happen if it were established for all time that the United Nations had the right to intervene wherever there existed within the boundaries of a certain State a racial, religious or linguistic minority?"[26] He was furious that the organization dared discuss French domestic affairs and resented the idea of having to explain their actions, especially concerning Algeria, which was legally part of France, to a foreign audience. Additionally, for him, UN members were violating a tacit agreement that non-Western countries had reached three years earlier regarding self-determination.

Algerian allies worked diligently during France's absence at the United Nations that fall and continued to push the organization to respond. On 11 November 1955, the secretary-general of the League of Arab States Abdul Khalik Hassouna sent a letter to Jose Maza, president of the UN General Assembly. He wrote about how Arab peoples were morally horrified at French action in Algeria. He asked that the United Nations intervene and stop the French military from executing "Algerian patriots whose only crime was to demand the God-given right to freedom and dignity advocated by the Charter of the United Nations."[27] Hassouna did not receive a favorable response.

An Indian UN delegate, Krishna Menon, pursued another course. Hoping to ease tensions and encourage the French government to find a suitable resolution to the conflict on its own, he suggested delegates cease discussing Algeria in the General Assembly's tenth session. Many delegates supported the idea, and on 25 November 1955 the General Assembly resolved "not to consider further the item."[28]

Menon's optimism for an early end to the war did not materialize by the UN General Assembly's eleventh session the following year. During this period, newly appointed governor-general Robert Lacoste proposed that the French National Assembly grant the government and the army "special powers" in Algeria.[29] These exceptional powers authorized colonial officials to expand economic projects, implement social and political reforms, and, most significant, take any measures that would maintain order and protect individuals and the territory.[30] When the French parliament approved Lacoste's proposal in March 1956, it essentially ended "individual liberty in Algeria" in favor of military rule.[31] Algerian supporters followed these developments and continued to urge the UN General Assembly to take a position on the "deteriorating situation" that "is a threat to peace and security, involves the infringement of the basic right of self-determination, and constitutes a flagrant violation of other fundamental human rights."[32] Henry Cabot Lodge, Jr., UN Security Council president at the time, acknowledged receiving the memorandum and said he would pass it on to the other members of the Security Council. But the United Nations still did not take any action.[33]

Since the outbreak of the war, neither the UN Security Council nor the General Assembly had taken a clear position on the national liberation struggle, even though it had received letters and compiled reports on the growing conflict.[34] Therefore, Algerian nationalists, suppressed at home as the French colonial state expanded its reach, pursued alternative means of garnering support and solidifying Third World internationalism. In the winter and spring months of 1956 the FLN sent representatives on a diplomatic mission to several Asian countries that had taken part in the Bandung Conference. The external FLN leadership in Cairo dispatched M'hamed Yazid and Hocine Lahouel to secure personal and financial pledges from political leaders and diplomats in support of the Algerian war effort.[35]

In March 1956, Yazid, a former Algerian People's Party (PPA) member who became the FLN figurehead in New York during the tenth, eleventh, and twelfth UN sessions and served as the Provisional Government of the Algerian Republic (GPRA) minister of information (1958–1962), and Lahouel, the secretary-general of the Movement for the Triumph of Democratic Liberties (MTLD) in 1950 who retired from political life after the Asia mission, spent four months traveling to Pakistan, India, Burma, Thailand, and Indonesia.[36] Before they arrived in Pakistan on 21 March, Hocine Aït Ahmed, the Algerian North Africa Liberation Committee representative in Cairo and founding FLN member who was the first to articulate the nationalists' sophisticated strategy, contacted the Pakistan Institute of International Affairs in Karachi, notifying personnel that Yazid and Lahouel were coming.[37] Sarwar Hasan, the Pakistan Institute's secretary, wrote to Aït Ahmed, saying he was "glad to learn" of their arrival "in Karachi to represent to the Pakistani people the seriousness of the situation in Algeria." He assured Aït Ahmed that "I shall do whatever I can do to help them. If they wish me to introduce them to Government leaders, that also I shall do. I need hardly say that all our sympathies are with the Arabs of North Africa in their gallant struggle for freedom."[38] Hasan's willingness to accommodate Yazid and Lahouel set the tone for the entire trip and foreshadowed the warm reception they would receive throughout Asia. Moreover, Hasan's response demonstrated a commitment to his Third World brethren and to putting the ideas discussed at Bandung into action.

Yazid and Lahouel sent regular reports to the Cairo delegation about their progress abroad, which included detailed notes on with whom they met, what level of support those individuals pledged (ideological, political, or financial), and Asian press stories about Algeria. Not only did their communiqués provide a practical account of their comings and goings, but they also enabled the representatives to get a broad overview of the degree to which their international outreach strategy was succeeding.

During their eight-day stay in Pakistan, Yazid and Lahouel met with the Syrian minister to Karachi, the Egyptian ambassador to Pakistan, and the Pakistani assistant secretary and secretary of the ministry of external affairs.[39] Though they did not meet the Pakistani president in person, Yazid and Lahouel remarked that he pledged support for Algeria in an address before parliament. In India, they met with the minister of foreign affairs and the Indian UN delegate Krishna Menon, who indicated that India supported the idea of Algerian independence "in principle," but deferred to "Arabs to take diplomatic initiatives."[40] They met with equally high-ranking officials in Burma, such as the minister of national defense and the president of the Chamber of Deputies, and claimed that "not a day goes by without being invited to lunch or dinner by ministers, vice-ministers, and deputies." They were especially touched by "our Burmese friends who leave us 'baba' by their kindness" and insisted that the Cairo leadership visit the Burmese delegation in Egypt and "transmit our thanks to their government."[41] Even though Yazid and Lahouel did not receive financial commitments or diplomatic pledges for their war effort in Pakistan or Burma, their victory, like that of the Algerian Red Crescent delegates who secured meetings with International Committee of the Red Cross delegates, was in getting an international audience to pay attention to Algeria and become invested in the war's outcome.

The Algerian representatives relied heavily on press statements to generate publicity for their trip and for their larger cause and continued to write to the Cairo leadership about the media. Yazid made frequent mention while in Karachi of the important and symbiotic role of the press, which, he said, "announced our arrival" and "every day publishes a communiqué on our activities."[42] When Yazid and Lahouel arrived in New Delhi, their first letter from India on 1 April said, "We issued a declaration to the press that was reproduced by a collection of newspapers. We also had the honor of the first-page photo. This morning *The Hindustan Standard* published a long article that we signed on the situation in Algeria."[43]

Yazid and Lahouel reported meeting with Syed Mahmud, the Indian minister of foreign affairs, during which they discussed "their point of view on recent French maneuvers." They explained nationalist strategy to him, sharing the primary aims of the FLN's internal delegation.[44] If the FLN was going to seriously challenge French colonial claims of Algerian barbarity, they had to make sure their allies knew of and understood their sophisticated political strategy. Yazid and Lahouel alerted the Cairo FLN representatives to Mahmud's upcoming trip there in two weeks, recommending that they schedule a meeting with him and continue nurturing this diplomatic relationship.[45]

Yazid and Lahouel also targeted other forms of media in India. "Yesterday we recorded a long interview on the radio . . . and we anticipate giving numerous conferences in the upcoming week"—a promise they kept.[46] On 6 April they hosted a press conference in New Delhi and explained why "the Algerian problem has reached a crucial phase." Citing the new French military offensive backed by the deployment of NATO troops and rising numbers of French soldiers in Algeria, they argued that "the Algerian people are facing not only one of the greatest modern armies but also the military coalition of NATO." For them, "the Algerian problem is not the concern of France alone but of all the world and particularly of the peoples who stand for the abolition of colonialism everywhere." Yazid and Lahouel ended their address with an appeal to uphold larger unifying principles and proclaimed that "the Algerian freedom movement needs the support of all freedom and peace-loving peoples and particularly of the Asian and African community so that a peaceful solution may be reached in Algeria."[47] This press conference, and their lengthy trip throughout Asia, contributed greatly to raising awareness about the Algerian war outside of Algeria and France and building a reliable political base upon which to rely at the United Nations. It also showed FLN political acumen in developing and carrying out a foreign policy agenda.

The external FLN delegation in Cairo also concentrated on establishing an African-Asian coalition in the United States and in anticipation of the UN General Assembly's eleventh session deployed Hocine Aït Ahmed to New York to begin this work.[48] On 8 March 1956, Mohamed Khider, Algerian delegate for the Cairo-based Committee of Liberation of North Africa, wrote a memo to the governments of the Afro-Asian nations that laid out the FLN's central points that Aït Ahmed would relay in New York. In Khider's address, he declared that "the moment has come for the Afro-Asian nations which pledged themselves to fight 'subjection of peoples to alien domination' and proclaimed as a principle 'abstention from the use of arrangements of collective defense to serve the particular interest of any of the big powers' to intervene to stop colonial aggression on Algeria." For Khider, the most pressing issue was for "Afro-Asian nations to act promptly and take practical measures to . . . enforce a peaceful settlement of the Algerian problem," a refrain Algerian delegates stressed repeatedly over the next six years.[49]

By the end of March, Aït Ahmed met with numerous permanent Arab delegations in New York and urged them to commit themselves to the Algerian problem. In a letter to "brothers" of the external delegation in Cairo, Aït Ahmed reported "the whole world is preoccupied with the Palestinian question" and that Arab delegates "preferred to wait around two weeks until they take up our question."[50] According to Aït Ahmed, the Arab delegates presented an additional obstacle. The ones with whom he consulted claimed "they could not bring the Algerian question before the Security Council without formal instructions from their governments." Though "in principle this is true," he wrote, "in practice, this is false, especially when" an issue "is approached collectively."[51]

To skirt this technicality Aït Ahmed embarked on a campaign to gather signatures and personal pledges from individuals from a variety of countries. He thought their signatures would contextualize the "global repercussions" of the Algerian conflict "and would place non-signatories in difficult political positions."[52] For maximum impact, he planned to submit the document to the press and suggested that it would help bolster media coverage of the nationalists' efforts, which at the time, Aït Ahmed thought "was not favorable to our cause."[53] Aït Ahmed also went on speaking tours around the United States as part of his massive publicity campaign.[54] He told the Cairo FLN leaders to continue exerting pressure on "Afro-Asian representatives in all of the Arab capitals" and to make sure "to contact the representatives of Iran, the USSR, and Yugoslavia who are the only countries willing to speak on our behalf."[55]

Aït Ahmed's campaign in the United States soon generated results. On 25 May 1956, Indian prime minister Jawaharlal Nehru made a statement in New York about the events in Algeria and linked them to "part of the great wave of national upsurges that has swept Asia and Africa in the last two generations."[56] In his eyes, "the grave developments in Algeria" had "reached the dimensions of a large-scale conflict with mounting violence with considerable forces and arms engaged and with no end . . . in sight." He reminded his audience that India's official position on all national liberation movements remained unchanged since Bandung. The Indian government had pledged its "unity with other independent governments of Asia and Africa" and "joined in declaring their support of the rights of the people of Algeria, Morocco, and Tunisia to self-determination and independence and appealing to the French Government to bring about a peaceful settlement of the issue without delay."[57] It remained imperative for Nehru to continue pursuing this outcome.

Nehru, as many other delegates in the Afro-Asian bloc, walked a fine diplomatic line, for in the next breath he was careful to mention that he recognized "the wisdom and statesmanship of the Government of France."[58] This would be a recurring issue for newly independent nations in the international global arena. On the one hand, bound by Third World solidarity and anticolonial struggle, they wanted to assert their independence from Western and American powers. But on the other hand, they did not want to completely isolate themselves on the world stage and risk economic alienation as they sought to build their postcolonial polities. In any event, Nehru's comments were a powerful indicator of the FLN support base.

Additional delegates from the Afro-Asia bloc started banning together at the United Nations, attempting to force a conversation about Algeria. On 12 April 1956, representatives from sixteen Asian and Middle Eastern countries sent a letter to the Security Council detailing French aggression and petitioning for more meaningful action in Algeria. The delegates, many from countries that participated in the Bandung Conference in April 1955, reminded the Security Council that the only reason they agreed to postpone discussing the Algerian issue in the tenth session was because they had been "inspired by the new constructive steps taken by France on the questions of Tunisia and Morocco, and was intended to give France an opportunity to reconsider its policy also on the question of Algeria. [The] postponement . . . was a gesture of conciliation."[59] They were disappointed by French government unwillingness to take seriously the demands of the Algerian people and wanted to go on record, again, for their belief that the United Nations "[could not] remain indifferent" to a situation that threatened peace and security.[60]

The Security Council did not assemble to discuss the contents of this April letter. On 13 June 1956 the same sixteen delegates sent a follow-up memorandum to the president of the Security Council, E. R. Walker (Australia).[61] They wrote, "[we] have the honour, upon instructions from our respective governments, to bring to the attention of the Security Council, under Article 35, paragraph 1, of the United Nations Charter, the grave situation in Algeria . . . which is likely to endanger the maintenance of international peace and security."[62] The Asian and Middle Eastern delegates reminded the Security Council of their "support of the rights of the peoples of Algeria to self-determination and independence" as articulated after Bandung and lamented the fact that "the French government refused to enter into negotiations with the representatives of the Algerian people to meet their legitimate demands" despite numerous appeals.[63] In their opinion, the United Nations could not turn away from the Algerian question as it had in 1955 when the General Assembly voted against including it on the agenda. They strongly urged the United Nations to revisit this serious matter.[64]

On 26 June, Security Council president Walker called a procedural meeting to discuss the two previously neglected letters.[65] He told the representatives not to raise specific concerns about what was happening in Algeria; those comments were intended for a later session should the item be included on the agenda. French ambassador Hervé Alphand and Iranian delegate Abdoh dominated the morning debate. Alphand spoke first and unequivocally dismissed a Soviet request to further postpone the issue. He wanted members to vote expeditiously—not to include Algeria onto the agenda— and avoid opening up the question to the General Assembly where the French would have to defend themselves and listen to inquiries from other nations. After Alphand finished his opening remarks, Abdoh took the floor, quickly emphasizing that "today, my delegation is far from being inspired by any spirit of animosity towards France, with which we have always enjoyed the most cordial relations. French culture has greatly influenced our education and our laws, and we owe the French people an immense intellectual debt." Diplomatic niceties did not mask his true intentions as he carried on:

> If we have joined with other nations in requesting the inscription of the Algerian question in the Council's agenda, we do so because we firmly believe that a Council debate on the matter would help the French Government, as well as the Algerian people, to find a just and equitable solution—a solution which would reflect the well-established traditions of France founded on the principles of liberty, equality, and fraternity. The fact that we are requesting the inclusion of this question in the agenda in no way diminishes our respect and our friendship for France. . . . My delegation hopes, therefore, that its attitude will be understood by other Member States as well as by France and that our statement may help the French to understand better the trend of events in Algeria.[66]

He, and the other Asian and Middle Eastern countries he represented, appealed to French pride about their revolutionary ideals and suggested that the Security Council would help government officials apply them to the Algerian people, but still he overtly implied that colonial administrators needed assistance interpreting Algerian aspirations.

Abdoh congratulated Alphand for France's "liberal attitude" toward Morocco and Tunisia and argued that Algeria was part of the same "movement towards liberation which has succeeded in numerous Asian and African countries" and "is one of the salient facts of our contemporary history."[67] The French government could not disregard "the awakening" of the Algerian people, and Abdoh warned against further divisions between Afro-Asian countries and the West if it did. Abdoh told the Security Council that he wanted to avoid this result, which went against the premise of cooperation at the United Nations. He read Article 35 of the UN Charter as evidence for why he was justified in bringing the Algerian question to the Security Council. And after reviewing the state of military operations, he concluded that what was happening in Algeria was nothing short of a civil war "whose effects go beyond the national level to the international level" and could serve as a "springboard for violence . . . contaminating the whole continent of Africa."[68] Of all of Abdoh's remarks this last point was the most significant and stood the best chance of gaining additional support for inscription onto the agenda. By this point in 1956, Asian and African delegates had met in Indonesia and declared their solidarity with the Algerian cause. The war had spilled over into Morocco. Egyptian president Nasser viewed an Algerian victory as integral to his vision for Pan-Arabism. And the Soviets were sending the FLN arms, heating up the Cold War race between them and the United States for influence in North Africa and the Middle East. And soon, other nationalist groups in sub-Saharan Africa turned to FLN strategies to articulate their own demands for national liberation. How then, Abdoh asked, could the Algerian conflict *not* be considered a threat to international peace and security?

The FLN asked the same question and promulgated similar lines of argument in its wartime journal *El Moudjahid*. Published in its November 1956 special edition, "Algerian Resistance," the editors' introduction focused on UN failure during the tenth session. Now, they claimed, the organization had to recognize the "absurd myth of French Algeria" and the risk it was taking by not intervening, for Algeria could be "a source of contamination for the outbreak of new wars" throughout the region.[69] Algerian historians have also suggested that by late 1955/early 1956, the war threatened peace and security by virtue of the large number of troops and French NATO units in Algeria. A surplus of arms was coming in from France, the United States, the Soviet Union, and North Africa, dispelling the notion that Algeria was an internal affair. By this point, France must have "implicitly recognized the seriousness of the situation" and desperately wanted to avoid "a grave threat to peace in the Mediterranean basin."[70] But French delegates would not openly admit this at the United Nations.

French representative Alphand complimented Iranian delegate Abdoh for his kind remarks about relations between their two countries but maintained that "France is doing no more in Algeria than exercising one of the most normal attributes of domestic sovereignty." Government efforts "[endeavored] to maintain public order which has been disturbed by rebellious citizens," and "prevent, or, if that has proved impossible, to punish the killings, the brutalities, fires and robberies which certain French-Algerians are committing against other French-Algerians, whether Christians or Mohammedans." In no way did their actions, according to Alphand, merit international investigation. In fact, he thought "it would be the most dangerous of precedents to recognize the right of the United Nations to intervene between the Government of a State and those of its citizens who are disturbing the peace."[71] Alphand's rebuttal of Abdoh bypassed the latter's carefully crafted arguments on international security and instead focused on UN intervention. Abdoh had never mentioned intervening in Algeria. In these meetings he concentrated on the United Nations Charter and its emphasis on international relations and peace. But Alphand, reading Article 2(7), redirected the debate and provided solid evidence against UN intervention that resonated with other powerful nations who feared any challenge to their sovereignty.

Alphand had one more way of discrediting the letter's request. He paid close attention to the Asian and Middle Eastern representatives' word choice and seized upon one damaging omission. In their letter to the Security Council, he noted, they wrote that "the situation had deteriorated to the extent that the United Nations could not remain indifferent to the threat to peace and security." Alphand "call[ed] attention to the fact that . . . the thirteen Asian-African States referred to peace and security without inserting the qualifying adjective 'international' which appears in Chapters VI and VII of the Charter." Even though the signatories likely meant the Algerian conflict posed an international threat, Alphand had grounds to argue that "not even the authors of the letter . . . have been bold enough to make that claim."[72]

The meeting adjourned and reconvened later that afternoon to vote. Before each representative explained his position, Abdoh cautioned those present that "the Council's policy of silence, a policy restrictive of freedom of discussion, is a serious infringement of its own moral authority. My delegation cannot but note that the Council's refusal to include certain items on its agenda occurs wherever there is a conflict of interests between a great Power and non-self-governing people."[73] Though often implied, smaller UN member states rarely publicly articulated this sentiment. The stakes of such a perception, real or imagined, threatened to undermine the entire organization in the eyes of current and future members and risked recreating the kind of power politics that led to world wars.

Abdoh's cautionary words proved insufficient. The agenda item was rejected by seven votes to two, with two abstentions, largely attributable to delegates' interpretation of Article 2(7) in the UN Charter.[74] Alphand, pleased with this result, told the Security Council that "France and France alone" was responsible "to settle the problems now arising in Algeria."[75] Trying to end the meeting and reduce political animosity, President Walker concluded that the council's decision "does not reflect any indifference towards the human suffering arising from the present situation in Algeria or any lack of consideration for the countries that submitted this matter to [us]." He affirmed his "deepest concern . . . over recent events in Algeria" and conveyed confidence in the French government's ability to find "just and peaceful solutions as speedily as possible."[76] Walker's empathy toward the Algerian people only yielded words of support, not action, and the same can be said of the other Western nations on the Security Council. But this would be the last time they could convincingly deny its international implications.

International Tidal Wave, 1956

The year 1956 was a critical one in which several major international developments increased FLN support, dramatizing their cause and adding pressure on France in the United Nations. The first set of events was Tunisian and Moroccan independence. The nature of French colonial rule in these countries differed from that in Algeria, primarily due to the shorter length of foreign domination (Tunisia, 1881–1956, and Morocco, 1912–1956) and because neither had been legally incorporated into France.[77] Moroccan and Tunisian nationalist parties, Istiqlal and Neo-Destour, respectively, had campaigned for independence since the 1920s, but the French government never devoted as many troops to putting down their rebellions, resulting in less loss of life on all sides. Both nations immediately became members in the United Nations and Moroccan king Mohammed V and Tunisian president Habib Bourguiba continually advocated on behalf of Algerian nationalists. They played a vital role in showing the international dimensions of military warfare and humanitarian crises, a point to which this chapter will return.

The second set of 1956 events that prompted some members to reconsider their positions on Algeria was the Suez Crisis and the Hungarian Revolution, culminating in the first and second UN emergency special sessions in November.[78] In the wake of a 1956 Soviet arms treaty with Egypt, the United States and Britain withdrew financial support for the Aswan Dam. Egyptian president Gamal Abdel Nasser responded by nationalizing the Suez Canal in July of that year, signaling his mission to oust Western imperialism from the Middle East. Despite American president Eisenhower's concerns about a Soviet presence in Egypt, he cautioned the new British prime minister, Anthony Eden, "that if an intervention did take place, 'the peoples of the Near East and of North Africa and, to some extent, all of Asia and all of Africa, would be consolidated against the West to a degree which, I fear, could not be overcome in a generation,'" revealing his Cold War motives.[79]

Eden did not heed the warning. On 29 October, the British, along with the French and Israelis, secretly invaded Egypt, staying until 7 November when the United States, the Soviet Union, and the United Nations forced them to withdraw. In the months leading up to the attack, Eden was reluctant to raise the issue at the United Nations. He worried that the Soviet Union would veto a British proposal and that the Security Council president would vote for policies sympathetic to the Egyptians.[80] The British administration engaged in a double game that fall, bringing the Suez issue to the United Nations, while simultaneously planning for military action. The backlash from the tripartite invasion was harsh and immediate. Eisenhower and Dulles were furious over Eden's breach of trust, claiming that the UN six principles of 13 October 1956, which Britain and France agreed to, appeared to have been a waste of time. Furthermore, Western imperial interests had been laid bare for the world to see, making the United States less likely to go out of its way to support the French in Algeria.

The Hungarian Revolution (23 October–10 November 1956) overlapped with the Suez Crisis and posed a quandary for members over whether the United Nations should also intervene there.[81] Student protests erupted the last week of October. When Soviet forces crushed the opposition ten days later, the UN had difficulty ascertaining information about the state of the uprising because, similar to the French, the Soviet and Soviet-controlled Hungarian governments reminded members of their "avowed policy of non-intervention in the internal affairs of other States."[82] French, British, and

American representatives sent a letter to the president of the Security Council saying they "[deplored] the use of Soviet military forces to suppress the efforts of the Hungarian people to reassert their rights," and that they wanted "the Security Council to instruct the Soviet and Hungarian Governments to start the negotiations immediately on withdrawal of Soviet forces." Their final call to "affirm the right of the Hungarian people to a government responsive to its national aspirations and dedicated to its independence and well-being" struck comparable chords with Algeria.[83]

The newly installed Hungarian officials made analogous arguments about the domestic nature of "the steps taken by [their] Government" against those whom they called "fascists, former capitalists and large landowners . . . considered . . . enemies of the people."[84] Péter Mód, Hungarian ambassador and permanent representative to the UN, claimed that "in the past there has been no point of law that has authorized the United Nations to make an inquiry in Hungary and it is even less authorized to do so today," and consequently he vehemently protested against placing the Hungary situation on the agenda of the General Assembly's eleventh and twelfth sessions. His rationale, also later articulated by the Soviet foreign minister Andrei Gromyko, relied on the preeminent principle of state sovereignty to deflect attention from the reality of opposition and repression. Mód and Gromyko's claims mimicked those of French delegate Alphand about Algeria, but the contentious and contradictory testimonies voiced during the second emergency session undermined their argument and increased international awareness regarding possible infractions that merited UN consideration. Alphand and French delegates who succeeded him strove to avoid conversations that sowed seeds of doubt about Algeria, but with Jordan and Libya's UN membership in 1955, and Morocco, Sudan, and Tunisia's in 1956, this quickly became more difficult.

A third factor to consider is Franco-American relations and the U.S. position on Algeria.[85] American diplomats had difficulty reaching a consensus about how to handle colonialism and the question of self-determination. High-ranking politicians, including President Eisenhower, knew that the success of future U.S. interactions with the British and French required that the United States avoid denouncing their empires. Yet, as more countries in the Third World sought and attained independence, American officials became preoccupied with curtailing Soviet encroachment, often in or close to French and British territories.[86]

In September 1955, Francis Wilcox, the assistant secretary of state for international organization affairs and primary representative of the United

States at the United Nations, thought it would be prudent to review American policy on the "colonial question," given the number of Bandung Conference participants and their resolutions. He suggested that the United States should uphold "the principle of equal rights and self-determination of people" and "earnestly strive by every peaceful means to promote self-government and to secure the independence of all countries whose peoples desire it and are able to undertake its responsibilities." He remained cautious and qualified American support for self-determination, remarking that, "while the principle has universal validity, it is not an absolute right."[87]

Wilcox's two main concerns were avoiding communist infiltration into newly independent nations and maintaining relationships with American allies. Fear of Soviet penetration dominated the U.S. position on colonial issues and, as historian Odd Arne Westad has argued, remained "at the core of American Third World involvement" during this period.[88] If the Americans did not preemptively support an independence movement, government officials thought that nationalists would turn to the Soviet Union for aid and, as historians Matthew Connelly and Jeffrey Byrne have shown for the Algerian case, they did.[89] Wilcox supported self-determination insofar as it was "attained resolutely and in an orderly manner," but he cautioned against "premature action" that could lead to "chaos and disorder."[90] His primary objective was ensuring American power and security, not the self-determination of people around the world. Throughout his tenure, he had to delicately balance the imminent threat of Soviet expansion into Algeria with these other factors.

Over the next two years, U.S. diplomats worked to support France privately at the United Nations. They tried to avoid making any public statements and, as UN records indicate, skirted voting on Algeria in the General Assembly until the last minute. But U.S. officials and delegates struggled to create a coherent policy toward France and Algeria, especially after Moroccan and Tunisian independence.[91] Their geopolitical significance, along with Algeria's, motivated President Eisenhower to avoid taking a firm position against France, while also realizing that the United States needed to articulate a more concrete position on decolonization and stop "walk[ing] a tightrope in terms of relations with the British and French on the one hand and their former colonies on the other."[92]

Inscribing Algeria onto the General Assembly Agenda

The confluence of international events did not alter French officials' fundamental belief that Algeria was a French matter, but it did cause them to speak about the conflict differently. They were also forced to contend with questions from an increasingly vocal UN Asian-African Group advocating a peaceful solution to the conflict. In the months leading up to the eleventh session, this group issued several statements about their growing concern over "the sharp deterioration of the Algerian question" and maintained that "the United Nations cannot stand passively by in so ominous a situation."[93] U Win, the chairman of the Asian-African Group and permanent representative of Burma to the United Nations, echoed these sentiments when he met with the UN secretary-general in May 1956. Win reportedly told him about "the deep anxiety and concern felt unanimously by all the members of the Asian-African Group over . . . the situation in Algeria which has led to death and bloodshed in terrifying proportions among the peoples of Algeria." He "refrained from suggesting to the Secretary-General any particular means in this regard." Instead, Win "implored him to make use of the prestige and respect which both his office and his person enjoy, in order to bring a speedy end to such a grave state of affairs in Algeria."[94] Win did not explicitly outline what he thought the secretary-general should do; nonetheless, his message was clear. The Algerian people were dying, and the United Nations stood by watching on the sidelines. If the UN wanted to preserve its reputation for promoting and ensuring peace, the secretary-general needed to take concrete action, the very least of which meant inscribing Algeria onto the General Assembly agenda.[95]

When the United Nations reconvened for its eleventh session in early 1957, the Algerian war had escalated considerably. The FLN had launched a series of attacks in the second half of 1956 and Radio Free Algeria began broadcasting instructions for a general strike at the beginning of January, set to coincide with the upcoming eleventh session.[96] The French government would not to be outdone by the FLN. French leader Guy Mollet gave General Massu full control of police powers, essentially granting carte blanche for the military sweeps that ensued in the casbah, poetically depicted in the iconic 1966 film *The Battle of Algiers*.

In preparation for another round of debates about Algeria at the UN, Mollet wrote what became known as the "9 January Declaration." In it, he reiterated his belief in a reformist position, "based upon the principles of equality, coexistence, and a recognition of Algeria's distinctiveness."[97] French foreign minister Christian Pineau used Mollet's declaration as his guide to preempt inscription discussions. In the First Committee meeting on 4 February 1957, Pineau explained that the new pacification policy—an effort to eliminate rebels and control the civilian population— was "essentially to free the Algerians from terror to which they were subjected, and to bring closer together the French and Moslem communities, and to increase their common trust in metropolitan France."[98] He tried to present pacification as beneficial to Algerians and demonstrate that rapprochement efforts would draw the conflict to a close, thereby eliminating the need for UN intervention. At no point did he use the term "special powers," nor did he mention forced relocation of civilians, French military use of torture, and the mounting number of French soldiers deployed to Algeria, all of which were occurring concurrently. In his opinion, the French government could successfully carry out this plan if it were not for the Soviet and Arab nations' actively interfering "in the internal affairs of France" by sending material and financial aid.[99]

Invoking the standard French trope that the conflict was an internal matter did not carry the same weight it had one year prior. Unlike in the tenth session, enough UN members expressed interest in discussing the matter further and passed Resolution 1012(XI) in the 654th Plenary Meeting.[100] The resolution still did not advocate intervention but it had evolved from the previous one fourteen months prior. Delegates from around the world openly discussed their apprehension regarding the rising death toll. Moreover, they reached a mutual agreement that participants needed *pourparlers* and that they needed to find a "peaceful" and "democratic" solution.[101] They did not define "appropriate means" but advised the warring parties to follow the parameters set forth in the UN Charter. This resolution may not have been enough to legitimize the FLN cause yet, but it was an important first step in dismantling the powerful Western alliance that had supported French attempts at prolonging empire and suppressing Algerians' right to self-determination. It also generated a brazen set of questions from Arab foreign ministers and leaders in regular contact with the FLN who asked, "Will France recognize the fact that the right of self-determination is an inherent right embodied in the Charter? Will France . . . start walking *not* behind history *but* with it—*not* with the spirit of the nineteenth century *but* with the spirit of the day; *not* with the spirit of domination and exploitation *but* with the spirit of inter-dependence and cooperation?"[102]

"The question of Algeria" did not go away. If anything Algerian nationalists and their allies exerted even more pressure on the UN to act in 1957 and 1958. In June 1957, three months before the twelfth session of the UN General Assembly was scheduled to begin, M'hamed Yazid, FLN delegate in New York, compiled a confidential report for the FLN delegation in Cairo detailing the three main areas he thought required the most attention: political considerations, tactical and practical preparation, and assembling a well-rounded Algerian delegation to show off the breadth and depth of the movement's appeal. He noted that the nationalists were up against a formidable and calculating French opponent who he anticipated would use the "magic" word, "elections," at the United Nations to illustrate that the colonial government took the situation seriously, while simultaneously trying to deflect international outrage.[103]

Yazid, the FLN point person on the ground in New York, was in a unique position to shape and refine the movement's strategy based on international reactions to its tactics. After the UN General Assembly's eleventh session ended, he wrote a memo to the external delegation in Cairo, reflecting on FLN successes and failures in New York. He thought the UN resolution was a success for both its content and because the nationalists "could use it as a trampoline for the next session." He did not think it possible for the FLN to obtain much more than that given the French delegation's "intelligent" approach that "spoke of a peaceful solution," which included a cease-fire, elections, and negotiations.[104]

Yazid wanted the political leadership to be better prepared for the twelfth session and suggested making tactical adjustments. Chief among them was securing additional funding for publicity, expanding the New York office, bringing Mohammed-Seddik Benyahia to New York, and expanding the pool of Algerian delegates who spoke English. He also wanted to round out an Algerian delegation to include representatives from the General Union of Algerian Workers (Union Générale des Travailleurs Algériens), the Algerian Red Crescent, the General Union of Algerian Muslim Students, and a female delegate to speak on behalf of Algerian women. Yazid warned against framing the Algerian question "within an Arab context." He thought it best to emphasize the North African context. "Naturally, [we] cannot forget our action within the Afro-Asian group relies entirely on support from the Arab countries."[105] Yazid's memo illustrates the multiple layers at which the international FLN strategy operated. He was abreast of the numerous diplomatic forces at play and, as much as possible, he laid the groundwork to speak to individual delegations' interests while paying close attention not alienate any of them.

One element Yazid did not account for over the summer was the number of additional advocates outside of the Afro-Asian bloc that would speak out on Algeria's behalf during the twelfth session of the General Assembly. On 20 September 1957, Irish delegate Frank Aiken, the first person to mention Algeria explicitly, delivered rousing words in support of the nationalist efforts and, similar to Iranian delegate Abdoh, appealed to French vanity. He said, "The case of Algeria deeply disturbs those of us who are the friends and admirers of the great French nation and of the noble and valiant French people. But the nature of the conflict there is one that leaves a country with Ireland's traditions no choice. As this case is to be considered by the General Assembly, we cannot do otherwise than support self-determination." Ireland's complex history with Britain likely predisposed many Irish to side with the FLN. Nonetheless, Aiken's public rebuke was one of the first times that a Western European country spoke out strongly against the colonial administration at the United Nations. "In the interest of the French people, in the interest of the French settlers, in the interest of the peace of mind of its friends, in the interest of world peace and for the glory of France," he urged the government "to declare its readiness to concede the right of self-determination to Algeria at the earliest practicable date to be fixed in agreement with this Organization."[106] Aiken's comments, though brief, proved powerful and lasting for weeks to come and ignited a healthy exchange between African, Asian, Soviet, European, and American representatives.

R. G. Casey, minister of state of external affairs for Australia, a former dominion of the British Empire, spoke next about Algeria and he did not refrain from conveying his disappointment in the French government for failing to comply with General Assembly Resolution 1012 (XI). His government, he stated, "deplores the fact that nothing tangible has been accomplished towards attaining the purposes stated in the resolution and is greatly disturbed by the constant deterioration of the situation, which merely prolongs the suffering and daily causes further large-scale loss of human life." Casey thought "there [was] nevertheless a clear and growing tendency on the part of world public opinion, including French opinion, to admit the need to recognize the legitimate aspirations of the Algerian people, not only on humanitarian grounds, but also in order to put an end to a situation fraught with danger to peace."[107] He condemned the UN for failing to intensify its efforts there. His suggesting international and French public opinion were moving toward supporting Algerian nationalist aspirations struck at the heart of French government fears. If other countries' leaders, even their own citizens, began sympathizing with the anticolonial struggle and focusing on humanitarian issues, colonial officials would have more difficulty convincing their rapidly eroding political base that they, and they alone, should handle the conflict. Based on French military actions to date, critics of the war had reason to suspect the French government did not prioritize a peaceful resolution.[108]

Taking into account the ongoing divisive events in Hungary, Hungarian first deputy minister for foreign affairs Dr. Endre Sik delivered a surprising condemnation of the UN and French government following Casey's plenary meeting. He contextualized the events in Algeria as part of a continuum of "hard struggle[s] against new forms of colonialism" with "right and justice . . . on their side." When many other delegates, even African and Asian ones, talked about what was happening in Algeria, they rarely used the term "war." Sik did. For him, 500,000 French soldiers fighting the population indicated "there is actually a war in progress." He implored the UN to "act in the spirit of the Charter" and "pass a resolution calling upon France to recognize the Algerian people's right to self-determination and to begin discussions with the representatives of the Algerian people without delay with a view to the immediate termination of the fighting."[109]

Other communist countries expressed their opposition to colonialism and criticized French actions, forming a second bloc within the UN protesting the war. Yugoslav secretary of state for foreign affairs Koča Popović echoed Sik's commentary about the necessity of "recognizing the Algerian people's right to self-determination."[110] He pointed out that "repression by force of arms is still the policy there and there is, so far, little sign of a cessation of hostilities." He believed the state of the conflict necessitated a "peaceful" solution "on an equitable basis acceptable to the parties concerned."[111] Popović thought both sides merited equal negotiating power, a claim French leaders strongly disputed. In the French view, the FLN, to which they referred as a terrorist organization, deserved criminal punishment consistent with military law, not equal rights before an international forum.

Arab delegates, strongly behind the idea of a peaceful solution, had grown noticeably frustrated with French officials who insisted that Algeria was part of France and therefore of no concern to them. In the General Assembly's twelfth session, the French delegation repeatedly vocalized these sentiments. Alternate Yemeni representative Tawfik Chamandi said that he was "surprised, and no doubt many people are surprised, at the intransigence of the French Government and its insistence on suppressing the Algerian nationalist movement by killing the Algerians and destroying their homes." Apparently, he continued, "this is the French way of influencing people and winning enemies. It is time for the French Government to come down to realities and admit that there is no way out of its dilemma except by recognizing the right of the Algerian people to self-determination and independence which is coming to them anyway."[112] Moroccan minister for foreign affairs and chairman of the delegation Ahmed Balafrej discussed the "direct and daily impact of this war on the internal situation in Morocco." He cautioned how it "might well poison our relations with France," a public political threat French officials did not appreciate.[113] Saudi Arabian minister of state for United Nations affairs Ahmad Shukairy asserted that "it [did] not require a genius to state the case for Algeria. In plain words, the Algerians, like any other people in the world, have an inherent right to sovereignty and independence. The position of France in Algeria is a position of imperialism—pure and simple—and no amount of eloquence can defend [it]."[114] And Egyptian minister for foreign affairs Dr. Mahmoud Fawzi called for an end to Algerian humiliation: "While the French Parliament indulges in its endless and barren debate, while it topples one ministry after another, and while we are made for the millionth time to hear the crazy notion that, because some French lawyers in Paris have written an article into their country's laws saying that Algeria is part of France, the people of Algeria must be treated as things and as serfs."[115] Their punitive words over the course of several days repeatedly attacked French colonial policy in a manner rarely seen at the United Nations and testified to the level of deep-seated anger over the war. Their comments also revealed a belief that Shukairy summarized as the Arab world's "obligation to sponsor the cause of Algeria," because "the Algerians are our kith and kin, and Algeria is an integral part of the Arab fatherland."[116] Within three years Asian, African, Middle Eastern, Soviet, even Irish representatives took a clear position against French action and, in front of hundreds, called for an end to the conflict in Algeria.

This amount of vitriol directed toward the French in such a public setting prompted officials to respond to the onslaught of verbal attacks and try to preserve their national reputation. Though UN military consequences were unlikely, persistent colonial violations, as articulated by Algerian allies, put the colonial administration on the defensive. For the first time, the French permanent representative to the United Nations Guillaume Georges-Picot told those assembled in the 700th Plenary Meeting that his country "did not oppose the inclusion of [Algeria] in the agenda of the present session, though this attitude in no way implies any renunciation of the fundamental rights to which [France] is entitled under Article 2, paragraph 7, of the Charter."[117]

Georges-Picot, as Hervé Alphand had done before him, concentrated on UN intervention rather than answer members' accusations that colonial efforts to preserve Algeria violated fundamental principles of the organization and its foundational text. Did they believe, he inquired, "they [were] right in encouraging outside intervention calculated to prolong the bloody phase of the struggle or in asking the United Nations to intervene in a conflict which it [had] neither the right nor the means to settle?" And did they think "their attitude had played an insignificant part in encouraging the rebels to reject, as they have done so far, the repeated French proposals for a cease-fire, followed by free elections?"[118] According to Georges-Picot, UN critics were disrupting French attempts to eradicate "anarchy and poverty, and probably even civil war" through pacification, reform, and development and asserted that it was "in the interests of the Algerian people and of world peace" to continue suppressing the FLN.[119] He abandoned the previous line of reasoning that Algeria was beyond the scope of UN debate and insinuated that French officials were pursuing a democratic end with free elections. He did not elaborate on the conditions required for a cease-fire at this point, nor was he ready to concede that Algeria was not part of France. However, the fact Georges-Picot constructed a careful rebuttal to members' concerns rather than merely ignoring them or shutting them down by citing Article 2(7) suggests the French delegation felt diplomatically isolated and compelled to win over international allies. American and British delegations, two that previously voted in support of the French position, remained noticeably quiet on the Algerian question during the General Assembly's twelfth session further amplifying the need for Georges-Picot to temper his tone.

Changing Tides Toward Self-Determination, 1958–1962

French representative Georges-Picot's diplomatic attempts earned France a degree of goodwill by the conclusion of the session in December 1957. But it quickly vanished in February 1958 when the French military bombed the Tunisian city of Sakiet Sidi Youssef, killing eighty people including women and children. This would be the first of many significant events in 1958 that shifted the course of the war and led to its end.

The Algerian-Tunisian border had long been a site of conflict between the French military and Algerian fighters, and after Tunisian independence, President Bourguiba committed to Algerian liberation, aided the transportation of arms to the FLN, and provided ALN troops with training grounds across his border. Bourguiba's assistance aggravated French military plans, but it did not stop targeted attacks against the FLN and ALN across the border. Historian Alistair Horne estimates that between September 1957 and January 1958 more than eighty shooting incidents occurred over the frontier but nothing as dramatic as the Sakiet Sidi Youssef bombing. In retaliation for French planes being shot down by what the military perceived as an FLN-base, B-26 bombers "flattened the village."[120]

In light of these events, Tunisian UN representative Mongi Slim wrote to the Security Council, informing it of "French aggression" against his country's sovereignty.[121] His letter and the several that followed that spring exposed an inconvenient truth. The war undeniably had reached international proportions and threatened the region's security, precisely the point Saudi UN representative Asad Al-Fiqih had tried to make three years prior. The French bombing of Sakiet Sidi Youssef was a "nightmare scenario" for American and British politicians. They feared that "French policy was bound to embroil Algeria's neighbors in the unwinnable struggle," first in Tunisia and then in Morocco and Libya. Soon, U.S. secretary of state Dulles told Ambassador Alphand, "France would find itself fighting the whole of North Africa, supported by Nasser's Egypt and other Arab states, and they would be armed and financed by the Soviet Union and communism."[122] From Dulles's perspective, French political leaders had lost control of the military and its actions threatened to incite a war across the entire Maghrib, an outcome he desperately wanted to avoid.

Dulles was worried that Ambassador Slim would take the Sakiet Sidi Youssef affair to the UN and place the United States "in an impossible dilemma" by asking it to vote against France. In order "to preserve [U.S.] credibility in the world organization and its coveted relations with the African and Asian bloc," Dulles worked with British representatives and offered to conduct a good offices mission aimed at restoring Franco-Tunisian relations. Nationalist newspaper *El Moudjahid* noted that the Americans wanted to avoid "unanimous disapproval" from the Third World.[123] Thwarting a public denouncement of the failing French Fourth Republic administration, Dulles and British diplomats mediated and temporarily restored their Western alliance. However, as historians Irwin Wall and Matthew Connelly have shown, Sakiet Sidi Youssef was a turning point in the war that demanded a drastically different approach if the French government wanted to avoid Algeria turning into a legitimate international confrontation.[124]

On 13 May 1958, three months after Sakiet Sidi Youssef, Charles de Gaulle returned to power, representing a second major shift in French policy. M'hamed Yazid, one of the FLN delegates in New York, immediately questioned what this would mean for the Algerian cause and wondered how it would impact the American position on the war.[125] Conservative French military leaders, such as Raoul Salan, initially supported de Gaulle and believed his vast experience, especially during World War II, would prove useful in suppressing the FLN and maintaining *Algérie française*. De Gaulle agreed to take power on the condition that his government would have full powers. He also announced his plans for a new constitution. In hindsight, "such an outcome," writes one historian, "underlines de Gaulle's razor-sharp political skills," for he anticipated many of the challenges ahead and gave himself room to maneuver.[126] Moreover, he was already looking ahead to international developments such as the European Economic Community and a loosely defined "Eurafrica," envisioning how to restore France's reputation on the world stage and a possible future that did not include formal empires.[127]

Historical tides were turning and de Gaulle was sensitive to them. He did not waste any time in launching a referendum campaign for a new constitution in September 1958, which would allow men and women in France and Algeria to cast a vote in favor or against Fifth Republic institutions. Ultimately, voters in France and Algeria demonstrated overwhelming support for de Gaulle's new constitution. In France voter turnout was 84.94 percent, of which 66.41 percent said yes. In Algeria, 80 percent of the population voted and 96 percent of those people voted in favor of the new constitution.[128] The referendum campaign was a huge success for de Gaulle, and he continued introducing new policies for Algeria through the fall of 1958, most notably the five-year Constantine Plan.

The FLN also underwent seismic changes that fall, culminating in the Provisional Government of the Algerian Republic (GPRA). The FLN leadership, constantly trying to find ways of presenting itself as a functional state, assembled in Cairo on 19 September and held a press conference to announce the new government. Ferhat Abbas, Benyoucef Benkhedda, and M'hamed Yazid, all dressed in suits standing before the Algerian flag, relied heavily on symbolism. If the nationalists were truly going "to challenge French sovereignty, they had to show [they] were not 'murderers' or 'criminals.' They had to exude gravitas. They had to project the image of respectable statesmen ready for national office."[129] It was not that the FLN inherently changed or adopted wildly different policies. Rather, the GPRA was another step in creating an easily recognizable diplomatic corps that performed like any other. Most of the FLN leaders assumed new titles. For example, Mohamed Khider became minister of state and Mohamed Debaghine became minister of foreign affairs. Their core mission for external recognition remained the same, and, if anything, their pursuit of Arab, African, and Asian support intensified.[130]

President Charles de Gaulle, forced to contend with the Provisional Government of the Algerian Republic's diplomatic efforts, worked quietly with military leaders and foreign officials to find a mutually agreeable solution to the Algerian conflict that would satisfy supporters of French Algeria and balance regional and international interests in the area. As did numerous French authorities before him, de Gaulle found this task nearly impossible. But given the pressure the French delegation now faced at the United Nations, in public and in private, he made a dramatic gesture that undeniably influenced the war's outcome and sheds light on how significant world opinion about France's reputation was to him.

On 16 September 1959, the same day the fourteenth session of the UN General Assembly began, de Gaulle delivered a shocking speech, the contents of which few were prepared for. He declared that "taking into account all the givens: Algerian, national and international, I consider necessary that the principle of self-determination be proclaimed from today."[131] His words were a momentous departure from previous French government's official position on Algeria. For the first time publicly, de Gaulle recognized Algeria's right to self-determination. Even though he did not spell out what "all the givens" were, the French president indicated the war was taking an unacceptable toll at home and tarnishing France's reputation.

Logistically, Algerians would choose between secession with no further connection to France, integration with continued access to French financial, military, and educational assistance, or Algerian self-government in a referendum. All of these options were in line with the UN Charter because they permitted the Algerian people to choose their form of government. De Gaulle's pronouncement was popular among the FLN, albeit still insufficient because it said nothing about full sovereignty and cease-fire conditions. French settlers and extreme-right military personnel thought de Gaulle had betrayed them. More than anything, his announcement revealed an acute awareness that Algeria was "a terrible burden" to French international relations. His speech was "a true watershed; nothing that went before was any longer relevant, and nothing could be the same again."[132]

The Provisional Government of the Algerian Republic led by Ferhat Abbas seized on de Gaulle's political concession. In a declaration circulated on 28 September 1959, Abbas reminded readers that "inscribed in the United Nations Charter, self-determination, meaning the right of peoples to have it, restores the exercise of sovereignty to the Algerian people." Fears that "open consultation" would result in "anarchy and misery" were unfounded, and failure to begin exploring ways to end the conflict "would only aggravate and pose a permanent threat to international peace and security," he said. The GPRA demonstrated knowledge of the UN Charter and the organization's priorities. It also showed that the Algerian leadership was following UN resolutions because this declaration ended by saying it was "ready to enter into *pourparlers* with the French government, and discuss the political and military conditions for cease-fire, [and] the conditions and guaranties for the application of self-determination."[133] The nationalists studied the United Nations and tracked the progression of debates closely enough that they creatively incorporated essential components of them into their own press statements and newspaper articles.

De Gaulle's tectonic shift also had important ramifications for the Algerian question in the United Nations. That fall African and Asian UN members still had to campaign for Algeria's inscription onto the agenda of the General Assembly's fifteenth session, and its allies continued to barrage the UN with letters on the Algerians' behalf.[134] These efforts soon bore fruit. When the United Nations convened in December, the General Assembly passed Resolution 1573.[135] This resolution differed significantly from previous ones. It acknowledged "the two parties concerned have accepted the right of self-determination as the basis for the solution of the Algerian problem," a direct reference to de Gaulle's 1959 speech. Up until this point, the French delegates had denied this right to the Algerian nationalists and people. But now, in front of the world and in writing, they had to recognize "the passionate yearning for freedom of all dependent peoples and the decisive role of such peoples in the attainment of their independence." The French government had to accept "the right of the Algerian people to self-determination and independence" and comply with UN efforts "to contribute towards the successful and just implementation of this right."[136]

Furthermore de Gaulle's concession enabled the United States to pursue openly a diplomatic "middle course."[137] For the first time in five years, the Americans could discreetly work with members of the French government and Algerian representatives to try to negotiate a settlement that factored in their geopolitical and Cold War concerns. U.S. officials wanted to limit their direct support of de Gaulle because it could "seriously" infringe upon their "ability to influence the Algerians directly," but they were particularly sensitive to earlier French threats that France would withdraw from NATO if Eisenhower and Dulles did not support *Algérie française*.[138]

The 1960 resolution coincided with the largest membership expansion since the UN's founding. Seventeen new countries were admitted, sixteen of which were African.[139] It was also passed in the same week as the Declaration on the Granting of Independence to Colonial Countries and Peoples, highlighting UN transformation during decolonization and the role of "Third World actors" as "principal arbiters of power."[140] Self-determination debates were among the most contentious in the early 1950s, particularly for France, Britain, and the United States, whose representatives went to great lengths to argue against it.[141] But by 1960, they were outnumbered and the international climate had changed.[142] They could no longer rely on their political preferences dominating the UN agenda.

In years past, French, Asian, Arab, and Soviet ambassadors delivered lengthy remarks about Algeria. In the 1960 General Assembly, African representatives, many of whom had recently gained independence from France, took center stage and discussed what they thought should happen there. For some, such as the minister of Mali Mamadou Aw, the stakes were clear. Aw thought the United Nations should take more concrete steps (intervention) in overseeing de Gaulle's call for Algerian self-determination. More than one year had passed since the French president's speech and the conflict raged on. Aw intuited that de Gaulle needed UN support to implement self-determination in order to "confront a minority in Algeria made up of settlers and a few officers who want a French Algeria." Aw suggested that the General Assembly show "some kind of indication of support from world opinion, which would tell France, tell ... the Algerians the desired guarantee."[143] Aw was not sure de Gaulle could carry out his project without such an endorsement.

Others, such as Ambassador Frédéric Guirma from Upper Volta, took a different approach and expressed trepidation at the idea of intervention. He told those members in the plenary meeting he respected the ideas of cooperation and wished his Algerian "brothers" well but that his country was "not prepared to intervene unconditionally in the dispute."[144] Guirma acknowledged the hard-fought battles of both sides, the Algerian people and "the heroic courage of General de Gaulle." And while he supported the principle of self-determination for the Algerians, his government was not prepared to take any more concrete steps against the French president.[145] Rapid membership expansion did not yield uniform voting records in the African bloc as Aw's and Guirma's opposing viewpoints reveal. As Western European countries and the United States hedged and voted on Algeria to preserve their national interests, so too did African nations. Upper Volta, though not a member of the French Community, foresaw potential future complications in its relationship with France if it came out strongly in favor of intervention in Algeria. Therefore, Guirma proceeded cautiously, trying to balance African solidarity with postcolonial diplomatic and economic realities.

Algeria did not become a voting member of the United Nations until 8 October 1962. Even though de Gaulle's self-determination speech and the December 1960 Declaration on the Granting of Independence to Colonial Countries and Peoples buoyed their chances for national liberation, Algerian nationalists and their supporters still had more work to do before the world recognized Algerian sovereignty.

Arab allies were the Algerians' most vocal supporters until the war's end and they persevered in their letter-writing campaign. The UAR National Congress in Cairo demanded that the UN secretary-general halt French aggression.[146] Fifteen men who worked for Iraqi Airways underlined their shared cultural heritage and told the UN that "Arab Algeria is, has been and shall be for Arab Algerians." They wanted the UN to recognize the GPRA as the legitimate political mouthpiece of the Algerian struggle because they thought this gesture would help bring a peaceful resolution to the conflict.[147] Egyptian president Gamal Abdel Nasser, Moroccan king Hassan II, Malian president Modibo Keita, GPRA president (1961–1962) Benyoucef Benkhedda, and representatives for Guinean president Sékou Touré and Ghanaian president Kwame Nkrumah convened a conference in Cairo in August 1961. At this meeting of the so-called Casablanca Powers, they reaffirmed their "support for the Algerian Provisional Government and to the Algerian people in their struggle for independence, with a view for safeguarding Algeria's unity and territorial integrity."[148] The United Nations received a copy of their communiqué and filed it with a report on UN resolutions pertaining to Algeria. Global pressure for Algerian independence did not let up. Algeria's allies maintained significant pressure in 1961 to ensure that the United Nations could not turn a blind eye any longer.

When Algerian independence seemed imminent in the spring of 1962, foreign governments outside of the Third World started recognizing the Provisional Government of the Algerian Republic. For example, in March 1962, the Soviet minister of foreign affairs conferred de jure status on the GPRA. French government officials were furious over what they called an "unfriendly gesture to France."[149] France had been diplomatically brought to its knees by this point, and, even still, government representatives could not stomach the fact that the Algerians had outplayed them on this unconventional battlefield.

Conclusion

Algeria at the United Nations truly was a matter of global concern, and even though Algerian nationalists did not make it there officially until 1962 when their country was accepted for membership, the Algerian question maintained a strong presence at the UN for the duration of the war. This is in large part attributable to the FLN's multidimensional international strategy that relied on Third World allies and a skilled diplomatic corps.

Algerian participation in the 1955 Bandung Conference, only six months into the war, solidified important contacts in the Third World and laid the foundation for representatives from Asia, the Middle East, and Africa to campaign at the UN for the Algerian cause. FLN delegates, namely M'hamed Yazid, Hocine Aït Ahmed, Hocine Lahouel, and Mohamed Khider, traveled abroad and carefully orchestrated diplomatic missions during which they met government officials, campaigned for political and financial support, and crafted a media and press offensive. Moreover, the nationalists benefited from international events beyond their control, including Moroccan and Tunisian independence, the Suez Crisis, the Hungarian Revolution, and escalating Cold War tensions. Charles de Gaulle's return to power introduced another series of unexpected events that significantly impacted the war's outcome.

The United Nations, as conceived in 1945, and its charter were unprepared for internal conflicts and decolonization, as evidenced by stalemate discussions over Articles 2, 34, and 35 between French representatives and Algerian allies. The original UN architects understood potential contradictions between self-determination and state sovereignty, especially as it pertained to existing empires. They were committed to international peace and security and wanted to implement safeguards against military aggression. However, after months of trying to resolve, or at least minimize, these contradictions, the final UN Charter opened the door for liberation movements and their allies to lodge viable complaints against colonial powers whose military action risked destabilizing entire regions and upsetting diplomatic relations.

The Algerian war obtained a reoccurring role at the United Nations and exposed institutional vulnerabilities but also unforeseen political possibilities. Algerian nationalists' success co-opting universal language and capitalizing on relationships with newly independent nations in the Third World capable of presenting a case on their behalf in international venues foreshadows a process that nonstate actors would hone and refine in the final decades of the twentieth century.[150] Moreover, it demonstrates the FLN's political acumen and success in changing the shape of UN debates and the structure of the organization and demanding their right to self-determination as outlined in the UN Charter.

Conclusion

Independence does not offer itself, it must be taken.

—Ferhat Abbas, 1960

In June 1961, President de Gaulle's administration and Provisional Government of the Algerian Republic (GPRA) leaders met on Lake Geneva to attempt negotiating a cease-fire to the war. Shortly thereafter, *El Moudjahid* published an article explaining why the talks broke down. The Algerian nationalists who had traveled to Evian, among them Belkacem Krim, Houari Boumediene, and the future first president of independent Algeria, Ahmed Ben Bella, firmly maintained their political position regarding the fundamental principles "of our struggle and of the hopes of an entire people. [They] call for independence of Algeria, territorial integrity of the country, [and] full and complete sovereignty of the people." The nationalist publication claimed that the French government knew these issues to be nonnegotiable. Despite this fact, according to a 25 June 1961 *El Moudjahid* article, French delegates came "to Evian with a secret ambition; curb [GPRA] positions on essential problems" and encourage the Algerian representatives "to abandon their principles." For the article's authors, failure to attain those political goals would "be serious" and "inexcusable." The stakes for the Algerians, and the colonized world more broadly, was "the solution to the colonial problem" and "recognition of a certain number of universal principles."[1]

The universal principles to which *El Moudjahid* referred, self-determination and national sovereignty, lay at the heart of the Algerian war. These concepts, old adages of international relations, had been recently renovated in the wake of World War II. The UN Charter, the Universal Declaration of Human Rights, and the Geneva Conventions of 1949 introduced a new vocabulary and set of rights to people around the world. They offered entry into a previously closed (to non-Western actors) international political arena and placed Third World actors on more equal footing with their American and European counterparts and armed them with language that was globally recognized as legitimate for making political claims. As Ferhat Abbas noted, colonized peoples did not achieve independence easily. The process was often long, violent, and riddled with disappointments. But 1950s revolutionaries who were committed to national liberation and freedom from imperial domination had an additional arsenal of rhetorical weapons to deploy against their oppressors, enabling them to (re)take their country.

The French and Algerians did not negotiate a cease-fire until March 1962 (Figure 14). They met again in Evian and decided on a several-month transition toward independence. In the final months of *Algérie francaise*, both sides worked to spell out agreeable conditions regarding specific economic policies

Figure 14. Members of the GPRA delegation at the negotiations for the Evian Accords, which established a cease-fire, 18 March 1962. (Corbis)

and rights to the Sahara, withdrawing French troops, and questions of citizenship that would shape future relations between the countries. On 18 March, after eleven days of tense discussions, representatives for French president Charles de Gaulle and the Provisional Government of the Algerian Republic signed a ninety-three-page document, which recognized Algerian sovereignty. Even though they interpreted the Evian agreement differently, de Gaulle made a television announcement declaring the accord "a common-sense solution." The GPRA heralded it as the culmination and justification for its efforts since 1954. The Algerian leadership believed the end of the war sent a message to the world that it had taken the country back. Algerian leaders emphasized that part of their success came from the "rights and freedom enshrined in the United Nations Charter," showing the charter's power and influence in molding the decolonization process.[2] GPRA premier Benyoucef Benkhedda released a cautiously optimistic statement about the Evian agreements. However, he knew difficult terrain lay ahead before Algerian sovereignty was fully restored.[3]

Between April and September 1962, nearly one million Europeans left Algeria for France, and their departure was swift and somewhat unexpected. The French government had anticipated that the repatriation process would take place gradually, over the course of several years. Instead, it was confronted with hundreds of thousands of individuals with various European backgrounds who left en masse, "a migration" that was "immediately named the 'exodus.'"[4] This rush to get out of Algeria also meant that most professionals, skilled laborers, and organizations departed for France and left the newly independent country "in crisis" and in dire need of trained personnel across all sectors of society.[5]

The Algerian leadership installed Ben Bella as head of state to begin the challenging task of nation building and repatriating hundreds of thousands of Algerian refugees who had been displaced during the war.[6] The celebratory and triumphant spirit of 1962 quickly dissipated as internal political struggles continued within the revolutionary guard. Algeria's new leaders confronted the daunting reality of having to address the technical and intellectual dearth the French left behind, as well as face the tremendous loss of life. The Ben Bella government (1962–1965) and subsequent Houari Boumediene regime (1965–1978) tried to address the economic and social deficiencies by developing a strong state and focusing on economic growth. These policies, especially after 1965, were ideologically founded on the notion of economic nationalism.[7] By concentrating on economic growth and nationalizing industry, these leaders aimed to improve the chronic underdevelopment from the colonial period, increase literacy and employment rates, and expand state infrastructure and available services. The new officials claimed they wanted to develop the public sector but their policies revealed they prioritized the private sector over the public one.

Postcolonial Algeria confronted a plethora of challenges that were often made worse by poor decisions that impeded social and political development. Nowhere is this fact more apparent than in the rapid unraveling of the leadership's purported commitment to rights and humanitarian practices that helped the nationalists win Algerian independence. On 19 June 1965, Boumediene, former National Liberation Army chief of staff along the Algerian-Moroccan border (1960–1962) and defense minister under Ben Bella, staged a bloodless coup. Operating under Boumediene's orders, armed men captured and imprisoned Ben Bella, the president of the National Assembly (Hadj Ben Alla), and two ministers (Mohamed Nekkache and Abderhamane Cherif). Their family members were not allowed to see them for several months, neither could their lawyers.[8] Rumors, which were later confirmed through reports, interviews, and medical examinations, began circulating about the poor treatment Algerian soldiers and policemen inflicted on them. Groups with a diverse membership from Europe and North Africa wrote letters to the United Nations on Ben Bella's behalf. They were alarmed by allegations of torture and the blatant disregard for human rights in Algeria.[9]

The United Nations continued to receive inquiries about the hundreds of political prisoners that Boumediene's security forces arrested in the summer and fall of 1965.[10] UN officials frequently were unable to obtain concrete information regarding their whereabouts and the security forces' alleged torture techniques akin to those infamously inflicted by the French army on Algerian soldiers and civilians during the Algerian war. The Boumediene regime remained tightlipped and relied on the tested notion that what happens within Algeria's borders is a private internal matter.

The dramatic violation of human rights under Boumediene raises important questions about the nature of power and authority in independent Algeria. Revolutionary theorist Frantz Fanon famously wrote that "decolonization is always a violent phenomenon."[11] The relationship between colonized and colonizer was marked by violence. The colonizer required the constant use of force in order to maintain his supremacy. Therefore, for Fanon, it is easy to understand how and why the colonized internalized violence and used it to overthrow their oppressors. But the colonized may have internalized violence so deeply that when they had the opportunity to run their own sovereign nations, they exercised the same methods of control over their own people.

The FLN waged a long war against the French on and off the battlefield, and a central component of the nationalists' strategy for internal and external recognition had been their proclaimed commitment to rights and humanitarianism. But this commitment had limitations. Once Algeria became independent, its heads of state were not particularly wed to upholding those pledges, as illustrated by Boumediene's coup and subsequent authoritarian regime. Moreover, they would rely on the same techniques as the French colonial government to try to keep international organizations and foreign inquiries at bay. The dubious human rights record in Algeria after 1962, however, does not discredit the innovative approach Algerian nationalists adopted to help them win the war and that was later emulated by nonstate actors for decades to come.

This book has shown how the post-1945 moment created international institutions and universal rights discourse about health, humanitarianism, and self-determination. Third World leaders used this language to articulate political claims that Western countries and imperial powers had to recognize. World War I began this process with the League of Nations and the circulation of self-determination as a universal concept, but these preliminary tools proved insufficient to fully articulate claims for sovereignty by people under European colonial rule. The scale of World War II's destruction, however, revitalized an internationalist spirit whereby American and Western diplomats reaffirmed their commitment to global security and went to considerable lengths to create institutions and doctrines that would ensure this goal. But the world had changed dramatically since the Paris Peace Conference in 1919, and the seeds for colonialism's collapse were in motion. Within five years of the Second World War's end, the International Committee of the Red Cross met to revise the Geneva Conventions and extend humanitarian protections, representatives from nearly fifty countries gathered in San Francisco to devise the United Nations and work out its charter, and human rights were redefined in influential documents such as the Universal Declaration of Human Rights. These, combined with ubiquitous frustration and discontent across the colonized world, furnished the ideal setting for waging a different kind of war against colonial governments.

The Algerian war is one of the most dramatic and ultimately successful cases in the history of decolonization. France's long and total rule of Algeria would not be relinquished easily; in order for nationalists to compete against the formidable French army and diehard advocates of *Algérie française*, they needed a strategy that went beyond the physical battlefield. The language of health, humanitarianism, and rights imparted the FLN with such ammunition and enabled its representatives to fashion themselves as diplomats and take their fight to the international arena. To that end, they developed a sophisticated local, regional, and international strategy that changed the face of national liberation movements and expanded political possibilities for nonstate actors.

When the FLN initiated the war in November 1954, most parts of the country were underdeveloped. Health was one area in which this was most pronounced. But chronic neglect also presented an opportunity for improvement and propaganda. The French and the Algerians seized the language of health and welfare and created health-service divisions that previously did not exist to win the hearts and minds of the people. Through their respective programs that distributed free medical care, they tried to project existing and aspiring state power and demonstrate their full commitment for the future. The French wartime programs, particularly the Special Administrative Sections (SAS) health-care initiatives reached a formidable number of patients and circulated among areas that previously had all but been ignored by the colonial state. Their efforts, notable and extensive, were undermined, however, by a constant shortage of funding, supplies, and participants. Given the level of need, it is not surprising the French medical programs were overwhelmed, yet the extent of their continued efforts indicates an awareness of how powerful a message the provision of health care could be.

The FLN also recognized the power of transmitting a message to the population, the French administration, and the international community through the adoption of a set of practices based on universal discourse. Its leadership created a domestic health-service division to do just that. Although it struggled during the first two years of the war, after the Soummam Congress in August 1956, Algerian doctors, nurses, and medical students were able to provide basic care to the people.

In line with the FLN proclamation to internationalize the conflict, representatives embarked upon expanding their medical division beyond the domestic realm and created the Algerian Red Crescent (CRA). This undertaking marked explicit engagement with one of the most influential universal rhetorics, humanitarianism, while broadening the reach of the nationalists' influence and donor base. By establishing the Algerian Red Crescent and recasting its image as humanitarian, the FLN demonstrated it was conversant in a particular language dating back a century. Algerian nationalists entered into a relationship with the Geneva-based International Committee of the Red Cross and its delegates and became part of a global network of national societies all committed to the tenants of humanitarianism. The Algerian Red Crescent and its international outreach and propaganda campaigns granted the nationalists access to a highly respected and internationally recognized group. Moreover, they offered a direct rebuttal of French depictions of them as barbaric and violent, incapable of running an independent Algeria.

Algerian leaders pursued an aggressive strategy of targeting international organizations and used them to their advantage. The ICRC had recently revised the Geneva Conventions but had not anticipated the conundrums of decolonization and internal conflicts. When the Algerian war broke out, the organization was still reeling from its failures during World War II and its silence and complicity in German atrocities, and, as such, its delegates were committed to restoring its image and reputation. But neither the ICRC representatives nor the Geneva Conventions were prepared for the sustained violence and relentless politicking by both the French and Algerians. Despite French officials' unwillingness to make meaningful changes based on the organization's mission reports, the Algerian leadership used the ICRC platform and relationships with particular delegates to harness the organization's moral authority and aid for political gain.

The Algerians set their sights on the ICRC for its humanitarian dimensions. They pursued the United Nations and its charter for their particular emphasis on self-determination and political rights. The UN Charter, unlike the revised Geneva Conventions of 1949, had anticipated decolonization, and its Western architects tried mercilessly to exclude concrete language that Third World leaders could use to achieve national liberation. But their efforts did not go far enough because the Algerian nationalists did exactly that. They dissected the charter and appropriated its language to make arguments for their sovereignty. Though not permitted to represent itself at the United Nations in an official capacity during the war, the Algerian leadership solicited and enlisted a throng of supporters in the Third World to advocate and present the nationalist case at the UN on its behalf, illustrating their collective strength and signaling a major shift in international relations.

The Algerian war was a seminal moment that exposed the failure of the French empire and republicanism and represented a watershed moment in decolonization. Nationalists, outnumbered and militarily outmaneuvered, bypassed the traditional means of waging war and adopted a comprehensive strategy that relied upon appropriating universal discourses that had been redefined after 1945. The post–World War II political climate produced important documents and international organizations that transformed the international arena and produced a language accessible to *all* political actors, whether they were imperial powers or Third World revolutionaries. The terminology was general, meant to protect as many people as possible, but, as Erez Manela has noted, "rhetoric in the international arena has unintended audiences, and actions beget unintended consequences."[12]

Algerian nationalists' actions are one example of these unintended consequences. They took potent rhetorics about health, humanitarianism, and rights, the same ones Western leaders applied to their own citizens, and framed them in such a way that they could not be ignored. They developed this strategy at home, first with the creation of its health-services division and focusing on the provision of basic health care, and then quickly expanded it beyond Algeria's borders with the Algerian Red Crescent. Nationalists' campaigns reached the corridors of the International Committee of the Red Cross and United Nations and successfully forced the Algerian question, and decolonization more broadly, onto their agendas.

These nonstate actors managed to take their particular quest for national liberation and turn it into an international affair. They would not permit the French to define the conflict as internal and therefore of little significance to any other country or group of people. Nationalists worked tirelessly to construct an image of themselves as modern global citizens entitled to the same rights and benefits as their Western counterparts. Additionally, they aimed to show the people and the world that they were capable of providing for the Algerian population. They were well versed in international diplomacy and, given the dangerous and violent circumstances of a colonial war, they did a remarkable job of acting like a functional state. The creative Algerian approach yielded fruitful results and garnered admiration and support from all corners of the globe. The nationalist strategy showed the tangible power of discourse and, when used with acumen, despite the odds, how political aspirations for sovereignty could be transformed into reality. The Algerians' struggle, and ultimately, their success, served as a compelling symbol of freedom from oppression and colonialism and influenced how claims were made for decades to come.

Notes

Introduction

1. Quoted in Mustapha Makaci, *Le Croissant-Rouge Algérien* (Algiers: Éditions Alpha, 2007), 131–138.

2. William Hitchcock, "Human Rights and the Laws of War: The Geneva Conventions of 1949," in *The Human Rights Revolution: An International History*, ed. Akira Iriye, Petra Goedde, and William Hitchcock (New York: Oxford University Press, 2012), 93–112.

3. Archives du Comité International de la Croix-Rouge (hereafter ACICR), B AG 202 008-007.1, Ferhat Abbas to ICRC president, 11 June 1960.

4. Matthew Connelly, *A Diplomatic Revolution: Algeria's Fight for Independence and the Origins of the Post–Cold War Era* (New York: Oxford University Press, 2002); Irwin Wall, *France, the United States, and the Algerian War* (Berkeley: University of California Press, 2001).

5. Most important, Raphaëlle Branche, *La torture et l'armée pendant la guerre d'Algérie* (Paris: Gallimard, 2001); Benjamin Brower, *A Desert Named Peace: The Violence of France's Empire in the Algerian Sahara, 1844–1902* (New York: Columbia University Press, 2011); Jim House and Neil MacMaster, *Paris 1961: Algerians, State Terror, and Memory* (Oxford: Oxford University Press, 2006); Marnia Lazreg, *Torture and the Twilight of Empire: From Algiers to Baghdad* (Princeton, N.J.: Princeton University Press, 2008); Fabian Klose, *Human Rights in the Shadow of Colonial Violence: The Wars of Independence in Kenya and Algeria* (Philadelphia: University of Pennsylvania Press, 2013); Pierre Vidal-Naquet, *La raison d'état* (Paris: Éditions de Minuit, 1962); Vidal-Naquet, *La torture dans la République: Essai d'histoire et de politique contemporaines, 1954–1962* (Paris: Éditions de Minuit, 1972); Vidal-Naquet, *Les crimes de l'armée française: Algérie, 1954–1962* (Paris: La Découverte & Syros, 2001).

6. Frantz Fanon, *A Dying Colonialism*, trans. Haakon Chevalier (New York: Grove Press, 1965); Fanon, *The Wretched of the Earth*, trans. Constance Farrington (New York: Grove Press, 1965).

7. Not all SAS efforts were directed at the health-care domain. It was an extensive program that included political, social, and economic components.

8. Grégor Mathias, *Les Sections Administratives Spécialisées en Algérie: Entre idéal et réalité, 1955–1962* (Paris: L'Harmattan, 1998), 11.

9. Sunil Amrith, *Decolonizing International Health: India and Southeast Asia, 1930–65* (New York: Palgrave Macmillan, 2006), 10. Gyan Prakash makes a similar argument in *Another Reason: Science and the Imagination of Modern India* (Princeton, N.J.: Princeton University Press, 1999), chap. 5. Throughout the book I use the term "Third World" (as opposed to global South) in an effort to historicize the prevalent 1950s and 1960s ideology as well as to reflect those states, national liberation movements, and individuals who actively crafted a Third World identity. For a

discussion on the use of Third World versus global South, see Odd Arne Westad, "The Cold War and the Third World," in *The Cold War in the Third World*, ed. Robert J. McMahon (New York: Oxford University Press, 2013), 208–219.

10. Mohammed Benaïssa Amir, *Contribution à l'étude de l'histoire de la santé en Algérie: Autour d'une expérience vécue en ALN Wilaya V* (Algiers: Office des Publications Universitaires, 1986), 109.

11. Studies of the International Committee of the Red Cross during the Algerian war that use newly available Red Cross archival material include Raphaëlle Branche, *Prisonniers du FLN* (Paris: Payot, 2014); and Klose, *Human Rights in the Shadow of Colonial Violence.*

12. Jean Bodin, *On Sovereignty: Four Chapters from "The Six Books of the Commonwealth,"* ed. and trans. Julian H. Franklin (Cambridge: Cambridge University Press, 1992); Stephan D. Krasner, *Sovereignty: Organized Hypocrisy* (Princeton, N.J.: Princeton University Press, 1999); Carl Schmitt, *Political Theology: Four Chapters on the Concept of Sovereignty* (Chicago: University of Chicago Press, 2006).

13. See Lauren Benton's excellent work, *A Search for Sovereignty: Law and Geography in European Empires, 1400–1900* (Cambridge: Cambridge University Press, 2009), esp. chap. 6. Also see Anthony Anghie, *Imperialism, Sovereignty and the Making of International Law* (Cambridge: Cambridge University Press, 2007); Olivier Beaud, *La puissance de l'état* (Paris: Presses Universitaires de France, 1994); Mary Dewhurst Lewis, *Divided Rule: Sovereignty and Empire in French Tunisia, 1881–1938* (Berkeley: University of California Press, 2014).

14. John Hutchinson and Anthony D. Smith, eds., *Nationalism* (Oxford: Oxford University Press, 1994).

15. John Darwin, "Decolonization and the End of Empire," in *The Oxford History of the British Empire*, vol. 5, *Historiography*, ed. Robin Winks (New York: Oxford University Press, 1999), 552; Dane Kennedy, "Imperial History and Post-Colonial Theory," in *The Decolonization Reader*, ed. James Le Sueur (New York: Routledge, 2003), 10–22.

16. Jeffrey James Byrne, "The Pilot Nation: An International History of Revolutionary Algeria, 1958–1965" (Ph.D. diss., London School of Economics, 2010); Jon Alterman, *Egypt and American Foreign Assistance, 1952–1956: Hopes Dashed* (New York: Palgrave Macmillan, 2002); Byrne, "The Pilot Nation"; Paul Thomas Chamberlin, *The Global Offensive: The United States, the Palestine Liberation Organization, and the Making of the Post–Cold War Order* (New York: Oxford University Press, 2012); Nathan Citino, *From Arab Nationalism to OPEC: Eisenhower, King Sa'ud, and the Making of U.S.-Saudi Relations* (Bloomington: Indiana University Press, 2002); Guy Laron, *Origins of the Suez Crisis: Postwar Development Diplomacy and the Struggle over Third World Industrialization, 1945–1956* (Baltimore: Johns Hopkins University Press, 2013); Salim Yaqub, *Containing Arab Nationalism: The Eisenhower Doctrine and the Middle East* (Chapel Hill: University of North Carolina, 2004).

17. Benjamin Stora, *La gangrène and l'oubli: La mémoire de la guerre d'Algérie* (Paris: La Découverte, 1991). This "amnesia," which lasted throughout the 1980s, stems from two sources. First, the 1962 Evian Accords stipulated that soldiers, nationalists, and policemen could not be prosecuted for their wartime actions, thus forcing a public and private silencing about the war. Second, archival material on the war years was extremely difficult to access in France and Algeria. The "amnesia" did not reflect a lack of historians' interest in the war. Raphaëlle Branche, "The State, the Historians, and the Algerian War in French Memory, 1991–2004," in *Contemporary History on Trial: Europe Since 1989 and the Role of the Expert Historian*, ed. Harriet Jones, Kjell Ostberg, and Nico Randeraad (Manchester: Manchester University Press, 2007), 159–173; Joshua Cole, "Massacres and Their Historians: Recent Histories on State Violence in France and Algeria in the Twentieth Century," *French Politics, Culture, and Society* 28, no.1 (Spring 2010): 106–126. Pierre Vidal-Naquet was one of the few French historians who wrote about Algeria and French military torture during the 1960s and 1970s. See *La raison d'état* and *La torture dans la République.*

18. Stora, *La gangrène and l'oubli*, 248.

19. Some of the most influential works published after 2000 include Branche, *La torture et l'armée pendant la guerre d'Algérie*; Sylvie Thénault, *Une drôle de justice: Les magistrats dans la guerre d'Algérie* (Paris: La Découverte, 2001); Vidal-Naquet, *Les crimes de l'armée française*.

20. Paul Aussaresses, *Services Spéciaux: Algérie, 1955–1957* (Paris: Perrin, 2001).

21. Louisette Ighilahriz, *Algérienne*, as told to Anne Nivat (Paris: Fayard/Calmann Lévy, 2001).

22. Claire Marynower, "Être socialiste dans l'Algérie colonial: Practiques, cultures et identités d'un milieu partisan dans le département d'Oran, 1919–1939" (Ph.D. diss., Sciences Po, 2013); Malika Rahal, "L'Union Démocratique du Manifeste Algérien (1946–1956): Histoire d'un parti politique; L'autre nationalisme algérien" (Ph.D. diss., Institut national des langues et civilisations orientales, 2007).

23. Some examples include Commandant Azzedine, *On nous appelait fellaghas* (Paris: Stock, 1976); Claudine Chaulet and Pierre Chaulet, *Le choix de l'Algérie: Deux voix, une mémoire* (Algiers: Éditions Barzakh, 2012); Messaoud Djennas, *Vivre, c'est croire: Mémoires, 1925–1991* (Algiers: Casbah, 2006); Ali Haroun, *La 7ᵉ wilaya: La guerre du FLN en France, 1954–1962* (Paris: Seuil, 1986); Mohamed Lemkami, *Les hommes de l'ombre: Mémoires d'un officier du MALG* (Algiers: Éditions ANEP, 2004); Michel Martini, *Chroniques des années algériennes, 1946–1962* (Saint-Denis: Éditions Bouchène, 2002); Mohamed Teguia, *L'Armée de libération nationale en wilaya IV* (Algiers: Casbah, 2006).

24. Raphaëlle Branche, "The Martyr's Torch: Memory and Power in Algeria," *Journal of North African Studies* 16, no. 3 (2011): 431–444.

25. Mohammed Harbi, *Aux origines du FLN* (Paris: Christian Bourgois, 1975); Harbi, *Le FLN, mirage et réalité* (Paris: Éditions Jeune Afrique, 1980); Mohammed Harbi and Gilbert Meynier, *Le FLN: Documents et histoire, 1954–1962* (Paris: Fayard, 2004); Gilbert Meynier, *Histoire intérieure du FLN, 1954–1962* (Algiers: Casbah, 2003); Daho Djerbal, *L'Organization Spéciale de la Fédération de France du FLN: Histoire de la lutte armée du FLN en France (1956–1962)* (Algiers: Éditions Chihab, 2012); Nedjib Sidi-Moussa, *Le MNA: Le Mouvement National Algérien (1954–1956)* (Paris: L'Harmattan, 2008).

26. Meynier, *Histoire intérieure du FLN*; Wall, *France, the United States, and the Algerian War*; Odd Arne Westad, *The Global Cold War: Third World Interventions and the Making of Our Times* (Cambridge: Cambridge University Press, 2005).

27. Connelly, *A Diplomatic Revolution*.

28. Byrne, "The Pilot Nation."

29. Mark Mazower, *No Enchanted Palace: The End of Empire and the Ideological Origins of the United Nations* (Princeton, N.J.: Princeton University Press, 2009), 7.

30. For the British case, see A. W. Brian Simpson, *Human Rights and the End of Empire: Britain and the Genesis of the European Convention* (Oxford: Oxford University Press, 2004).

31. Erez Manela, *The Wilsonian Moment: Self-Determination and the International Origins of Anticolonial Nationalism* (Oxford: Oxford University Press, 2007).

32. The League of Nations, the precursor to the United Nations, provided a public forum in which leaders could debate the political and social questions of the day. But during the interwar period anticolonial leaders and nonstate actors did not play a decisive role in these discussions. Susan Pedersen, "Back to the League of Nations," *American Historical Review* 112, no. 4 (2007): 1091–1117.

33. Frederick Cooper, *Citizenship Between Empire and Nation: Remaking France and French West Africa, 1945–1960* (Princeton, N.J.: Princeton University Press, 2014).

34. Patricia Clavin, *Securing the World Economy. The Reinvention of the League of Nations, 1920–1946* (Oxford: Oxford University Press, 2013); Mark Mazower, *Governing the World: The History of an Idea* (New York: Penguin Press, 2012); Pedersen, "Back to the League of Nations."

35. Samuel Moyn and Jan Eckel would disagree. Moyn goes so far as to argue that "recent attempts to place anticolonialism in human rights history must first face up to an era when the human rights idea has no movement and anticolonialism, a powerful movement, used other

concepts. Human rights, as we understand them today, did not take shape until the 1970s." Samuel Moyn, "Imperialism, Self-Determination, and the Rise of Human Rights," in *The Human Rights Revolution: An International History,* ed. Akira Iriye, Petra Goedde, and William Hitchcock (New York: Oxford University Press, 2012), 161. Moyn presents a version of the same argument in Samuel Moyn, *The Last Utopia: Human Rights in History* (Cambridge, Mass.: Harvard University Press, 2010), chap. 3. Eckel's position is slightly more nuanced. While he challenges that "the ideas and the politics of human rights" were key components in the decolonization process, which led to indepen- dence, he acknowledges that human rights served as a "sporadic strategy of legitimizing their strug- gle against colonialism." Jan Eckel, "Human Rights and Decolonization: New Perspective and Open Questions," *Humanity* 1, no. 1 (2010): 111–135, quote at 112–113. For a similar argument to Eckel's, see Andreas Eckert, "African Nationalists and Human Rights," in *Human Rights in the Twentieth Century,* ed. Stefan-Ludwig Hoffmann (Cambridge: Cambridge University Press, 2011), 283–300.

36. Kenneth Cmiel, "The Recent History of Human Rights," *American Historical Review* 109, no. 1 (2004): 117–135; and Hitchcock, "Human Rights and the Laws of War," 96.

37. Cmiel, "Recent History of Human Rights," 125. On the role of the Third World and social rights, see Roland Burke, "Some Rights Are More Equal Than Others: The Third World and the Transformation of Economic and Social Rights," *Humanity* 3, no. 3 (2012): 427–448.

38. Akira Iriye and Petra Goedde, "Introduction: Human Rights as History," in *The Human Rights Revolution: An International History,* ed. Akira Iriye, Petra Goedde, and William Hitchcock (New York: Oxford University Press, 2012), 3–24, Stefan-Ludwig Hoffmann, "Introduction: Gene- alogies of Human Rights," in *Human Rights in the Twentieth Century,* ed. Stefan-Ludwig Hoffmann (Cambridge: Cambridge University Press, 2011), 1–26.

39. Cmiel, "Recent History of Human Rights," 127.

40. Many scholars argue that the 1970s is when the human rights regime truly took shape. Jan Eckel and Samuel Moyn, eds., *The Breakthrough: Human Rights in the 1970s* (Philadelphia: Univer- sity of Pennsylvania Press, 2013); Barbara J. Keys, *Reclaiming American Virtue: The Human Rights Revolutions of the 1970s* (Cambridge, Mass.: Harvard University Press, 2014); Sarah Snyder, *Human Rights Activism and the End of the Cold War: A Transnational History of the Helsinki Network* (Cambridge: Cambridge University Press, 2011).

41. Moyn, *The Last Utopia.* For examples of how anticolonial nationalists used the language of human rights, see Roland Burke, *Decolonization and the Evolution of International Human Rights* (Philadelphia: University of Pennsylvania Press, 2010); Daniel Maul, *Human Rights, Development, and Decolonization: The International Labor Organization, 1940–1970* (New York: Palgrave Mac- millan, 2012); Bradley Simpson, "Self-Determination, the End of Empire, and the Fragmented Dis- course of Human Rights in the 1970s," *Humanity* 4, no. 2 (2013): 239–260; Meredith Terretta, " 'We Had Been Fooled into Thinking That the UN Watched Over the Whole World': Human Rights, UN Trust Territories, and Africa's Decolonization," *Human Rights Quarterly* 34, no. 2 (2012): 329–360. Fabian Klose's work provides a necessary intervention in the history of human rights and decoloni- zation. He argues that the evolution of the human rights regime was intimately connected to the end of empire. He compares British Kenya and French Algeria and shows how the colonial regimes implemented states of emergency to bypass applying universal rights in the colonies. The French and British were keenly aware that their use of excessive violence served as sources of government embarrassment and therefore went to great lengths to cover up the blatant tension between simul- taneously advocating for human rights and violating them. Klose, *Human Rights in the Shadow of Colonial Violence*; Klose, "Source of Embarrassment: Human Rights, State of Emergency, and the Wars of Decolonization," in *Human Rights in the Twentieth Century,* ed. Stefan-Ludwig Hoffmann (Cambridge: Cambridge University Press, 2011), 237–257; Klose, "The Colonial Testing Ground: The International Committee of the Red Cross and the Violent End of Empire," *Humanity* 2, no. 1 (2011): 107–126.

42. Frederick Cooper's *Decolonization and African Society* was a pioneering work that showed

the power of making claims based on universal discourse in European colonies. He demonstrated how "African labor movements seized the new discourse of administrators," pertaining to the labor crisis in the 1930s and 1940s, "and turned assertions of control into demands for entitlements: if colonial officials wanted Africans to work like their idealized European workers, they should pay them on a similar scale and bargain with them in good faith." Frederick Cooper, *Decolonization and African Society: The Labor Question in French and British Africa* (Cambridge: Cambridge University Press, 1996), 3.

43. For the influence of Cuba's revolution and role in African decolonization, see Piero Gleijeses, *Conflicting Missions: Havana, Washington, and Africa, 1959–1976* (Chapel Hill: University of North Carolina Press, 2002). The Palestine Liberation Organization employed similar tactics as the FLN by targeting the international arena to legitimize their claims. See Chamberlin, *The Global Offensive.*

Chapter 1. The Long Road to War

1. Initially Ben M'hidi's death was called a suicide, but it was later revealed members of the French military killed him on 3 or 4 March 1957 while in custody.

2. The ten agenda items were objectives and reasons for the meeting, general overview of military, financial, and political matters for each region in Algeria, political platform, standardization of military, political, and administrative matters, FLN doctrines and institutions, acceptable National Liberation Army (ALN) terminology, FLN and ALN reports, material needs, major issues to concentrate on, such as cease-fire conditions, negotiations, and the United Nations, and, finally, diverse matters including Kabylia. Procès-verbal du Congrès de la Soummam, 20 August 1956, in Mohammed Harbi, *Les archives de la révolution algérienne* (Paris: Éditions Jeune Afrique, 1981), 160–161.

3. Ibid., 161–162.

4. Ibid., 162.

5. Ibid., 163–164.

6. The seventeen primary CNRA members were Mustapha Ben Boulaïd, Youcef Zighoud, Belkacem Krim, Amar Ouamrane, Mohamed Larbi Ben M'hidi, Rabah Bitat, Ramdane Abane, Benyoucef Benkhedda, Idir Aïssat, Mohamed Boudiaf, Hocine Aït Ahmed, Mohamed Khider, Ahmed Ben Bella, Mohammed Lamine, Ferhat Abbas, Tewfik El Madani, and M'hamed Yazid. The seventeen CNRA substitute members were Ben Boulaid's assistant, Lakhdar Bentobbal, Saïd Mohammedi, Slimane Dehiles, Abdelhafid Boussouf, Ali Mellah, Mohammed-Seddik Benyahia, Mohamed Lebjaoui, Abdelmalek Temmam, Saad Dahlab, the General Union of Algerian Workers (UGTA, two spots), Salah Louanchi, Tayeb Taalbi, Abdelhamid Mehri, Ahmed Francis, and Brahim Mezhoudi.

7. Harbi, *Les archives*, 165. Dahlab was in prison during the Soummam Congress and was replaced by Temam Abdelmalek.

8. Ibid., 166–167.

9. Letter from Ben Bella to the Direction Exécutive du FLN, fall 1956, in Harbi, *Les archives de la révolution algérienne*, 168.

10. Connelly, *A Diplomatic Revolution.*

11. On the French conquest of Algeria, see Osama Abi-Mershed, *Apostles of Modernity: Saint-Simonians and the Civilizing Mission in Algeria* (Stanford, Calif.: Stanford University Press, 2010); Patricia Lorcin, *Imperial Identities: Stereotyping, Prejudice and Race in Colonial Algeria* (New York: I. B. Tauris, 1995); Jennifer Sessions, *By Sword and Plow: France and the Conquest of Algeria* (Ithaca, N.Y.: Cornell University Press, 2011); John Ruedy, *Modern Algeria: The Origins and Development of a Nation* (Bloomington: Indiana University Press, 1992).

12. On colonial violence in nineteenth-century Algeria, see Brower, *A Desert Named Peace.*

13. On French colonial rule in Algeria and its consequences between 1870 and 1920, see Pierre Bourdieu and Abdelmalek Sayad, *Le déracinement: La crise de l'agriculture traditionelle en Algérie* (Paris: Éditions de Minuit, 1964); Allan Christelow, *Muslim Law Courts and the French Colonial State in Algeria* (Princeton, N.J.: Princeton University Press, 1985); Kamel Kateb, *Européens, "indigènes," et juifs en Algérie (1830–1962): Répresentations et réalités des populations* (Paris: Institut national d'études démographiques, 2001); David Prochaska, *Making Algeria French: Colonialism in Bône, 1870–1920* (Cambridge: Cambridge University Press, 1990); George R. Trumbull IV, *An Empire of Facts: Colonial Power, Cultural Knowledge, and Islam in Algeria, 1870–1914* (Cambridge: Cambridge University Press, 2009). For recent work on Jews in Algeria, see Jessica Hammerman, "The Heart of the Diaspora: Algerian Jews During the War for Independence" (Ph.D. diss., City University of New York, 2013); Ethan Katz, "Jews and Muslims in the Shadow of Marianne: Conflicting Identities and Republican Culture in France (1914–1975)" (Ph.D. diss., University of Wisconsin–Madison, 2009); Joshua Schreier, *Arabs of the Jewish Faith: The Civilizing Mission in Colonia Algeria* (New Brunswick, N.J.: Rutgers University Press, 2010); Sarah Abrevaya Stein, *Jews and the Fate of French Algeria* (Chicago: University of Chicago Press, 2014).

14. Charles-Robert Ageron, *Histoire de l'Algérie contemporaine*, vol. 2, *De l'insurrection de 1871 au déclenchement de la guerre de libération (1954)* (Paris: Presses Universitaires de France, 1979), 232. Also see Ageron, "Le mouvement 'Jeune Algérien' de 1900 à 1923," in *Études maghrébines: Mélanges*, Charles-André Julien, ed. (Paris: Presses Universitaires de France, 1964), 217–243; John Ruedy, "Chérif Benhabylès and the Young Algerians," in *Franco-Arab Encounters: Studies in Memory of David Gordon*, ed. L. Carl Brown and Matthew S. Gordon (Syracuse, N.Y.: Syracuse University Press, 1997); Mahfoud Smati, *Les jeunes algériens: Correspondances et rapports, 1837–1918* (Algiers: Thala, 2011).

15. Ophthalmologist Belkacem Benthami, one of the few Algerian doctors in Algiers, was among the signatories. For an account of Benthami's role in Algerian politics and local medical community, see Hannah-Louise Clark, "Doctoring the *Bled*: Medical Auxiliaries and the Administration of Rural Life in Colonial Algeria, 1904–1954" (Ph.D. diss., Princeton University, 2014), chap. 2.

16. " Le Manifeste jeune algérien, (juin 1912)" in Claude Collot and Jean-Robert Henry, eds., *Le mouvement national algérien: Textes, 1912–1954* (Paris: L'Harmattan, 1978), 23–24.

17. There is a discrepancy among scholars as to the number of wounded during World War I; Martin Evans cites 57,000, whereas John Ruedy and Charles-Robert Ageron cite 72,000. Evans, *Algeria: France's Undeclared War* (Oxford: Oxford University Press), 44; Ruedy, *Modern Algeria*, 111; Ageron, *Histoire de l'Algérie contemporaine*, 261.

18. Alice Conklin, *A Mission to Civilize: The Republican Idea of Empire in France and West Africa, 1895–1930* (Stanford, Calif.: Stanford University Press, 1997); Richard Fogarty, *Race and War in France: Colonial Subjects in the French Army, 1914–1918* (Baltimore; Johns Hopkins University Press, 2012); Richard Fogarty and Andrew Jarboe, eds., *Empires in World War I: Shifting Frontiers and Imperial Dynamics in a Global Conflict* (New York: I. B. Tauris, 2014).

19. "President Woodrow Wilson's Fourteen Points," at http://avalon.law.yale.edu/20th_century/wilson14.asp (accessed on 26 May 2014).

20. Erez Manela, *The Wilsonian Moment: Self-Determination and the International Origins of Anticolonial Nationalism* (Oxford: Oxford University Press, 2007).

21. "Mémoire adressé au Congrès de la Paix par le Comité Algéro-Tunisien en Janvier 1919," in Collot and Henry, *Le mouvement national algérien*, 25–30; "La 'Fraternité algérienne' (janvier 1922)," in Collot and Henry, *Le mouvement national algérien*, 30–31.

22. The clergy (*'ulamā*) in Algeria and across the Arab world tested one such vision. They articulated a clear platform for spiritual renewal. They gravitated toward modern religious reform (*islāh*) and participated in the *salafiyya* movement. The *'ulamā* were primarily concerned with inner personal and cultural reform, not political reform or independence through violence. The *'ulamā*, and

especially 'Abd al-Hamid Ben Badis (1889–1940), enjoyed moderate success in Algeria but charismatic leaders promoting qualitative changes to daily life under French rule appealed to a broader demographic. James McDougall, "The Shabiba Islamiyya of Algiers: Education, Authority and Colonial Control, 1921–57," *Comparative Studies of South Asia, Africa and the Middle East* 24, no. 1 (2004): 18–25; McDougall, *History and the Culture of Nationalism in Algeria* (Cambridge: Cambridge University Press, 2006); Abdelkader Djeghloul, "La formation des intellectuels algériens modernes, 1880–1930," *Revue algérienne des sciences juridiques, économiques et politiques* 22, no. 4 (1985): 639–664; Mahfoud Kaddache, *Histoire du nationalism algérien. Question nationale et politique algérienne, 1919–1951* (Algiers: ENAL, 1993); Jean-Claude Vatin, "Seduction and Sedition: Islamic Polemical Discourses in the Maghreb," in *Islam and the Political Economy of Meaning: Comparative Studies of Muslim Discourse*, ed. William R. Roff (Berkeley: University of California Press, 1987).

23. Ferhat Abbas, *Le jeune Algérien (1930): De la colonie vers la province* (Paris: Garnier, 1981).

24. Evans, *Algeria*, 56.

25. Ferhat Abbas, "Mon testament politique," in Charles-Robert Ageron, "Un manuscrit inédit de Ferhat Abbas: 'Mon testament politique,'" *Revue française d'histoire d'outre mer* 81, no. 303 (1994): 188.

26. "Interview de Ferhat Abbas au journal tunisien *L'Action*, janvier 1956," in Harbi and Meynier, *Le FLN*, 222.

27. UN ARMS, S-0188-005-08, Department of Political and Security Council Affairs, Confidential Note on Algeria, 20 June 1956.

28. Mahfoud Bennoune, "The Introduction of Nationalism to Rural Algeria, 1919–1954," *Maghreb Review* 2, no. 3 (1977): 1–12; Emmanuel Sivan, "The Étoile Nord Africaine and the Genesis of Algerian Nationalism," *Maghreb Review* 3, nos. 5–6 (1978), 17–22; Benjamin Stora, *Messali Hadj: Pionnier du nationalisme algérien 1898–1974* (Paris: L'Harmattan, 1986). For an overarching account of the development of Algerian nationalism, see André Nouschi, *La naissance du nationalisme algérien* (Paris: Éditions de Minuit, 1962).

29. Ruedy, *Modern Algeria*, 137.

30. Sivan, "The Étoile Nord Africaine," 17–22.

31. Evans, *Algeria*, 65.

32. Ibid.

33. Ageron, *Histoire de l'Algérie contemporaine*, 389–402.

34. Ibid., 449.

35. Quoted in Ageron, *Histoire de l'Algérie contemporaine*, 453.

36. Ruedy, *Modern Algeria*, 141.

37. Quoted in Ageron, *Histoire de l'Algérie contemporaine*, 392.

38. Mohammed Harbi, *Le FLN: Mirage et Réalité* (Paris: Éditions J.A., 1980), 23.

39. "L'Algérie devant le conflit colonial: Manifeste du peuple algérien," in Collot and Henry, *Le mouvement national algérien*, 162.

40. Hocine Aït Ahmed, *Mémoires d'un combattant* (Algiers: Barzah, 2009), 24.

41. Jean-Pierre Peyroulou, *Guelma, 1945: Une subversion française dans l'Algérie coloniale* (Paris: La Découverte, 2009), 26.

42. In addition to launching air assaults on Europe and invading France and Italy from North Africa in the final years of World War II, the American presence in Morocco and Algeria set a precedent for the United States "to intervene in France's empire as well as its domestic affairs" after 1945. Ferhat Abbas did not factor in American foreign policy interests nor could he have foreseen Algeria's strategic place in the Cold War. Connelly, *A Diplomatic Revolution*, 41.

43. Ruedy, *Modern Algeria*, 145.

44. Paul Gordon Lauren, *The Evolution of International Human Rights: Visions Seen* (Philadelphia: University of Pennsylvania Press, 2003), 138.

45. Nnamdi Azikiwe, a Nigerian nationalist and future president of the country, wrote about

"the electrifying impact" of the Atlantic Charter on West African populations in *The Atlantic Charter and British West Africa, Memorandum on Postwar Reconstruction of the Colonies and Protectorates in British West Africa* (Lagos: West African Press Delegation to Great Britain, 1943), 12. Nelson Mandela, the first president of post-apartheid South Africa, mentions that the Atlantic Charter also inspired the African National Congress, in his memoir *Long Walk to Freedom: The Autobiography of Nelson Mandela* (Boston: Back Bay Books, 1994), 83.

46. "L'Algérie devant le conflit colonial, Manifeste du peuple algérien," in Collot and Henry, *Le mouvement national algérien*, 163.

47. Ibid., 163–164.

48. Istiqlal (Independence), a Moroccan nationalist party, published a similar manifesto on 11 January 1944 with the following four demands: "an independent Morocco under Sidi Mohammed; that Sidi Mohammed himself should negotiate independence; that Morocco should sign the Atlantic Charter and take part in the peace conference; and that the Sultan should establish a democratic government." C. R. Pennell, *Morocco Since 1830: A History* (London: Hurst, 2000), 265.

49. Ruedy, *Modern Algeria*, 146.

50. Ageron, *Histoire de l'Algérie contemporaine*, 567.

51. "Statuts de l'Association des Amis du Manifeste et de la Liberté," in Collot and Henry, *Le mouvement national algérien*, 186.

52. Quoted in Ageron, *Histoire de l'Algérie contemporaine*, 570.

53. Ageron, *Histoire de l'Algérie contemporaine*, 572–573.

54. Peyroulou's *Guelma, 1945* is the leading work on this subject; he argues that the demonstrations were not an articulation of Algerian nationalism, but rather a settler insurrection (13). Also see Marcel Reggui, *Les massacres de Guelma, Algérie, mai 1945: Une enquête inédite sur la furie des milices coloniales* (Paris: La Découverte, 2006); Martin Thomas, "The Sétif Uprising and the Savage Economics of Colonialism," in *The French Colonial Mind*, vol. 2, *Violence, Military Encounters, and Colonialism*, ed. Martin Thomas (Lincoln: University of Nebraska Press, 2011), 140–173.

55. Evans, *Algeria*, 89. The death toll is disputed. John Ruedy explains: "French government estimates spoke of 1,500 dead, the army of 6,000 to 8,000, American sources from 7,000 to 40,000 and some Algerian nationalists of 45,000." Ruedy, *Modern Algeria*, 149.

56. Meynier, *Histoire intérieure du FLN*, 68.

57. "Mise au point du Bureau central des A.M.L." (18 May 1945), in Collot and Henry, *Le mouvement national algérien*, 208.

58. For a history of the UDMA, see Malika Rahal, "L'Union Démocratique du Manifeste Algérien"; and Rahal, "La place des réformistes dans le mouvement national algérien," *Vingtième Siècle: Revue d'histoire* 83 (2004): 161–171.

59. Harbi, *Le FLN*, 90.

60. Ibid., 114–117.

61. Jacques Simon, ed., *Biographies de Messali Hadj* (Paris: L'Harmattan, 2009).

62. 'Allal al-Fasi, *Al-harakat al-istiqlaliyya fi-l-Maghrib al-'Arabi* (Tangier: Abd al Salam Gassus, n.d.).

63. Connelly, *A Diplomatic Revolution*, 41.

64. Kenneth Perkins, *A History of Modern Tunisia* (Cambridge: Cambridge University Press, 2004), 110.

65. Ibid., 117.

66. Pennell, *Morocco Since 1830*, 276.

67. For histories of the conflict, see Anthony Clayton, *The Wars of French Decolonisation* (Harlow: Longman, 1994); William J. Duiker, "Ho Chi Minh and the Strategy of People's War," in *The First Vietnam War: Colonial Conflict and Cold War Crisis*, ed. Mark Atwood Lawrence and Fredrik Logevall (Cambridge, Mass.: Harvard University Press, 2007); Nicola Cooper, *France in Indochina: Colonial Encounters* (Oxford: Berg, 2001); Gilbert Bodinier, ed., *Le retour de la France en Indochine*,

1945–46 (Vincennes: SHAT, 1987); Bodinier, ed., *Indochine 1947: Règlement politique et solution militaire* (Vincennes: SHAT, 1987); David Schalk, *War and the Ivory Tower: Algeria and Vietnam* (Oxford: Oxford University Press, 1991).

68. For an analysis of the impact of the memory of French military defeat in Indochina, see, Stephen Tyre, "The Memory of French Military Defeat at Dien Bien Phu and the Defence of French Algeria," in *Defeat and Memory: Cultural Histories of Military Defeat in the Modern Era*, ed. Jenny Macleod (London: Palgrave Macmillan, 2008), 214–232.

69. On the cost of the war, see Hugues Tertrais, *La piastre et le fusil: Le coût de la guerre d'Indochine, 1945–1954* (Paris: Comité pour l'histoire économique et financière, 2002).

70. Norman Howard-Jones, *The Scientific Background of the International Sanitary Conferences, 1851–1938* (Geneva: World Health Organization, 1975); Amy Staples, *The Birth of Development: How the World Bank, Food and Agriculture Organization, and World Health Organization Changed the World, 1945–1965* (Kent, Ohio: Kent State University Press, 2006), esp. chap. 8; "International Sanitary Conferences," at http://ocp.hul.harvard.edu/contagion/sanitaryconferences.html (accessed 26 May 2014).

71. Susan Gross Solomon, Lion Murard, and Patrick Zylberman, eds., *Shifting Boundaries of Public Health: Europe in the Twentieth Century* (Rochester, N.Y.: University of Rochester Press, 2008). For histories of the League of Nations Health Organization, see Martin Davis Dubin, "The League of Nations Health Organization," in *International Health Organizations and Movements, 1918–1938*, ed. Paul Weindling (Cambridge: Cambridge University Press, 1995), 56–80; and Iris Borowy, *Coming to Terms with World Health: The League of Nations Health Organization, 1921–1946* (Frankfurt: Peter Lang, 2009).

72. Heather Bell, "Midwifery Training and Female Circumcision in the Inter-War Anglo-Egyptian Sudan," *Journal of African History* 39, no. 2 (1998): 293–312; Nancy Rose Hunt, *A Colonial Lexicon: Of Birth Ritual, Medicalization, and Mobility in the Congo* (Durham, N.C.: Duke University Press, 1999); Carol Summers, "Intimate Colonialism: The Imperial Production of Reproduction in Uganda, 1907–1925," *Signs* 16, no. 4 (1991): 787–807; Lynn Thomas, *Politics of the Womb: Women, Reproduction, and the State in Kenya* (Berkeley: University of California Press, 2003).

73. Heather Bell, *Frontiers of Medicine in the Anglo-Egyptian Sudan, 1899–1940* (Oxford: Clarendon Press, 1999); John Iliffe, *East African Doctors: A History of the Modern Profession* (Cambridge: Cambridge University Press, 1998); Megan Vaughan, *Curing Their Ills: Colonial Power and African Illness* (Stanford, Calif.: Stanford University Press, 1991).

74. Sokhieng Au, *Mixed Medicines: Health and Culture in Colonial Cambodia* (Chicago: University of Chicago Press, 2011); Prakash, *Another Reason*; Julie Livingston, *Debility and the Moral Imagination in Botswana* (Bloomington: Indiana University Press, 2005); Maryinez Lyons, "The Power to Heal: African Medical Auxiliaries in Colonial Belgian Congo and Uganda," in *Contesting Colonial Hegemony: State and Society in Africa and India*, ed. Dagmar Engels and Shula Marks (London: British Academic Press, 1994).

75. Kirk Hoppe, *Lords of the Fly: Sleeping Sickness Control in British East Africa, 1900–1960* (Westport, Conn.: Praeger, 2003); Maryinez Lyons, *The Colonial Disease: A Social History of Sleeping Sickness in Northern Zaire, 1900–1940* (Cambridge: Cambridge University Press, 1992); Deborah Neill, "Paul Ehrlich's Colonial Connections: Scientific Networks and Sleeping Sickness Drug Therapy Research, 1900–1914," *Social History of Medicine* 22, no. 1 (2009): 61–77; Randall Packard, "Maize, Cattle, and Mosquitoes: The Political Economy of Health and Disease in Colonial Swaziland," *Journal of African History* 25, no. 2 (1984): 189–212; Michael Worboys, "The Comparative History of Sleeping Sickness in East and Central Africa, 1900–1914," *History of Science* 32 (1994): 89–102.

76. Ageron, *Histoire de l'Algérie contemporaine*, 472–473.

77. Joseph Hodge, *Triumph of the Expert: Agrarian Doctrines of Development and the Legacies of British Colonialism* (Athens: Ohio University Press, 2007), 16–17.

78. Helen Tilley, *Africa as a Living Laboratory: Empire, Development, and the Problem of Scientific Knowledge, 1870–1950* (Chicago: University of Chicago Press, 2011).

79. On health programs in other colonial contexts, see Amrith, *Decolonizing International Health*; and Jessica Pearson-Patel, "From the Civilizing Mission to International Development: France, the United Nations, and the Politics of Family Health in Postwar Africa, 1940–1960" (Ph.D. diss., New York University, 2013).

80. On international development, see Staples, *The Birth of Development*.

81. Manela, *The Wilsonian Moment*.

82. Lauren, The *Evolution of International Human Rights*, 138. See Douglas Brinkley and David Facey-Crowther, eds., *The Atlantic Charter* (New York: St. Martin's Press, 1994). The Universal Declaration of Human Rights (UDHR) was conceived to have three parts: a declaration, a binding convention, and specific measures for implementation. Ultimately forty-eight states voted in favor of the UDHR in December 1948, but unfortunately it did not successfully outline practical methods for implementation. The UDHR helped to shape the Geneva Conventions of 1949. See M. Glen Johnson and Janusz Symonides, *The Universal Declaration of Human Rights: A History of Its Creation and Implementation, 1948–1998* (Paris: UNESO, 1998); William Korey, *NGOs and the Universal Declaration of Human Rights: A Curious Grapevine* (New York: St. Martin's Press, 1998); Johannes Morsink, *The Universal Declaration of Human Rights: Origins, Drafting, and Intent* (Philadelphia: University of Pennsylvania Press, 1999).

83. For general histories of the United Nations, see Robert C. Hilderbrand, *Dumbarton Oaks: The Origins of the United Nations and the Search for Postwar Security* (Chapel Hill: University of North Carolina Press, 1990); Paul Kennedy, *The Parliament of Man: The Past, Present, and Future of the United Nations* (New York: Random House, 2006); Mazower, *No Enchanted Palace*; Stephen Schlesinger, *Act of Creation: The Founding of the United Nations* (New York: Westview Press, 2003). For a history of human rights and the UN, see Roger Normand and Sarah Zaidi, *Human Rights at the UN: The Political History of Universal Justice* (Bloomington: Indiana University Press, 2008).

84. For treatment of the interplay between sovereignty, human rights, and empire, see James J. Sheehan, "The Problem of Sovereignty in European History," *American Historical Review* 111, no. 1 (2006): 1–15; Jeremy Adelman, "An Age of Imperial Revolutions," *American Historical Review* 113, no. 2 (2008): 319–340; Eric Weitz, "From the Vienna to the Paris System: International Politics and the Entangled Histories of Human Rights, Forced Deportations, and Civilizing Missions," *American Historical Review* 113, no. 5 (2008): 1313–1343; Bonny Ibhawoh, *Imperialism and Human Rights: Colonial Discourses of Rights and Liberation in African History* (Albany: State University of New York Press, 2007); Mikael Rask Madsen, "France, the UK, and the 'Boomerang' of the Internationalisation of Human Rights (1945–2000)," in *Human Rights Brought Home: Socio-Legal Perspectives on Human Rights in the National Context*, ed. Simon Halliday and Patrick Schmidt (Oxford: Hart, 2004); Anthony Pagden, "Human Rights, Natural Rights, and Europe's Imperial Legacy," *Political Theory* 31, no. 2 (2003), 171–199.

85. Ageron, *Histoire de l'Algérie contemporaine*, 571.

86. Among the most pressing cases between 1951 and 1953 were Tunisia's and Morocco's right to self-determination. See Martin Thomas, "France Accused: French North Africa Before the United Nations, 1952–1962," *Contemporary European History* 10, no. 1 (2001): 96–103.

87. Article 1(2) of the UN Charter states, "To develop friendly relations among nations based on respect for the principle of equal rights and self-determination of peoples, and to take other appropriate measures to strengthen universal peace." http://www.un.org/en/documents/charter/chapter1.shtml. However, this position frequently bristled against foreign policy interests. For example, NARA, RG 59, General Record of the Department of State, Lot 60D257, Box 18, Discussion of Dilemmas of U.S. Foreign Policy Objectives with Respect to Colonial Areas, 26 August 1952;

NARA RG 59, General Record of the Department of State, Lot 60D257, Box 18, Further Discussion of Dilemmas of U.S. Foreign Policy Objectives with Respect to Colonial Areas, 28 August 1952.

88. Thomas, "France Accused," 92.

89. Lauren, *The Evolution of International Human Rights*, 394–395.

90. NARA, RG 59, Bureau of International Organization Affairs, 1945–1974, Lot 82D211, Box 29, Memorandum on Conversation, 14 November 1952. For a history of Eleanor Roosevelt's role in advocating for human rights, see Mary Ann Glendon, *A World Made New: Eleanor Roosevelt and the Universal Declaration of Human Rights* (New York: Random House, 2001); and Allida Black, ed., *The Eleanor Roosevelt Papers: The Human Rights Years, 1945–1948* (Charlottesville: University of Virginia Press, 2010); Black, *The Eleanor Roosevelt Papers: The Human Rights Years, 1949–1952* (Charlottesville: University of Virginia Press, 2012).

91. For example, when Britain ratified the European Convention for the Protection of Human Rights and Fundamental Freedoms in 1953, the Foreign Office wanted to convince Europeans that Britain "was a good European" citizen and that it was committed to strengthening "the Western European bloc." Its representatives perceived the convention as a "feather in [their] caps," not a tool for colonial liberation. A. W. Brian Simpson, *Human Rights and the End of Empire*, 3–5.

92. Susan Pedersen makes a similar argument about how the League of Nations provided an international forum with shared administrative and ethical norms for states of different types and varying degrees of power. Pedersen, "Back to the League of Nations." For important histories of the League of Nations, see Donald S. Birn, *The League of Nations Union, 1918–1945* (Oxford: Oxford University Press, 1981); Michael D. Callahan, *Mandates and Empire: The League of Nations and Africa, 1914–1931* (Brighton: Sussex Academic Press, 1999); *The League of Nations, 1920–1946: Organization and Accomplishments; A Retrospective of the First Organization for the Establishment of World Peace* (New York: United Nations, 1996); F. S. Northedge, *The League of Nations: Its Life and Times, 1920–1946* (New York: Holmes & Meier, 1986).

93. David Forsythe, *The Humanitarians: The International Committee of the Red Cross* (Cambridge: Cambridge University Press, 2005), 55.

94. For further discussion of the Geneva Conventions see Chapter 5.

95. For an account of the Geneva Conventions revisions process, see Geoffrey Best, *War and Law Since 1945* (New York: Oxford University Press, 1994).

96. Mark Lewis, *The Birth of the New Justice: The Internationalization of Crime and Punishment, 1919–1950* (New York: Oxford University Press, 2014), chap. 8.

97. Ibid., 233. Lewis argues that European governments sought more specific protections for POWs and civilian populations depending on their experience with Nazi Germany during World War II.

98. Ibid., 234. Also see International Committee of the Red Cross, *Commission of Government Experts for the Study of Conventions for the Protection of War Victims, Geneva, April 14 to 26, 1947: Preliminary Documents Submitted by the International Committee of the Red Cross*, vol. 3, *Condition and Protection of Civilians in Time of War* (Geneva, 1947), 2–3.

99. The 1957 Mélouza massacres, a tragic event in which the FLN killed nearly three hundred followers of the Algerian Nationalist Movement, a rival political group, is an example of the continued struggle for power within the Algerian leadership.

Chapter 2. Medical Pacification and the Sections Administratives Spécialisées

1. FLN Proclamation, 1 November 1954, in Harbi, *Les archives de la révolution algérienne*, 101–102.

2. Ibid.

3. Phillip C. Naylor, *France and Algeria: A History of Decolonization and Transformation* (Gainesville: University Press of Florida, 2000), 18.

4. Quoted in Alistair Horne, *A Savage War of Peace: Algeria, 1954–1962* (New York: New York Review of Books, 2006), 98.

5. Ibid.

6. On 5 February 1955, Mendès-France lost a vote of confidence 319 to 273 at the National Assembly.

7. On the Vichy period, see Robert Paxton, *Vichy France: Old Guard and New Order, 1940–1944* (New York: Norton, 1975). For an analysis of how the memory of Vichy and Indochina impacted French resistance to the Algerian war, see Martin Evans, *The Memory of Resistance: French Opposition to the Algerian War, 1954–1962* (Oxford: Berg, 1997), chaps. 1–6.

8. Patrick Eveno and Jean Planchais, eds., *La guerre d'Algérie: Dossier et témoignages* (Paris: La Découverte/Le Monde, 1989), 103–106.

9. Ibid., 103.

10. Evans, *Algeria*, 132.

11. Eveno and Planchais, *La guerre d'Algérie*, 105.

12. David Galula, *The Pacification of Algeria, 1956–1958* (Santa Monica, Calif.: Rand Corporation, 2006), 12–13.

13. I use the term *pacification* without quotation marks throughout the book. This is not meant to exonerate the French military's violent tactics nor does it suggest colonial authorities did not frequently use this word as a euphemism for coercive measures. However, this chapter and the rest of the book emphasize the peaceful components of the pacification strategy. Consequently, I chose not to use quotation marks.

14. Mathias, *Les Sections Administratives Spécialisées*, 11.

15. Sylvie Thénault, *Histoire de la guerre d'indépendance algérienne* (Paris: Flammarion, 2005), 94.

16. Clark, "Doctoring the *Bled*," 1–4.

17. Mathias, *Les Sections Administratives Spécialisées*, 11; and Fanon, *A Dying Colonialism*.

18. Yvonne Turin, *Affrontements culturels dans l'Algérie coloniale: Écoles, médecines, religion, 1830–1880* (Paris: François Maspero, 1971), 21.

19. Ibid., 306.

20. Ibid., 77–83.

21. On medicine and the military during the colonization process, see Claire Fredj, "Les médecins de l'armée et les soins aux colons en Algérie (1848–1851)," *Annales de démographie historique* 113, no. 1 (2007): 127–154; William Gallois, *The Administration of Sickness: Medicine and Ethics in Nineteenth-Century Algeria* (London: Palgrave Macmillan, 2008); Patricia Lorcin, *Imperial Identities*; Lorcin, "Imperialism, Colonial Identity, and Race in Algeria, 1830–1870: The Role of the French Medical Corps," *Isis* 90, no. 4 (1999): 653–679; Yvonne Turin, "'Médecine de propagande' et colonisation, l'expérience de Bouffarick, en 1835," *Revue de l'Occident musulman et de la Méditerranée* 8, no. 1 (1970): 185–194. On treating the local population and their responses, see Claire Fredj, "Encadrer la naissance dans l'Algérie colonial: Personnels de santé et assistance à la mère et à l'enfant 'indigènes' (XIXe–début du XXe siècle)," *Annales de démographie historique* 122, no. 2 (2011): 169–203; Fredj, "'Et il les envoya prêcher le royaume de Dieu et guérir les malades . . .' (Luc, IX, 2): Soigner les populations au Sahara; L'hôpital mixte de Ghardaïa (1895–1910)," *Histoire, monde et cultures religieuses* 22, no. 2 (2012): 55–89; William Gallois, "Local Responses to French Medical Imperialism in Late Nineteenth-Century Algeria," *Social History of Medicine* 20, no. 2 (2007): 315–331; Bertrand Taithe, "Entre deux mondes: Médecins indigènes et médecine indigène en Algérie, 1860–1905," in *La santé des populations civiles et militaires: Nouvelles approches et nouvelles sources hospitalières, XVIIe–XVIIIe siècles*, ed. Élisabeth Belmas and Serenella Nonnis-Vigilante (Villeneuve d'Ascq: Presses Universitaires Septentrion, 2010), 99–112.

22. Nancy Gallagher, *Medicine and Power in Tunisia, 1780–1900* (Cambridge: Cambridge University Press, 1983); Anne Marcovich, "French Colonial Medicine and Colonial Rule: Algeria and Indochina," in *Disease, Medicine, and Empire: Perspectives on Western Medicine and the Experience of European Expansion*, ed. Roy MacLeod and Milton Lewis (New York: Routledge, 1988), 103–117; Anne-Marie Moulin, "Tropical Without the Tropics: The Turning-Point of Pastorian Medicine in North Africa," in *Warm Climates and Western Medicine: The Emergence of Tropical Medicine, 1500–1900*, ed. David Arnold (Atlanta: Rodopi, 1996), 160–180; Michael A. Osborne, *The Emergence of Tropical Medicine in France* (Chicago: University of Chicago Press, 2014).

23. Raymond Féry, *L'oeuvre médicale française en Algérie* (Calvisson: Éditions Jacques Gandini, 1994), 15.

24. Marcovich, "French Colonial Medicine," 106; Turin, *Affrontements culturels*, 11.

25. A large literature exists on medicine as a tool of European empires. See Daniel Headrick, *The Tools of Empire* (New York: Oxford University Press, 1981); Deepak Kumar, ed., *Science and Empire: Essays in Indian Context, 1700–1947* (Delhi: Anamika Prakashan, 1991); Roy MacLeod and Milton Lewis, eds., *Disease, Medicine, and Empire: Perspectives on Western Medicine and the Experience of European Expansion* (New York: Routledge, 1988); Teresa Meade and Mark Walker, eds., *Science, Medicine, and Cultural Imperialism* (New York: St. Martin's Press, 1991); Vicente Navarro, ed., *Imperialism, Health and Medicine* (London: Pluto Press, 1982); Bisamoy Pati and Mark Harrison, eds., *Health, Medicine, and Empire: Perspectives on Colonial India* (Hyderabad, India: Orient Longman, 2001); Patrick Petitjean, Catherine Jami, and Anne-Marie Moulin, eds., *Science and Empires: Historical Studies About Scientific Development and European Expansion* (Dordrecht: Kluwer, 1992); Lewis Pyenson, "Why Science May Serve Political Ends: Cultural Imperialism and the Mission to Civilize," *Berichte zur Wissenschaftgeschichte* 13 (1990): 69–81; Pyenson, *Civilizing Mission: Exact Sciences and French Overseas Expansion* (Baltimore: Johns Hopkins University Press, 1993). However, recent scholarship has analyzed how local actors made use of medicine and science to increase their social status and professional opportunities. Warwick Anderson and Hans Pols, "Scientific Patriotism: Medical Science and National Self-Fashioning in Southeast Asia," *Comparative Studies in Society and History* 1, no. 54 (2012): 93–113; Sylvia Chiffoleau, *Médecines et médecins en Egypte: Construction d'une identité professionnelle et projet médical* (Paris: L'Harmattan, 1997); Khaled Fahmy, "Medicine and Power: Towards a Social History of Medicine in Nineteenth-Century Egypt," in *New Frontiers in the Social History of the Middle East*, ed. Enid Hill (Cairo: American University in Cairo Press, 2001), 15–62; Clark, "Doctoring the *Bled*"; Cyrus Schayegh, *Who Is Knowledgeable Is Strong: Science, Class, and the Formation of Modern Iranian Society, 1900–1950* (Berkeley: University of California Press, 2009).

26. Turin, *Affrontements culturels*, 328.

27. Lorcin, "Imperialism, Colonial Identity, and Race," 655; Turin, *Affrontements culturels*, 145. Also see Fredj, "Les médecins de l'armée."

28. See M. W. Hilton-Simpson, *Arab Medicine and Surgery: A Study of the Healing Art in Algeria* (London: Oxford University Press, 1922); Marcovich, "French Colonial Medicine."

29. Hilton-Simpson, *Arab Medicine and Surgery*, 12–13.

30. Turin, *Affrontements culturels*, 317–318. However, these fears were not unique to non-Western cultures, and they continue to influence contemporary debate about vaccinations. For a discussion on the measles-mumps-rubella (MMR) vaccine debate in the United Kingdom and vaccination trials in the Gambia, see Melissa Leach and James Fairhead, *Vaccine Anxieties: Global Science, Child Health and Society* (London: Earthscan, 2007).

31. Ruedy, *Modern Algeria*, 45–79.

32. Gallois, *Administration of Sickness*, 9; Lorcin, *Imperial Identities*, 118–145.

33. See Féry, *L'oeuvre médicale française*, 13–14; and Lorcin, "Imperialism, Colonial Identity, and Race," 661–664. A similar process of medical transmission occurred with French psychiatrists in North Africa. Psychiatrists acted as medical pioneers in the nineteenth century. Their

Orientalist prejudices shaped their ideas about North African Muslims and ascribed to them "primitive mentalities" and "criminal impulsiveness" that excluded them from the rest of humanity. Richard Keller, *Colonial Madness: Psychiatry in French North Africa* (Chicago: University of Chicago Press, 2007), 7.

34. This is a process similar to that described by Megan Vaughan as occurring in East and Central Africa in the twentieth century. She writes that "in British colonial Africa, medicine and its associated disciplines played an important part in constructing the African as an object of knowledge, and elaborated classification systems and practices which have to be seen as intrinsic to the operation of colonial power." Vaughan, *Curing Their Ills*, 8. But not every early interaction between French physicians and North Africans was fraught with conflict. Nancy Gallagher's work on Tunisia provides an instructive example of how Europeans and Arabs practiced medicine side by side in the nineteenth century.

35. Quoted in Clark, "Doctoring the *Bled*," 12. Previously this quote was anonymously attributed in Gallagher, *Medicine and Power in Tunisia*, 95. Clark found the original reference that Tunisian medics attributed to Jonnart. Archives Nationales d'Outre-Mer, Aix-en-Provence, France (hereafter ANOM), ALG GGA 25H/30/5, Report by M. Malinas and M. Constivint, (1903/4), reference on 2.

36. Féry, *L'oeuvre médicale française*, 32; Marcovich, "French Colonial Medicine," 106; Keller, *Colonial Madness*, chaps. 2 and 3. But as Clark points out, only a small number of Algerians who needed medical care were able to take advantage of the free consultations because they were concentrated in the *centres de colonisation*, not the *douars* where the majority of the Algerian population resided. Clark, "Doctoring the *Bled*," 15.

37. Keller, *Colonial Madness*, 56. Hospitals in Egypt expanded in a similar pattern at the turn of the century. Most of the better hospitals with updated equipment and trained staff were privately owned and frequented by the European communities. Even though Egypt was not subject to the same kind of formal colonization, nor did it have a dominant settler community, it is still a useful comparison to gain a broader understanding of colonial public health in this period. Nancy Gallagher, *Egypt's Other Wars: Epidemics and the Politics of Public Health* (Syracuse, N.Y.: Syracuse University Press, 1990), 10. Philip Curtin makes a similar argument in *The Health of European Troops in the Conquest of Africa* (Cambridge: Cambridge University Press, 1998).

38. Mustapha Bourkaïb, *Contribution à l'étude de l'assistance médicale aux indigènes d'Algérie: Hôpitaux et infirmeries* (Algiers: Adolphe Jourdan, 1915), 30.

39. Keller, *Colonial Madness*, 85.

40. Hannah-Louise Clark's work makes an important contribution to the history of medicine in Algeria between 1900 and 1950, a period frequently overlooked in favor of the nineteenth century and the war for national liberation. Clark, "Doctoring the *Bled*."

41. Féry, *L'oeuvre médicale française*, 33.

42. Bourkaïb, *Contribution à l'étude*, 32.

43. Ibid., 38.

44. Féry, *L'oeuvre médicale française*, 53.

45. In 1944, primary school enrollment for Muslim students had reached 110,000, just under 9 percent of children between ages seven and fourteen. Ruedy, *Modern Algeria*, 126.

46. Archives du Service Historique de l'Armée de Terre, Vincennes, France (hereafter SHAT), 1H 2571, Gouvernement Général de l'Algérie, *Service de l'Information, Alger: Projets pour 1955–56*. This figure does not include military hospitals.

47. ANOM SAS DOC/3, Conférence de M. Marguerite, Médecin-Inspecteur Général des Services de la Santé Publique au Gouvernement de l'Algérie, Cours d'Administration Communale, Algiers, 1955.

48. Ibid.

49. Ibid.

50. Robert Lacoste, *Algérie: Quelques aspects des problèmes économiques et sociaux* (Algiers: Baconnier, 1957), SHAT 1H 2571.

51. The most notable laws and ordinances of the period were the ordinance of 24 September 1945 and subsequently the law of 9 August 1950, which regulated the midwife profession, and law no. 51-443 of 19 April 1951, which clarified physician, dentist, and pharmacist procedures. ANOM GGA 81F/1638.

52. ANOM GGA 81F/1603, *Journal Officiel de la République Française*, 7 October 1953.

53. Interview, Jean-Paul Grangaud, 10 March 2007, Algiers.

54. Interview, Jeanine Belkhodja, 25 March 2007, Algiers.

55. In August 1955, Algerians killed a small number of European civilians and the French carried out vicious reprisal killings. The number of casualties is contested. Alistair Horne cites thirty-seven Europeans deaths, while Jacques Soustelle claimed seventy-one had been murdered. The French responded by killing disproportionate numbers of Algerians, some claiming as high as twelve thousand. Horne, *A Savage War of Peace*, 119–123. Prior to the massacres, the FLN had forbid targeting European civilians. And John Ruedy writes that until Philippeville, "the war had little impact on the settlers." Ruedy, *Modern Algeria*, 162.

56. For example, see Galula, *The Pacification of Algeria*.

57. Lazreg, *Torture and the Twilight of Empire*, 15. Also see Alf Andrew Heggoy, *Insurgency and Counterinsurgency in Algeria* (Bloomington: Indiana University Press, 1972); and Vidal-Naquet, *Les crimes de l'armée française*.

58. For a discussion of the global origins of revolutionary warfare, see Ian Beckett, ed., *The Roots of Counter-Insurgency: Armies and Guerrilla Warfare, 1900–1945* (London: Blandford Press, 1988); and Paul Villatoux and Marie-Catherine Villatoux, *La République et son armée face au "péril subversif": Guerre et action psychologiques en France, 1945–1960* (Paris: Les Indes Savantes, 2005), for an analysis of the ways in which France developed new methods of subversive warfare in Indochina and Algeria.

59. Lazreg, *Torture and the Twilight of Empire*, 17.

60. Jacques Frémeaux, "Les SAS (sections administratives spécialisées)," *Guerres mondiales et conflits contemporains* 208, no. 4 (2002): 56.

61. Todd Shepard, *The Invention of Decolonization: The Algerian War and the Remaking of France* (Ithaca, N.Y.: Cornell University Press, 2006), 47.

62. James Le Sueur, *Uncivil War: Intellectuals and Identity Politics During the Decolonization of Algeria* (Lincoln: University of Nebraska Press, 2005), 63.

63. Mathias, *Les Sections Administratives Spécialisées*, 11–14. Soustelle conceived of a second initiative in 1955, the Service des Centres Sociaux, which targeted the education sphere. Germaine Tillion, a French anthropologist who conducted fieldwork in the Aurès region between 1934 and 1940 and was considered one of the leading French experts on Algeria, was asked to assist the colonial government in this endeavor. Tillion argued that education was one of the most crucial elements that could improve a population's social condition, and that the colonial regime could no longer deny responsibility for Algeria's situation. It needed to start building schools, medical facilities, and provide job opportunities. See Germaine Tillion, *L'Algérie en 1957* (Paris: Éditions de Minuit, 1957). For the role of women in the Centres Sociaux, see Andrée Dore-Audibert, *Les Françaises d'Algérie dans la guerre de libération* (Paris: Éditions Karthala, 1995). Religious organizations were also operational during this time, trying to provide basic services. For an analysis of Christian activism in Algeria, see Darcie Fontaine, "Decolonizing Christianity: Grassroots Ecumenism in France and Algeria, 1940–1962" (Ph.D. diss., Rutgers University, 2011).

64. ANOM SAS DOC/3, *Sections Administratives Spécialisées: Goums et Harkas; Instructions Comptables (Algiers, 1955)*, pamphlet published by the official press of the governor-general.

65. Ibid.

66. Ibid.

67. Frémeaux, "Les SAS," 58.

68. Mathias, *Les Sections Administratives Spécialisées*, 107.

69. SHAT 1H 2539, Général Salan, *Participation de l'Armée aux tâches de pacification* (Algiers, 1958).

70. Lazreg, *Torture and the Twilight of Empire*, 28.

71. For an example of a monthly medical report, see ANOM 2 SAS 141, "Fiche mensuelle d'activité médico-sociale."

72. Peter Paret, *French Revolutionary Warfare from Indochina to Algeria: The Analysis of a Political and Military Doctrine* (New York: Frederick A. Praeger, 1964), 47.

73. Consistent record keeping of this nature was rare.

74. Mathias, *Les Sections Administratives Spécialisées*, 33–35.

75. Ibid., 7.

76. General Physician Inspector Debenedetti, "Service de santé militaire et assistance médicale gratuite aux populations autochtones en Algérie," *Revue du Corps de Santé Militaire* 1 (March 1958), 3–4.

77. ANOM 81F/1626, "Bulletin Mensuel de Statistique Générale," May 1955.

78. Mathias, *Les Sections Administratives Spécialisées*, 29.

79. Armand Frémont, "Le contingent: Témoignage et réflexion," in *La guerre d'Algérie et les Français*, ed. Jean-Pierre Rioux (Paris: Fayard, 1990), 80.

80. ANOM GGA 1K/460, Enquêtes administratives par les hôpitaux civils d'Alger et l'hôpital civil de Beni-Messous, 1955; ANOM GGA 1K/713, Enquêtes demandés par Hôpitaux Civil d'Alger, 1956.

81. ANOM GGA 1K/460, Enquêtes administratives par les hôpitaux civils d'Alger et l'hôpital civil de Beni-Messous, 1955, "Notice of Information" from the Algiers prefect J. Petit to the director of the Blida Psychiatric Hospital, 7 November 1955.

82. ANOM GGA 1K/460, Enquêtes administratives par les hôpitaux civils d'Alger et l'hôpital civil de Beni-Messous, 1955.

83. ANOM GGA 1K/460, Enquêtes administratives par les hôpitaux civils d'Alger et l'hôpital civil de Beni-Messous, 1955, Sous-préfet, M. Platt, 5 July 1955, Orléansville.

84. ANOM GGA 1K/460, Enquêtes administratives par les hôpitaux civils d'Alger et l'hôpital civil de Beni-Messous, 1955, Sous-préfet, M. Platt, 5 July 1955, Orléansville.

85. ANOM GGA 1K/460, Enquêtes administratives par les hôpitaux civils d'Alger et l'hôpital civil de Beni-Messous, 1955, letter from the prefect J. Petit to the director of the Tlemcen civil hospital, 21 November 1955.

86. ANOM GGA 12 CAB 12, Santé publique, Cabinet Lacoste. Letter from Robert Lacoste, July 1956.

87. Bell, *Frontiers of Medicine*; Lyons, "The Power to Heal"; Vaughan, *Curing Their Ills*.

88. SHAT 1H 3868, Service note by General Bucournau, "Action sur les milieux féminines en Algérie—Emploi des Equipes médico-sociales itinérantes," 7 June 1960, Batna; SHAT 1H 4064, General Alix, notice no. 257, "relative à l'action sur les milieux féminines en Algérie," 27 March 1960.

89. Lazreg, *Torture and the Twilight of Empire*, 147.

90. Diane Sambron, *Femmes musulmanes: Guerre d'Algérie, 1954–1962* (Paris: Éditions Autrement, 2007), 72.

91. ANOM 14 CAB 56, General Allard to the General Delegate of Algeria, 26 January 1959, Algiers.

92. SHAT 1H 2570, Étude sur la mise en oeuvre d'une campagne psychologique en vue de renforcer les mesures sanitaires dans les troupes d'Algérie et accroître l'effort de la santé publique auprès des populations, n.d. [after August 1956].

93. SHAT 1H 3988/D/4, "Synthèse Trimestrielle d'Activité des EMSI," written by General de Rendette, 13 March 1961, Oran.

94. SHAT IH 3501/D/1, Lieutenant Colonel Adrian to all practicing AMG physicians, 27 June 1958, Algiers.

95. ANOM GGA 81F/1617, *Hygiène Publique*, Contrôle sanitaire aux frontières, 1948–1958.

96. Ordinance no. 58-10006 of 23 October 1958, decrees no. 60-313 of 28 March 1960 and no. 60-360 of 9 April 1960 respectively. ANOM GGA 81F/1638, Marcel Blanc to governor-general Paul Delouvrier, 14 March 1960, Algiers.

97. ANOM GGA 81F/1637, Director of Social Action E. Sirvent to Foreign Minister, 28 February 1962, Algiers.

98. Mr. Sirvent recommended that Edgardo Roson Duenas, a doctor living in Madrid, be considered to practice medicine in Algeria, ibid.

99. SHAT 1H 3501/D/1, Lieutenant Colonel Horville to Director of Health Services for the Region of Algiers, 14 May 1960, Algiers.

100. SHAT 1H 3501/D/1, Lieutenant Colonel Massonie, Director of Health Services in the eastern Algiers region, to all physician units, 13 December 1958, Algiers.

101. SHAT1H 3501/D/1, letter signed by General Director of Social Action Mr. Besancenez for General Salan to the general commanders of the army corps unit, 20 June 1958.

102. ANOM 5 SAS 54, Département de Tizi-Ouzou (ou département de Grande Kabylie), SAS d'Afir, 1958–1960.

103. For additional SAS medical notebooks, see ANOM 9 SAS 196, Département de Sétif, SAS de la Réunion, 1958–1962; and ANOM 3 SAS 74, Département de Médea, SAS de l'antenne d'Aïn Rich, 1959–1962.

104. Fanon, *A Dying Colonialism*, 123.

105. Specifically, Fanon was referring to his experience working in hospitals in Lyon and Blida, both urban environments in which the population interacted more regularly with the settler population.

106. Fanon, *A Dying Colonialism*, 126.

107. Also see Pierre Lefebvre, *Histoire de la médecine aux armées*, vol. 3, *De 1914 à nos jours* (Paris: Lavauzelle, 1987); Pierre Miquel, *La Guerre d'Algérie: Images inédites des archives militaires* (Paris: Chêne, 1993).

108. *Le Service de santé des armées en Algérie, 1830–1958* (Paris: SPEI, 1958), iv.

109. Frémeaux, "Les SAS," 67.

110. Jacques Soustelle, *L'espérance trahie, 1958–1961* (Paris: Éditions de l'Alma, 1962), 20.

111. Ibid., 24.

112. Heggoy, *Insurgency and Counterinsurgency*, 188–211; Lazreg, *Torture and the Twilight of Empire*, 145–150.

Chapter 3. "See Our Arms, See Our Physicians"

1. Martini, *Chroniques des années algériennes*, 27–62.

2. Ibid., 65.

3. Ibid., 83.

4. Michel Martini continued to personally assist in the armed struggle for national liberation. He was arrested in July 1956, subsequently imprisoned in Oran for one year, and exiled to Tunis, where he spent the remaining war years working as a surgeon in Sfax Hospital and Charles Nicolle Hospital. He returned to Algeria after the cease-fire in 1962 and worked in various hospitals until his retirement in 1987.

5. Martini, *Chroniques des années algériennes*, 65.

6. Amir, *Contribution à l'étude*, 109.

7. Harbi, *Le FLN*, 170.

8. See Horne, *A Savage War of Peace*, 135. Horne uses the all-encompassing term "European" to describe victims that were not Algerian. In the mid-nineteenth century, French, Maltese, Italian, Spanish, German, and Swiss settled in Algeria. Evans, *Algeria*, 14. One hundred years later, their descendants likely were French citizens, but their origins could be traced back to other parts of Europe. I will use the term "French" to describe this population living in Algeria.

9. Charles-Robert Ageron, "Complots et purges dans l'armée de libération algérienne, 1958–1961," *Vingtième Siècle: Revue d'histoire* 59, no. 1 (1998): 15–27.

10. Ibid.

11. William Quandt has shown how the "FLN made revolution itself the icon to be worshipped," and how "glory was accorded to the 'one million martyrs.'" This ideological model wrought serious consequences to any person or group that tried to operate outside of it and assert an alternative political vision. William Quandt, *Between Ballots and Bullets: Algeria's Transition from Authoritarianism* (Washington, D.C.: Brookings Institution Press, 1998), 21. The most notable example is the decade-long civil conflict that erupted after the FLN canceled parliamentary elections in January 1992 when the Islamic Salvation Front (Front Islamique du Salut, FIS) was poised to win at the polls. See Hugh Roberts, *The Battlefield Algeria, 1988–2002: Studies in a Broken Polity* (New York: Verso, 2003); Luis Martinez, *La guerre civile en Algérie, 1990–1998* (Paris: Karthala, 1998); Quandt, *Between Ballots and Bullets*.

12. For example, in November 1955, Ramdane Abane, a former Algerian People's Party member, wrote a letter expressing his disapproval of Ahmed Ben Bella and his dispatches from Cairo. Abane was critical of Ben Bella because he was "5,000 kilometers from Algeria, far from territorial realities," and he reproached him for being more "Maghribi than Algerian." Meynier, *Histoire intérieure du FLN*, 171–172; 4 November 1955 letter in Mabrouk Belhocine, *Le courrier Alger–le Caire 1954–1956* (Algiers: Casbah, 2000), 109.

13. Horne, *A Savage War of Peace*, 135.

14. Connelly, *A Diplomatic Revolution*, 74.

15. Ageron, *Histoire de l'Algérie contemporaine*, 538–540.

16. UN ARMS, S-0188-005-07, Department of Political and Security Council Affairs, Working Paper No. 381, 8 September 1955.

17. Ruedy, *Modern Algeria*, 126.

18. Ibid.

19. Mostéfa Khiati, *Les blouses blanches de la révolution* (Algiers: Éditions ANEP, 2011), 13.

20. Ibid., 15.

21. Amir, *Contribution à l'étude*; Ahmed Benkhaled, *Chroniques médicales algériennes: Les années de braise* (Algiers: Houma, 2004); Mohammed Guentari, *Organisation politico-administrative et militaire de la Révolution algérienne de 1954 à 1962* (Algiers: Office des publications universitaires, 2000); Khiati and Benkhaled's works feature one or two pages on this period while the remainder of the books are devoted to the later years.

22. Lazreg, *Torture and the Twilight of Empire*, 84.

23. Azzedine, *On nous appelait fellaghas*, 78.

24. Ibid., 79.

25. *Séminaire sur le développement d'un système national de santé: L'expérience algérienne*, (Algiers: Ministère de la Santé, 1983), 41; Benkhaled, *Chroniques médicales algériennes*, 23–24; Amir, *Contribution à l'étude*, 103; Farouk Benatia, *Les actions humanitaires pendant la lutte de liberation, 1954–1962* (Algiers: Éditions Dahlab, 1997), 73.

26. Azzedine, *On nous appelait fellaghas*, 78.

27. Interview, Youcef Khatib (Colonel Hassan), 23 June 2009, Algiers.

28. Azzedine, *On nous appelait fellaghas*, 157, 144.

29. *Séminaire sur le développement d'un système national de santé*, 41; Harbi, *Le FLN*, 170.

30. Benkhaled, *Chroniques médicales algériennes*, 22.

31. Khiati, *Les blouses blanches*, 16–18.

32. Teguia, *L'Armée de libération nationale en wilaya IV*, 69.

33. Khiati, *Les blouses blanches*, 79.

34. Ibid.

35. This claim is refuted by several scholars including Lazreg, *Torture and the Twilight of Empire*, 77–84; Ruedy, *Modern Algeria*, 162–167.

36. "Actes de la Journée Commémorative du 19 mai 1956: Journée de l'étudiant," Bulletin d'Information de la Faculté de Médecine d'Alger, 19 May 2007, no. 3.

37. Quoted in Khiati, *Les blouses blanches*, 81.

38. Ibid.

39. Guy Pervillé, *Les étudiants algériens de l'université française, 1880–1962* (Paris: CNRS, 1984), 132–133; Mostéfa Khiati, *Histoire de la médecine en Algérie* (Algiers: Éditions ANEP, 2000), 28.

40. Khiati, *Les blouses blanches*, 82–83.

41. Benkhaled, *Chroniques médicales algériennes*, 24.

42. Meynier, *Histoire intérieure du FLN*, 511.

43. "ALN forme ses cadres: Des infirmiers d'élite," *El Moudjahid*, 15 January 1959, 130–131.

44. Khiati, *Les blouses blanches*, 85.

45. Ibid.

46. Messaoud Djennas, *Vivre, c'est croire*, 243.

47. Ibid., 252.

48. Bensalem Djamel-Eddine, *Voyez nos armes, voyez nos médecins: Chronique de la Zone 1, Wilaya III* (Algiers: Entreprise National du Livre, 1984), 17–24.

49. Amir, *Contribution à l'étude*, 103–105.

50. Djamila Amrane, "La femme algérienne et la guerre de libération nationale," quoted in Marnia Lazreg, *The Eloquence of Silence: Algerian Women in Question* (New York: Routledge, 1994), 121.

51. Azzedine, *On nous appelait fellaghas*, 148–149.

52. Lazreg, *The Eloquence of Silence*, 125.

53. Meynier, *Histoire intérieure du FLN*, 191–195.

54. Wilaya 1, Aurès region; Wilaya 2, North Constantine region; Wilaya 3, Kabylia region; Wilaya 4, Algiers region; Wilaya 5, Oran region; and Wilaya 6, Sahara and the surrounding area.

55. Benkhaled, *Chroniques médicales algériennes*, 35–36.

56. Ibid., 35–37; SHAT 1H 1691/1, FLN Service de Santé, Organisation du service de santé rebelle, 1957–1960, Informational notice written by French army general Raoul Salan, Tenth Military Region, Algiers, 1 June 1957. Copies of recovered internal FLN-ALN documents and medical reports are also attached to Salan's letter.

57. SHAT 1H 1691/2, FLN Service de Santé, Organisation du service de santé rebelle, 1957–1960, FLN-ALN service notice from Wilaya 4, Zone 1 captain Mr. Lakhdar, 8 December 1956. Though Benkhaled and material in file 1H 1691 suggest that monthly reports were written, I only saw a few in 1H 1691, and none in the Algerian archives.

58. SHAT 1H 1691/2, FLN Service de Santé; and SHAT 1H 2582/1, Armée de Libération National. During a tactical operation, the French military discovered letters and ALN services directives detailing rudimentary skills it expected medical personnel to perform.

59. Quote is from Omnia El Shakry, *The Great Social Laboratory: Subjects of Knowledge in Colonial and Postcolonial Egypt* (Stanford, Calif.: Stanford University Press, 2007), 17, regarding Egypt (but applicable to the situation in Algeria as well); James Ferguson makes a similar argument about Zambia in *Expectations of Modernity: Myths and Meanings of Urban Life on the Zambian Copperbelt* (Berkeley: University of California Press, 1999).

60. SHAT 1H 1691/2, FLN Service de Santé, Organisation du service de santé rebelle, FLN-ALN service notice from Wilaya 4, Zone 1 captain Mr. Lakhdar, 8 December 1956.

61. SHAT 1H 1691/D2, FLN Service de Santé, Organisation du service de santé rebelle, 1957–1960, report on social conditions written by ALN medical assistant in Wilaya 4, Zone 1, 7 February 1957.

62. SHAT 1H 2582/1, Armée de Libération, October 1956 monthly report, Wilaya 4.

63. Djamel-Eddine, *Voyez nos armes*, 98–99.

64. Sandra Sufian, *Healing the Land and the Nation: Malaria and the Zionist Project in Palestine, 1920–1947* (Chicago: University of Chicago Press, 2007). Sufian's study focuses on Palestine under the British Mandate (1920–1947) and argues that the antimalaria campaigns supported by the Zionist movement were a deliberate effort to reshape both the physical bodies of Jews and the physical landscape of the land.

65. SHAT 1H 1691/2, FLN Service de Santé, Organisation du service de santé rebelle, Informational notice, General Raoul Salan, 1 June 1957.

66. SHAT 1H 2582/1, ALN-FLN circular regarding Wilaya 2 health-services division rules and regulations, 9 December 1956.

67. Ibid.

68. SHAT 1H 1691/2, FLN Service de Santé, Organisation du service de santé rebelle, "Règlement du Blessé de l'A.L.N." (n.d., after summer 1957).

69. Ibid.

70. Amir, *Contribution à l'étude*, 129.

71. Ibid., 131.

72. *Séminaire sur le développement d'un système national de santé*, 46–47.

73. Interview, Mohamed Toumi, 20 June 2009, Algiers.

74. Teguia, *L'Armée de libération nationale*, 72.

75. Martini lived and worked in Algeria beginning in March 1955. He met Germaine Tillion and other members of the Algerian Communist Party who influenced his political orientation. In 1956, French authorities arrested him for his alleged political activities and exiled him. He went to Tunisia, where he stayed and treated patients, until he returned to Algeria in July 1962. He became an Algerian citizen in 1964. He chronicles this period in his life in *Chroniques des années algériennes*.

76. Martini, *Chroniques*, 224.

77. SHAT 1H 1691/2, FLN Service de Santé, Organisation du service de santé rebelle, report written by a medical assistant "Mahmoud", Wilaya 4, Zone 1, 7 February 1957.

78. SHAT IH 1691/2, FLN Service de Santé, Organisation du service de santé rebelle, report written by medical assistant "Rachid," Wilaya 3, July and August 1959.

79. SHAT 1H 2582, FLN-ALN, Information notice on female combatants, Tenth Military Region, Constantine Army Corps, 7 November 1957.

80. Lazreg, *The Eloquence of Silence*, 118–141; Sambron, *Femmes musulmanes*; Natalya Vince, *Our Fighting Sisters: Nation, memory and gender in Algeria, 1954–2012* (Manchester, Manchester University Press, 2015); Vince, "La mémoire des femmes algériennes de la guerre de libération algérienne," *Raison présente* 175, no. 3 (2010): 79–92.

81. SHAT 1H 2582, FLN-ALN, "Note de Service aux Commissaires Politiques," after summer 1956.

82. Ibid.

83. ANOM GGA 12 CAB/12, Santé Publique, 1956, Cabinet Lacoste, Robert Lacoste, governor-general of Algeria, to René Coty, French president, 9 June 1956.

84. ANOM GGA 11 CAB/83, Cabinet Soustelle, Decrees on Nitrate and Chloride, "Official Notice on Nitrate and Chloride Products," 1955.

85. Ibid.

86. Ibid.

87. ANOM 81F/1467, Ministère d'État Chargé des Affaires Algériennes, Report to the Council

of Ministers from the Minister of the Interior, Henri Queuille, and the Minster of Public Health and of the Population, 2 May 1951, Paris. The 1951 decree specifically stated it applied to metropolitan France as well as to Algeria.

88. ANOM GGA 12 CAB/243, Cabinet Lacoste, 1957. The Service of the Central Pharmacy of the governor general responds to a note of concern regarding a pharmacy closure in Sétif, 13 May 1957.

89. ANOM 12 CAB/243, note on general social action written by civil cabinet director Pierre Hosteing, 25 March 1957.

90. ANOM 12 CAB/243, M. Lafont de Sentenac, social action director general, to Pierre Hosteing, civil cabinet director, 23 April 1957.

91. SHAT 1H 1691/3. Drawn from two photographs under derogation. "Jeu de photographie du matériel médico-chirurgical et des produits pharmaceutiques contenus dans la trousse d'urgence récupérée sur le H.L.L. Bachir Saadi Ben Ahmed, Infirmier-Major du 72. Bataillon rallié à El-Ma-El-Abiod," 5 December 1960.

92. SHAT 1H 1691/2, Letter from Colonel A. Brunet to the general of the Central Oran Zone, 16 May 1960.

93. ANA GPRA 78(i), "Plan du travail du CRA établi à l'intérieur de CCE," internal Algerian Red Crescent work plan, signed by Hadj Omar Boukli-Hacène, CRA president, Comité Centrale, Tunis, 26 September 1957.

94. Azzedine, *On nous appelait fellaghas*, 157.

95. Interview, Commandant Azzedine, 7 March 2007, Algiers; interview, Jeanine Belkhodja, 25 March 2007, Algiers; Djennas, *Vivre, c'est croire*, 252–256.

96. ACICR B AG 225 008 010, Condamnations de médecins et d'infirmières en Algérie, 1958. André François-Poncet, CRF president, to Léopold Boissier, ICRC president, 22 December 1958, Paris.

97. ACICR B AG 202 008 004, Condamnations de médecins en Algérie, 1957–1960, "Personnel sanitaire poursuivi lors de conflits intérieurs," report from ICRC representative Jean-Pierre Schoenholzer, 16 March 1959.

98. "Les bons offices de M. de Preux," *El Moudjahid*, 3 March 1958.

99. ACICR B AG 225 008 010, Condamnations de médecins et d'infirmières en Algérie, 1958, Dr. Bentami, CRA representative, to Léopold Boissier, ICRC president, 2 June 1958, Geneva.

100. ACICR B AG 225 008 010, Condamnations de médecins et d'infirmières en Algérie, 1958, M. Henri Langlais to ICRC delegate Michel, 18 December 1958, Paris.

101. In an annex to his letter, Langlais provided the names of those eleven men: Paul Estorges, Ahmed Aroua, Rachid Bouyayed, Hamidou Tethy, Belouzdad Mustapha, Kerbouche Rabah, Bendadis Lakdar, Medjebeur, Klouche Mostepha, Smati Azzedine, and Smati Mohamed. Ibid. I have reprinted the names as they appear in the letter, however, the last seven names appear to invert the first and last names.

102. Benarbia Mohamed, Djennas Messaoud, Maouche Mohand, Hachemane Larbi ben Mohamed, Krouri Benaissa, Mokretat Karoubi were the six physicians the French released. Ibid. I have reprinted the names as they appear in the letter, however, all six names appear to invert the first and last names.

103. Djamel-Eddine, *Voyez nos armes*, 81–82, 85–86.

104. Azzedine, *On nous appelait fellaghas*, 66; Djamel-Eddine, *Voyez nos armes*, 102.

105. SHAT 1H 2582, Armée de Libération, Wilaya 4 monthly report, May 1957.

106. SHAT 1H 3092, Croissant-Rouge Algérien. A recovered CRA tract that had been thrown out of an unidentified car window on 9 May 1962 and found near Relizane.

107. Interview, Pierre Chaulet, 8 March 2007, Algiers.

108. Ibid.; interview, Salim Hafiz, 10 June 2009, Algiers; interview, Colonel Hassan, 23 June 2009, Algiers.

109. Interview, Pierre Chaulet, 8 March 2007, Algiers.

110. Azzedine, *On nous appelait fellaghas*, 18–19; Djennas, *Vivre, c'est croire*, 260.

111. Interview, Pierre Chaulet, 8 March 2007, Algiers. His recent memoir, written with his wife, details his life and reasons for staying Algeria after 1962. Chaulet and Chaulet, *Choix de l'Algérie*.

112. See "Histoire de l'Algérie médicale," http://www.santémaghreb.com/algérie/hist/index.asp.

113. Interview, Jeanine Belkhodja, 25 March 2007, Algiers.

114. Ibid.

115. Ibid.

116. ACICR B AG 202 008 004, Condamnations de médecins en Algérie, 1957–1960. H. Langlais, Foreign Affairs Ministry, to William Michel, head of the ICRC delegation to Algeria, 23 April 1958, Paris.

117. André Morice, the minister of defense under the Maurice Bourgès-Maunoury government, wanted to "asphyxiate" the rebels by completely blocking the borders. The Morice Line was an electrified fence that ran five hundred kilometers along the western border with Morocco and four hundred kilometers along the eastern border with Tunisia. This fence greatly contributed to the decrease in arms and supplies upon which the FLN-ALN relied. By 1959, roughly 200 arms entered Algeria per month, as compared to 1,000–1,200 in 1957. Thénault, *Histoire de la guerre d'indépendance algérienne*, 175.

118. Interview, Jeanine Belkhodja, 25 March 2007, Algiers.

119. Evans, *The Memory of Resistance*. For a history of Grangaud's life, see his biography, Abderrahmane Djelfaoui, *Grangaud: D'Alger à El-Djazair* (Algiers: Casbah, 2000). I had the opportunity to meet with Grangaud in 2007 and 2008 and over the course of our discussions he explained that his political views evolved in opposition to his father's, who believed "100 percent in the civilizing mission" and in *Algérie française*. Interview, Grangaud, 13 February 2008, Algiers.

120. Khiati, *Les blouses blanches*, 389.

121. Darcie Fontaine, "Decolonizing Christianity," 271; Fontaine, "Treason or Charity? Christian Missions on Trial and the Decolonization of Algeria," *International Journal of Middle East Studies* 44, no. 4 (2012): 733–753.

122. Gérard Zwang, *Chirurgien du contingent: Suez-Algérie, mai 1956– octobre 1958*, ed. Jean-Charles Jauffret (Montpellier: Université Paul Valéry, 2000); Pierre Godeau, *Une aventure algérienne* (Paris: Flammarion, 2001); Marie-Claude Leloup-Colonna, *Souvenirs d'une toubiba: Algérie, 1957–1963* (Paris: L'Harmattan, 2004).

123. Joël Gaucher, *Révélateur d'images: Témoignage autobiographique* (La Roche-sur-Yon: Siloë, 2006), 36.

124. Ibid., 80.

125. ANOM 91 4F/19, Commissariat central d'Alger, 1949–1962. Letter from Algiers Police Prefecture to the Algiers chief of police, 12 December 1961, Algiers.

126. Gaucher, *Révélateur d'images*, 141.

127. "Une promotion d'infirmières algériennes au Caire," *El Moudjahid*, 8 December 1958, 98.

128. Amir, *Contribution à l'étude*, 110.

129. "Le Litva emporte nos blessés vers Odessa," *El Moudjahid*, 24 November 1960, 319; "Actualité: Pour nos blessés," *El Moudjahid*, 15 April 1961, 459.

130. "Actualité et point to repère: Des blessés de l'ALN partent pour l'USSR et la Tchecoslovaquie," *El Moudjahid*, 31 August 1959, 441; "Le Litva emporte nos blessés vers Odessa," 319; "Actualité: Pour nos blessés," 459.

131. Interview, Jeanine Belkhodja, 25 March 2007, Algiers; Ian Young, *The Private Life of Islam* (London: Allen Lane, 1974).

132. Gleijeses, *Conflicting Missions*, 9.

133. "Actualité et point de repère," 441; Connelly, *A Diplomatic Revolution*; Westad, *The Global Cold War*.

134. Gleijeses, *Conflicting Missions*, 36.

135. Ibid.

136. In *The Wretched of the Earth* and *A Dying Colonialism*, Fanon depicted a one-dimensional colonial reality in which only two categories existed: the colonizer and colonized. He struggled to envision the possibility of transcending colonial categories, wherein health-care professionals, no matter what their background or political orientation, prioritized their commitment to patients' health and well-being above all else. Not every medical interaction was an "ordeal" as he put it. Fanon, *A Dying Colonialism*, 128–129.

137. Byrne, "The Pilot Nation"; Connelly, *A Diplomatic Revolution*; Wall, *France, the United States, and the Algerian War*.

Chapter 4. Internationalizing Humanitarianism

1. Algerian National Archives (hereafter ANA), GPRA 78(i), "Plan du travail du CRA établi à l'intérieur de CCE," internal Algerian Red Crescent work plan, signed by Hadj Omar Boukli-Hacène, CRA president, Comité Centrale, Tunis, 26 September 1957.

2. John Hutchinson, *Champions of Charity: War and the Rise of the Red Cross* (Boulder, Colo.: Westview Press, 1996), 176.

3. Forsythe, *The Humanitarians*, 21.

4. Ibid., 305.

5. Quoted in Hutchinson, *Champions of Charity*, 183.

6. Geoffrey Best, *Humanity in Warfare: The Modern History of the International Law of Armed Conflict* (London: Weidenfeld and Nicolson, 1980), 142.

7. Caroline Moorehead, *Dunant's Dream: War, Switzerland and the History of the Red Cross* (London: HarperCollins, 1998), 345.

8. Ibid.

9. French Red Cross web site, http://www.croix-rouge.fr.

10. ANOM GGA 1K/678, French Red Cross reports, 1942–1957.

11. ACICR B AG 121 078 001-007, summary of a meeting between Mr. Lossier and Mrs. Zarrins regarding Red Cross action in Africa, 2 April 1954.

12. Ibid.

13. ANA GPRA 78(i), "Plan du travail du CRA établi à l'intérieur de CCE."

14. "Le médecin, un combatant?" *Vie et Bonté*, no. 69, September–October 1955, 16–17.

15. "Visite de M. André François-Poncet, président de la C.R.F., en Algérie," *Vie et Bonté*, no. 78, September–October 1956, 1.

16. Archives de la Croix-Rouge Française (hereafter CRF), "Rapport sur les activités de la Croix-Rouge Française en Algérie au cours de l'année 1955," May 1956, 2.

17. ANOM GGA 1K/678, French Red Cross reports, 1942–1957, memo on the French Red Cross by Jacques Pernet, Office of the Prefect, Algiers, 21 April 1956.

18. CRF, "Rapport sur les activités de la Croix-Rouge Française en Algérie au cours de l'année 1955," May 1956, 1.

19. ACICR B AG 121 078 001-007, Léonce Imbert to ICRC president Léopold Boissier, 11 June 1956.

20. CRF, "Rapport sur les activités de la Croix-Rouge Française en Algérie au cours de l'année 1957," April 1957, 1.

21. Ibid.

22. Ibid., 2.

23. These news sources repeatedly published articles about CRF visits to French military and civilian hospitals. Often, CRF nurses would pose alongside injured French soldiers and the caption would describe the rejuvenating nature of their visits. Around Christmas, the CRF made an extra effort to visit hospitals around the country and hand out gifts to the French soldiers.

24. Interview, Colonel Hassan, 23 June 2009, Algiers.

25. ANA GPRA 78(i), "Plan du travail du CRA établi à l'intérieur de CCE."

26. ACICR B AG 121 078 001-007, letters from Dr. M. Chaouky, Damascus, to League of Red Cross and Red Crescent Society President, 22 July 1957, and Dr. Moustafa Khalifeh, Amman, to League of Red Cross and Red Crescent Society Secretary General, 14 August 1957.

27. Ibid.

28. ACICR 121 078 001-007, French Red Cross president André François-Poncet to ICRC president Léopold Boissier, 6 September 1957.

29. ACICR B AG 121 078 001-007, Pierre Gaillard, ICRC delegate to Roger Gallopin, ICRC executive director, 9 June 1958.

30. Makaci, *Le Croissant-Rouge Algérien*, 82. This work draws on the author's experiences and on notes he took in the late 1950s and includes an annex with invaluable CRA documents, correspondence, and pictures from the war years.

31. Ibid., 82–83.

32. ANA GPRA 78(i), "Plan du travail du CRA établi à l'intérieur de CCE."

33. Ibid.

34. Algerian leaders in Tetouan, Morocco first contacted Boumediène Bensmaine and pharmacist Merad Abdellah to compile a report entitled "The Algerian Red Crescent Organization." This organization was modeled on the Tunisian Red Crescent. Benatia, *Les actions humanitaires*, 80.

35. Makaci, *Le Croissant-Rouge Algérien*, 84.

36. ACICR B AG 210 008 001, Prisonniers français en mains rebelles, 1956–1957, report from ICRC representative Pierre Gaillard, regarding his meeting with CRA representative and Geneva delegate Dr. Bentami, Geneva, 15 October 1957.

37. El Shakry, *The Great Social Laboratory*, 14. Frederick Cooper has shown how African laborers made effective claims by seizing "the new discourse of [French and British] administrators and [turning] assertions of control into demands for entitlements: if colonial officials wanted Africans to work like their idealized European workers, they should pay them on a similar scale and bargain with them in good faith." Cooper, *Decolonization and African Society*, 3.

38. Benatia, *Les actions humanitaires*, 255.

39. Ibid., 80. Morocco and Tunisia had already established emergency care committees in early 1957 to assist the massive influx of Algerian refugees into their respective territories. However, the committees were plagued with insufficient funds to meet the level of care and assistance the refugees required. ANA GPRA 78(h), "Rapport général d'activité du CRA," Cairo, 1957.

40. The international political dimension is also outlined in an early CRA work plan written by unnamed CCE members in 1957, ANA GPRA 78(i), "Plan du travail du CRA établi à l'intérieur de CCE."

41. The FLN claimed its army, the ALN, followed the Geneva Conventions and treated French prisoners of war accordingly. While this may have been true in some instances, as Raphaëlle Branche argues, the FLN would have had difficulty providing food and shelter for prisoners given the nature of guerrilla warfare. The ALN would have been moving frequently, and its leaders barely had enough supplies for themselves, let alone enough to give to French prisoners. Branche, *Prisonniers du FLN*, chaps. 1 and 2.

42. Makaci, *Le Croissant-Rouge Algérien*, 82.

43. ANA GPRA 78(h), "Rapport général d'activité du CRA," Cairo, 1957.

44. Ibid.

45. Benatia, *Les actions humanitaires*, 81.

46. Quoted in Benatia, *Les actions humanitaires*, 265.

47. March 1957 was not the first time ICRC representatives met with Algerian nationalists. Mohamed Khider and Ahmed Ben Bella were in contact with the ICRC in March 1956. In a letter written from Cairo, they explained the FLN would adhere to the Geneva Conventions if the ICRC could get the French to do the same. Khider even promised to obtain lists of prisoners and told ICRC delegate David de Traz that he would try to facilitate visits with the prisoners. Khider and Ben Bella were arrested on 22 October 1956 and were unable to see through these promises. Branche, *Prisonniers du FLN*, 81–84.

48. ACICR B AG 210 008 003, confidential report on the Algerian Red Crescent written by Claude Pilloud, Rabat, 18 March 1957.

49. Ibid.

50. SHAT 1H 1755/1, Croissant-Rouge Algérien, Algerian Red Crescent activities in Libya, 10 September 1957, Paris.

51. SHAT 1H 1755/1, Croissant-Rouge Algérien, information notice on the Arab League and International Red Cross activities in Algeria, 28 October 1957.

52. Makaci, *Le Croissant-Rouge Algérien*, 102.

53. Benatia, *Les actions humanitaires*, 87.

54. ACICR B AG 202 008 004, Condamnations de médecins en Algérie, 1957–1960, Resolution XVII of the Nineteenth International Conference of the Red Cross, New Delhi, 1957.

55. "La Croix-Rouge Internationale condamne l'attitude du gouvernement français," *El Moudjahid*, 15 December 1957, 8.

56. During the second half of May 1958, de Gaulle negotiated the terms of his return to power. The National Assembly raised constitutional objections to de Gaulle's proposals, resulting in an impasse. After much deliberation, President René Coty threatened to resign if the Assembly rejected de Gaulle's conditions. The vote passed 329 to 224. Horne, *A Savage War of Peace*, 297–298. De Gaulle faced tremendous opposition to this because, for many, it was reminiscent of Marshal Philippe Pétain's request for full powers in 1940. Julian Jackson, "General de Gaulle and His Enemies: Anti-Gaullism in France Since 1940," *Transactions of the Royal Historical Society*, 6th ser., 9 (1999): 54.

57. The four governors during this period were Roger Léonard (12 April 1951 to 26 January 1955), Jacques Soustelle (26 January 1955 to 1 February 1956), Georges Catroux (1 February 1956 to 9 February 1956), and Robert Lacoste (9 February 1956 to 13 May 1958).

58. Horne, *A Savage War of Peace*, 299.

59. For an analysis of the 1958 constitution and its implication for Algerian citizenship, see Shepard, *The Invention of Decolonization*. For de Gaulle's personal reflections on this period, see Charles de Gaulle, *Discours et messages*, vol. 3, *Avec le renouveau, mai 1958–juillet 1962* (Paris: Plon, 1970); de Gaulle, *Lettres, notes et carnets: Juin 1951–mai 1958* (Paris: Plon, 1985); and de Gaulle, *Lettres, notes et carnets: Juin 1958–décembre 1960* (Paris: Plon, 1985). For secondary accounts, see Jean Daniel, *De Gaulle et l'Algérie* (Paris: Seuil, 1986); and Michael Kettle, *De Gaulle and Algeria, 1940–1960: From Mers El-Kébir to the Algiers Barricades* (London: Quartet, 1993).

60. Horne, *A Savage War of Peace*, 317.

61. A complete list of the fifteen countries in the order the GPRA received their support: United Arab Emirates, Iraq, Libya (19 September 1958), Tunisia, Morocco, Saudi Arabia, Jordan (20 September 1958), Palestine, Yemen (21 September 1958), China (22 September 1958), Korea (25 September 1958), Vietnam (26 September 1958), Sudan, Indonesia (1958), Mongolia (27 September 1958). ANA GPRA/44, 11 October 1959, Cairo.

62. Branche, *La torture et l'armée pendant la guerre d'Algérie*, 14. Raphaëlle Branche has written extensively on torture; see Branche, "La torture pendant la guerre," in *La guerre d'Algérie, 1954–2004: La fin de l'amnésie*, ed. Mohammed Harbi and Benjamin Stora (Paris: Laffont, 2004),

381–402; Françoise Sironi and Raphaëlle Branche, "Torture and the Border of Humanity," *International Social Science Journal* 54, no. 174 (2002): 539–548; Sylvie Thénault and Raphaëlle Branche, "L'impossible procès de la torture pendant la guerre d'Algérie," in *Justice, politique et République: De l'affaire Dreyfus à la guerre d'Algérie*, ed. Marc-Olivier Baruch and Vincent Duclert (Brussels: Complexe/IHTP, 2002), 243–260; Branche, "Les entretiens avec d'anciens soldats: Une source pour l'histoire de la torture pendant la guerre d'Algérie," in *La guerre d'Algérie au miroir des décolonisations françaises: En l'honneur de Charles-Robert Ageron* (Paris: SFHOM, 2000), 593–606.

63. SHAT 1H 1152, Torture, Coupures de presses contre la torture. "La torture, thème de propagande du FLN," GOAA, July 1960. The three-page document cites cases such as Raymonde Peschard, Maurice Audin, and Djamila Bouhired as examples of FLN propaganda. It explains how with each instance the FLN exaggerated the details or made accusations the administration could refute.

64. The twelve members were Paul Béteille, Maurice Garçon, Pierre Daure, Robert Delavignette, André François-Poncet, Paul Haag, Jean Moliérac, Marcel Oudinot, Émile Pierret-Gérard, Charles Richet, Robert de Vernejoul, and General Henri Zeller. Raphaëlle Branche, "La Commission de sauvegarde pendant la guerre d'Algérie: Chronique d'un échec annoncé," *Vingtième Siècle* 61 (1999): 16–17.

65. Branche, *La torture et l'armée pendant la guerre d'Algérie*, 151.

66. For a report on Aïn Isser, submitted by commission member Robert Delavignette, see Vidal-Naquet, *Les crimes de l'armée française*, 100–102.

67. Branche, "La Commission de sauvegarde pendant la guerre d'Algérie," 28.

68. Ibid.

69. Ibid.

70. Other personal accounts that described time in captivity, bodily harm, or physical scars that were the result of torture were published often in *Le Monde* and *Libération* during 1958–1960. One example is Dénis Berger's retelling of an encounter he had with an Algerian while detained. The Algerian prisoner told him he had been tortured with electricity. Berger says he saw the long thin scars covering the man's body. "Un nouveau témoignage sur 'La Gangrène,'" *Le Monde* 12 December 1959. Additional accounts of torture include Amar Belkhodja, *L'affaire Hamdani Adda* (Tiaret: Éditions Mekhloufi, n.d., ca. 1985); Simone de Beauvoir and Gisèle Halimi, *Djamila Boupacha: The Story of the Torture of a Young Algerian Girl Which Shocked Liberal French Opinion*, trans. Peter Green (New York: Macmillan, 1962); Jean-Luc Einaudi, *La ferme Améziane: Enquête sur un centre de torture pendant la guerre d'Algérie* (Paris: L'Harmattan, 1991); Thénault, *Une drôle de justice*; Vidal-Naquet, *La torture dans la République*; Rita Maran, *Torture: The Role of Ideology in the French-Algerian War* (New York: Praeger, 1989).

71. Henri Alleg, *The Question*, trans. John Calder (New York: George Braziller, 1958), 9–10.

72. Jean-Paul Sartre, "A Victory," in Alleg, *The Question*, 13–36.

73. Fontaine, "Decolonizing Christianity"; Le Sueur, *Uncivil War*, 147–238; Paul Clay Sorum, *Intellectuals and Decolonization in France* (Chapel Hill: University of North Carolina Press, 1977).

74. SHAT 1H 1152, "La torture, thème de propagande du FLN," GOAA, July 1960.

75. James McDougall, "Savage Wars? Codes of Violence in Algeria, 1830s–1990s," *Third World Quarterly* 26, no. 1 (2005): 117. These caricatures of violence persisted through the 1990s and were invoked to explain the civil conflict in Algeria. See Roberts, *The Battlefield, Algeria, 1988–2002*.

76. *France-Soir*, 12 May 1958, quoted in Thénault, *Histoire de la guerre*, 160; see also 88.

77. Mélouza has become the commonly used name for this event but the killings actually took place at Mechta Kasba. Mohammedi Saïd, the local commander and new head of Wilaya 3, gave the order to carry out the massacre. Later he was sanctioned by other FLN-ALN members for his controversial decision. This is yet another example of internal divisions among the FLN leadership.

Moula Bouaziz, "Guerre, violence politique et crises en Wilaya III: Contribution à l'étude de la guerre de libération d'Algérie (1954–1962)" (Ph.D. diss., L'École des Hautes Études en Sciences Sociales [EHESS], 2011).

78. Le Sueur, *Uncivil War*, 198.

79. Thénault, *Histoire de la guerre*, 88.

80. The Green Book was republished in 2001 amid the public and controversial debate about torture in France. Jean-Pierre Rondeau, ed., *Aspects véritables de la rébellion algérienne: Suivi de Algérie médicale; Documents publiés à l'origine par le Cabinet du Ministre du Ministère de l'Algérie* (Paris: Dualpha, 2001), 13–14.

81. These included bans on smoking, drinking, and any form of employment by Europeans.

82. Quoted in Le Sueur, *Uncivil War*, 198.

83. Ibid., 200.

84. Ibid., 202–203.

85. SHAT 1H 1152, "La torture, theme de propagande du FLN," GOAA, July 1960.

86. *International Red Cross Handbook* (Geneva: International Committee of the Red Cross, 1983), 551.

87. *The Geneva Conventions of August 12, 1949* (Geneva: International Committee of the Red Cross, 2007).

88. Branche, *Prisonniers du FLN*, 72.

89. "Guerre d'Algérie: Mémoires d'un délégué du CICR," at http://www.icrc.org/fre/resources/documents/misc/algeria-history-al-insani-2011-04-01.htm (accessed 9 August 2014).

90. ACICR B AG 229 008-001, report about a meeting between Dr. Bentami, Dr. Gailland, and M. Gaillard, 18 March 1958.

91. Branche, *Prisonniers du FLN*, 32.

92. ACICR B AG 210 008 001, Prisonniers en mains rebelles, 1956–1957, report by ICRC representative I. Zreikat regarding a meeting with CRA delegate Dr. Bentami, 14 June 1957, Geneva; ACICR B AG 210 008 001, Prisonniers français en mains rebelles, 1956–1957, report by ICRC representative Pierre Gaillard regarding a meeting with CRA representative Dr. Bentami, 10 July 1957, Geneva.

93. ANA GPRA 83(5), "Libération de prisonniers français par l'ALN 1958," official notice from Ferhat Abbas, GPRA president, 14 October 1958, Cairo.

94. Ibid.

95. Photographs were a major source of FLN propaganda. See Marie Chominot, "Guerre des images, guerre sans image? Pratiques et usages de la photographie pendant la guerre d'indépendance algérienne (1954–1962)" (Ph.D. diss., EHESS, 2008); Chominot, "Quand la photographie vint à la Révolution: Petite contribution à l'histoire des services d'information du FLN pendant la guerre d'indépendance algérienne," in *Images du Maghreb, images au Maghreb (XIXe–XXe siècles): Une révolution du visuel?* ed. Omar Carlier (Paris: L'Harmattan, 2010), 239–255; Laurent Gervereau and Benjamin Stora, eds., *Photographier la guerre d'Algérie* (Paris: Marval, 2004).

96. ANA GPRA 83(5), "Libération de prisonniers français par l'ALN 1958," letter written by "Nadir," who worked for the minister of external affairs, 1 December 1958, Cairo.

97. Ibid.

98. The prisoners were Vincent Morales, Jacques Reléa, Jean Jacob, and Jean Vialaron.

99. *Le Monde* reported the release of these four French prisoners in the 19–20 October 1958 edition with an article titled "Le FLN annonce comme imminente la libération d'un groupe de prisonniers français: Deux délégués de la Croix-Rouge attendus à Tunis." It published a second story on 21 October 1958 titled "Libérés par le FLN à Tunis: Quatres prisonniers français sont attendus ce soir à Paris." The latter was a front-page story.

100. ACICR B AG 062-035.12, informational notice written by Pierre Gaillard, 22 October 1958.

101. "Pour le respect des lois de la guerre," *El Moudjahid*, 1 November 1958, 15. This article is accompanied by a picture of smiling French soldiers at the press conference.

102. ANA GPRA 17(a), "Communiqué du M.I. sous le titre: Libération des six prisonniers français par Amirouche," Cairo, 9 November 1958.

103. ANA GPRA 83(5), "Libération de prisonniers français par l'ALN, 1958," note from external affairs representative "Nadir," 1 December 1958, Cairo.

104. CICR Procès-verbal de Remises de Prisonniers, submitted by C. Vautier and P. Gaillard, 20 February 1959, reprinted in Makaci, *Le Croissant-Rouge Algérien*, 164.

105. ANA GPRA 83(5), "Libération de prisonniers français par l'ALN, 1958."

106. "Premier Décret du Gouvernement Provisoire de la République Algérienne," *El Moudjahid*, 10 October 1958, 15.

107. "Interview de M. Benbahmed, président du Croissant-Rouge Algérien," *El Moudjahid*, 22 June 1959, 9.

108. ACICR B AG 229 008 002, "Libération de 6 prisonniers civils par l'ALN, 1958," letter from "Georges" to Gilbert Eugène, negotiator in Castellane, France, 19 October 1958.

109. ACICR B AG 229 008 002, "Libération de 6 prisonniers civils par l'ALN, 1958," letter from Colonel Amirouche to the army, 22 October 1958, Wilaya 3.

110. ANA GPRA 81(7), "Libération de prisonniers par le FLN, 1959," letter from FLN representative in Madrid (illegible) to GPRA minister of armed forces, 10 June 1958, Madrid.

111. Dalila Aït-El-Djoudi, *La guerre d'Algérie vue par l'ALN, 1954–1962: L'armée française sous le regard des combattants algériens* (Paris: Éditions Autrement, 2007), 191. Also see Branche, *Prisonniers du FLN*.

112. "Rapport spécial militaire," ALN directive regarding Wilaya 3, 1957, quoted in Aït-El-Djoudi, *La guerre d'Algérie*, 192.

113. "L'exécution par le FLN de trois prisonniers français est un pas de plus vers une guerre totale," and "L'exécution par le FLN de trois militaires français," *Le Monde*, 11–12 May 1958, Sunday–Monday edition. According to *Le Monde*, an ALN military tribunal sentenced René Decourteix, Robert Richomme, and Jacques Feuillebois to death for torturing, raping, and assassinating civilians in Roum-el-Souk.

114. The unspecified ICRC delegate was likely Claude Pilloud or Pierre Gaillard. ACICR B AG 210 008 003, "Prisonniers français en mains rebelles, 1957–1960," letter from ALN officer (illegible) in Tunis to the Red Cross, 26 July 1958.

115. Ibid.

116. UN GAOR Resolution A/RES/1389 (XIV), "Refugees from Algeria in Morocco and Tunisia," 841st Plenary Meeting, 20 November 1959.

117. Michel Cornaton, *Les regroupements de la décolonisation en Algérie* (Paris: Éditions Ouvrières, 1967), 63; Harbi, *Le FLN*, 208. Cornaton's work on regroupment centers used Inspection Générale des Regroupements de la Population (IGRP) reports and fieldwork in Algeria to substantiate his analysis. French archives on this subject remained closed for nearly thirty years after *Les regroupements* was published. Cornaton's claims were corroborated when archival material on the subject became available.

118. Cornaton, *Les regroupements*, 62–63.

119. Keith Sutton, "Army Administration Tensions over Algeria's Centres de Regroupement, 1954–1962," *British Journal of Middle Eastern Studies* 26, no. 2 (1999): 256; SHAT 1H 2030, Centres de Regroupements, Général de Corps d'Armée Crepin to Général Commandant la Région Territoriale et le Corps d'Armée d'Oran, d'Alger, de Constantine (n.d.)

120. Sutton, "Army Administration Tensions," 257. Sylvie Thénault estimates that nearly 400,000 Algerians lived in regroupment centers by early 1958. Thénault, *Histoire de la guerre*, 99.

121. Bourdieu and Sayad, *Le Déracinement*, 13.

122. Horne, *A Savage War of Peace*, 331.

123. Thénault, *Histoire de la guerre*, 99.

124. Sutton, "Army Administration Tensions," 249. On regroupment, also see Keith Sutton, "Population Resettlement—Traumatic Upheavals and the Algerian Experience," *Journal of Modern African Studies* 15, no. 2 (1977): 279–300; Sutton, "Algeria's Socialist Villages—a Reassessment," *Journal of Modern African Studies* 22, no. 2 (1984): 223–248.

125. ANOM GGA 81F/1026, Situation des réfugiés algériens en Tunisie et au Maroc, 1957–1962. Report on Algerian refugees in Morocco sent to the Division of Information, Paris, 1 June 1959.

126. ANOM GGA 81F/1026, Situation des réfugiés algériens en Tunisie et au Maroc, 1957–1962. Report on the number of Algerian refugees in Tunisia from April 1958 to March 1959. Annex to "Fiche au sujet des réfugiés algériens de Tunisie" sent to the Division of Information in Paris on 14 April 1959.

127. ANOM 81F/528, Croissant-Rouge Algérien, CRA pamphlet *Les Réfugiés Algériens*, exact date unknown, but likely published after spring 1959. The original pamphlet had English and French text side by side.

128. Ibid.

129. ANOM GGA 81F/528, Croissant-Rouge Algérien, letter written by Lieutenant-Colonel Bourdoncle, chef du 2ème Bureau to the Commandement en Chef des Forces en Algérie about the bilingual FLN propaganda document retrieved 3 November 1959 from the dead body of an Algerian rebel who appeared to have been in Algeria recently, 5 December 1959.

130. ANA GPRA 78(j), Croissant-Rouge Algérien, 1958–1962, "Appel du CRA aux pays Arabes," letter from Benkhedda to the minister of external affairs, 10 November 1958.

131. Ibid.

132. ACICR B AG 280 008 002, Secours demandés par le CRA, CICR, 1957–1963, letter from ICRC representative Pierre Gaillard to ICRC delegate de Traz, 23 January 1958, Geneva.

133. ANA GPRA 78(d), Croissant-Rouge Algérien, 1958–1962, "Besoins des Réfugiés Algériens," letter from Zahidallah Agish Reish, Libyan Red Crescent, Central Committee, Ministry of Health, Benghazi, Libya, no date [late 1958]. The sum is given in dollars because that is how it is described in the document.

134. ANA GPRA 78(f), Besoins des Réfugiés, Secours aux Refugies Algérien en Tunisie et au Maroc, Dons en nature reçus par le CRA, 31 December 1959.

135. ANA GPRA 98(a), Croissant-Rouge Algérien, 1960–1961, CRA report, "Dons en nature reçus au CRA pendant la première quinzaine du mois janvier 1961"; and ANA GPRA 34, "Éxpédition de médicaments de Beyrouth, 1961," Note d'Ait Chaalal, chef de la mission diplomatique au Liban, adressé au Ministre des Affaires extérieures au Caire, portant l'expédition des médicaments au profit du CRA, 5 June 1961, Beirut.

136. ANA GPRA 53, report on motions delegates from several countries adopted at the WHO conference, May 1959.

137. ANA GPRA 53(1c), telegram from unnamed official in Damascus to FLN-ALN minister of external affairs regarding the Jordanian government's willingness to include a CRA delegate, 19 September 1959.

138. Makaci, *Le Croissant-Rouge Algérien*, 163.

139. ACICR B AG 280 008 002, "Secours demandés par le CRA, 1957–1963," letter from J. P. Robert-Tissot, ICRC delegate in Tunisia, to Edward Windhall, director of the Assistance Bureau, 15 February 1958.

140. ANA GPRA 53(1c), MAE/MAS, telegram from the minister of external affairs to CRA delegate in Rabat, 19 September 1959; Niek Pas, *Les Pays-Bas et la guerre d'Algérie* (Algiers: Barzakh, 2013), 104–108.

141. ANA GPRA 107, Report on Mostefa Lakhal, CRA vice president, and his trip to Turkey, Ankara, 3 September 1961.

142. SHAT 1H 1755/1, Croissant-Rouge Algérien, French report on CRA activity, 18 March 1958.

143. ANA GPRA 98(a), CRA report, "Dons en nature reçus par le Croissant Rouge Algérien pendant la première quinzaine du mois de Novembre 1960."

144. ANA GPRA 99, Soins CICR médicaux au Chef de Mission 1960/61, Aide aux réfugiés 1961, letter from Morocco mission chief Chawki Mostefa to minister of social and cultural affairs, Rabat, 12 July 1960.

145. ANA GPRA 78(m), Correspondance émanant du Croisant Rouge Algérien, 1959–1962, letter from CRA president Benbahmed to U.N. Dhebar, president of Indian National Committee for Algeria, 11 January 1961, Tunis.

146. Richard Brace and Joan Brace, *Algerian Voices* (Princeton, N.J.: Van Nostrand, 1965), 93.

147. ACICR B AG 122 008-001, letter from the Algerian Red Crescent president to the Norwegian Red Cross president, 23 May 1959, Tunis.

148. ACICR B AG 122 008-001, letters from Haakon Mathiesen to ICRC, 5 June 1959; and Mr. F. H. A. de Graff to ICRC president, 3 July 1959.

149. ACICR B AG 122 008-001, letter from Roger Gallopin to Haakon Mathiesen, 16 June 1959.

150. ACICR BAG 122 008-001, letter from Haakon Mathiesen to the Algerian Red Crescent in Tunis, 29 June 1959.

151. ACICR B AG 122 008-001, letter from Evelyn Bark, British Red Cross international relations and relief adviser, to Roger Gallopin and Henry Dunning, 5 June 1959.

152. Even though the Netherlands and Great Britain's Red Cross societies did not officially recognize the Red Crescent, they sent a variety of supplies for Algerian refugees between January and March 1959. ACICR B AG 122 008-001, Algerian Red Crescent, London Delegation, "An Account of the Plight and Needs of the Algerian Refugees in Morocco & Tunisia," May 1959.

153. The conflict in Syria is a recent example. "Rushing to Aid in Syrian War, but Claiming No Side," *New York Times*, 3 June 2013. Humanitarian aid can also lead to unintended consequences, such as providing support for an insurgent military. On the moral and political quandaries this poses for humanitarian organizations, see David Rieff, *A Bed for the Night: Humanitarianism in Crisis* (New York: Simon and Schuster, 2002). On Rwanda, see Alison Des Forges, *"Leave None to Tell the Story": Genocide in Rwanda* (New York: Human Rights Watch, 1999).

Chapter 5. The International Committee of the Red Cross in Algeria

Epigraph: ACICR B AG 040-020, Applicability of the Geneva Conventions in actual conflicts, Geneva, 7 September 1965.

1. The ICRC's experience with Mussolini during the Italo-Ethiopian war foreshadowed how it could be manipulated for political ends in a colonial context. See Rainer Baudendistel, *Between Bombs and Good Intentions: The Red Cross and the Italo-Ethiopian War, 1935–36* (New York: Berghahn Books, 2006).

2. Important work on the history of the ICRC includes Pierre Boissier, *Histoire du Comité international de la Croix-Rouge* (Geneva: Institut Henry-Dunant, 1978); François Bugnion, *The International Committee of the Red Cross and the Protection of War Victims*, trans. Patricia Colberg, Edward Markee, and Nicolas Sommer (Oxford: Macmillan Education, 2003); Forsythe, *The Humanitarians*; David Forsythe and Barbara Ann Rieffer-Flanagan, *The International Committee of the Red Cross: A Neutral Humanitarian Actor* (London: Routledge, 2007); Ian Reid, *The Evolution of the Red Cross* (Geneva: Henry Dunant Institute, 1975). Red Cross inaction during the Holocaust stained the organization's reputation. See Jean-Claude Favez, *The Red Cross and the Holocaust*, ed. and trans. John Fletcher and Beryl Fletcher (Cambridge: Cambridge University Press, 1999).

3. The three preexisting conventions provided protections for wounded soldiers and POWs.

4. *The Geneva Conventions of August 12, 1949* (Geneva: ICRC, 2007), 2.

5. For an account of the Geneva Conventions revision process, see Best, *Law and War Since 1945*, chaps. 4 and 5; G. I. A. D. Draper, *The Red Cross Conventions* (New York: Praeger, 1958); Mark Lewis, *The Birth of the New Justice*, chap. 8; Jean Pictet, *Les Conventions de Genève du 12 août 1949: Commentaire* (Geneva: Comité international de la Croix-Rouge, 1952).

6. Geneva Convention for the Amelioration of the Condition of the Wounded and Sick in Armed Forces in the Field; Geneva Convention for the Amelioration of the Condition of Wounded, Sick and Shipwrecked Members of Armed Forces at Sea; Geneva Convention Relative to the Treatment of Prisoners of War; and Geneva Convention Relative to the Protection of Civilian Persons in Time of War. *The Geneva Conventions of August 12, 1949*, 3–5.

7. ACICR B AG 040-020, Applicability of the Geneva Conventions in actual conflicts, Geneva, 7 September 1965.

8. Heather Wilson, *International Law and the Use of Force by National Liberation Movements* (Oxford: Clarendon Press, 1988), 43.

9. Klose, "The Colonial Testing Ground," 109. For a discussion of colonial violence in Kenya and Algeria, see Klose, *Human Rights in the Shadow of Colonial Violence*.

10. *The Geneva Conventions of August 12, 1949*, 24.

11. ACICR, Presidential Council Reports, verbal proceedings, 16 December 1954.

12. ACICR B AG 012 004, Red Cross principles and rules for action, report by Henri Coursier on the question of internal troubles, 18 January 1955.

13. ACICR B AG 012 004, Red Cross principles and rules for action, internal report on ICRC intervention in civil wars and internal conflicts, n.d.

14. Ibid.

15. Ibid.

16. ACICR B AG 012 004, report by Henri Coursier on the question of internal troubles, 18 January 1955.

17. ACICR B AG 013 008, Political, religious, and cultural questions relating to the Red Cross concept; action in favor of peace: letter to Pierre Gaillard concerning the British Red Cross in Kenya, 29 June 1955.

18. Quoted in Klose, "The Colonial Testing Ground," 112.

19. ACICR, Presidential Council Reports, verbal proceedings, Pierre Gaillard, "Note for the Committee," 7 June 1955.

20. For the role of national societies and their relationship with the ICRC, see *International Red Cross Handbook*, 591–614; Forsythe, *The Humanitarians*, 126–128.

21. Magali Herrmann, "Le CICR et la guerre d'Algérie: Une guerre sans nom, des prisonniers sans statut, 1954–1958" (Mémoire de license, Université de Genève, 2006), 2005 interview with Pierre Gaillard, 99–100.

22. Ibid., 100.

23. ACICR B AG 200 008-001, note from Pierre Gaillard to ICRC, 8 November 1954. At the time, the CRF only had a few Algerian members and it concentrated its recruitment efforts on the French living in Algeria, not the native population.

24. ACICR B AG 013 008, William Michel to Jean Pictet, 8 December 1955.

25. Herrmann, "Le CICR et la guerre d'Algérie," Gaillard interview, 99.

26. Ibid., 100–101.

27. ACICR B AG 200 008-001, ICRC meeting report, 16 November 1954.

28. ANOM GGA 11 CAB 37, Pierre Mendès-France to W. H. Michel, Head of the ICRC delegation in France, 2 February 1955.

29. ACICR, Presidential Council Reports, verbal proceedings, 16 December 1954.

30. France ratified them in 1951.

31. Herrmann, "Le CICR et la guerre d'Algérie," Gaillard interview, 106.

32. Raphaëlle Branche, "Entre droit humanitaire et intérêts politiques: Les missions algériennes du CICR," *Revue Historique* 301, no. 1 (1999): 105–106.

33. In his 2 February 1955 letter, Mendès-France granted the ICRC access to Algeria only if the delegates also visited detention centers in Morocco.

34. ANOM GGA 11 CAB 37, Report on detention sites in Morocco and Algeria that ICRC delegates visited between 28 February and 18 April 1955.

35. Herrmann, "Le CICR et la guerre d'Algérie," Gaillard interview, 102.

36. ANOM GGA 11 CAB 37, Report on detention sites in Morocco and Algeria that ICRC delegates visited between 28 February and 18 April 1955. For a discussion of suspended juridical practices in Algeria during the war, see Thénault, *Une drôle de justice.*

37. Maurice Faivre, *La Croix-Rouge pendant la guerre d'Algérie: Un éclairage nouveau sur les victimes et les internés* (Panazol: Lavauzelle, 2007), 16.

38. Herrmann, "Le CICR et la guerre d'Algérie," Gaillard interview, 103–104.

39. Faivre, *La Croix-Rouge,* 16. The report recommended that Algerians detained for actions related to the "events" should be separated from those who had been arrested for unrelated crimes. Presumably, the rationale was to keep the two groups apart so that those arrested for unrelated crimes did not learn about the war and become indoctrinated in prison. But the ICRC report did not explain this point outright.

40. ANOM GGA 11 CAB 37, Report on detention sites in Morocco and Algeria that ICRC delegates visited between 28 February and 18 April 1955.

41. Ibid.

42. Nicholas Berry, *War and the Red Cross: The Unspoken Mission* (New York: St. Martin's Press, 1997), 39.

43. Forsythe, *The Humanitarians,* 2.

44. Berry, *War and the Red Cross,* 1–3.

45. *International Red Cross Handbook,* 555.

46. ACICR B AG 200 008 001, Pierre Gaillard, "Note for the Committee," 24 May 1955.

47. Ibid.

48. ACICR B AG 200 008-001, Mohamed Khider and Ahmed Ben Bella to David de Traz, 2 March 1956.

49. ACICR B AG 008 001, Albert Camus, François Mauriac, Professor Massignon, Henri Roser, Maurice Voge, Malek Bennabi, Abdelaziz Khaldi, Joséphine Oliva, and Pierre Martin to Léopold Boissier, 16 March 1956.

50. ACICR B AG 008 001, Léopold Boissier to Pierre Martin, 20 March 1956.

51. ANOM GGA 12 CAB 96, Guy Mollet to Léopold Boissier, 6 April 1956; emphasis added.

52. Faivre, *La Croix-Rouge,* 17.

53. ANOM 81F/142, Étienne Dennery to the Minister of Foreign Affairs, 3 July 1956.

54. They carried out the third mission from 15 October to 3 November 1956, the fourth mission from 15 May to 6 July 1957, and fifth one from 23 November to 21 December 1957.

55. Mohamed Ben Ahmed, "Pierre Gaillard: Un humanitaire dans la guerre d'Algérie," *L'Humanitaire Maghreb* 5 (June 2003): 19.

56. Françoise Perret, "L'action du Comité international de la Croix-Rouge pendant la guerre d'Algérie (1954–1962)," *International Review of the Red Cross* 86, no. 856 (2004): 928.

57. Faivre, *La Croix-Rouge,* 19.

58. Ibid, 20.

59. Ibid.

60. *The Geneva Conventions of August 12, 1949,* 75.

61. Herrmann, "Le CICR et la guerre d'Algérie," Gaillard interview, 104.

62. Herrmann, "Le CICR et la guerre d'Algérie," 47.

63. ACICR B AG 210 008 001, note written by ICRC representative George Hoffman to the Central Red Cross Agency concerning French prisoners held by the FLN, Tunis, 11 December 1957.

64. Herrmann, "Le CICR et la guerre d'Algérie," Gaillard interview, 113–114.

65. Ibid.

66. ANOM GGA 12 CAB 243, L. Marcou to Pierre Hosteing, 10 December 1957.

67. ANOM GGA 12 CAB 243, Pierre Hosteing to L. Marcou, 16 December 1957.

68. ANA GPRA 78(a), Léopold Boissier, ICRC president, to the GPRA, 12 April 1958.

69. ANA GPRA 78(a), Léopold Boissier to the French government, 28 May 1958.

70. ANOM GGA 81F 142, "Projet de réponse au Comité International de la Croix-Rouge," (n.d.).

71. Ibid.

72. Perret, "L'action du Comité international," 940; ANOM GGA 81F 142, "Projet de réponse au Comité International de la Croix-Rouge."

73. Makaci, Le Croissant-Rouge Algérien, 144–145.

74. Mohamed Ben Ahmed, "Jacques Moreillon: Le droit humanitaire suit la pratique . . . il ne le précède pas," L'Humanitaire Maghreb 5 (June 2003): 22.

75. Le CICR et le conflit algérien (Geneva: Comité International de la Croix-Rouge, 1962), 8.

76. See Perret, "L'action du Comité international," 929; Thènault, Histoire de la guerre, 174.

77. Le CICR et le conflit algérien, 8–9.

78. ACICR B AG 251 008-007, instructions for Pierre Gaillard written by Roger Gallopin, Geneva, 28 November 1958.

79. ACICR B AG 251 008-007, Report on the sixth ICRC mission to Algeria, 5–23 December 1958.

80. Ibid.

81. Ibid.

82. ICRC delegates visited eighty-two sites from 15 October to 27 November 1959.

83. Beuve-Méry, a founder of Le Monde, also taught courses on the ethical responsibilities of the press.

84. ACICR B AG 063 026-030, confidential letter from Roger Gallopin to M. L. Biaggi de Blasys, 19 January 1960.

85. Joseph Rovan, "Témoignage sur Edmond Michelet, garde des Sceaux," in La Guerre d'Algérie et les Français, ed. Jean-Pierre Rioux (Paris: Fayard, 1990), 277.

86. Ibid., 276.

87. ACICR B AG 063 026-030, Gallopin to Biaggi de Blasys, 19 January 1960.

88. Among his early accomplishments as police chief was the 7 October 1958 ordinance, which allowed "Algerians to be held under arrest for two weeks, giving police and military time to interrogate individuals, while the Interior Minister was granted powers to hold Algerians in detention camps without trial or to return them into the hands of the army in Algeria." House and MacMaster, Paris 1961, 68–69.

89. Ibid., 103.

90. Faivre, La Croix-Rouge, 2004 interview with Pierre Gaillard, 70.

91. Vidal-Naquet, La raison d'état, 6; Branche, "La torture et l'armée," 348. In Branche's "Entre droit humanitaire et intérêt politiques," she writes that in a January 1997 interview with Gosselin, he told her he had taken the report to Le Monde journalist Pierre Viansson-Ponté.

92. French prime minister's statement published in Le Monde, 5 January 1960, p. 3.

93. "Après la publication d'une analyse du rapport de la Croix-Rouge internationale," Le Monde, 6 January 1960.

94. ACICR B AG 063 026-030, confidential note from Edmond Muller, 11 January 1960, Cairo; ACICR B AG 063 026-030, report on press reactions by Roger Du Pasquier, February 1960.

95. *Le Monde*, 5 January 1960, 1.

96. ACICR B AG 063 026-030, letters from Gallopin to Biaggi de Blasys, 19 January 1960; Laurent Vust to Roger Gallopin, 11 January 1960; report by Roger Du Pasquier, February 1960.

97. ACICR B AG 063 026-030, informational note from Léopold Boissier, 8 January 1960, Geneva.

98. Ibid.

99. Faivre, *La Croix-Rouge*, Gaillard interview, 70.

100. Moorehead, *Dunant's Dream*, 591.

101. *Le Monde*, 5 January 1960, 3.

102. ACICR B AG 251 008 010, Report on the eighth ICRC Mission to Algeria.

103. ACICR B AG 251 008 011, Report on the ninth ICRC Mission to Algeria.

104. ACICR B AG 251 008 016, Report on the tenth ICRC Mission to Algeria.

105. The OAS was a paramilitary group of French generals, including Raoul Salan, Edmond Jouhaud, Pierre Lagaillarde, and Jean-Jacques Susini, that aimed to stop Algerian independence. They formed the group after the January 1961 referendum on self-determination and enacted extreme violence throughout Algeria for the next eighteen months. For histories of the OAS, see Arnaud Déroulade, *OAS: Étude d'une organization secrète* (Hélette, France: Curutchet, 1997); Anne-Marie Duranton-Crabol, *Le temps de l'OAS* (Brussels: Editions Complexe, 1995); Georges Fleury, *Histoire secrète de l'OAS* (Paris: Grasset, 2002); Alexander Harrison, *Challenging De Gaulle: The OAS and the Counterrevolution in Algeria, 1954–1962* (New York: Praeger, 1989).

106. The *harkis* were Algerians who fought with the French army during the war. On the memory of *harkis*, see Saïd Boualam, *Les harkis au service de la France* (Paris: France-Empire, 1963); Vincent Crapanzano, *The Harkis: The Wound That Never Heals* (Chicago: University of Chicago Press, 2011); Jean-Jacques Jordi and Mohand Hamoumou, *Les harkis, une mémoire enfouie* (Paris: Autrement, 1999); Martin Evans, "The *Harkis*: The Experience and Memory of France's Muslim Auxiliaries," in *The Algerian War and the French Army, 1954–62: Experiences, Images, Testimonies*, ed. Martin S. Alexander, Martin Evans, and J. F. V. Keiger (New York: Palgrave Macmillan, 2002), 117–133; Michel Roux, *Les harkis, ou Les oubliés de l'histoire* (Paris: La Découverte, 1991).

107. Quoted in Faivre, *La Croix-Rouge*, Pierre Gaillard's mission in Algeria, 9 October 1962, 113–114.

108. Ibid., 115.

109. SHAT 1H 3210/ D4, Agreement between the ICRC and the Algerian government, signed by Ahmed Ben Bella and Roger Gallopin, no date, likely 1962.

110. ACICR, Presidential Council Reports, verbal proceedings, 1954 and 1955; and Herrmann, "Le CICR et la guerre d'Algérie," Gaillard interview, 112.

111. Forsythe, *The Humanitarians*, 92–94, and 242–278; David Forsythe, "Legal Management of Internal War: The 1977 Protocol on Non-International Armed Conflicts," *American Journal of International Law* 72, no. 2 (April 1978): 272–295.

Chapter 6. Global Diplomacy and the Fight for Self-Determination

1. Connelly, *A Diplomatic Revolution*; Wall, *France, the United States, and the Algerian War*; Klose, *Human Rights in the Shadow of Colonial Violence*; Thomas, "France Accused."

2. Robert Malley, *The Call from Algeria: Third Worldism, Revolution and the Turn to Islam* (Berkeley: University of California Press, 1996), 2.

3. In 1945, the United Nations had fifty-one members. By the end of 1960, it had one hundred members, many of which were African and Asian. Adam Roberts and Benedict Kingsbury, eds., *United Nations, Divided World: The UN's Roles in International Relations* (Oxford: Clarendon Press,

1998), 7. After 1945, the largest number of new countries were admitted for UN membership in 1955 and 1960, sixteen and seventeen, respectively, and coincided with national liberation movements. For analysis on how this new demographic impacted the UN, see Sunil Amrith and Glenda Sluga, "New Histories of the United Nations," *Journal of World History* 19, no. 3, (2008): 251–274; Yassin El-Ayouty, *United Nations and Decolonization: The Role of Afro-Asia* (The Hague, Netherlands: Martinus Nijhoff, 1971); Evan Luard, *A History of the United Nations*, vol. 2, *The Age of Decolonization, 1955–1965* (New York: Palgrave Macmillan, 1989); Robert A. Hill and Edmond Keller, eds., *Trustee for the Human Community: Ralph J. Bunche, the United Nations, and the Decolonization of Africa* (Athens: Ohio University Press, 2010).

4. Burke, *Decolonization and the Evolution of International Rights*, 36.

5. Mazower, *No Enchanted Palace* and *Governing the World*.

6. The UN and its charter's applicability were tested immediately by colonial questions. In 1946, Indian prime minister Jawaharlal Nehru brought the first colonial issue to the General Assembly: South Africa's discriminatory practices toward Indians. He challenged a European country's right to rule abroad and publicly disputed what South African prime minister Jan Smuts considered an "instrument of the white man's alliance." Mazower, *No Enchanted Palace*, 165. Crises in Malaya (1948–1960) and Indochina (1945–1954) had drawn additional attention to the unresolved problem of how to defend global security while simultaneously respecting state sovereignty.

7. FLN proclamation, 1 November 1954, in André Mandouze, ed., *La révolution algérienne par les textes* (Algiers: Éditions ANEP, 2006), 150.

8. According to GPRA records at the Algerian National Archives (ANA), this is the FLN's first international outreach after 1 November 1954 pertaining to bringing its case to the United Nations.

9. ANA GPRA 001/008/013, telegram from Abed Bou Hafa to Mohamed Khider about bringing the Algerian question to the United Nations Security Council, 14 December 1954.

10. "Terrorisme en Afrique du Nord: Plusieurs tués en Algérie au cours d'attaques simultanées de postes de police," *Le Monde*, 2 November 1954, p. 1. The *New York Times* ran a headline with comparable language, "Terrorist Bands Kill 7 in Algeria; French Send Aid," 2 November 1954, p. 1.

11. "Après la série d'attentats commis dimanche en Algérie, le calme est revenue dans l'algérois et en oranie," *Le Monde*, 3 November 1954, p. 1. In contrast, the French communist newspaper *L'Humanité* covered the story under the headlines "Stop Repression in Algeria, Massive Arrests" (2 November 1954, p. 1) and "Armored Vehicles in Action Against Algerians in the Aurès Mountains" (3 November 1954, p. 1).

12. United Nations, Security Council, Official Records (UN SCOR) Document S/3341, Permanent Representative Asad Al-Faqih to the President of the Security Council, 5 January 1955.

13. Ibid.

14. A UN Working Paper on the Algerian situation confirmed the deployment of French troops during the first year of the war. UN ARMS, S-0188-005-07, Department of Political and Security Council Affairs, Working Paper No. 381, 8 September 1955.

15. UN SCOR Document S/3341, Asad Al-Faqih to the president of the Security Council, 5 January 1955.

16. Jeffrey Byrne uses the term "guerrilla diplomats" to describe the FLN external delegation that acted as ambassadors around the world. Byrne, "The Pilot Nation," 41.

17. Scholars of international relations and political science have written most of the histories of the Bandung Conference. See Roeslan Abdulgani, *The Bandung Connection: The Asia-Africa Conference in Bandung in 1955,* trans. Molly Bondar (Singapore: Gunung Agung, 1981); A. Appadorai, *The Bandung Conference* (New Delhi: Indian Council of World Affairs, 1955); George Mc-Turnan Kahin, *The African-Asian Conference: Bandung, Indonesia, April 1955* (Ithaca, N.Y.: Cornell University Press, 1956); David Kimche, *The Afro-Asian Movement: Ideology and Foreign Policy of*

the Third World (New York: Halstead Press, 1973); Robert Mortimer, *The Third World Coalition in International Politics* (New York: Praeger, 1980); Robert Vitalis, "The Midnight Ride of Kwame Nkrumah and Other Fables of Bandung," *Humanity* 4, no. 2 (2013): 261–288. For a discussion of the impact of human rights at Bandung, see Roland Burke, "The Compelling Dialogue of Freedom: Human Rights at the Bandung Conference," *Human Rights Quarterly* 28, no. 4 (2006): 947–965; Burke, *Decolonization and the Evolution of International Human Rights*, 13–34.

18. Christopher Lee, ed., *Making a World After Empire: The Bandung Moment and Its Political Afterlives* (Athens: Ohio University Press, 2010), 3.

19. Quoted in Lee, *Making a World*, 5. For participant speeches, see *Asia-Africa Speaks from Bandung* (Jakarta: Ministry of Foreign Affairs, Republic of Indonesia, 1955).

20. I thank Roland Burke for kindly sharing an overview of unpublished Bandung Conference proceedings with me. Indian Council of World Affairs Library. Record produced by the Secretariat of the Asian-African Conference. AAC/SR/4, Summary Record of the meeting with Dr. Ali Sastroamidjojo.

21. Meynier, *Histoire intérieur du FLN*, 581.

22. Bandung Conference proceedings. AAC/SR/4, Summary Record of the meeting with Dr. Ali Sastroamidjojo.

23. Quoted in Byrne, "The Pilot Nation," 297.

24. Mohamed Alwan, *Algeria Before the United Nations* (New York: Robert Speller & Sons, 1959), 16–17.

25. Ibid, 30–31.

26. United Nations, General Assembly Official Records (UN GAOR), Tenth Session, 530th Plenary Meeting, 30 September 1955, 73–75.

27. UN ARMS, S-0442-0189-03, Secretary-General of the League of Arab States to president of the UN General Assembly, 11 November 1955.

28. Alwan, *Algeria Before the United Nations*, 17; and UN GAOR, Resolution A/RES/909(X), 25 November 1955.

29. Evans, *The Memory of Resistance*, 137–171.

30. Benjamin Stora, *Histoire de la guerre d'Algérie, 1954–1962* (Paris: La Découverte, 1993), 20.

31. Ibid., 21.

32. UN ARMS, S-0442-0189-03, exploratory memorandum on the Algerian question submitted to the Security Council, signed by UN members from Afghanistan, Burma, Ceylon, Egypt, India, Indonesia, Iran, Iraq, Jordan, Lebanon, Libya, Pakistan, Philippines, Saudi Arabia, Syria, and Yemen, 12 April 1956.

33. UN ARMS, S-0442-0189-03, Henry Cabot Lodge, Jr., to Dr. Sudjarwo Tjondronegoro, 18 April 1956.

34. For example, see UN ARMS, S-0188-005-08, confidential note on Algeria, 20 June 1956, which explains the political and military developments that year.

35. International relations scholars call this strategy employed by nonstate actors "boomerang theory," a process that enables them to "bypass their state and directly search out international allies to try and bring pressure on their states from outside." Margaret E. Keck and Kathryn Sikkink, *Activists Beyond Borders: Advocacy Networks in International Politics* (Ithaca, N.Y.: Cornell University Press, 1998), 12. I thank Cristina Balboa for bringing this literature to my attention.

36. There is a discrepancy in the spelling of Yazid and Lahouel's first names in the Algerian documents. I use "M'hamed" and "Hocine," which appear in Achour Cheurfi, *Dictionnaire de la révolution algérienne, 1954–1962* (Algiers: Casbah, 2004). Alternative spellings, "M'hammed," "Mohammed," and "Hussein" also appear in GPRA files, reports, international press statements, and correspondence.

37. In 1948, Aït Ahmed, a twenty-seven-year-old member of the Algerian People's Party Political Office, wrote a thirty-page memorandum that laid out the tenets of revolution. In it, he explained

the necessity of incorporating different political ideologies as well as launching a comprehensive plan that moved beyond general terrorism. "Rapport d'Aït Ahmed, membre du Bureau Politique du PPA, au Comité Central, décembre 1948," in Harbi, *Les archives de la révolution algérienne*, 15–49.

38. ANA GPRA 002/003/010, Sarwar Hasan to Hocine Aït Ahmed, 13 March 1956.

39. ANA GPRA 002/003/010, letter from M'hamed Yazid to the external delegation in Cairo, 23 March 1956; and from M'hamed Yazid and Hocine Lahouel to the external delegation in Cairo, 28 March 1958.

40. ANA GPRA 002/003/010, M'hamed Yazid and Hocine Lahouel to the external delegation in Cairo, 18 April 1956.

41. ANA GPRA 002/003/010, M'hamed Yazid and Hocine Lahouel to the external delegation in Cairo, 12 May 1956.

42. ANA GPRA 002/003/010, M'hamed Yazid to the external delegation in Cairo, 23 March 1956.

43. ANA GPRA 002/003/010, letter from Hocine Lahouel and M'hamed Yazid to the external delegation, 1 April 1956.

44. Ibid.

45. Ibid.

46. Ibid.

47. ANA GPRA 002/003/010, text of statement by Hocine Lahouel and M'hamed Yazid, members of the Algerian delegation representing the National Liberation Front, at a press conference at New Delhi on Friday, 6 April 1956.

48. Matthew Connelly conducted interviews with Yazid, chronicling his time in New York as an FLN delegate. See Connelly, *A Diplomatic Revolution*, esp. chap. 5, which focuses primarily on 1957 and 1958.

49. ANA GPRA 001/008/015, Mohamed Khider, memo to the Governments of the Afro-Asian Nations, 8 March 1956.

50. ANA GPRA 001 /011 /021, Hocine Aït Ahmed to the external delegation in Cairo, 30 March 1956.

51. Ibid.

52. Ibid.

53. Ibid.

54. ANA GPRA 001 /011 /016, note from the Department of Public Relations, United African Nationalist Movement, New York, 4 July 1956.

55. ANA GPRA 001/011/021, letter from Hocine Aït Ahmed to the external delegation in Cairo, 30 March 1956.

56. ANA GPRA 002/003/015, prime minister Nehru "Statement on Algeria," 25 May 1956.

57. Ibid.

58. Ibid.

59. UN ARMS, S-0442-0189-03, exploratory memorandum on the Algerian question, submitted to the Security Council, signed by UN members from Afghanistan, Burma, Ceylon, Egypt, India, Indonesia, Iran, Iraq, Jordan, Lebanon, Libya, Pakistan, the Philippines, Saudi Arabia, Syria, and Yemen, 12 April 1956.

60. Ibid.

61. The eleven countries on the Security Council in 1956 were Australia, Belgium, the Republic of China, Cuba, France, Iran, Peru, the Union of Soviet Socialist Republics, the United Kingdom of Great Britain and Northern Ireland, the United States of America, and Yugoslavia. Of this group the five permanent members were the Republic of China, France, the Soviet Union, the United Kingdom, and the United States.

62. UN SCOR Document S/3589, letter from representatives of Afghanistan, Egypt, Indonesia, Iran, Iraq, Jordan, Lebanon, Libya, Pakistan, Saudi Arabia, Syria, Thailand, and Yemen to the president of the Security Council, 16 April 1956.

63. Ibid. Self-determination was not a new concept put forth in the 1950s. The term took on significance for colonies when Woodrow Wilson began discussing it during World War I. See Manela, *The Wilsonian Moment*. During the interwar and World War II years, self-determination continued to plague Western leaders. See Mark Mazower, *Dark Continent: Europe's Twentieth Century* (New York: Vintage Books, 2000).

64. UN SCOR Document, S/3589, Representatives of Afghanistan, Egypt, Indonesia, Iran, Iraq, Jordan, Lebanon, Libya, Pakistan, Saudi Arabia, Syria, Thailand, and Yemen to the president of the Security Council, 16 April 1956.

65. UN SCOR, Eleventh Year, 730th Meeting, 26 June 1956, 5.

66. Ibid., 729th Meeting, 26 June 1956, 6.

67. Ibid.

68. Ibid., 11–12.

69. "Introduction de la 2ème édition," in "Résistance algérienne," special issue no. 4, *El Moudjahid*, November 1956, 58.

70. Khalfa Mameri, *Les Nations Unies face à la "Question algérienne," 1954–1962* (Algiers: Société nationale d'édition et de diffusion, 1969), 24.

71. UN SCOR, Eleventh Year, 729th Meeting, 26 June 1956, 16.

72. Ibid., 17.

73. UN SCOR, Eleventh Year, 730th Meeting, 26 June 1956, 3.

74. The American, Australian, Belgian, British, Cuban, French, and Peruvian delegations voted against it; the Iranian and Soviet Union delegations voted for its inclusion; and the Chinese and Yugoslav delegations abstained.

75. UN SCOR, Eleventh Year, 730th Meeting, 26 June 1956, 16.

76. Ibid.

77. For comprehensive histories of Morocco and Tunisia, see Pennell, *Morocco Since 1830*; and Perkins, *A History of Modern Tunisia*.

78. The first emergency special session took place in New York from 1 to 10 November; the second emergency special session, from 4 until 10 November. Representatives of Afghanistan, Australia, Colombia, the Dominican Republic, France, Indonesia, Iraq, the Soviet Union, and the United States served as the Credentials Committee for both sessions.

79. Quoted in Westad, *The Global Cold War*, 125.

80. William Roger Louis, "The United Nations and the Suez Crisis: British Ambivalence Towards the Pope on the East River," in *Ends of British Imperialism: The Scramble for Empire, Suez and Decolonization* (New York: I. B. Tauris, 2006), 669.

81. For histories of the Hungarian Revolution, see Hannah Arendt, "Totalitarian Imperialism: Reflections on the Hungarian Revolution," *Journal of Politics* 20, no. 1 (1958): 5–43; László Eörsi, *Hungarian Revolution of 1956: Myths and Realities*, trans. Mario D. Fenyo (Boulder, Colo.: Social Science Monographs, 2006); and David Pryce-Jones, *The Hungarian Revolution* (London: Benn, 1969).

82. UN SCOR Document S/3730, letter from the representatives of France, the United Kingdom of Great Britain and Northern Ireland, and the United States to the president of the Security Council, concerning "The Situation in Hungary," 3 November 1956.

83. Ibid.

84. UN GAOR, Twelfth Session, 684th Plenary Meeting, 23 September 1957, 75.

85. See Wall, *France, the United States, and the Algerian War*; and Connelly, *A Diplomatic Revolution*.

86. For examples of American diplomatic thinking about the first year of the Algerian war, see U.S. Department of State, *Foreign Relations of the United States*, 1952–1954, vol. 11, part 1, Africa, pp. 382–405.

87. NARA, RG 59, International Organizations and the United Nations, Subject Files of the

Office of United Nations Political and Security Affairs, 1945–1957, Box 11, Francis Wilcox, report on the U.S. approach to colonial questions in the United Nations, 14 September 1955.

88. Westad, *The Global Cold War*, 110.

89. American fears were not totally unfounded. As Westad has shown, the United States and the Soviet Union battled not only for the hearts and minds of people from Cuba to Angola, and from Ethiopia to Iran, but also for ideological and military supremacy. Westad, *The Global Cold War*. For additional perspectives on the impact of the Cold War in Algeria, see Connelly, *A Diplomatic Revolution*; and Byrne, "The Pilot Nation."

90. NARA, RG 59, International Organizations and the United Nations, Subject Files of the Office of United Nations Political and Security Affairs, 1945–1957, Box 11, Wilcox report, 14 September 1955.

91. During the tenth, eleventh, and twelfth sessions, the United States voted against the inclusion of Algeria on the agenda, and American officials continued to send arms and helicopters to France as part of the NATO agreement. Even though they insisted the shipments were not to be used as part of the French war effort in Algeria, on occasion American State Department officers received word that the French military brought that equipment to Algeria. NARA, RG 59, Africa Lot Files, Office of Northern African Affairs, 1944–1963, Box 1, memorandum of conversation between Sheikh Abdullah al-Khayyal, ambassador of Saudi Arabia, Raymon Hare, deputy undersecretary for political affairs, and Hermann Eilts, officer-in-charge, Arabian Peninsula affairs, 5 October 1960; and letter from Charles Yost at the American Embassy in Rabat, Morocco, to William Witman II, director, Office of North African Affairs, 28 September 1960.

92. Connelly, *A Diplomatic Revolution*, 120.

93. ANA GPRA 001/008/012, Statement from the Asian-African Group to be distributed to governments, 26 April 1956.

94. ANA GPRA 002/003/014, confidential report from U Win, chairman of the Asian-African Group, on his interview with the secretary-general of the United Nations on Tuesday, 8 May 1956, New York, 15 May 1956.

95. African and Asian UN representatives sent additional letters that conveyed a similar message. See, for example, UN ARMS, S-0442-0189-04, letter from nineteen UN members to Dag Hammarskjöld about the deteriorating situation in Algeria and the systematic violence used by the French, 15 April 1957; telegram from Arab League to UN about Algerian situation, 10 September 1958.

96. Frantz Fanon, "This Is the Voice of Algeria," in *A Dying Colonialism* (New York: Grove Press, 1994).

97. Evans, *Algeria*, 192.

98. Quoted in Alwan, *Algeria Before the United Nations*, 34. Also see UN GAOR, Eleventh Session, First Committee, 831st Meeting, 4 February 1957, 105.

99. Quoted in Alwan, *Algeria Before the United Nations*, 35.

100. "The General Assembly, having heard the statements made by various delegations and discussed the question of Algeria, having regard to the situation in Algeria which is causing much suffering and loss of human lives, expresses the hope that, in a spirit of co-operation, a peaceful, democratic and just solution will be found through appropriate means, in conformity with the principles of the Charter of the United Nations." UN GAOR, Resolution A/RES/1012(XI), 654th Plenary Meeting, 15 February 1957.

101. *Pourparlers* are informal preliminary discussions.

102. *Algeria Speaks: The Case for Algeria at the 12th UN General Assembly*, prepared by the Arab States Delegation Office, United Nations Section (New York: Arab States Delegations Office, 1958), 18, emphasis in the original.

103. ANA GPRA 004/002/027, confidential report written by M'hamed Yazid to the external delegation in Cairo, regarding preparation for the twelfth UN session, New York, 19 June 1957.

104. Ibid.

105. Ibid.

106. UN GAOR, Twelfth Session, 682nd Plenary Meeting, 20 September 1957, 48.

107. Ibid., 687th Plenary Meeting, 25 September 1957, 137.

108. France's critics had cause for concern. The UN compiled a report in November 1957 that questioned French military tactics against the FLN. It detailed how the military could likely keep fighting the Algerian "rebels" for "an indefinite period of time" because "the burden of the Algerian war . . . does not exceed 4 per cent of French national income." UN ARMS, S-0188-005-09, confidential note on the military situation in Algeria, 8 November 1957.

109. UN GAOR, Twelfth Session, 687th Plenary Meeting, 25 September 1957, 146.

110. Ibid., 688th Plenary Meeting, 25 September 1957, 149.

111. Ibid.

112. UN GAOR, Twelfth Session, 692nd Plenary Meeting, 27 September 1957, 199.

113. Ibid., 694th Plenary Meeting, 30 September 1957, 218.

114. Ibid., 697th Plenary Meeting, 2 October 1957, 232.

115. Ibid., 699th Plenary Meeting, 3 October 1957, 259.

116. *Algeria Speaks*, 5.

117. UN GAOR, Twelfth Session, 700th Plenary Meeting, 3 October 1957, 277.

118. Ibid.

119. Ibid.

120. Horne, *A Savage War of Peace*, 249.

121. UN GAOR Document S/4013, letter from Tunisian UN representative Mongi Slim to the president of the Security Council, 29 May 1958.

122. Wall, *France, the United States, and the Algerian War*, 100.

123. Ibid, 114; "L'Algérie et les bon offices Anglo-Americains," *El Moudjahid*, 28 February 1958, 341.

124. Wall, *France, the United States, and the Algerian War*, 99; Connelly, *A Diplomatic Revolution*, 160–170.

125. ANA GPRA 004/002/051, report written by M'hamed Yazid, FLN New York office, 29 May 1958; ANA GPRA 004/001/042, report written by M'hamed Yazid on the American attitude toward the Algerian question, FLN New York office, June 1958.

126. Evans, *Algeria*, 236.

127. On Eurafrica, see Yves Montarsolo, *L'Eurafrique: Contrepoint de l'idée d'Europe; Le cas français de la fin de la deuxième guerre mondiale aux négociations des traités de Rome* (Aix-en-Provence: Publications de l'Université de Provence, 2010).

128. Evans, *Algeria*, 240. These numbers seem high, a fact Evans also acknowledges.

129. Ibid., 241.

130. ANA GPRA 004/001/043, letter written by M'hamed Yazid about pursuing African support for the Algerian cause at the next Accra Conference, FLN New York office, June 1958; ANA GPRA 004/001/066, report written by M'hamed Yazid in New York, 16 December 1958.

131. Quoted in Connelly, *A Diplomatic Revolution*, 209.

132. Horne, *A Savage War of Peace*, 346.

133. "Déclaration *in extenso* du GPRA," 28 September 1959, in Mandouze, *La révolution algérienne par les textes*, 134–135.

134. UN ARMS, S-0442-0189-04, letter from UN Asian-African Group to Dag Hammarskjöld, 14 September 1960. For examples of letters that various groups sent the UN in October and November 1960, see UN ARMS, S-0442-0189-09, letter from the General Union of Muslim Algerian Students in Tunis, 22 October 1960; letter from the Youth Council of Madagascar, 4 November 1960; letter from the Secretariat of the Iraqi Women's Society, 9 November 1960; letter from Ceylon University Student's Federation, 10 November 1960; letter from Iraqi Bar Association in Baghdad, 29 November 1960.

135. UN GAOR Resolution A/RES/1573(XV) "Question of Algeria," 19 December 1960.

136. Ibid.

137. NARA, RG 59, Africa Lot Files, Office of Northern African Affairs, 1944–1963, Box 1, talking points on Algeria for the meeting with the Joint Chiefs of Staff, 8 December 1960.

138. Ibid.

139. In 1960 Cameroon, Central African Republic, Chad, Congo (Brazzaville), Congo (Leopoldville), Cyprus, Dahomey, Gabon, Ivory Coast, Malagasy Republic, Mali, Niger, Nigeria, Senegal, Somalia, Togo, and Upper Volta were admitted to the United Nations. http://www.un.org/en/members/growth.shtml, accessed 26 July 2012.

140. Burke, *Decolonization and the Evolution of International Human Rights*, 1–3.

141. Ibid., 35.

142. There were several other international events in 1960 that help explain the adoption of the Declaration on the Granting of Independence to Colonial Countries and Peoples. They include British prime minister Harold Macmillan's "Winds of Change" speech, Congolese independence, and the Addis Ababa Conference of Independent African States. El-Ayouty, *United Nations and Decolonization*, 207–213.

143. UN GAOR, Fifteenth Session, 926th Plenary Meeting, 19 December 1960, 1421.

144. Ibid., 1423.

145. Ibid., 1424.

146. UN ARMS, S-0442-0189-04, letter from Dr. Anwar No'man, executive director of the UAR National Congress, Cairo branch, to UN secretary-general D. Hammarskjöld, 17 December 1960.

147. UN ARMS, S-0442-0189-09, fifteen identical form letters to the Chairman of the UN from Iraqi men, ages twenty-one to fifty, employed by Iraqi Airways, no date.

148. UN ARMS, S-0442-0189-05, letter from Abdel-Hamid Khaled Hamdy, acting director of UNIC in Cairo, to William C. Powell, External Relations Division, OPI, 1 September 1961.

149. UN ARMS, S-0884-0001-10, statement by USSR Ministry of Foreign Affairs, 29 March 1962.

150. See Chamberlain, *The Global Offensive*.

Conclusion

1. Quoted in Mandouze, *La révolution algérienne par les textes*, 186–187.

2. Evans, *Algeria*, 311.

3. US ARMS, S-0884-0001-10, statement by Benyoucef Benkhedda to the Algerian people, Tunis, 9 May 1962.

4. Shepard, *The Invention of Decolonization*, 207.

5. Mostefa Khiati, *Quelle santé pour les Algériens* (Algiers: Éditions Maghreb Relations, 1990), 4.

6. The United Nations and the International Committee of the Red Cross offered vital assistance in this endeavor. UN ARMS, S-0884-0001-12, report on contributions of money and tents received in response to High Commissioner's appeals on behalf of Algerian refugees, 27 April 1962; interim report by the United Nations High Commissioner for refugees on the operation for the repatriation of Algerian refugees, 11 June 1962; statement on aid sought for 600,000 Algerians, UNHCR and League of Red Cross Societies launch joint appeal for $8.3 million, 21 June 1962; ACICR B AG 234 008-004, refugees in diverse countries, 1961–1968.

7. Mahfoud Bennoune, *The Making of Contemporary Algeria, 1830–1987: Colonial Upheavals and Post-Independence Development* (Cambridge: Cambridge University Press, 1988), 7.

8. United Nations Office at Geneva (UNOG) Archives, SO 215/1 ALG, 1961–1965, Memo from the Director the Popular Resistance Organization (L'Organisation de la Resistance Populaire)

to all International Organizations, 5 September 1965; confidential letter to UN Secretary-General U Thant, 6 September 1965.

9. UNOG, SO 215/1 ALG, 1966–1967, "*Livre Blanc des tortures et sévices, Algérie, Septembre–Novembre* 1965," by the Committee for the Defense of Ahmed Ben Bella and the Other Victims of Repression in Algeria, 1 March 1966.

10. UNOG, SO 215/1 ALG, 1961–1965, letter to UN Secretary-General, 3 November 1965; SO 215/1 ALG, 1966–1967, letter to Chairman of Human Rights Commission, September 1966.

11. Fanon, *The Wretched of the Earth*, 29.

12. Manela, *The Wilsonian Moment*, 225.

Bibliography

Primary Sources: Archival

Algeria

Algerian National Archives (ANA)
    Croissant-Rouge Algérien
    Gouvernement Provisoire de la République Algérienne
Bibliothèque des Glycines

France

Archives de la Croix-Rouge Française (CRF)
Bibliothèque Interuniversitaire de Médecine (BIUM)
Archives Nationales d'Outre-Mer (ANOM)
    81F
    Alger-Constantine SAS
    Cabinet Civil (CAB)
    Préfecture d'Alger
Centre d'accueil et de recherches des Archives nationales (CARAN)
    F1a 5060
Établissement de communication et de production audiovisuelle de la défense (ECPAD)
Service Historique de l'Armée de Terre (SHAT)
    Série 1H
Val-de-Grâce Library

Switzerland

Archives of the International Committee of the Red Cross (ACICR)
    B AG 060
    B AG 062
    B AG 063
    B AG 121
    B AG 200
    B AG 202
    B AG 210
    B AG 225

B AG 229
B AG 234
B AG 251
B AG 280
Rapports du Conseil de la Présidence, 1954–1960
International Committee of the Red Cross Library
United Nations Office at Geneva (UNOG) Archives
    SO 215/1 ALG
    SO 227
    SO 262/1

United States

Library of Congress
National Archives and Records Administration, College Park, MD (NARA)
    Record Group 59
United Nations Archives and Records Management Section (UN ARMS)
    S-0188-005
    S-0442-0189
    S-0884-0001

Primary Sources: Interviews in Algeria

Jeanine Belkhodja
Pierre Chaulet
Jean-Paul Grangaud
Salim Hafiz
Youcef Khatib (Colonel Hassan)
Mohamed Toumi
Rabah Zérari (Commandant Azzedine)

Newspapers and Magazines

L'Echo d'Alger
L'Esprit
Libération
Le Monde
El Moudjahid
New York Times
Témoignage chrétien
Vie et Bonté

Primary Sources: Printed

Abbas, Ferhat. *Le jeune Algérien (1930): De la colonie vers la province.* Paris: Garnier, 1981.
"Actes de la Journée Commémorative du 19 mai 1956: Journée de l'étudiant." Bulletin d'Information de la Faculté de Médecine d'Alger, 19 May 2007, no. 3.
Algeria Speaks: The Case for Algeria at the 12th UN General Assembly. Prepared by the Arab States Delegations Office, United Nations Section. New York: Arab States Delegations Office, 1958.
Alleg, Henri. *La Question.* Paris: Minuit, 1958.
———. *The Question.* Trans. John Calder. New York: George Braziller, 1958.
Asia-Africa Speaks from Bandung. Jakarta: Ministry of Foreign Affairs, Republic of Indonesia, 1955.
Aussaresses, Paul. *Services Spéciaux: Algérie, 1955–1957.* Paris: Perrin, 2001.
Azikiwe, Nnamdi. *The Atlantic Charter and British West Africa, Memorandum on Postwar Reconstruction of the Colonies and Protectorates in British West Africa.* Lagos: West African Press Delegation to Great Britain, 1943.
Azzedine, Commandant. *On nous appelait fellaghas.* Paris: Stock, 1976.
Bourkaïb, Mustapha. *Contribution à l'étude de l'assistance médicale aux indigènes d'Algérie: Hôpitaux et infirmeries.* Algiers: Adolphe Jourdan, 1915.
Le CICR et le conflit algérien. Geneva: Comité International de la Croix-Rouge, 1962.
Debenedetti, Inspector. "Service de santé militaire et assistance médicale gratuite aux populations autochtones en Algérie." *Revue du Corps de Santé Militaire* 1 (March 1958).
De Gaulle, Charles. *Discours et messages.* Vol. 3, *Avec le renouveau, mai 1958–juillet 1962.* Paris: Plon, 1970.
———. *Lettres, notes et carnets: Juin 1951–mai 1958.* Paris: Plon, 1985.
———. *Lettres, notes et carnets: Juin 1958–décembre 1960.* Paris: Plon, 1985.
Fanon, Frantz. *A Dying Colonialism.* Trans. Haakon Chevalier. New York: Grove Press, 1965.
———. *The Wretched of the Earth.* Trans. Constance Farrington. New York: Grove Press, 1965.
Feraoun, Mouloud. *Journal, 1955–1962: Reflections on the French-Algerian War.* Trans. Mary Ellen Wolf. Lincoln: University of Nebraska Press, 2000.
International Committee of the Red Cross. *Commission of Government Experts for the Study of Conventions for the Protection of War Victims, Geneva, April 14 to 26, 1947: Preliminary Documents Submitted by the International Committee of the Red Cross.* Vol. 3, *Condition and Protection of Civilians in Time of War.* Geneva, 1947.
Lacoste, Robert. *Algérie: Quelques aspects des problèmes économiques et sociaux.* Algiers: Baconnier, 1957.
Mandela, Nelson. *Long Walk to Freedom: The Autobiography of Nelson Mandela.* Boston: Back Bay Books, 1994.
Salan, Raoul. *Participation de l'Armée aux tâches de pacification.* Algiers, 1958.
Sections Administratives Spécialisées, Goums et Harkas: Instructions comptables. Algiers, 1955.
Séminaire sur le développement d'un système national de santé: L'expérience algérienne. Algiers: Ministère de la Santé, 1983.
Le Service de santé des armées en Algérie, 1830–1958. Paris: SPEI, 1958.
Soustelle, Jacques. *L'espérance trahie, 1958–1961.* Paris: Éditions de l'Alma, 1962.
Tillion, Germaine. *L'Algérie en 1957.* Paris: Éditions de Minuit, 1957.
Toumi, Mohamed. "La Médecine au Maquis." *Bulletin d'Information de la Faculté de Médecine d'Alger,* 19 May 2007.
United Nations, General Assembly, Official Records (UN GAOR)
United Nations, Security Council, Official Records (UN SCOR)
U.S. Department of State. *Foreign Relations of the United States, 1952–1954.* Vol. 11, *Africa and South Asia.*

——. *Foreign Relations of the United States, 1955–1957.* Vol. 18, *Africa.*
——. *Foreign Relations of the United States, 1958–1960.* Vol. 13, *Arab-Israeli Dispute; United Arab Republic; North Africa.*
——. *Foreign Relations of the United States, 1961–1963.* Vol. 21, *Africa.*

Secondary Sources

Abdulgani, Roeslan. *The Bandung Connection: The Asia-Africa Conference in Bandung in 1955.* Trans. Molly Bondar. Singapore: Gunung Agung, 1981.
Abi-Mershed, Osama. *Apostles of Modernity: Saint-Simonians and the Civilizing Mission in Algeria.* Stanford, Calif.: Stanford University Press, 2010.
Adelman, Jeremy. "An Age of Imperial Revolutions." *American Historical Review* 113, no. 2 (2008): 319–340.
Ageron, Charles-Robert. "Complots et purges dans l'armée de libération algérienne, 1958–1961." *Vingtième Siècle: Revue d'histoire* 59, no. 1 (1998): 15–27.
——. *Histoire de l'Algérie contemporaine.* Vol. 2, *De l'insurrection de 1871 au déclenchement de la guerre de libération (1954).* Paris: Presses Universitaires de France, 1979.
——. "Un manuscrit inédit de Ferhat Abbas: 'Mon testament politique.'" *Revue française d'histoire d'outre mer* 81, no. 303 (1994): 181–197.
——. "Le mouvement 'Jeune Algérien' de 1900–1923." In *Études maghrébines: Mélanges Charles-André Julien,* ed. Pierre Marthelot and André Raymond, 217–243. Paris: Presses Universitaires de France, 1964.
Aït Ahmed, Hocine. *Mémoires d'un combatant.* Algiers: Barzah, 2009.
Aït-El-Djoudi, Dalila. *La guerre d'Algérie vue par l'ALN, 1954–1962: L'armée française sous le regard des combattants algériens.* Paris: Éditions Autrement, 2007.
Al-Fasi, 'Allal. *Al-harakat al-istiqlaliyya fi-l-Maghrib al-'Arabi.* Tangier: Abd al Salam Gassus, n.d.
Alterman, Jon. *Egypt and American Foreign Assistance, 1952–1956: Hopes Dashed.* New York: Palgrave Macmillan, 2002.
Alwan, Mohamed. *Algeria Before the United Nations.* New York: Robert Speller & Sons, 1959.
Amir, Mohammed Benaïssa. *Contribution à l'étude de l'histoire de la santé en Algérie: Autour d'une expérience vécue en ALN Wilaya V.* Algiers: Office des Publications Universitaires, 1986.
Amrith, Sunil. *Decolonizing International Health: India and Southeast Asia, 1930–65.* New York: Palgrave Macmillan, 2006.
Amrith, Sunil, and Glenda Sluga. "New Histories of the United Nations." *Journal of World History* 19, no. 3 (2008): 251–274.
Anderson, Warwick, and Hans Pols. "Scientific Patriotism: Medical Science and National Self-Fashioning in Southeast Asia." *Comparative Studies in Society and History* 1, no. 54 (2012): 93–113.
Anghie, Anthony. *Imperialism, Sovereignty and the Making of International Law.* Cambridge: Cambridge University Press, 2007.
Appadorai, A. *The Bandung Conference.* New Delhi: Indian Council of World Affairs, 1955.
Arendt, Hannah. "Totalitarian Imperialism: Reflections on the Hungarian Revolution." *Journal of Politics* 20, no. 1 (1958): 5–43.
Au, Sokhieng. *Mixed Medicines: Health and Culture in Colonial Cambodia.* Chicago: University of Chicago University Press, 2011.
Baudendistel, Rainer. *Between Bombs and Good Intentions: The Red Cross and the Italo-Ethiopian War, 1935–36.* New York: Berghahn Books, 2006.
Beaud, Olivier. *La puissance de l'état.* Paris: Presses Universitaires de France, 1994.
Beauvoir, Simone de, and Gisèle Halimi. *Djamila Boupacha: The Story of the Torture of a Young*

Algerian Girl Which Shocked Liberal French Opinion. Trans. Peter Green. New York: Macmillan, 1962.

Beckett, Ian, ed. *The Roots of Counter-Insurgency: Armies and Guerilla Warfare, 1900–1945.* London: Blandford Press, 1988.

Belhocine, Mabrouk. *Le courrier Alger–le Caire, 1954–1956.* Algiers: Casbah, 2000.

Belkhodja, Amar. *L'affaire Hamdani Adda.* Tiaret: Éditions Mekhloufi, n.d., ca. 1985.

Bell, Heather. *Frontiers of Medicine in the Anglo-Egyptian Sudan, 1899–1940.* Oxford: Clarendon Press, 1999.

———. "Midwifery Training and Female Circumcision in the Inter-War Anglo-Egyptian Sudan." *Journal of African History* 39, no. 2 (1998): 293–312.

Ben Ahmed, Mohamed. "Jacques Moreillon: Le droit humanitaire suit la pratique . . . il ne le précède pas." *L'Humanitaire Maghreb* 5 (June 2003): 22.

———. "Pierre Gaillard: Un humanitaire dans la guerre d'Algérie." *L'Humanitaire Maghreb* 5 (June 2003): 18–21.

Benatia, Farouk. *Les actions humanitaires pendant la lutte de libération, 1954–1962.* Algiers: Éditions Dahlab, 1997.

Benkhaled, Ahmed. *Chroniques médicales algériennes: Les années de braise.* Algiers: Éditions Houma, 2004.

Bennoune, Mahfoud. "The Introduction of Nationalism to Rural Algeria, 1919–1954." *Maghreb Review* 2, no. 3, (1977): 1–12.

———. *The Making of Contemporary Algeria, 1830–1987: Colonial Upheavals and Post-Independence Development.* Cambridge: Cambridge University Press, 1988.

Benton, Lauren. *A Search for Sovereignty: Law and Geography in European Empires, 1400–1900.* Cambridge: Cambridge University Press, 2009.

Berry, Nicholas. *War and the Red Cross: The Unspoken Mission.* New York: St. Martin's Press, 1997.

Best, Geoffrey. *Humanity in Warfare: The Modern History of the International Law of Armed Conflict.* London: Weidenfeld and Nicolson, 1980.

———. *War and Law Since 1945.* New York: Oxford University Press, 1994.

Birn, Donald S. *The League of Nations Union, 1918–1945.* Oxford: Oxford University Press, 1981.

Black, Allida, ed. *The Eleanor Roosevelt Papers: The Human Rights Years, 1945–1948.* Charlottesville: University of Virginia Press, 2010.

———. *The Eleanor Roosevelt Papers: The Human Rights Years, 1949–1952.* Charlottesville: University of Virginia Press, 2012.

Bodin, Jean. *On Sovereignty: Four Chapters from "The Six Books of the Commonwealth."* Ed. and trans. Julian H. Franklin. Cambridge: Cambridge University Press, 1992.

Bodinier, Gilbert, ed. *Indochine 1947: Règlement politique et solution militaire.* Vincennes: Service Historique de l'Armée de Terre, 1987.

———. *Le retour de la France en Indochine, 1945–1946.* Vincennes: Service Historique de l'Armée de Terre, 1987.

Boissier, Pierre. *Histoire du Comité international de la Croix-Rouge.* Geneva: Institut Henry-Dunant, 1978.

Borowy, Iris. *Coming to Terms with World Health: The League of Nations Health Organization, 1921–1946.* Frankfurt: Peter Lang, 2009.

Boualam, Saïd. *Les harkis au service de la France.* Paris: France Empire, 1963.

Bouaziz, Moula. "Guerre, violence politique et crises en Wilaya III: Contribution à l'étude de la guerre de libération d'Algérie (1954–1962)." Ph.D. diss., L'École des Hautes Études en Sciences Sociales [EHESS], 2011.

Bourdieu, Pierre, and Abdelmalek Sayad. *Le déracinement: La crise de l'agriculture traditionnelle en Algérie.* Paris: Éditions de Minuit, 1964.

Brace, Richard, and Joan Brace. *Algerian Voices.* Princeton, N.J.: Van Nostrand, 1965.

Branche, Raphaëlle. "La Commission de sauvegarde pendant la guerre d'Algérie: Chronique d'un échec annoncé." *Vingtième Siècle: Revue d'histoire* 61 (1999): 14–29.

———. "Entre droit humanitaire et intérêts politiques: Les missions algériennes du CICR." *Revue Historique* 301, no. 1 (1999): 101–125.

———. "Les entretiens avec d'anciens soldats: Une source pour l'histoire de la torture pendant la guerre d'Algérie." In *La guerre d'Algérie au miroir des décolonisations françaises: En l'honneur de Charles-Robert Ageron*, 593–606. Paris: Société française d'histoire d'outre-mer (SFHOM), 2000.

———. "The Martyr's Torch: Memory and Power in Algeria." *Journal of North African Studies* 16, no. 3 (2011): 431–444.

———. *Prisonniers du FLN*. Paris: Payot, 2014.

———. "The State, the Historians, and the Algerian War in French Memory, 1991–2004." In *Contemporary History on Trial: Europe Since 1989 and the Role of the Expert Historian*, ed. Harriet Jones, Kjell Ostberg, and Nico Randeraad, 159–173. Manchester: Manchester University Press, 2013.

———. *La torture et l'armée pendant la guerre d'Algérie*. Paris: Gallimard, 2001.

———. "La torture pendant la guerre." In *La guerre d'Algérie, 1954–2004: La fin de l'amnésie*, ed. Mohammed Harbi and Benjamin Stora, 381–402. Paris: Laffont, 2004.

Brett, Michael. "Legislating for Inequality in Algeria: The Senatus-Consulte of July 1865." *Bulletin of the School of Oriental and African Studies, University of London* 51, no. 3 (1988): 440–461.

Brinkley, Douglas, and David Facey-Crowther, eds. *The Atlantic Charter*. New York: St. Martin's Press, 1994.

Brocheux, Pierre, and Daniel Hémery. *Indochine: La colonisation ambiguë (1858–1954)*. Paris: La Découverte, 1995.

Brower, Benjamin. *A Desert Named Peace: The Violence of France's Empire in the Algerian Sahara, 1844–1902*. New York: Columbia University Press, 2011.

Bugnion, François. *The International Committee of the Red Cross and the Protection of War Victims*. Trans. Patricia Colberg, Edward Markee, and Nicolas Sommer. Oxford: Macmillan Education, 2003.

Burke, Roland. "The Compelling Dialogue of Freedom: Human Rights at the Bandung Conference." *Human Rights Quarterly* 28, no. 4 (2006): 947–965.

———. *Decolonization and the Evolution of International Human Rights*. Philadelphia: University of Pennsylvania Press, 2010.

———. "Some Rights Are More Equal Than Others: The Third World and the Transformation of Economic and Social Rights." *Humanity* 3, no. 3 (2012): 427–448.

Byrne, Jeffrey James. "The Pilot Nation: An International History of Revolutionary Algeria, 1958–1965." Ph.D. diss., London School of Economics, 2011.

Callahan, Michael D. *Mandates and Empire: The League of Nations and Africa, 1914–1931*. Brighton: Sussex Academic Press, 1999.

Chamberlin, Paul Thomas. *The Global Offensive: The United States, the Palestine Liberation Organization, and the Making of the Post–Cold War Order*. New York: Oxford University Press, 2012.

Chaulet, Claudine, and Pierre Chaulet. *Le choix de l'Algérie: Deux voix, une mémoire*. Algiers: Éditions Barzakh, 2012.

Cheurfi, Achour. *Dictionnaire de la révolution algérienne, 1954–1962*. Algiers: Casbah, 2004.

Chiffoleau, Sylvia. *Médecines et médecins en Egypte: Construction d'une identité professionnelle et projet médical*. Paris: L'Harmattan, 1997.

Chominot, Marie. "Guerre des images, guerre sans image? Pratiques et usages de la photographie pendant la guerre d'indépendance algérienne (1954–1962)." Ph.D. diss., EHESS, 2008.

———. "Quand la photographie vint à la Révolution: Petite contribution à l'histoire des services d'information du FLN pendant la guerre d'indépendance algérienne." In *Images du Maghreb*, *images au Maghreb (XIXᵉ-XXᵉ siècles): Une révolution du visuel?*, ed. Omar Carlier, 239–255. Paris: L'Harmattan, 2010.

Christelow, Allan. *Muslim Law Courts and the French Colonial State in Algeria*. Princeton, N.J.: Princeton University Press, 1985.

Citino, Nathan. *From Arab Nationalism to OPEC: Eisenhower, King Sa'ud, and the Making of U.S.-Saudi Relations*. Bloomington: Indiana University Press, 2002.

Clark, Hannah-Louise. "Doctoring the *Bled*: Medical Auxiliaries and the Administration of Rural Life in Colonial Algeria, 1904–1954." Ph.D. diss., Princeton University, 2014.

Clavin, Patricia. *Securing the World Economy. The Reinvention of the League of Nations, 1920–1946.* Oxford: Oxford University Press, 2013.

Clayton, Anthony. *The Wars of French Decolonisation*. Harlow: Longman, 1994.

Cmiel, Kenneth. "The Recent History of Human Rights." *American Historical Review* 109, no. 1 (2004): 117–135.

Cole, Joshua. "Massacres and Their Historians: Recent Histories on State Violence in France and Algeria in the Twentieth Century." *French Politics, Culture, and Society* 28, no.1 (2010): 106–126.

Collot, Claude, and Jean-Robert Henry, eds. *Le mouvement national algérien: Textes, 1912–1954.* Paris: L'Harmattan, 1978.

Conklin, Alice. *A Mission to Civilize: The Republican Idea of Empire in France and West Africa, 1895–1930*. Stanford, Calif.: Stanford University Press, 1997.

Connelly, Matthew. *A Diplomatic Revolution: Algeria's Fight for Independence and the Origins of the Post–Cold War Era*. New York: Oxford University Press, 2002.

Cooper, Frederick. *Citizenship Between Empire and Nation: Remaking France and French West Africa, 1945–1960*. Princeton, N.J.: Princeton University Press, 2014.

———. *Decolonization and African Society: The Labor Question in French and British Africa*. Cambridge: Cambridge University Press, 1996.

Cooper, Nicola. *France in Indochina: Colonial Encounters*. Oxford: Berg, 2001.

Cornaton, Michel. *Les regroupements de la décolonisation en Algérie*. Paris: Éditions Ouvrières, 1967.

Crapanzano, Vincent. *The Harkis: The Wound That Never Heals*. Chicago: University of Chicago Press, 2011.

Curtin, Philip. *The Health of European Troops in the Conquest of Africa*. Cambridge: Cambridge University Press, 1998.

Daniel, Jean. *De Gaulle et l'Algérie*. Paris: Seuil, 1986.

Darwin, John. "Decolonization and the End of Empire." In *The Oxford History of the British Empire*, vol. 5, *Historiography*, ed. Robin Winks, 541–557. New York: Oxford University Press, 1999.

Déroulade, Arnaud. *OAS: Étude d'une organization secrète*. Hélette, France: Curutchet, 1997.

Des Forges, Alison. *"Leave None to Tell the Story": Genocide in Rwanda*. New York: Human Rights Watch, 1999.

Djamel-Eddine, Bensalem. *Voyez nos armes, voyez nos médecins: Chronique de la Zone 1, Wilaya III*. Algiers: Entreprise Nationale du Livre, 1985.

Djeghloul, Abdelkader. "La formation des intellectuels algériens modernes, 1880–1930." *Revue algérienne des sciences juridique, économique et politique* 22, no. 4 (December 1985): 639–664.

Djelfaoui, Abderrahmane. *Grangaud: D'Alger à El-Djazair*. Algiers: Casbah, 2000.

Djennas, Messaoud. *Vivre, c'est croire: Mémoires, 1925–1991*. Algiers: Casbah, 2006.

Djerbal, Daho. *L'Organization Spéciale de la Fédération de France du FLN: Histoire de la lutte armée du FLN en France (1956–1962)*. Algiers: Éditions Chihab, 2012.

Dore-Audibert, Andrée. *Les Françaises d'Algérie dans la guerre de libération*. Paris: Éditions Karthala, 1995.

Draper, G. I. A. D. *The Red Cross Conventions*. New York: Praeger, 1958.

Dubin, Martin Davis. "The League of Nations Health Organization." In *International Health Organizations and Movements, 1918–1938*, ed. Paul Weindling, 56–80. Cambridge: Cambridge University Press, 1995.

Duiker, William J.. "Ho Chi Minh and the Strategy of People's War." In *The First Vietnam War: Colonial Conflict and Cold War Crisis*, ed. Mark Atwood Lawrence and Fredrik Logevall, 152–174. Cambridge, Mass.: Harvard University Press, 2007.

Duranton-Crabol, Anne-Marie. *Le temps de l'OAS*. Brussels: Editions Complexe, 1995.

Eckel, Jan. "Human Rights and Decolonization: New Perspective and Open Questions." *Humanity* 1, no. 1 (2010): 111–135.

Eckel, Jan, and Samuel Moyn, eds. *The Breakthrough: Human Rights in the 1970s*. Philadelphia: University of Pennsylvania Press, 2013.

Eckert, Andreas. "African Nationalists and Human Rights." In *Human Rights in the Twentieth Century*, ed. Stefan-Ludwig Hoffmann, 283–300. Cambridge: Cambridge University Press, 2011.

Einaudi, Jean-Luc. *La ferme Améziane: Enquête sur un centre de torture pendant la guerre d'Algérie*. Paris: L'Harmattan, 1991.

El-Ayouty, Yassin. *United Nations and Decolonization: The Role of Afro-Asia*. The Hague, Netherlands: Martinus Nijhoff, 1971.

El Shakry, Omnia. *The Great Social Laboratory: Subjects of Knowledge in Colonial and Postcolonial Egypt*. Stanford, Calif.: Stanford University Press, 2007.

Eörsi, László. *Hungarian Revolution of 1956: Myths and Realities*. Trans. Mario D. Fenyo. Boulder, Colo.: Social Science Monographs, 2006.

Evans, Martin. *Algeria: France's Undeclared War*. Oxford: Oxford University Press, 2012.

———. "The Harkis: The Experience and Memory of France's Muslim Auxiliaries." In *The Algerian War and the French Army, 1954–62: Experiences, Images, Testimonies*, ed. Martin S. Alexander, Martin Evans, and J. F. V. Keiger, 117–133. New York: Palgrave Macmillan, 2002.

———. *The Memory of Resistance: French Opposition to the Algerian War, 1954–1962*. Oxford: Berg, 1997.

Eveno, Patrick, and Jean Planchais, eds. *La guerre d'Algérie: Dossier et témoignages*. Paris: La Découverte/Le Monde, 1989.

Fahmy, Khaled. "Medicine and Power: Towards a Social History of Medicine in Nineteenth-Century Egypt." In *New Frontiers in the Social History of the Middle East*, ed. Enid Hill, 15–62. Cairo: American University in Cairo Press, 2001.

Faivre, Maurice, *La Croix-Rouge pendant la guerre d'Algérie: Un éclairage nouveau sur les victimes et les internes*. Panazol: Lavauzelle, 2007.

Favez, Jean-Claude. *The Red Cross and the Holocaust*. Ed. and trans. John Fletcher and Beryl Fletcher. Cambridge: Cambridge University Press, 1999.

Ferguson, James. *Expectations of Modernity: Myths and Meanings of Urban Life on the Zambian Copperbelt*. Berkeley: University of California Press, 1999.

Féry, Raymond. *L'oeuvre médicale française en Algérie*. Calvisson: Éditions Jacques Gandini, 1994.

Fleury, Georges. *Histoire secrète de l'OAS*. Paris: Grasset, 2002.

Fogarty, Richard. *Race and War in France: Colonial Subjects in the French Army, 1914–1918*. Baltimore: Johns Hopkins University Press, 2008.

Fogarty, Richard, and Andrew Jarboe, eds. *Empires in World War I: Shifting Frontiers and Imperial Dynamics in a Global Conflict*. New York: I. B. Tauris, 2014.

Fontaine, Darcie. "Decolonizing Christianity: Grassroots Ecumenism in France and Algeria, 1940–1962." Ph.D. diss., Rutgers University, 2011.

———. "Treason or Charity? Christian Missions on Trial and the Decolonization of Algeria." *International Journal of Middle East Studies* 44, no. 4 (2012): 733–753.

Forsythe, David. *The Humanitarians: The International Committee of the Red Cross*. Cambridge: Cambridge University Press, 2005.

——. "Legal Management of Internal War: The 1977 Protocol on Non-International Armed Conflicts." *American Journal of International Law* 72, no. 2 (April 1978): 272–295.

Forsythe, David, and Barbara Ann Rieffer-Flanagan. *The International Committee of the Red Cross: A Neutral Humanitarian Actor.* London: Routledge, 2007.

Fredj, Claire. "Encadrer la naissance dans l'Algérie colonial: Personnels de santé et assistance à la mère et à l'enfant 'indigènes' (XIXe–début du XXe siècle)." *Annales de démographie historique* 122, no. 2 (2012): 169–203.

——. " 'Et il les envoya prêcher le royaume de Dieu et guérir les malades . . .' (Luc, IX, 2): Soigner les populations au Sahara; L'hôpital mixte de Ghardaïa (1895–1910)." *Histoire, monde et cultures religieuses* 22, no. 2 (2012): 55–89.

——. "Les médecins de l'armée et les soins aux colons en Algérie (1848–1851)." *Annales de démographie historique* 113, no. 1 (2007): 127–154.

Frémeaux, Jacques. "Les SAS (sections administratives spécialisées)." *Guerres mondiales et conflicts contemporains* 208, no. 4 (2002): 55–68.

Frémont, Armand. "Le contingent: Témoignage et réflexion." In *La guerre d'Algérie et les Français,* ed. Jean-Pierre Rioux. Paris: Fayard, 1990.

Gallagher, Nancy. *Egypt's Other Wars: Epidemics and the Politics of Public Health.* Syracuse, N.Y.: Syracuse University Press, 1990.

——. *Medicine and Power in Tunisia, 1780–1900.* Cambridge: Cambridge University Press, 1983.

Gallissot, René. *L'économie de l'Afrique du Nord.* Paris: Presses Universitaires de France, 1961.

Gallois, William. *The Administration of Sickness: Medicine and Ethics in Nineteenth-Century Algeria.* London: Palgrave Macmillan, 2008.

——. "Local Responses to French Medical Imperialism in Late Nineteenth-Century Algeria." *Social History of Medicine* 20, no. 2 (2007): 315–331.

Galula, David. *The Pacification of Algeria, 1956–1958.* Santa Monica, Calif.: Rand Corporation, 2006.

Gaucher, Joël. *Révélateur d'images: Témoignage autobiographique.* La Roche-sur-Yon: Siloë, 2006.

The Geneva Conventions of August 12, 1949. Geneva: International Committee of the Red Cross, 2007.

Gervereau, Laurent, and Benjamin Stora, eds. *Photographier la guerre d'Algérie.* Paris: Marval, 2004.

Gleijeses, Piero. *Conflicting Missions: Havana, Washington, and Africa, 1959–1976.* Chapel Hill: University of North Carolina Press, 2002.

Glendon, Mary Ann. *A World Made New: Eleanor Roosevelt and the Universal Declaration of Human Rights.* New York: Random House, 2001.

Godeau, Pierre. *Une aventure algérienne.* Paris: Flammarion, 2001.

Guentari, Mohammed. *Organisation politico-administrative et militaire de la Révolution algérienne de 1954 à 1962.* Algiers: Office des publications universitaires, 2000.

Hammerman, Jessica. "The Heart of the Diaspora: Algerian Jews During the War for Independence." Ph.D. diss., City University of New York, 2013.

Harbi, Mohammed. *Aux origines du FLN.* Paris: Christian Bourgois, 1975.

——. *Les archives de la révolution algérienne.* Paris: Éditions Jeune Afrique, 1981.

——. *Le FLN, mirage et réalité.* Paris: Éditions Jeune Afrique, 1980.

Harbi, Mohammed, and Gilbert Meynier. *Le FLN: Documents et histoire, 1954–1962.* Paris: Fayard, 2004.

Haroun, Ali. *La 7e wilaya: La guerre du FLN en France, 1954–1962.* Paris: Seuil, 1986.

Harrison, Alexander. *Challenging De Gaulle: The OAS and the Counterrevolution in Algeria, 1954–1962.* New York: Praeger, 1989.

Headrick, Daniel. *The Tools of Empire.* New York: Oxford University Press, 1981.

Heggoy, Alf Andrew. *Insurgency and Counterinsurgency in Algeria.* Bloomington: Indiana University Press, 1972.

Herrmann, Magali. "Le CICR et la guerre d'Algérie: Une guerre sans nom, des prisonniers sans statut, 1954–1958." Mémoire de license, Université de Genève, 2006.

Hilderbrand, Robert C. *Dumbarton Oaks: The Origins of the United Nations and the Search for Postwar Security*. Chapel Hill: University of North Carolina Press, 1990.

Hill, Robert A., and Edmond Keller, eds. *Trustee for the Human Community: Ralph J. Bunche, the United Nations, and the Decolonization of Africa*. Athens: Ohio University Press, 2010.

Hilton-Simpson, M. W. *Arab Medicine and Surgery: A Study of the Healing Art in Algeria*. London: Oxford University Press, 1922.

Hitchcock, William. "Human Rights and the Laws of War: The Geneva Conventions of 1949." In *The Human Rights Revolution: An International History*, ed. Akira Iriye, Petra Goedde, and William Hitchcock, 93–112. New York: Oxford University Press, 2012.

Hodge, Joseph. *Triumph of the Expert: Agrarian Doctrines of Development and the Legacies of British Colonialism*. Athens: Ohio University Press, 2007.

Hoffmann, Stefan-Ludwig. "Introduction: Genealogies of Human Rights." In *Human Rights in the Twentieth Century*, ed. Stefan-Ludwig Hoffmann. Cambridge: Cambridge University Press, 2011.

Hoppe, Kirk. *Lords of the Fly: Sleeping Sickness Control in British East Africa, 1900–1960*. Westport, Conn.: Praeger, 2003.

Horne, Alistair. *A Savage War of Peace: Algeria, 1954–1962*. New York: New York Review of Books, 2006.

House, Jim, and Neil MacMaster. *Paris 1961: Algerians, State Terror, and Memory*. Oxford: Oxford University Press, 2006.

Howard-Jones, Norman. *The Scientific Background of the International Sanitary Conferences, 1851–1938*. Geneva: World Health Organization, 1975.

Hunt, Nancy Rose. *A Colonial Lexicon: Of Birth Ritual, Medicalization, and Mobility in the Congo*. Durham, N.C.: Duke University Press, 1999.

Hutchinson, John. *Champions of Charity: War and the Rise of the Red Cross*. Boulder, Colo.: Westview Press, 1996.

Hutchinson, John, and Anthony D. Smith, eds. *Nationalism*. Oxford: Oxford University Press, 1994.

Ibhawoh, Bonny. *Imperialism and Human Rights: Colonial Discourses of Rights and Liberation in African History*. Albany: State University of New York Press, 2007.

Ighilahriz, Louisette. *Algérienne*. As told to Anne Nivat. Paris: Fayard/Calmann Levy, 2001.

Iliffe, John. *East African Doctors: A History of the Modern Profession*. Cambridge: Cambridge University Press, 1998.

International Red Cross Handbook. Geneva: International Committee of the Red Cross, 1983.

Iriye, Akira. *Global Community: The Role of International Organizations in the Making of the Contemporary World*. Berkeley: University of California Press, 2002.

Iriye, Akira, and Petra Goedde, "Introduction: Human Rights as History." In *The Human Rights Revolution: An International History*, ed. Akira Iriye, Petra Goedde, and William Hitchcock, 3–24. New York: Oxford University Press, 2012.

Jackson, Julian. "General de Gaulle and His Enemies: Anti-Gaullism in France Since 1940." *Transactions of the Royal Historical Society*, 6th ser., 9 (1999): 43–65.

Johnson, M. Glen, and Janusz Symonides. *The Universal Declaration of Human Rights: A History of Its Creation and Implementation, 1948–1998*. Paris: UNESO, 1998.

Jordi, Jean-Jacques, and Mohand Hamoumou. *Les harkis, une mémoire enfouie*. Paris: Autrement, 1999.

Kaddache, Mahfoud. *Histoire du nationalism algérien: Question nationale et politique algérienne, 1919–1951*. Algiers: ENAL, 1993.

Kahin, George McTurnan. *The African-Asian Conference: Bandung, Indonesia, April 1955.* Ithaca, N.Y.: Cornell University Press, 1956.

Kateb, Kamel. *Européens, "indigènes," et juifs en Algérie (1830–1962): Répresentations et réalités des populations.* Paris: Institut national d'études démographiques, 2001.

Katz, Ethan. "Jews and Muslims in the Shadow of Marianne: Conflicting Identities and Republican Culture in France (1914–1975)." Ph.D. diss., University of Wisconsin–Madison, 2009.

Keck, Margaret E., and Kathryn Sikkink. *Activists Beyond Borders: Advocacy Networks in International Politics.* Ithaca, N.Y.: Cornell University Press, 1998.

Keller, Richard. *Colonial Madness: Psychiatry in French North Africa.* Chicago: University of Chicago Press, 2007.

Kennedy, Dane. "Imperial History and Post-Colonial Theory." In *The Decolonization Reader,* ed. James D. Le Sueur, 10–22. New York: Routledge, 2003.

Kennedy, Paul. *The Parliament of Man: The Past, Present, and Future of the United Nations.* New York: Random House, 2006.

Kettle, Michael. *De Gaulle and Algeria, 1940–1960: From Mers El-Kébir to the Algiers Barricades.* London: Quartet, 1993.

Keys, Barbara J. *Reclaiming American Virtue: The Human Rights Revolution of the 1970s.* Cambridge, Mass.: Harvard University Press, 2014.

Khiati, Mostéfa. *Les blouses blanches de la révolution.* Algiers: Éditions ANEP, 2011.

———. *Histoire de la médecine en Algérie.* Algiers: Éditions ANEP, 2000.

———. *Quelle santé pour les Algériens.* Algiers: Éditions Maghreb Relations, 1990.

Kimche, David. *The Afro-Asian Movement: Ideology and Foreign Policy of the Third World.* New York: Halstead Press, 1973.

Klose, Fabian. "The Colonial Testing Ground: The International Committee of the Red Cross and the Violent End of Empire." *Humanity* 2, no. 1 (2011): 107–126.

———. *Human Rights in the Shadow of Colonial Violence: The Wars of Independence in Kenya and Algeria.* Trans. Dona Geyer. Philadelphia: University of Pennsylvania Press, 2013.

———. "Source of Embarrassment: Human Rights, State of Emergency, and the Wars of Decolonization." In *Human Rights in the Twentieth Century,* ed. Stefan-Ludwig Hoffmann, 237–257. Cambridge: Cambridge University Press, 2011.

Korey, William. *NGOs and the Universal Declaration of Human Rights: A Curious Grapevine.* New York: St. Martin's Press, 1998.

Krasner, Stephan D. *Sovereignty: Organized Hypocrisy.* Princeton, N.J.: Princeton University Press, 1999.

Kumar, Deepak, ed. *Science and Empire: Essays in Indian Context, 1700–1947.* Delhi: Anamika Prakashan, 1991.

Laron, Guy. *Origins of the Suez Crisis: Postwar Development Diplomacy and the Struggle over Third World Industrialization, 1945–1956.* Baltimore: Johns Hopkins University Press, 2013.

Lauren, Paul Gordon. *The Evolution of International Human Rights: Visions Seen.* Philadelphia: University of Pennsylvania Press, 2003.

Lazreg, Marnia. *The Eloquence of Silence: Algerian Women in Question.* New York: Routledge, 1994.

———. *Torture and the Twilight of Empire: From Algiers to Baghdad.* Princeton, N.J.: Princeton University Press, 2008.

Leach, Melissa, and James Fairhead. *Vaccine Anxieties: Global Science, Child Health and Society.* London: Earthscan, 2007.

The League of Nations, 1920–1946: Organization and Accomplishments; A Retrospective of the First Organization for the Establishment of World Peace. New York: United Nations, 1996.

Lee, Christopher, ed. *Making a World After Empire: The Bandung Moment and Its Political Afterlives.* Athens: Ohio University Press, 2010.

Lefebvre, Pierre, ed. *Histoire de la médecine aux armées*. Vol. 3, *De 1914 à nos jours*. Paris: Lavauzelle, 1987.

Leloup-Colonna, Marie-Claude. *Souvenirs d'une toubiba: Algérie, 1957–1963*. Paris: L'Harmattan, 2004.

Lemkami, Mohamed. *Les hommes de l'ombre: Mémoires d'un officier du MALG*. Algiers: Éditions ANEP, 2004.

Le Sueur, James. *Uncivil War: Intellectuals and Identity Politics During the Decolonization of Algeria*. Lincoln: University of Nebraska Press, 2005.

Lewis, Mark. *The Birth of the New Justice: The Internationalization of Crime and Punishment, 1919–1950*. New York: Oxford University Press, 2014.

Lewis, Mary Dewhurst. *Divided Rule: Sovereignty and Empire in French Tunisia, 1881–1938*. Berkeley: University of California Press, 2014.

Livingston, Julie. *Debility and the Moral Imagination in Botswana*. Bloomington: Indiana University Press, 2005.

Lorcin, Patricia. *Imperial Identities: Stereotyping, Prejudice and Race in Colonial Algeria*. London: I. B. Tauris, 1995.

———. "Imperialism, Colonial Identity, and Race in Algeria, 1830–1870: The Role of the French Medical Corps." *Isis* 90, no. 4 (1999): 653–679.

Louis, William Roger. "The United Nations and the Suez Crisis: British Ambivalence Towards the Pope on the East River." In *Ends of British Imperialism: The Scramble for Empire, Suez and Decolonization*, 665–688. New York: I. B. Tauris, 2006.

Luard, Evan. *A History of the United Nations*. Vol. 2, *The Age of Decolonization, 1955–1965*. New York: Palgrave Macmillan, 1989.

Lyons, Maryinez. *The Colonial Disease: A Social History of Sleeping Sickness in Northern Zaire, 1900–1940*. Cambridge: Cambridge University Press, 1992.

———. "The Power to Heal: African Medical Auxiliaries in Colonial Belgian Congo and Uganda." In *Contesting Colonial Hegemony: State and Society in Africa and India*, ed. Dagmar Engels and Shula Marks, 202–223. London: British Academic Press, 1994.

MacLeod, Roy, and Milton Lewis, eds. *Disease, Medicine, and Empire: Perspectives on Western Medicine and the Experience of the European Expansion*. New York: Routledge, 1988.

Madsen, Mikael Rask. "France, the UK, and the 'Boomerang' of the Internationalisation of Human Rights (1945–2000)." In *Human Rights Brought Home: Socio-Legal Perspectives on Human Rights in the National Context*, ed. Simon Halliday and Patrick Schmidt, 57–86. Oxford: Hart, 2004.

Makaci, Mustapha. *Le Croissant-Rouge Algérien*. Algiers: Éditions Alpha, 2007.

Malley, Robert. *The Call from Algeria: Third Worldism, Revolution and the Turn to Islam*. Berkeley: University of California Press, 1996.

Mameri, Khalfa. *Les Nations Unies face à la "Question algérienne," 1954–1962*. Algiers: Société nationale d'édition et de diffusion, 1969.

Mandouze, André, ed. *La révolution algérienne par les textes*. Algiers: Éditions ANEP, 2006.

Manela, Erez. *The Wilsonian Moment: Self-Determination and the International Origins of Anticolonial Nationalism*. Oxford: Oxford University Press, 2007.

Maran, Rita. *Torture: The Role of Ideology in the French-Algerian War*. New York: Praeger, 1989.

Marcovich, Anne. "French Colonial Medicine and Colonial Rule: Algeria and Indochina." In *Disease, Medicine, and Empire: Perspectives on Western Medicine and the Experience of European Expansion*, ed. Roy MacLeod and Milton Lewis, 103–117. New York: Routledge, 1988.

Martinez, Luis. *La guerre civile en Algérie, 1990–1998*. Paris: Karthala, 1998.

Martini, Michel. *Chroniques des années algériennes, 1946–1962*. Saint-Denis: Éditions Bouchène, 2002.

Marynower, Claire, "Être socialiste dans l'Algérie colonial: Pratiques, cultures et identités d'un milieu partisan dans le département d'Oran, 1919–1939." Ph.D. diss., Sciences Po, 2013.

Mathias, Grégor. *Les Sections Administratives Spécialisées en Algérie: Entre idéal et réalité, 1955–1962*. Paris: L'Harmattan, 1998.

Maul, Daniel. *Human Rights, Development, and Decolonization: The International Labor Organization, 1940–1970*. New York: Palgrave Macmillan, 2012.

Mazower, Mark. *Dark Continent: Europe's Twentieth Century*. New York: Vintage Books, 2000.

———. *Governing the World: The History of an Idea*. New York: Penguin Press, 2012.

———. *No Enchanted Palace: The End of Empire and the Ideological Origins of the United Nations*. Princeton, N.J.: Princeton University Press, 2009.

McDougall, James. *History and the Culture of Nationalism in Algeria*. Cambridge: Cambridge University Press, 2006.

———. "Savage Wars? Codes of Violence in Algeria, 1830s–1990s." *Third World Quarterly* 26, no. 1 (2005): 117–131.

———. "The Shabiba Islamiyya of Algiers: Education, Authority and Colonial Control, 1921–57." *Comparative Studies of South Asia, Africa and the Middle East* 24, no. 1 (2004): 18–25.

Meade, Teresa, and Mark Walker, eds. *Science, Medicine, and Cultural Imperialism*. New York: St. Martin's Press, 1991.

Meynier, Gilbert. *Histoire intérieure du FLN, 1954–1962*. Algiers: Casbah, 2003.

Miquel, Pierre. *La guerre d'Algérie: Images inédites des archives militaires*. Paris: Chêne, 1993.

Moorehead, Caroline. *Dunant's Dream: War, Switzerland and the History of the Red Cross*. London: HarperCollins, 1998.

Morsink, Johannes. *The Universal Declaration of Human Rights: Origins, Drafting, and Intent*. Philadelphia: University of Pennsylvania Press, 1999.

Mortimer, Robert. *The Third World Coalition in International Politics*. New York: Praeger, 1980.

Moulin, Anne-Marie. "Tropical Without the Tropics: The Turning-Point of Pastorian Medicine in North Africa." In *Warm Climates and Western Medicine: The Emergence of Tropical Medicine, 1500–1900*, ed. David Arnold, 160–180. Atlanta: Rodopi, 1996.

Moyn, Samuel. "Imperialism, Self-Determination, and the Rise of Human Rights." In *The Human Rights Revolution: An International History*, ed. Akira Iriye, Petra Goedde, and William Hitchcock, 159–178. New York: Oxford University Press, 2012.

———. *The Last Utopia: Human Rights in History*. Cambridge, Mass.: Harvard University Press, 2010.

Navarro, Vincente, ed. *Imperialism, Health and Medicine*. London: Pluto Press, 1982.

Naylor, Phillip C. *France and Algeria: A History of Decolonization and Transformation*. Gainesville: University Press of Florida, 2000.

Neill, Deborah. "Paul Ehrlich's Colonial Connections: Scientific Networks and Sleeping Sickness Drug Therapy Research, 1900–1914." *Social History of Medicine* 22, no. 1 (2009): 61–71.

Normand, Roger, and Sarah Zaidi. *Human Rights at the UN: The Political History of Universal Justice*. Bloomington: Indiana University Press, 2008.

Northedge, F. S. *The League of Nations: Its Life and Times, 1920–1946*. New York: Holmes & Meier, 1986.

Nouschi, André. *La naissance du nationalisme algérien*. Paris: Éditions de Minuit, 1962.

Onyedum, Jennifer Johnson. "Humanize the Conflict: Algerian Health Care Organizations and Propaganda Campaigns, 1954–1962." *International Journal of Middle East Studies* 44, no. 4 (2012): 713–731.

Osborne, Michael A. *The Emergence of Tropical Medicine in France*. Chicago: University of Chicago Press, 2014.

Packard, Randall. "Maize, Cattle, and Mosquitoes: The Political Economy of Health and Disease in Colonial Swaziland." *Journal of African History* 25, no. 2 (1984): 189–212.

Pagden, Anthony. "Human Rights, Natural Rights, and Europe's Imperial Legacy." *Political Theory* 31, no. 2 (2003): 171–199.

Paret, Peter. *French Revolutionary Warfare from Indochina to Algeria: The Analysis of a Political and Military Doctrine.* New York: Frederick A. Praeger, 1964.

Pas, Niek. *Les Pays-Bas et la guerre d'Algérie.* Algiers: Barzakh, 2013.

Pati, Bisamoy, and Mark Harrison, eds. *Health, Medicine, and Empire: Perspectives on Colonial India.* Hyderabad, India: Orient Longman, 2001.

Paxton, Robert. *Vichy France: Old Guard and New Order, 1940–1944.* New York: Norton, 1975.

Pearson-Patel, Jessica. "From the Civilizing Mission to International Development: France, the United Nations, and the Politics of Family Health in Postwar Africa, 1940–1960." Ph.D. diss., New York University, 2013.

Pedersen, Susan. "Back to the League of Nations." *American Historical Review* 112, no. 4 (2007): 1091–1117.

Pennell, C. R. *Morocco Since 1830: A History.* London: Hurst, 2000.

Perkins, Kenneth. *A History of Modern Tunisia.* Cambridge: Cambridge University Press, 2004.

Perret, Françoise. "L'action du Comité international de la Croix-Rouge pendant la guerre d'Algérie (1954–1962)." *International Review of the Red Cross* 86, no. 856 (December 2004): 917–951.

Pervillé, Guy. *Les étudiants algériens de l'université française, 1880–1962.* Paris: CNRS, 1984.

Petitjean, Patrick, Catherine Jami, and Anne-Marie Moulin, eds. *Science and Empires: Historical Studies About Scientific Development and European Expansion.* Dordrecht: Kluwer, 1992.

Peyroulou, Jean-Pierre. *Guelma, 1945: Une subversion française dans l'Algérie coloniale.* Paris: La Découverte, 2009.

Pictet, Jean. *Les Conventions de Genève du 12 août 1949: Commentaire.* Geneva: Comité international de la Croix-Rouge, 1952.

Prakash, Gyan. *Another Reason: Science and the Imagination of Modern India.* Princeton, N.J.: Princeton University Press, 1999.

Prochaska, David. *Making Algeria French: Colonialism in Bône, 1870–1920.* Cambridge: Cambridge University Press, 1990.

Pryce-Jones, David. *The Hungarian Revolution.* London: Benn, 1969.

Pyenson, Lewis. *Civilizing Mission: Exact Sciences and French Overseas Expansion.* Baltimore: Johns Hopkins University Press, 1993.

———. "Why Science May Serve Political Ends: Cultural Imperialism and the Mission to Civilize." *Berichte zur Wissenschaftgeschichte* 13 (1990): 69–81.

Quandt, William. *Between Ballots and Bullets: Algeria's Transition from Authoritarianism.* Washington, D.C.: Brookings Institution Press, 1998.

Rahal, Malika. "La place des réformistes dans le mouvement national algérien." *Vingtième Siècle: Revue d'histoire* 83 (2004): 161–171.

———. "L'Union Démocratique du Manifeste Algérien (1946–1956): Histoire d'un parti politique; L'autre nationalisme algérien." Ph.D. diss., Institut national des langues et civilisations orientales, 2007.

Reggui, Marcel. *Les massacres de Guelma, Algérie, mai 1945: Une enquête inédite sur la furie des milices colonials.* Paris: La Découverte, 2006.

Reid, Ian. *The Evolution of the Red Cross.* Geneva: Henry Dunant Institute, 1975.

Rieff, David. *A Bed for the Night: Humanitarianism in Crisis.* New York: Simon and Schuster, 2002.

Rioux, Jean-Pierre, ed. *La Guerre d'Algérie et les Français.* Paris: Fayard, 1990.

Roberts, Adam, and Benedict Kingsbury, eds. *United Nations, Divided World: The UN's Roles in International Relations.* Oxford: Clarendon Press, 1998.

Roberts, Hugh. *The Battlefield, Algeria, 1988–2002: Studies in a Broken Polity.* London: Verso, 2003.

Rondeau, Jean-Pierre, ed. *Aspects véritables de la rébellion algérienne: Suivi de Algérie médicale; Documents publiés à l'origine par le Cabinet du Ministre du Ministère de l'Algérie.* Paris: Dualpha, 2001.

Rosenberg, Clifford. "The International Politics of Vaccine Testing in Interwar Algiers." *American Historical Review* 117, no. 3 (2012): 671–697.

Roux, Michel. *Les harkis, ou Les oubliés de l'histoire.* Paris: La Découverte, 1991.

Rovan, Joseph. "Témoignage sur Edmond Michelet, garde des Sceaux." In *La Guerre d'Algérie et les Français,* ed. Jean-Pierre Rioux, 276–278. Paris: Fayard, 1990.

Ruedy, John. "Chérif Benhabylès and the Young Algerians." In *Franco-Arab Encounters: Studies in Memory of David Gordon,* ed. L. Carl Brown and Matthew S. Gordon, 345–369. Syracuse, N.Y.: Syracuse University Press, 1997.

———. *Modern Algeria: The Origins and Development of a Nation.* Bloomington: Indiana University Press, 1992.

Sambron, Diane. *Femmes musulmanes: Guerre d'Algérie, 1954–1962.* Paris: Éditions Autrement, 2007.

Schalk, David. *War and the Ivory Tower: Algeria and Vietnam.* Oxford: Oxford University Press, 1991.

Schayegh, Cyrus. *Who Is Knowledgeable Is Strong: Science, Class, and the Formation of Modern Iranian Society, 1900–1950.* Berkeley: University of California Press, 2009.

Schlesinger, Stephen. *Act of Creation: The Founding of the United Nations.* New York: Westview Press, 2003.

Schmitt, Carl. *Political Theology: Four Chapters on the Concept of Sovereignty.* Chicago: University of Chicago Press, 2006.

Schreier, Joshua. *Arabs of the Jewish Faith: The Civilizing Mission in Colonial Algeria.* New Brunswick, N.J.,: Rutgers University Press, 2010.

Sessions, Jennifer. *By Sword and Plow: France and the Conquest of Algeria.* Ithaca, N.Y.: Cornell University Press, 2011.

Sheehan, James J. "The Problem of Sovereignty in European History." *American Historical Review* 111, no. 1 (2006): 1–15.

Shepard, Todd. *The Invention of Decolonization: The Algerian War and the Remaking of France.* Ithaca, N.Y.: Cornell University Press, 2006.

Sidi-Moussa, Nedjib. *Le MNA: Le Mouvement National Algérien (1954–1956).* Paris: L'Harmattan, 2008.

Simon, Jacques, ed. *Biographies de Messali Hadj.* Paris: L'Harmattan, 2009.

Simpson, A. W. Brian. *Human Rights and the End of Empire: Britain and the Genesis of the European Convention.* Oxford: Oxford University Press, 2004.

Simpson, Bradley. "Self-Determination, the End of Empire, and the Fragmented Discourse of Human Rights in the 1970s." *Humanity* 4, no. 2 (2013): 239–260.

Sironi, Françoise, and Raphaëlle Branche. "Torture and the Border of Humanity." *International Social Science Journal* 54, no. 174 (2002): 539–548.

Sivan, Emmanuel. "The Étoile Nord Africaine and the Genesis of Algerian Nationalism." *Maghreb Review* 3, nos. 5–6 (1978): 17–22.

Smati, Mahfoud. *Les jeunes algériens: Correspondances et rapports, 1837–1918.* Algiers: Thala, 2011.

Snyder, Sarah. *Human Rights Activism and the End of the Cold War: A Transnational History of the Helsinki Network.* Cambridge: Cambridge University Press, 2011.

Solomon, Susan Gross, Lion Murard, and Patrick Zylberman, eds. *Shifting Boundaries of Public Health: Europe in the Twentieth Century.* Rochester, N.Y.: University of Rochester Press, 2008.

Sorum, Paul Clay. *Intellectuals and Decolonization in France.* Chapel Hill: University of North Carolina Press, 1977.

Staples, Amy. *The Birth of Development: How the World Bank, Food and Agriculture Organization, and World Health Organization Changed the World, 1945–1965.* Kent, Ohio: Kent State University Press, 2006.

Stein, Sarah Abrevaya. *Jews and the Fate of French Algeria*. Chicago: University of Chicago Press, 2014.

Stora, Benjamin. *La gangrène et l'oubli: La mémoire de la guerre d'Algérie*. Paris: La Découverte, 1991.

———. *Histoire de la guerre d'Algérie, 1954–1962*. Paris: La Découverte, 1993.

———. *Messali Hadj: Pionnier du nationalisme algérien, 1898–1974*. Paris: L'Harmattan, 1986.

Sufian, Sandra. *Healing the Land and the Nation: Malaria and the Zionist Project in Palestine, 1920–1947*. Chicago: University of Chicago Press, 2007.

Summers, Carol. "Intimate Colonialism: The Imperial Production of Reproduction in Uganda, 1907–1925." *Signs* 16, no. 4 (1991): 787–808.

Sutton, Keith. "Algeria's Socialist Villages—a Reassessment." *Journal of Modern African Studies* 22, no. 2 (1984): 223–248.

———. "Army Administration Tensions over Algeria's Centres de Regroupement, 1954–1962." *British Journal of Middle Eastern Studies* 26, no. 2 (1999): 243–270.

———. "Population Resettlement—Traumatic Upheavals and the Algerian Experience." *Journal of Modern African Studies* 15, no. 2 (1977): 279–300.

Taithe, Bertrand. "Entre deux mondes: Médecins indigènes et médecine indigène en Algérie, 1860–1905." In *La santé des populations civiles et militaires: Nouvelles approches et nouvelles sources hospitalières, XVIIe–XVIIIe siècles*, ed. Élisabeth Belmas and Serenella Nonnis-Vigilante, 99–112. Villeneuve d'Ascq: Presses Universitaires Septentrion, 2010.

Teguia, Mohamed. *L'Armée de Libération Nationale en Wilaya IV*. Algiers: Casbah, 2002.

Terretta, Meredith. "'We Had Been Fooled into Thinking That the UN Watched Over the Whole World': Human Rights, UN Trust Territories, and Africa's Decolonization." *Human Rights Quarterly* 34, no. 2 (2012): 329–360.

Tertrais, Hugues. *La piastre et le fusil: Le coût de la guerre d'Indochine, 1945–1954*. Paris: Comité pour l'histoire économique et financière, 2002.

Thénault, Sylvie. *Une drôle de justice: Les magistrats dans la guerre d'Algérie*. Paris: La Découverte, 2001.

———. *Histoire de la guerre d'indépendance Algérienne*. Paris: Flammarion, 2005.

Thénault, Sylvie, and Raphaëlle Branche. "L'impossible procès de la torture pendant la guerre d'Algérie." In *Justice, politique et République: De l'affaire Dreyfus à la guerre d'Algérie*, ed. Marc-Olivier Baruch and Vincent Duclert, 243–260. Brussels: Complexe/IHTP, 2002.

Thomas, Lynn. *Politics of the Womb: Women, Reproduction, and the State in Kenya*. Berkeley: University of California Press, 2003.

Thomas, Martin, "France Accused: French North Africa Before the United Nations, 1952–1962." *Contemporary European History* 10, no. 1 (2001): 96–103.

———. "The Sétif Uprising and the Savage Economics of Colonialism." In *The French Colonial Mind*, vol. 2, *Violence, Military Encounters, and Colonialism*, ed. Martin Thomas, 140–173. Lincoln: University of Nebraska Press, 2011.

Thomas, Martin, L. J. Butler, and Bob Moore, eds. *Crises of Empire: Decolonization and Europe's Imperial States, 1918–1975*. London: Hodder Education, 2008.

Tilley, Helen. *Africa as a Living Laboratory: Empire, Development, and the Problem of Scientific Knowledge, 1870–1950*. Chicago: University of Chicago Press, 2011.

Trumbull, George R., IV. *An Empire of Facts: Colonial Power, Cultural Knowledge, and Islam in Algeria, 1870–1914*. Cambridge: Cambridge University Press, 2009.

Turin, Yvonne. *Affrontements culturels dans l'Algérie coloniale: Écoles, médecines, religion, 1830–1880*. Paris: François Maspero, 1971.

———. "'Médecine de propagande' et colonisation, l'expérience de Bouffarick, en 1835." *Revue de l'Occident musulman et de la Méditerranée* 8, no. 1 (1970): 185–194.

Tyre, Stephen. "The Memory of French Military Defeat at Dien Bien Phu and the Defence of

French Algeria." In *Defeat and Memory: Cultural Histories of Military Defeat in the Modern Era*, ed. Jenny Macleod, 214–232. London: Palgrave Macmillan, 2008.

Vatin, Jean-Claude. "Seduction and Sedition: Islamic Polemical Discourses in the Maghreb." In *Islam and the Political Economy of Meaning: Comparative Studies in Muslim Discourse*, ed. William R. Roff. Berkeley: University of California Press, 1987.

Vaughan, Megan. *Curing Their Ills: Colonial Power and African Illness*. Stanford, Calif.: Stanford University Press, 1991.

Vidal-Naquet, Pierre. *Les crimes de l'armée française: Algérie, 1954–1962*. Paris: La Découverte & Syros, 2001.

———. *La raison d'état*. Paris: Éditions de Minuit, 1962.

———. *La torture dans la République: Essai d'histoire et de politique contemporaines, 1954–1962*. Paris: Éditions de Minuit, 1972.

Villatoux, Paul, and Marie-Catherine Villatoux. *La République et son armée face au "péril subversif": Guerre et action psychologiques en France, 1945–1960*. Paris: Les Indes Savantes, 2005.

Vince, Natalya. "La mémoire des femmes algériennes de la guerre de libération algérienne." *Raison présente* 175, no. 3 (2010): 79–92.

———. *Our Fighting Sisters: Nation, Memory and Gender in Algeria, 1954–2012*. Manchester: Manchester University Press, 2015.

Vitalis, Robert. "The Midnight Ride of Kwame Nkrumah and Other Fables of Bandung." *Humanity* 4, no. 2 (2013): 261–288.

Wall, Irwin. *France, the United States, and the Algerian War*. Berkeley: University of California Press, 2001.

Weitz, Eric. "From the Vienna to the Paris System: International Politics and the Entangled Histories of Human Rights, Forced Deportations, and Civilizing Missions." *American Historical Review* 113, no. 5 (2008): 1313–1343.

Westad, Odd Arne. *The Global Cold War: Third World Interventions and the Making of Our Times*. Cambridge: Cambridge University Press, 2005.

Wilson, Heather. *International Law and the Use of Force by National Liberation Movements*. Oxford: Clarendon Press, 1988.

Worboys, Michael. "The Comparative History of Sleeping Sickness in East and Central Africa, 1900–1914." *History of Science* 32 (1994): 89–102.

Yaqub, Salim. *Containing Arab Nationalism: The Eisenhower Doctrine and the Middle East*. Chapel Hill: University of North Carolina Press, 2004.

Young, Ian. *The Private Life of Islam*. London: Allen Lane, 1974.

Zwang, Gérard. *Chirurgien du contingent: Suez-Algérie, mai 1956–octobre 1958*. Ed. Jean-Charles Jauffret. Montpellier: Université Paul Valéry, 2000.

Index

A c k n o w l e d g m e n t s

This journey started many years ago and I have accrued many intellectual and personal debts along the way. My interest in African history dates back to my undergraduate studies at Brown University, where under the guidance of Nancy Jacobs, I discovered the possibility of becoming a professional historian. I am especially indebted to her, the Mellon Mays Undergraduate Fellowship, and the Institute for the Recruitment of Teachers for providing invaluable mentorship and professional guidance over the course of my education and career.

At Princeton Univerity I had the good fortune of working with James McDougall whose passion and vast knowledge of the Maghrib is nothing short of inspiring. He kindled and nurtured my interest in Algerian history and offered precise comments at various stages of the project. Philip Nord read numerous incarnations and always made countless helpful suggestions. The argument and big picture are stronger as a result of his discerning eye. Helen Tilley introduced me to the history of medicine and offered much-needed perspective. Deans Karen Jackson-Weaver and David Redman provided critical research support and important words of encouragement. In graduate school I was lucky to have been surrounded by some of the sharpest minds and kindest spirits. Carolyn Biltoft, Hannah Louise Clark, Darcie Fontaine, Monica Huerta, Hannah Weiss Muller, Paul Ocobock, Abi Ocobock, and Elena Schneider made seminars, research, and writing stimulating, and, more important, fun.

At the History Department at the City College of New York, my friends and colleagues have made me feel welcome and have provided a vibrant and dynamic intellectual home. Clifford Rosenberg, who has read and commented on more drafts along the way than anyone could ever hope for, and Emily Greble, who has offered endless encouragement in professional and personal matters, deserve special mention. I thank Beth Baron, Richard Boles, Lale Can, Gregory Downs, Andreas Killen, Anne Kornhauser, Adrienne Petty, and

Judith Stein for reading chapters at critical junctures in the process and for creating an enviable working environment. Deans Geraldine Murphy and Eric Weitz were staunch advocates of my work and Moe Liu-D'Albero helped me navigate endless paperwork. I appreciate my students more than they know, notably those in my Algerian War class who allowed me to work through many of the ideas contained in these pages. Their intellectual curiosity makes teaching a joy.

Over the course of working on this project, I am grateful to have participated in the National History Center Decolonization Seminar, where William Roger Louis, Philippa Levine, Dane Kennedy, Jason Parker, Pillarisetti Sudhir, and the seminar participants encouraged me to think about Algeria and decolonization more broadly. Emmanuel Blanchard, Raphaëlle Branche, Frederick Cooper, Claire Fredj, Abosede George, Patricia Lorcin, Gregory Mann, Jean-Pierre Peyroulou, Malika Rahal, Emmanuelle Saada, Joshua Schreier, Todd Shepard, Rhiannon Stephens, and Sylvie Thénault have shared critical insights about French, Algerian, and African history. It was a pleasure to learn from and discuss human rights and international history with Matthew Connelly, Jan Eckel, Mark Mazower, and Samuel Moyn. At Lehman College I enjoyed many conversations with and benefited from the support of Timothy Alborn, Evelyn Ackerman, Mark Christian, Bertrade Ngo-Ngijol Banoum, Jim Jervis, Cindy Lobel, Anne Rice, Robyn Spencer, Chuck Wooldridge, and Amanda Wunder. The Faculty Fellowship Publication Program introduced me to a wonderful group of thoughtful and conscientious scholars at CUNY, notably Mark Lewis, Teresita Levy, Megan Moran, Isabel Martinez, Cristina Balboa, and Virginia Sanchez-Korrol, who read and commented on several parts of the manuscript.

I benefited greatly from panelists and discussants who read and debated my research in a variety of forums, including the American Historical Association, the Columbia University Seminar Beyond France, the Columbia University Seminar on Contemporary Africa, the Middle East Studies Association Annual Meeting, French Colonial Historical Studies, the Dissections Seminar at the CUNY Graduate School, the Wellcome Unit for the History of Medicine at Oxford University, and diverse conferences and workshops in Paris, Tunis, and Gießen, Germany. I received valuable feedback and encountered probing questions that helped me develop and refine my ideas.

The research for this book would not have been possible without the generous funding from many sources, including a Humanities Enrichment Grant awarded by the Division of Humanities and Art at the City College of

New York, the Simon H. Rifkind Center for Humanities, a PSC-CUNY Award, the Faculty Fellowship Publication Program, a CEMA Research Grant awarded by the American Institute for Maghrib Studies, the SSRC-MMUF Proposal Writing and Development Seminar, a Princeton University Department of History Research Grant, a Center for Health and Wellbeing Grant, support from the Princeton University Center for African-American Studies, an Andrew W. Mellon Fellowship in Humanistic Studies, and a Foreign Language Area Studies Award to study Arabic.

Furthermore, countless archivists and librarians have assisted me along the way. The book would have looked very different without the dedicated archivists at the Algerian National Archives. Not only did Abdelmadjid Chikhi, Samia Benali, Zineb Chergui, Houriyya Rebba, and Naouel Sai make the working environment in the reading room warm and receptive, but they also went to great lengths to find important Algerian Red Crescent and Provisional Government of the Algerian Republic files. The librarians at the Glycines in Algiers were also quite knowledgeable and helpful in pointing me toward colonial health records. I owe my gratitude to the Algerian men and women who welcomed me into their homes and offices and shared private and personal stories about themselves and their families. Jean-Paul Grangaud, Pierre Chaulet, Jeanine Belkhodja, Commandant Azzedine, Salim Hafiz, Mohamed Toumi, and Colonel Hassan were open and willing to revisit and explain quite difficult times in their lives. Daho Djerbal was a lovely academic anchor in Algiers. His office was a delightful refuge and his introductions were essential. Mohamed Mebtoul was encouraging and eager to share health-related materials with me. Robert Parks and Karim Waras at the Centre d'Etudes Maghrébines en Algérie greatly facilitated my research trips to Algeria and warmly received me each time. Madame Décuber always graciously accommodated me at the Service Historique de l'Armée de Terre; Daniel Hick unearthed wonderful files at the Archives Nationales d'Outre-Mer; Fabrizio Bensi's mastery of the Archives du Comité International de la Croix Rouge proved critical to maximizing the use of my time in Geneva, as did Coralie Esmeralda Dussex's assistance in the ICRC photo library. Neytcho Iltchev, Sylvie Carlon-Riera, and Maria del Ma Sanchez at the United Nations archives in Geneva enthusiastically tracked down material on human rights in Algeria. My thanks to the archivists at the Etablissement de communication et de production audiovisuelle de la défense for showing me captivating images of the French military during the war.

At the University of Pennsylvania, my editor, Peter Agree, and the series editor, Bert B. Lockwood, have supported and championed this project from the moment we met, successfully steering it into port, shall we say. Peter's relentless enthusiasm, steadfast dedication, and exceptionally timely, thoughtful, and thorough responses assuaged this first-time author. I could not have asked for a more encouraging editor. A mere thank you is hardly sufficient. John Ackerman was an early advocate of my work and I greatly appreciate his interest and efforts to move the manuscript forward. Benjamin Brower and Roland Burke reviewed the entire manuscript and they each provided detailed comments and suggestions that, without a doubt, strengthened the book. Their attentive readings, phone conversations, and e-mail exchanges far exceeded what I could have hoped for. Noreen O'Connor-Abel and Jennifer Shenk provided invaluable assistance in the final stages.

I would never have survived the research and writing phases of this book without the support and encouragement of my friends and family. Okwudiri Onyedum was instrumental and made so much of this possible. Muriam Haleh Davis, Javiela Evangelista, and David Stevens have sustained me through thick and thin. Kristen Shockley, Shannon Reilly, Katie Flanagan, and Andrea Pappas have cheered me on and provided much needed distractions. Simon Tetelbaum, Jane Leeke, and Kofi Kankam have supported me from near and far. The Pavanellos and the Delpédro's generously welcomed me in their homes while I researched in Geneva. Kenny Johnson and the Barnes family have nutured me from a young age and been there for all of life's important moments. Katie Kozin, Kathy Bacuyag Payson, and Marie Walcott have enriched my life in more ways than I could ever explain. Their friendship—kind, understanding, patient, daring, and unapologetic—inspires me every day.

A heartfelt thank you to Craig Daigle for all of the above, everything, and more.

Finally, it is with great pleasure that I dedicate this book to my mom, who has taught me strength, fortitude, and perseverance and has always encouraged me to follow my dreams and pursue my happiness.